78909

the digital designer's

jargon buster

D1407151

the digital designer's
jargon
buster

ILEX

ALASTAIR CAMPBELL

78909

First published in the United Kingdom in 2004 by

I L E X

The Old Candlemakers
West Street
Lewes
East Sussex BN7 2NZ

THE LIBRARY

 **THE SURREY INSTITUTE OF ART & DESIGN**

741.
601
4
CAM

ILEX is an imprint of The Ilex Press Ltd
Visit us on the Web at:
www.ilex-press.com

Copyright © 2004 The Ilex Press Limited

This book was conceived by
ILEX, Cambridge, England

Publisher Alastair Campbell
Executive Publisher Sophie Collins
Creative Director Peter Bridgewater
Editorial Director Steve Luck
Editor Adam Juniper
Design Manager Tony Seddon
Designer Ginny Zeal
Artwork Administrator Joanna Clinch

Commissioning Editor Alan Buckingham
Development Art Director Graham Davis
Technical Art Editor Nicholas Rowland

Any copy of this book issued by the publisher as a paperback is sold
subject to the condition that it shall not by way of trade or otherwise be
lent, resold, hired out or otherwise circulated without the publisher's prior
consent in any form of binding or cover other than that in which it is
published and without a similar condition including these words being
imposed on a subsequent purchaser.

British Library Cataloguing-in-Publication Data
A catalogue record for this book is available from the British Library

ISBN 1-904705-35-9

All rights reserved. No part of this publication may be reproduced or used
in any form, or by any means – graphic, electronic or mechanical,
including photocopying, recording or information storage-and-retrieval
systems – without the prior permission of the publisher.

Printed and bound in China

For more information on this title please visit
www.ddjbuk.web-linked.com

In any skill, trade or profession there will be words that are taken for granted, yet mean nothing to the uninitiated. Whether it's the archaic language on your self-assessment tax form or the Latinate names spouted by your gardener, it's easy to be made to feel like a second-class citizen by those in the know. Jargon is the key to their power, and for no-one is the breadth and depth of that mysterious language more complicated than for designers.

There was a time when that wasn't so. Talent notwithstanding, to be a designer you simply had to be handy with a Rotring pen, a 10A scalpel and some Cow Gum (remember that?). It didn't hurt to have a cool haircut, too. Now it's another story: the computer has welded traditional crafts to modern technology, consolidating decades of typographical knowledge, scientific research into colour, mathematical algorithms, and staggering advances in photography, then dumping it all onto the same screen, all in front of a single designer. You.

As well as hijacking – or, more kindly, borrowing from – the vast vernacular already on hand, computers have also brought their own terminology to the field of design. Indeed, many of the modern designer's mainstays – Web design, to use the obvious example – exist thanks to the marriage of computer technology to conventional graphic skills.

In short, there are truckloads of words out there; they need translating and that is what this book does. Drawing on the talents behind ILEX's wealth of creative titles, we've built the most comprehensive, up-to-date guide to the digital designer's lexicon. Our contributors include professional photographers, 3D designers, video editors, graphic designers, typographers and more. Between them you can pretty much guarantee that, if you need to know it, it's in here.

The following abbreviations are
used throughout this book:

aud
  audio

com
  computers

fin
  finishing/binding

gen
  general

har
  hardware

int
  Internet

Mac
  Mac specific

pap
  paper

pho
  photographic

pre
  prepress

pri
  printing

sof
  software

typ
  typographical

Win
  Windows specific

ABBREVIATIONS

@ *(int)* → *commercial a*

AA *(gen) abb.:* author's alteration. → *author's alteration*

AAAA *(gen) abb.:* American Association of Advertising Agencies.

ABA *(gen) abb.:* American Booksellers Association. Body that issues an annual Book Buyers Handbook, the standard reference work for publishers.

aberration *(pho)* The flaw in a photographic lens by which light rays are improperly focused, resulting in image blurring.

ablation plate *(pri)* A plate used in digital offset litho printing. Requiring no chemical processing, ablation plates can be digitally imaged directly onto the printing press using a laser. → *offset litho(graphy)*

abort *(com)* → *cancel (2)*

abrasion *(pap)* → *scuffing*

abrasion resistance *(pri)* The property of a printing plate that enables the plate to resist rubbing without its surface being worn away.

A/B-Roll *(aud)* A system of video editing where video is taken from two or more sources, placed on two separate tracks – Video A and Video B – and transitions applied between the two. Software like Adobe Premiere Pro does away with the A/B-Roll concept, instead using multiple tracks that can be grouped and nested on a single timeline, offering more flexibility and control.

absolute leading *(typ)* A fixed amount of space between lines of text, generally measured in points. → *leading*

absolute page number *(gen)* The position of a page relative to the first page of the document, regardless of the numbering system used. For example, in a publication where a six-page section of prelims uses, say, roman numerals, or none at all, and page 1 identifies the start of the main text, the absolute page number of the first page of text is seven.

absolute path *(com)* The path, or route, taken to locate a file by starting at the highest level and searching through each directory (or folder) until the file is found. The path is spelled out by listing each directory en route. → *access path*

absolute URL *(int)* A complete address, or 'uniform resource locator' (URL), which takes you to a specific location in a website rather than its home page. An absolute URL will contain the full file path to the page document location on the host server and will appear, for example, as 'http://www.yoursite.com/extrainfo/aboutyou /yourhouse.htm'. → *URL*

absolute value *(gen)* A change in the value of a property that is made in direct relationship to a fixed value.

absorbency/absorption *(pri)* The property of a paper or other material to absorb liquids such as ink. In printing, absorption is not only determined by the fibre structure of the

A

paper, but also by the consistency of the ink and the pressure of the printing plates. Incorrect absorption can lead to printing problems such as strike through and drying failure. → *strike through*

AC *(gen) abb.*: author's correction. → *author's alteration*

accelerator board/card *(com)* A circuit board added to a computer, generally as an optional extra, to speed up various operations. It can either function generally, as with the central processing unit (CPU), or specifically, as with some graphics tasks.
→ *central processing unit; circuit board; expansion card/board*

accent *(typ)* A symbol attached to a letterform to indicate pronunciation of a word, usually in a particular language. Can also be used to indicate certain pronunciations, as in dictionaries.

accent characters *(typ)* The characters on a keyboard that generate accents in particular typographic letters. The keyboard characters are usually used in conjunction with 'modifier' keys, such as Shift, Option and Control, or a combination of these.
→ *accent; character (1); modifier key*

access path *(com)* The description of the route taken to access a file, created when the file is opened. → *absolute path*

access provider *(int)* → *Internet service provider; ISP*

access time *(com)* The time taken by a disk drive to access data. This is measured as an average of the 'seek' time (the time the drive head takes to find the data), and 'latency' time (the time the data sector takes to rotate under the head). Also known as 'average access time'. → *sector*

accordion/concertina fold *(fin)* A method of folding paper in which parallel folds are made in opposite directions to form pleats. Also called 'z-fold', or 'fan fold'.
→ *fold/folding*

acetate *(gen)* → *cellulose acetate*

achromatic *(gen)* A colour that has no saturation, or 'chroma', such as black or white. → *chroma*

achromatic colour removal *(pre)* A method of colour correction by which an extended degree of 'undercolour removal' (UCR) can take place. With conventional UCR, most of the colour and tone is generated by the three process colours, with black providing the deeper shadow tones. In achromatic reproduction, however, the absolute minimum of each colour required is computed, black being added to enhance the depth of colour. → *achromatic; chroma (2); grey component replacement; undercolour removal*

acid *(pri)* A solution of iron perchloride, used to etch the image cylinders in gravure printing. → *acid resist; etch*

acid fixer *(pho)* → *fix*

acid resist *(pri)* A protective layer applied to offset litho plates, which resists the acid being used to etch the plate, thus limiting the areas being etched. → *acid*

acid stop bath *(pho)* → *stop bath*

acoustic *(aud)* While the actual definition of this word refers to sound, it is often used to define an instrument that can be played without the aid of electric amplification, such as an acoustic guitar.

ACR *(pre) abb.*: achromatic colour removal. → *achromatic colour removal*

Acrobat *(com)* → *Adobe Acrobat*

acronym *(gen)* A single word made up from several words by using initial letters or syllables of some of the words (although not necessarily all) – for example, laser (light amplification by stimulated emission of radiation) and bit (binary digit). Abbreviations, such as ISBN and UCR,

Accordion folds result in pleats

AC

which are made up from the initial letters of a collection of words but do not form a word in themselves, are incorrectly considered acronyms.

active *(com)* In computer interfaces and applications, items selected for editing or other modification are described as being 'active'. Active items are distinguished, for example, by highlighting (text), or by the appearance of 'handles' on boxes (graphics). → *active icon; active window*

active desktop *(int)* A term coined by Microsoft to describe the interface built into its Internet Explorer Web browser, which merges the Windows operating system's desktop into the browser's window.

active hyperlink *(int)* A currently selected link (being clicked on) in a Web browser, usually differentiated from other links that appear on the same page by being displayed in another colour.

active icon *(com)* The status of the currently selected icon in a window or on the desktop, indicated by some form of highlighting. → *icon*

active matrix display *(com)* An LCD (liquid crystal display) monitor technology that is generated by using tiny transistors. → *LCD; passive matrix display*

ActiveMovie *(int)* → *DirectShow*

active window *(com)* The frontmost desktop or document window. Usually, only the contents of the active window can be modified by the user, although some types of window, such as floating palettes, allow their contents to be modified simultaneously. The active window is usually indicated by a bold title bar and active scroll bars. → *scroll bar; title bar*

ActiveX Controls *(int)* Microsoft's proprietary technology for enhancing interactive webpages. Like Java 'applets', ActiveX Controls can be downloaded from the Internet but, unlike Java applets, they are not platform-independent and are mainly supported only in Microsoft Windows environments. → *Java*

acutance *(pho)* The quality of an edge in a photographic image.

acute *(typ)* → *accent*

adaptive smoothing *(com)* Smoothing that is applied to a path, in some drawing and 3D applications, only where it is required rather than uniformly. → *smoothing*

ADB *(com) abb.:* Apple Desktop Bus. → *Apple Desktop Bus*

addendum/addenda *(gen)* Material supplementary to the main content of a book, printed separately at the beginning or end of the text.

additive colour mixing *(gen)* The mixing of red, green and blue light to create white light with all at equal strength, or one of the millions of other colours when mixed selectively. The basis of all screen display and digital image capture.

additive colours *(gen)* The colour model describing the primary colours of transmitted light: red, green and blue (RGB). Additive colours can be mixed to form all other colours in photographic reproduction and computer display monitors. → *colour model*

additivity failure *(pri)* The failure of the combined value of each overprinting ink film to achieve the correct ink density, resulting in thinly printed colours.

An **active** folder (top) and normal (below)

The **active hyperlink** has a different colour

1	AC Propulsion Inc.	tzerro
2	Audi	A4 duo 3
3	Celco Profil srl	CIP 025
4	Chevrolet, GM	S-10 Electric Pickup
5	Citroen, PSA	Berlingo electric
6	Citroen, PSA	Saxo electric
7	City Com	CityEl
8	DaimlerChrysler		electric

add-on board *(com)* ➔ *expansion card/board*

address (1) *(com)* The number or code identifying the location of data in a computer's memory. An address can be 'logical' – used when an instruction is executed – or 'physical', when the computer translates the logical address into a physical location on a disk drive, for example.

address (2) *(int)* A string of letters or numbers used by Internet users to communicate with each other via e-mail. Also an informal name for a website URL. ➔ *e-mail; URL; World Wide Web*

adhesive binding *(fin)* A method of binding that involves gluing the pages or signatures together rather than sewing or stitching them, although some binding methods combine both processes.
➔ *binding; bookbinding; cut back binding; signature (1)*

adhesive decal *(pri)* ➔ *decal*

adhesive stitch binding *(fin)* A method of adhesive binding in which signatures are stitched with heat-activated plastic-coated wire. ➔ *adhesive binding; binding; bookbinding; signature (1)*

adjustment layer *(com)* A specialized layer that can be handled as a conventional layer but is also designed to affect layers below it in the image 'stack'. Effects that can be applied via an adjustment layer include changes in levels, brightness/contrast, colour balance and even posterization. These changes do not actually modify the underlying pixels. If the adjustment layer is removed, the image will revert to its previous appearance. Conversely, an adjustment layer's adjustments can be permanently embedded in the image (or in the underlying layers) by selecting the appropriate layer merge command (such as Merge Down).

Adobe *(com)* Software developer whose products are widely used by professionals and amateurs for many creative tasks, such as Web design, graphic design and video editing. Photoshop, Photoshop Elements, Illustrator, Acrobat, InDesign and the video-editing package Premiere are some of its most successful products.

Adobe Acrobat *(com)* Application that creates the proprietary 'portable document format' (PDF) file, which has fonts and pictures embedded in the document, enabling it to be viewed and printed on different computer systems. The term 'Acrobat' is often used to describe the file format as well as the software that creates it. The application comes in two versions: full, which can create the PDF file format, or the free version, which simply reads the document (also known as Acrobat Reader).
➔ *portable document format*

The **address** line in a Web browser

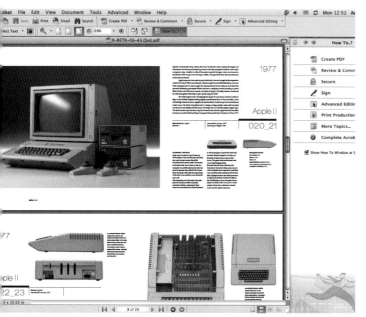

Viewing a PDF in
Adobe Acrobat

Adobe Font Metrics (AFM) *(com)* A specification for storing, in a text file, font information such as character width, kerning, ascent and descent. → *metrics*

Adobe Gamma *(com)* Adobe's display calibration application, which enables Windows users (and pre-OS X Macs) to adjust brightness and contrast values of their monitor by eye for improved colour display accuracy. Replaced in OS X by the 'colour' tab of the Displays System Preferences panel.

Adobe RGB (1998) *(com)* A large colour space encompassing the majority of printed CMYK and many of the smaller RGB gamuts. Adobe RGB (1998) is gaining acceptance as an RGB colour space for files made for printing purposes.

Adobe Type Manager (ATM) *(com)* A utility for managing, displaying and printing fonts. ATM improves the display (and printing, on non-PostScript printers) of PostScript Type 1 fonts by using the outlines contained within their corresponding printer files, rather than relying on the jagged screen fonts. Not required by Mac OS X.

ADR *(aud) abb.:* automated dialogue replacement. A method of 'voicing over' existing dialogue in a video soundtrack, for example.

ADSL *(int) abb.:* Asymmetrical Digital Subscriber Line. A high-speed communications link often referred to as 'broadband'. Provides permanent high-speed Internet access using regular telephone lines and without affecting voice calls. It is 'asymmetric' in that data is received faster than sent (typically 512kbps downstream, 256kbps up). → *ISDN*

ADT *(aud) abb.:* automatic double-tracking. An analog studio technique whereby a sound – a bass line, for example – is copied to another track and played back almost simultaneously to 'fatten up' the result. This effect can now be achieved more easily by using digital delay, but more accurate digital reproduction of this effect is also possible with some plug-in effects.

advance copies/advances *(fin)* The first delivery of copies of a printed job so that the quality of binding and reproduction can be checked and approved.

advance sheets *(pri)* → *folded and collated*

advert(isement) *(gen)* A public notice selling goods or services and printed or broadcast in a variety of media. → *display advertisement*

aerate *(pri)* The separation of sheets of paper, prior to printing, either by blowing air or by manual sifting.

AFE *(com) abb.:* Apple File Exchange. → *Apple File Exchange*

AFK *(gen) abb.:* away from keyboard.

AFM *(com) abb.:* Adobe Font Metrics. → *Adobe Font Metrics*

Afterburner *(int)* Proprietary file compression software for the purpose of compressing and delivering Macromedia Director film strips on the Internet.

after-tack *(pri)* An undesirable sticky property retained by printed ink after it should have dried (without tackiness).

against the grain *(fin)* Folding, marking or feeding paper at right angles to the direction ('grain') of paper fibres. Also called 'cross-grain'. → *graining*

agate *(typ)* A measurement of column depth in newspaper and magazine classified advertisements. Fourteen agates equal one inch. → *agate line; column inch/ centimetre*

agate line *(pri)* A fixed measurement of space, used in newspaper and magazine classified advertisements – 14 agate lines are equal to one column inch. → *agate*

AI *(gen)* abb: artificial intelligence. → *artificial intelligence*

AIF/AIFF *(aud)* Audio Interchange File Format. A file format devised by Apple Computer for making and storing sounds on computers, standard on the Mac, but common on Windows machines too. The AIFF standard is also the underlying format for audio on compact discs. → *file format*

AIGA *(gen)* abb.: American Institute of Graphic Arts. Founded in 1914 to uphold the standard of the graphic arts in the United States.

air bar *(pri)* A device on a printing press that prevents a double image from being printed.

air bells *(pap)* A blistering defect in paper.

airbrush/airbrushing *(gen)* A tool (invented in the USA around 1900) used in illustration and photographic retouching, in which a fine spray of paint or ink is propelled by compressed air. → *Airbrush tool*

Airbrush tool *(com)* A tool used in some graphic applications, such as Photoshop, to simulate the behaviour and effect of a mechanical airbrush. → *airbrush*

air-knife coater *(pap)* A device used in making coated papers, in which a jet of compressed air removes surplus coating from the paper. → *coated paper*

air pull *(pri)* When ink is flooded across the screen during screen printing without contacting the surface to be printed.

Alaska seal *(fin)* An imitation sealskin binding material, made from animal hide such as cow or sheep.

album binding *(fin)* A volume that is bound along its short side rather than along its long side, as is more common. → *binding; bookbinding*

album paper *(pap)* Antique finish paper made from wood pulp, used mainly for the pages of photograph albums.

albumen plate *(pri)* An obsolescent type of plate used in lithographic printing, in which a photosensitive surface made from albumen is applied to a plate.

alert *(com)* An audible or visible warning on a computer alerting you to a specific situation – usually an error. → *alert box*

alert box *(com)* A message box that appears on screen, giving information or a warning, and which usually requires no action by the user other than an acknowledgement. → *alert*

The Photoshop **Airbrush tool** icon

alfa grass *(pap)* A variety of esparto grass used to make paper. → *esparto*

algorithm *(com)* A predetermined procedure for solving a specific problem. → *algorithmically defined*

algorithmically defined *(com)* Usually used to describe a font in which each character is drawn 'on-the-fly' according to the calculations made by a software program, rather than residing on the computer as a predrawn font file.

AFTER-TACK

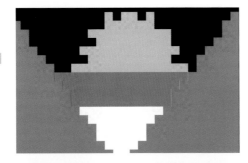

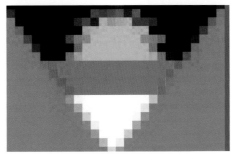

The jagged edges of **aliasing** (above) and with anti-aliasing applied (below)

alias *(com)* A duplicate of a file icon, but not of the file itself, thus occupying very little space. An alias (or Shortcut in Windows) is a means of convenient access to a file which may, for example, be buried deep in the file hierarchy or reside on a different, networked computer. → *network*

aliasing *(com)* The jagged appearance of bitmapped images or fonts occuring either when the resolution is insufficient, or when they have been enlarged. This is caused by the square pixels that make up the image becoming visible to the eye. Sometimes called 'jaggies', 'staircasing' or 'stairstepping', it can also refer to distortion of sound waveforms caused by difficulties processing higher frequencies. It is removed by means of an anti-aliasing filter. → *anti-aliasing; bitmapped font; bitmap graphic; image; resolution (1)*

aligned left/right/centre *(typ)* → *unjustified*

aligning numerals *(typ)* → *lining figures/numerals*

alignment *(gen)* The placement of type or images so that they line up according to an invisible line, either horizontally or vertically.

Unjustified text, for example, is generally aligned left, right or centred. Also called 'lining up' or 'line up'. → *bumped out (1); ranged left/right (UK);*

alley *(gen)* The spaces, or 'gutters', between columns in tabular matter. → *gutter margin*

all in hand *(pre)* The stage of the publishing process when the job is in the hands of the typesetter. → *all up*

allocation block *(com)* The predefined, or 'formatted', space on a hard disk where data files are stored. Only one file is permitted per allocation block, so if the file is small but the allocation block is large, space is wasted. Allocation blocks grow larger as disk capacity increases, so less storage is wasted if high capacity disks are divided into smaller 'partitions'. → *format (4); partitioning*

all up *(pre)* The stage of the publishing process when the job is in the hands of the printer. → *all in hand*

alphabet length *(typ)* The measurement, in points, of the entire length of the 26 alphabet characters in a font of any one size set in lower case. Therefore 39 characters have a length of 1.5 alphabets. → *character (1); point (1)*

alpha channel *(com)* The place where information regarding the transparency of a pixel is stored. In image files, this is a separate channel – additional to the three RGB or four CMYK channels – where

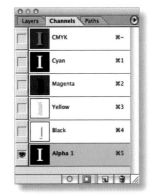

The **alpha channel** selected for editing

'masks' are stored. It simulates the physical material used in platemaking to shield parts of a plate from light. ➔ *CMYK; mask (1)*

alpha matte *(com)* A feature used to define areas of an image that will drop out, appearing transparent when previewed or rendered. For example, in a black alpha matte, any black areas of the image will become invisible, allowing imagery in the layer behind to show through.

alphanumeric set *(typ)* The complete set of alphabet characters, numbers, punctuation and associated symbols and accents of a font.

alpha test *(com)* The first testing, usually by the team developing it, of a software program in order to discover and eliminate errors ('debugging'). ➔ *alpha version*

alpha version *(com)* The first version of a newly developed software program, prior to testing and eventual release. ➔ *alpha test; beta version; release version*

Alt key *(com)* ➔ *modifier key*

aluminium ink *(pri)* Ink that contains particles of aluminium, giving the printed result a silvery property.

ambience *(aud)* In the recording process, this often refers to the reverberations produced by an analog instrument or a vocalist that are shaped by the room or environment in which they are released. Some engineers will place microphones in various parts of a room to capture some of the ambient sound while an instrument is being recorded, and will then incorporate these sounds into the mix to achieve a more natural and complex result. Most of these effects can be emulated digitally, but it can be difficult to reproduce more complex environments.

ambient *(com)* A term used in 3D modelling software to describe a light source with no focus or direction, such as that which results from bouncing off all objects in a scene. ➔ *ambience*

ambient light *(gen)* The natural light source in any scene. Many image creation and 3D applications offer their own version of ambient light.

American book sizes *(fin)* Modern book sizes. ➔ *book sizes; British book sizes*

Traditional US book sizes

Name	Size; in inches	in millimetres
Thirtysixmo (36mo)	4 x 3⅓	102 x 85
Medium Thirtytwomo (Med. 32mo)	4¼ x 3	121 x 76
Medium Twentyfourmo (Med. 24mo)	5½ x 5⅝	140 x 92
Medium Eighteenmo (Med. 18mo)	6⅔ x 4	169 x 102
Medium Sixteenmo (Med. 16mo)	6¾ x 4½	171 x 114
Cap Octavo (Cap 8vo)	7 x 7½	184 x 178
Duodecimo (12mo)	7½ x 4½	191 x 114
Crown Octavo (Cr. 8vo)	7½ x 5	191 x 127
Post Octavo (Post 8vo)	7½ x 5½	191 x 140
Medium Duodecimo (Med. 12mo)	7⅔ x 5⅛	195 x 130
Demy Octavo (Dy. 8vo)	8 x 5½	203 x 140
Small Quarto (Sm. 4to)	8½ x 7	216 x 178
Broad Quarto (Br. 4to) (varies)	8½ x 7	216 x 178
Medium Octavo (Med. 8vo)	9½ x 6	241 x 152
Royal Octavo (Roy. 8vo)	10 x 6½	254 x 162
Super Royal Octavo (S. Roy. 8vo)	10½ x 7	267 x 178
Imperial Quarto (Imp. 4to)	11 x 15	279 x 381
Imperial Octavo (Imp. 8vo)	11½ x 8¼	292 x 210

American joints *(fin)* → *French joints*

American russia *(fin)* A strong bookbinding material made from cowhide.
→ *bookbinding; russia cowhide*

ampersand *(typ)* The sign '&' used to represent the word 'and'. Sometimes called a 'short and'.

amplification *(aud)* The process by which sounds are made audible or louder.

amplitude *(aud)* The strength or volume of a sound. In a graphical illustration of a waveform, the amplitude generally refers to the distance by which the highest peak (positive amplitude) and the lowest peak (negative amplitude) deviate from the centre of the sound wave; however, amplitude can be measured at any point along the waveform. Put more simply, the amplitude represents the level of the signal, or the amount of pressure exerted by the sound source on surrounding air molecules. An increase in volume increases the amplitude of the signal.

amplitude modulated screening *(pre)* An alternative name for a conventional halftone screen – in other words, those that break up a continuous tone image into a regular pattern of different sized dots.

AM screening *(pre)* abb.: amplitude modulated screening. → *amplitude modulated screening; frequency modulated screening; halftone (1)*

analog computer *(com)* A computer that uses a physical variable such as voltage to process information or make calculations.
→ *analog*

analog/analogue *(gen)* The use of signals or information processed by a physical variation such as light or voltage, as distinct from digital signals. As applied to sound, the term usually refers to that which is not produced through digital means, such as traditional reel-to-reel tape recording. However, strictly speaking, all sound that is heard is analog, because it has to be played through amplifier, loudspeakers or headphones – which produce sound waves rather than digital signals. → *digital*

anamorphic scan *(pre)* An image scanned and subsequently manipulated to give it disproportionate dimensions.

anastigmatic lens *(pre)* A photographic lens used in conventional repro to prevent blurring of the subject.

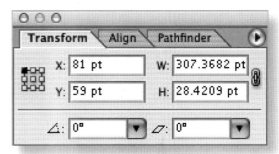

anchor (1) *(com)* The facility, available in many applications, to define a fixed point, such as top left or top right, for an item such as a text or graphic box or a page ruler. Accordingly, values attributed to the item relate to the anchor point. In some applications, graphics or rules can be anchored to text so that they flow with it.

anchor (2) *(int)* A text or graphic element with an HTML tag, which provides a specific target location within a page for a hyperlink. → *HTML; tag (1)*

Anchor Point *(com)* A control point used in Premiere to control the motion or intensity of an effect in relation to the timeline.

angle bar *(pri)* A metal bar on a web printing press that turns paper between two units of the press. → *web printing*

angle of view (1) *(gen)* The angle between opposite faces of a viewing pyramid (the structure created by drawing two lines from the centre of a view to its edges). The more extreme the perspective, the greater the angle.

A palette giving values relating to an **anchor (1)**

angle of view (2) *(pho)* The amount of a scene included in a photographic picture, determined by a combination of the focal length of the lens and the film format.
→ *film format; focal length*

aniline *(pri)* An oily liquid – deriving from a nitrobenzine base – that is used in the preparation of dyes and of volatile, quick-drying aniline ink.

aniline printing *(pri)* → *flexography*

anilox system *(pri)* The method of inking used in flexographic printing. → *flexography*

animal-sized *(pap)* Paper that has been hardened or 'sized' by being passed through a bath of animal glue or gelatine. → *engine-sized; size; tub-sized*

animated GIF *(int)* A 'GIF' (Graphics Interchange Format) file comprised of multiple images, simulating an animation when played back in a Web browser. → *GIF*

animation *(gen)* The process of creating a moving image by rapidly moving from one still image to the next. Traditionally, this was achieved through a laborious process of drawing or painting each 'frame' (a single step in the animation) manually onto

cellulose acetate sheets called 'cels', or 'cells'. However, animations today are more commonly created with specialist software that renders sequences in a variety of formats, typically QuickTime, AVI, Flash and animated GIFs. → *animated GIF; AVI; cel (1); frame (2); QuickTime*

Animation *(com)* A 'lossless' compression method ('codec') used by QuickTime, which will work with all bit depths. Since it is very sensitive to picture changes, the Animation codec works best for creating sequences in images that were rendered digitally.
→ *animation value; bit depth; codec (1); keyframe; QuickTime*

animation value *(com)* The value applied to a keyframe in an animation sequence which represents a change in the object's property and, in turn, determines how the animation of a sequence is interpolated.
→ *Animation; animation; keyframe; interpolate/interpolation; QuickTime*

annex *(fin)* A supplement to a publication that is bound into the main body of the publication.

annotation (1) *(gen)* An identification number or text label added to an illustration.

annotation (2) *(gen)* Notes printed as an explanation in the margin of a text.

anodized plate *(pri)* A standard aluminium litho plate that has been given a fine grain and then electrolytically hardened, making it suitable for a 'deep-etch' image that is capable of sustaining print runs of up to 500,000. → *deep-etch (ing); offset litho(graphy)*

anonymous FTP *(int)* A means of accessing files on a remote computer across the Internet using the File Transfer Protocol (FTP) service, but without having to provide a predefined password or other login name. Access is normally achieved by logging in with a username of 'anonymous' and using an e-mail address as the password. → *File Transfer Protocol; log on*

Several frames of an **animated GIF**

*!?

ANSI *(gen) abb.:* American National Standards Institute. A US organization devoted to defining standards such as those used for programming languages. ANSI represents the United States at the International Standards Organization (ISO).

anti-aliasing *(gen)* The smoothing of jagged edges on diagonal lines created in an imaging program, by giving intermediate values to pixels between the steps. This is especially common with text. The effect is achieved by blending the colour at the edge of the image with its background, averaging the density of the range of pixels involved. Can also be applied to filter texture programs such as those used in 3D applications.

antihalation backing *(pre)* In platemaking, the protective coating on the non-emulsion side of reprographic film, which prevents light from reflecting back onto the emulsion and thus damaging the image. ➔ *halation*

antiqua *(typ)* A group of roman type designs based on early North Italian scripts. Also used in German to describe roman type, as distinct from 'fraktur', the German name for black letter type. ➔ *black letter*

There is a variety of **anti-aliasing** settings available in Photoshop that affect type

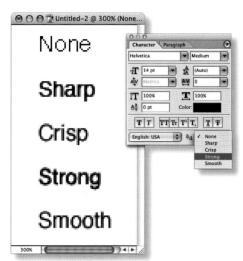

antiquarian *(pap)* The largest known size of handmade paper, introduced by James Whatman in the 18th century, and measuring 1350 x 790mm (53 x 31in). ➔ *paper sizes*

antique gold edges *(fin)* The finish given to gilt edges that are either left unburnished or which are washed over with water after burnishing. ➔ *art gilt edges; gilt edges*

antique laid *(pap)* ➔ *antique paper*

antique paper *(pap)* Generally, any rough-surfaced paper, but originally used to describe laid paper that had been made in moulds where the chain wires were attached directly to the supports of the mould, giving the paper a rough finish. Antique wove is a light but bulky rough-surfaced paper of a good quality.

antique wove *(pap)* ➔ *antique paper*

anti-set-off sprayer/antisetoff (US) *(pri)* A device attached to a printing press that sprays a film of resinous solution or powder onto the printed paper as it leaves the press, thus preventing set-off by keeping the sheets separate. ➔ *set-off*

AOL *(int) abb.:* America Online. One of the world's largest Internet service providers (ISP), now merged with entertainment giant Time Warner. ➔ *Internet Service Provider*

APA *(gen) abb.:* American Publishers' Association.

'A' paper sizes *(pap)* A-series paper sizes ➔ *ISO A-series paper sizes*

aperture *(pho)* A variable opening in a camera lens, controlled by a diaphragm, which allows light to reach the film. The size of aperture is measured by the 'f-number', or 'f-stop'. ➔ *f-number/f-stop*

aperture priority *(pho)* A mode in automatic cameras by which you select the aperture manually, the shutter speed then being set automatically according to the camera's metering system. The opposite of shutter priority. ➜ *aperture; shutter priority*

API *(com) abb.:* application programming interface. ➜ *application programming interface*

apochromatic lens *(pre)* A photographic lens used for colour separations, which has been corrected for colour and astigmatic aberrations. ➜ *astigmatism; colour separation*

append *(com)* The facility within some applications to import user-defined formatting into one document from another, placing it after existing data. ➜ *formatting*

appendix *(gen)* Information, usually reference material, printed at the end of a work.

Apple Desktop Bus (ADB) *(com)* The standard connection bus on old, pre-USB Macintosh computers for connecting input devices such as the mouse, keyboard, digitizing tablets, etc. ➜ *bus (1)*

Apple event *(com)* A feature of the Macintosh Operating System that allows one application to send messages and trigger events in another.

Apple File Exchange *(com)* Outdated software, supplied with old versions of the Macintosh Operating System, that provided support for Microsoft DOS format disks and helped link IBM-compatible PC file formats with equivalent Macintosh applications.

Apple menu *(com)* A menu item on a Macintosh computer, identified by the Apple logo, which is generally available in all applications and where key controls and system information can be accessed. In older systems, with rainbow-coloured Apple logos, this meant the 'Chooser' for selecting network resources, and memory information. On newer (Mac OS X and above) computers, it allows access to recent applications and documents, 'About This Mac' information and shutdown and logging off options, much as the 'Start' button does on Windows computers.

Apple Remote Access *(com)* A Macintosh application that enables one Mac to connect to another via a modem, and then remotely control and access all the files and network services available to it, such as printers, servers, etc. ➜ *network; server*

Apple RGB *(com)* An older colour space based on the original Apple 13-inch colour monitor and Photoshop 4 standards, with a lower gamma setting (1.8) than Adobe RGB or sRGB (both have gamma 2.2). No longer widely used.

AppleScript *(com)* The scripting feature built into the Mac OS to allow the user to write scripts that will automate common tasks. Many applications support AppleScript, enabling scripts to perform automatic operations within those programs. ➜ *droplet; script (1)*

AppleShare *(com)* A feature of the Mac OS allowing computers to share files across a network. ➜ *network*

applet *(int)* Although a general term that can be applied to any small application that performs a specific task, such as the calculator, an applet is also used to describe a small application written in the Java programming language, which is downloaded by an Internet browser to perform specific tasks. ➜ *browser (1); Internet; Java*

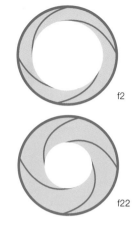

f2

f22

The wider the **aperture,** the lower the 'f-number'

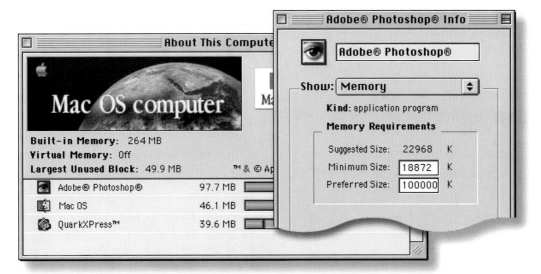

Older operating
systems required the
user to play an active
part in managing
application memory

AppleTalk *(com)* The protocol built into the Mac
OS enabling the computer to communicate
with other computers or hardware devices,
such as printers, across a network. The
hardware cabling used to connect
computers via AppleTalk is generally
Ethernet. ➔ *Ethernet; network*

application *(com)* A software program written
to enable the user to create and modify
documents for a specific purpose, thus
distinguishing it from operating system
software and utilities (software that improves
the functioning of your computer rather than
enabling you to create anything). Typical
application groups include those for page
layout, graphics, image-editing, word
processing and spreadsheets.

application memory (heap) *(com)* The
portion of the computer's memory (RAM)
occupied for use by an application when it
is launched or opened. The application heap
is reserved for use only by that application,
and separates it from the memory reserved
for other applications or the computer's
operating system. ➔ *application memory
size/partition; operating system; random
access memory (RAM)*

application memory size/partition *(com)*
The amount of memory (RAM), measured
in megabytes, reserved by an application
when it is being used. ➔ *application
memory (heap); random access memory
(RAM)*

application menu *(com)* A standard menu
that lists all opened applications and
enables you to switch between them.
➔ *menu*

application programming interface (API)
(com) A set of routines, protocols and tools
for building software applications, making it
easier for a programmer to develop a
program by providing all the building blocks.

application (support) file *(com)* A file used
by applications for specific operations that
are unique to that application, such as
checking spelling or providing help.

APR *(pre)* abb.: automatic picture replacement.
➔ *automatic picture replacement*

apron *(pri)* White space added to the margins of
the text area on a page to accommodate a
foldout.

Aqua-trol *(pri)* The proprietary name (American
Type Founders Company) of a device for
removing moisture from the inking system
of a lithographic printing press.

aquatint *(pri)* An intaglio printing process that builds up even or graded tones using resin and varnish. Although once used as a commercial process, aquatints are now used only for limited edition fine art prints.
→ *intaglio*

ARA *(com) abb.:* Apple Remote Access.
→ *Apple Remote Access*

arabesque *(typ)* A design found in decorative fonts of curving stems, leaves and flowers, originally deriving from the Islamic ornamental depiction of the acanthus vine.
→ *dingbat; flower; ornament*

Arabic numerals *(typ)* The characters '1234567890'. Although described as 'Arabic', thus presuming their origin, these numeric symbols have been traced back to Hindi symbols used in India. → *Roman numerals*

archetype *(gen)* The correct version of a manuscript or printed work, marked or otherwise, that is used for amending later versions.

Archie *(int)* An outdated Internet service that logs the whereabouts of files so that they can be located for downloading. Once found, files are downloaded using FTP.
→ *File Transfer Protocol*

archival backup *(com)* A backup routine that copies files on your hard disk without overwriting, or replacing, previously backed up versions of those files. Consequently, archival backups just keep growing!
→ *backup/backing up*

archival paper *(pap)* Special acid-free paper used for printing volumes intended for long-lasting storage. → *archival printing*

archival printing *(pri)* The printing of works for long-lasting storage, using special techniques. → *archival paper*

archive *(com)* Any file or collection of files that has been backed up for storage or compressed to free up disk space.
→ *archival backup*

Area light *(com)* A special light type that emits from a 2D area rather than a point.

argument *(com)* A term used to describe the words or numbers on which a formula or mathematical function is carried out. The input used to generate the answer.

arpeggio *(aud)* A musical term, referring to the playing in rapid succession of a series of individual notes. The notes make up a chord, but are played individually instead of all together.

arrow pointer *(com)* → *pointer*

art canvas *(fin)* A rough-surfaced binding material used for binding cased books.
→ *bookbinding; case (1); cased/casebound*

An **arabesque** of the letter 'A'

artefact *(gen)* Any flaw in a digital image, such as 'noise'. Most artefacts are undesirable, although adding noise can create a grainy texture if appropriate. A typical example of an artefact would be clumps of pixels appearing in a video clip.

art gilt edges *(fin)* Gilt-edged books in which the edges have been coloured, usually with a tint of the binding, prior to the gold being applied. → *antique gold edges; gilt edges*

artificial intelligence (AI) *(com)* Software programs that learn from criteria provided by the user and which are thus able to modify results.

artificial light *(gen)* Any light source not naturally occurring in the environment, but usually used to describe incandescent, tungsten or fluorescent lighting.

artificial parchment *(pap)* → *parchment*

art-lined envelope *(pap)* An envelope lined on its interior with an extra-fine paper that is generally coloured or patterned.

art paper *(pap)* A high-quality paper with a smooth surface. Originally, the surface was achieved by applying china clay to a base paper, but it is now more common for art

papers to be coated by other processes such as 'blade coaters'. Art paper can be gloss or matt. → *blade coater; coated paper*

art vellum *(pap)* A strong, imitation animal parchment paper used for bindings and certificates. → *parchment; vellum*

art(work) *(gen)* Any matter prepared for reproduction, but generally used to mean illustrations and photographs, thus distinguishing them from text.

ASA *(pho) abb.:* American Standards Association. The US Association that defined the scale used for rating the speed (light-sensitivity) of photographic film.

ascender

ascender *(typ)* The part of a lower case character that extends above its body (or 'x-height') as with the letters b, d, f, h, k, l and t. → *character (1); x-height*

ascent *(typ)* The amount of space required to accommodate a font. The ascent value is determined by the font designer and is the value used by many page-layout applications for leading and aligning boxes. It is measured from the baseline.
→ *baseline; leading*

ASCII *(com)* (pron.: *asskee*) Acronym for the American Standard Code for Information Interchange. A code that assigns a unique number to the 256 letters, numbers and symbols (including carriage returns and tabs) that can be typed on a keyboard.

ASCII is the cross-platform, computer industry-standard, text-only file format.
→ *cross-platform*

ASIO *(aud)* (PC/Mac) Audio Streaming Input/Output. A Steinberg-developed soundcard driver with low latency times. An extremely powerful and reliable system for software synthesis that sits outside the operating system. Recommended and supported by most sequencers and soft synths.

A-sizes *(pap)* → *ISO A-series paper sizes*

aspect ratio *(gen)* The ratio of the width of an image to its height, expressed as x:y. For example, the aspect ratio of an image measuring 200 x 100 pixels is 2:1.

ASPIC *(pre)* Acronym for Author's Symbolic Prepress Interfacing Codes. A means of translating typographic formatting of text output on a word processor into a language that a typesetting machine will understand.

assembled negative *(pre)* The combination of line and halftone negative film used for platemaking in offset litho printing.
→ *assembly; flat (1); offset litho(graphy); plate (3)*

assembly *(pre)* The gathering together and arrangement of all the separate components used to make final film, or 'flats', in platemaking. Also called 'stripping', 'film assembly', 'film make-up' or 'image assembly'. → *film assembly; flat (1)*

associative linking *(int)* Hyperlinks organized by association rather than by formal classification.

asterisk *(typ)* A star-shaped symbol (*), generally used as a reference mark within text to indicate a footnote.

astigmatism *(pho)* A defect in photographic lenses that causes distortion.
→ *apochromatic lens*

as to press *(pri)* Proofs that show the final position of images before printing in gravure printed magazines. → *gravure*

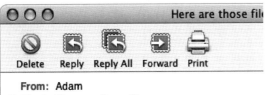

Here are those fil[...]

Delete | Reply | Reply All | Forward | Print

From: Adam
Subject: **Here are those files**
Date: 5 April 2004 15:25:34 BST
To: Eve

▶ 1 Attachment, 83.4 KB (Save All...)

Hi Eve,

Here is that file you asked for:

Eden A-Z.pdf (83.4 KB)

--
Adam

Asymmetrical Digital Subscriber Line (ADSL) *(int)* → *ADSL*

asynchronous *(com)* A communications protocol in which data bits are transmitted one after the other, with start-and-stop bits denoting the beginning and end of each character transmitted. In terms of communication, this allows data to be sent back and forth without being subject to rigid timing signals. → *synchronous communication/transmission*

asynchronous transfer mode (ATM) *(com)* A very fast communications technology in which data can be transferred at extremely high speeds.

atlas folio *(pap)* The largest folio paper size, measuring 432 x 660mm (17 x 26in). → *folio (2); paper sizes*

ATM (1) *(com) abb.:* Adobe Type Manager. → *Adobe Type Manager; printer font; screen font; Type 1 font*

ATM (2) *(int)* → *asynchronous transfer mode*

attaching *(fin)* A binding method in which a narrow strip of strong paper is used to attach the end leaves of the book block to the boards, as distinct from casing-in. → *binding; casing-in*

attachment *(int)* An external file such as an image or text document 'attached' to an e-mail message for electronic transmission. → *e-mail*

attenuation *(aud)* This usually refers to equalizer settings, when certain frequencies are manually or automatically attenuated or 'cut back' in an effort to alter the sound or draw attention to other frequencies.

attribute (1) *(int)* A characteristic of an HTML tag, which is identified alongside the tag in order to describe, modify or extend it. → *attribute (2); HTML; tag (1)*

attribute (2) *(com)* The specification applied to a character, box or other item. Character attributes include font, size, style, colour, shade, scaling, kerning, etc.

audio-visual aids *(gen)* The name given to display equipment used for teaching and training, such as projectors and computers.

authentication *(int)* The process of verifying the identity of someone attempting to access a remote computer or server, via a network or the Internet, usually by means of a user ID and/or password. → *anonymous FTP; Internet; server*

authoring *(com)* The act of constructing a multimedia presentation or website, usually with reference to manipulating the scripting language. → *authoring tool/application/ software/program; HTML; script (1)*

authoring tool/application/software/ program *(com)* Software that enables you to create interactive presentations, such as those used in multimedia, websites, and software programming. Authoring programs typically provide text, drawing, painting, animation and audio features, and combine these with a scripting language that

An e-mail with an **attachment**

```
on mouseDown
    show bg grc "GoFirst"
end mouseDown

on MouseUp
    hide bg grc "GoFirst"
    go to card "Index"
end MouseUp

on MouseLeave
    hide bg grc "GoFirst"
end MouseLeave
```

Some code in an **authoring** application

determines how each element behaves. For example, a scripted instruction attached to a button will tell the computer to display a different page or perform a task, such as playing a film. ➔ *authoring; script (1)*

author's alteration/correction *(gen)* Alterations made to a text by its author, that deviate from the original copy. These corrections are marked on the author's proof and are distinguished from typesetting errors, especially in cases where additional charges may be made for implementing the corrections. ➔ *author's proof*

author's proof *(gen)* Galley or laser proofs, usually of text, supplied to an author for correction. These proofs will have previously been read by a proofreader, who will have marked all typesetting errors. ➔ *author's alteration/correction; galley proof*

autoflow *(com)* A feature of page-layout, word processing and graphics applications, which flows running text automatically from one page or box to another. ➔ *automatic text box; auto page insertion*

auto-key event *(com)* A command, called an 'event' in programming terms, generated repeatedly when a character key is held down on the keyboard. ➔ *auto-key rate; auto-key threshold; event; keyboard event*

auto-key rate *(com)* The rate at which a character key repeats when it is held down. ➔ *auto-key event; auto-key threshold*

auto-key threshold *(com)* The length of time a character key must be held down before it begins repeating. ➔ *auto-key event; auto-key rate*

auto leading *(com)* The facility of an application to adjust the leading automatically as the size of text is adjusted. Auto leading is usually expressed as a percentage of the font size. ➔ *leading*

automated dialogue replacement (ADR) *(aud)* ➔ *ADR*

automated publication *(gen)* Published work of which a digital copy is kept for automatic updating.

automatic font downloading *(com)* ➔ *font downloading*

automatic double-tracking (ADT) *(aud)* ➔ *ADT*

automatic hyphenation *(com)* The facility of an application to divide words by placing a hyphen automatically at the end of a line, the second part of the word being carried over to the next line of text. The placement of the hyphen usually occurs at predefined syllable junctures. ➔ *hyphenation and justification (H&Js, H/Js)*

automatic picture replacement (APR) *(pre)* The 'open prepress interface' (OPI) procedure whereby low-resolution scanned images are used for page-layout purposes, and are automatically replaced by the high-resolution files prior to film output. ➔ *Desktop Color Separation; open prepress interface (OPI)*

automatic text box *(com)* A text box into which text flows when a page is automatically inserted. This is a feature of most page-layout and word processing applications ➔ *auto page insertion; text box; text chain*

automatic text chain *(com)* ➔ *text chain*

automatic transfer press *(pri)* A type of web press that allows a change of plates without interrupting the run. While one job is running, another is prepared on a second unit.

auto page insertion *(com)* A feature of some applications that automatically adds pages if the amount of text on a page exceeds the space available to accommodate it. ➔ *autoflow; automatic text box*

autopaster *(pri)* ➔ *flying paster*

autoplate machine *(pri)* Used in rotary printing, this is a moulding cylinder that has 'flong' (a papier-maché-like material) placed around it to make the curved 'stereos' used for printing. → *stereo (type); flong*

autopositive *(pho)* A photographic material that provides a positive image without a negative version being required. → *auto-reversing film*

auto-reversing film *(pre)* A photographic material that provides a negative copy from a negative film original without an intermediate positive being required. Also known as 'autoscreen'. → *autopositive*

autotrace *(com)* A feature of some drawing applications that will automatically create a vector path by tracing around the solid elements of a bitmapped image. → *bit map/bitmap; bitmap graphic; vector*

A/UX *(com)* A version of the AT&T UNIX Operating System that could be used on Macintosh computers. → *operating system*

auxiliary dictionary *(com)* A dictionary file, available in many applications, which allows user-defined spellings to be stored and re-used in addition to the program's built-in dictionary. → *exception dictionary*

auxiliary file *(com)* → *application (support) file*

auxiliary roll stand *(pri)* A stand for holding an additional roll of paper on a web-fed printing press, which allows continuous printing while the first roll is replaced. → *automatic transfer press; web (1)*

AVA *(gen) abb.:* audio-visual aids. → *audio-visual aids*

Avatar *(int)* The incarnation of a human being in a virtual reality environment, game, or a networked multi-user environment. Avatars are a kind of alter ego used by some computer users to represent themselves when they interact with other users. → *virtual reality*

AVI *(com)* Audio Video Interleaved. A Microsoft media file format used within Windows, and the default file format for captured video files on Windows-based systems. Microsoft has now replaced it with 'DirectShow', but it is also used as an Internet streaming and non-streaming format. → *codec (1); DirectShow; QuickTime*

AVOption *(aud)* This is Digidesign's Plug-and-Play compatible, two-card interface that enables the importing of video and audio from high-end Avid video workstations, or any NTSC or PAL sources such as video tape, directly into a Pro Tools video track.

a/w *(gen) abb.:* artwork. → *art(work)*

axial lighting *(pho)* The technique of lighting a photographic subject by shining a light along the lens axis, thus casting few or no shadows.

axis *(gen)* (plural: axes) An imaginary line that defines the centre of the 3D universe. In turn, the x, y and z axes (width, height and depth, respectively) define each of the three dimensions of an object. The axis along which an object rotates is the axis of rotation.

azure *(pap)* In papermaking, the term describing paler shades of blue paper.

azured tooling *(fin)* The 'hatched' effect in hand-tooled bindings, deriving from the heraldic device of using horizontal parallel lines to indicate blue. → *binding*

3D space is defined by the x, y and z **axes**

Bb

back *(fin)* The part of a book formed nearest to the edge at which it is bound and after it is stitched.

backbone (1) *(fin)* → *spine*

backbone (2) *(com)* The main high-speed connection between nodes linking networked devices. → *network*

back cornering *(fin)* The removal of small chips from the four innermost corners of the boards of a book to make it easier to open after it is covered. → *boards*

back cylinder *(pri)* → *impression cylinder*

backed (1) *(pri)* A sheet that has had its reverse side printed. → *backs (2); back up/backing up (2)*

backed (2) *(fin)* Used during the binding process to describe a volume after backing, but before casing-in. → *binding; casing-in*

back edge curl/tail-end hook *(pri)* An aberration that occurs at the tail end of a press, either when light papers cling to the blanket cylinder of a sheet-fed litho press, or when too much ink is applied at this edge, causing curling. This may result in misregister in later printings. → *blanket cylinder*

back (edge) margin *(gen)* The margin closest to the spine on a page which forms part of a bound volume. Also called the 'inner margin', 'binding margin' or 'gutter margin'. → *spine*

back end *(com)* A general term describing the part of the computing process when heavy-duty data processing is carried out – by servers or imagesetters, for example – as distinct from the 'front end', where data is input by the user. → *front end (1); server*

background (1) *(com)* Any software activity, such as printing, which takes place while you are working on other software in the foreground.

background (2) *(gen)* The area of an image upon which the principal subject, or foreground, sits.

background colour/tint *(com)* In graphics applications, a colour or tint that has been applied to the background of any item, such as a page, text box or illustration.

backing (away) *(pri)* A printing problem that occurs as a result of an inadequate supply of ink to the fountain roller, resulting in a lighter printed image.

backing strip *(fin)* → *back lining*

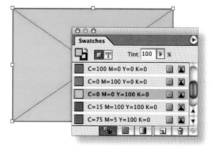

Applying a **background colour** in Adobe InDesign

back (jacket) flap *(gen)* → *jacket flaps*

backlighting *(pho)* The principal light source that shines from behind the subject and is directed (broadly) towards the camera lens. This tends to give a lot of contrast, with silhouettes. A specific form of backlighting is called contre jour. Many cameras feature backlight controls that increase aperture (or exposure time) to compensate for backlighting and to prevent the silhouetting of foreground objects.

back lining *(fin)* A fabric or paper strip glued to the back of a book to reinforce the binding before casing-in. → *casing-in*

back mark *(pri)* → *back(step) mark*

back printing *(pri)* Printing on the underside of a translucent material. Also called 'reverse printing'. As distinct from backing up.

back projection *(pho)* The technique of displaying an image behind a photographic subject by projecting it onto a translucent screen from behind. → *front projection*

backs (1) *(fin)* → *back (edge) margin*

backs (2) *(pri)* Printed sheets to be printed (backed up) on the reverse side. The term also describes the printing plates to be used in backing up. → *backed (1); backup/ backing up (2);*

back scatter *(pho)* A photographic 'snowstorm' effect achieved by lighting the subject with a flashgun placed under bubbling water.

backside cache *(com)* A dedicated chip for temporary storage of frequently accessed data. The term indicates it is connected directly to the main CPU of a computer, thus bypassing the speed limitations of the main data transfer bus (the path along which data travels). → *cache*

backslanted type *(typ)* → *contra italic*

backslash *(typ)* → *slash*

The unwanted specks in this photo are known as **back scatter**

back(step) collation *(pri)* The collation of printed signatures by reference to printed marks on the back fold of each section. → *back(step) mark; signature (1); collate*

back(step) mark *(pri)* A black mark printed on a sheet to show where the final fold will be. If the sheet forms a volume made out of several signatures, each back(step) mark is placed in a slightly different position, so that when all the signatures are collated the marks form a stepped sequence that indicates whether the signatures are in the correct order or if any are missing. Also called a 'collating mark'. → *back(step) collation; collate; signature (1)*

back-to-back *(pri)* Printing on both sides of a sheet. → *backup/backing up (2)*

backup/backing up (1) *(com)* To duplicate data files as a precaution against damage to or loss of the originals. Backup copies can be made on the same disk as the original (not recommended), on another hard disk, or on other kinds of media such as CDs, DVDs and tapes. For ultimate security, backups should be stored in a different location from the original. → *archival backup; backup, global/baseline; backup, incremental; backup, mirror image; backup, same disk; backup set*

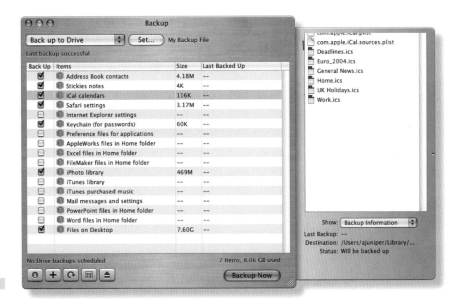

Backing up files using Apple's **Backup**

backup/backing up (2) *(pri)* The printing of the reverse side of a printed sheet. After backing up, the sheet is described as 'backed'. Also called 'perfecting'.
→ *backed (1); backs (2); backup registration; perfecting*

backup, global/baseline *(com)* A backup routine in which the entire contents of your hard disk is duplicated, creating a snapshot of your disk at one moment in time. Global backups usually form the first copy, or backup 'set', of your hard disk, and from then on backups to that set are either 'archival' or 'incremental'. → *archival backup; backup/backing up (1); backup, incremental; backup set*

backup, incremental *(com)* A copy to a backup set of only those files on your hard disk that have been modified since the last time you backed up the disk. With some software, an incremental backup may replace previously backed up versions of newly modified files, so you need to create an archival backup if you want to keep earlier versions. → *archival backup; backup/backing up (1); backup set*

backup, mirror-image *(com)* An exact copy of one hard disk to another, replacing any data that may previously have been stored on the target disk. → *backup/backing up (1)*

backup registration *(pri)* The correct registration of a printed sheet relative to the printing on the other side. → *backup/backing up (2)*

backup, same disk *(com)* A copy of files made to the disk on which the originals reside. As a general backup strategy, same disk backups are not advised, and should only be used, for example, to keep temporary copies of the file you are working on as a precaution against data corruption. → *backup/backing up (1)*

backup set *(com)* The collection of disks, tapes or files that form the backed-up copy of your hard disk. Also called a 'storage set'. → *backup/backing up (1)*

B

bad break *(typ)* Used in typesetting to describe text breaking in an undesirable place. Examples are beginning a page with the last word (orphan), or short line (widow), of a paragraph. The term is also applied to an incorrectly hyphenated word. ➔ *orphan; widow (line)*

bad colour *(pri)* In printing, uneven colour caused either by mechanical faults such as erratic ink distribution, or by operator faults during make-ready. ➔ *make-ready*

bad copy *(gen)* A heavily corrected manuscript, making it difficult to read.

bagged *(gen)* Describes a publication that is placed in a pack along with another publication or a promotional item.

ballooning *(com)* An aberration in cheaper monitors when voltage fluctuations, which occur during the switch from light images to dark, cause the image to spread out.
➔ *monitor; pincushion*

band *(fin)* ➔ *head/tail band*

banding *(pre)* An aberration that occurs in the electronic reproduction of graduated tints, when the ratio of halftone screen ruling and output resolution is incorrect, causing a 'stepped' appearance. The maximum number of achievable levels of tone is 256 (the PostScript limit) for each of the four process colours (CMYK). To calculate the optimum imagesetter resolution, multiply the halftone screen ruling by 16 (the square root of 256 – each imagesetter dot is constructed on a matrix of 16 x 16 pixels). Therefore, to minimize the chance of banding in a single colour image to be printed with a halftone screen ruling of 150lpi, the maximum levels of grey can be achieved if it is output by the imagesetter at 2400dpi (150 x 16). Banding can also occur when the percentage values of a large area of a graduated single colour tint are very close. ➔ *CMYK; halftone (2); imagesetter; PostScript; resolution (2)*

bandwidth *(int)* The measure of the speed at which information is passed between two points, which may be between modems, across a bus, or from memory to disk. The broader the bandwidth, the faster data flows. Similarly, the bandwidth of a set of loudspeakers is the range of frequencies across which it can reproduce sound; a wider bandwidth allows for a greater range of sounds, and thus better sound reproduction. Bandwidth is usually measured in cycles per second (hertz) or in kilobits per second (kbps). ➔ *bus (1)*

bank *(com)* Another term for roll, or rotation about an object's local z-axis. Also applies when an object rotates along its motion vector.

banker envelope *(pap)* An envelope that has its flap along the longer edge.

bank paper *(pap)* A thin, uncoated writing or typing paper typically between 45 and 63gsm. Similar papers in heavier weights are called 'bonds', while lighter weights are 'manifolds'. ➔ *bond paper*

banner (1) *(gen)* A headline that occupies the full width of a page of a newspaper or magazine.

banner (2) *(int)* An image used to attract attention on a webpage, usually an advertisement.

bar code *(gen)* A product identification and coding system in which a number is represented by a pattern of bars of varying thickness, which can be optically scanned to extract information. There are a number

A **banner** advertisement for Powergen

of systems employed for encoding information, the most common being UPC (Universal Product Code) and EAN (European Article Number). Also called 'optical bar recognition' (OBR), or 'optical mark recognition' (OMR). ➔ *UPC*

barn doors *(pho)* Flaps attached to a photographic light to control the direction and amount of light emitted. Many presentation applications contain features that emulate the effect of barn doors on lights.

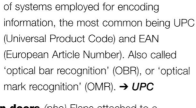

A light with **barn doors** fitted

baryta paper *(pap)* A very smooth paper, traditionally used for making reproduction-quality proofs from metal type.

base alignment *(typ)* The alignment of type characters of differing sizes or fonts along their baselines. ➔ *baseline*

base artwork *(pre)* Camera-ready art, used in photomechanical reproduction, which contains text matter and keylines, but to which other elements such as halftone images and tints must be added at film stage. ➔ *camera-ready copy/art (CRC); halftone (1); keyline (1)*

base film *(pre)* In photomechanical reproduction, the basic negative or positive film substrate onto which other film components such as halftone images are mounted, or 'stripped'. ➔ *halftone (1); stripping (2)*

base lighting *(pho)* The technique of lighting a photographic subject from beneath by projecting the light upwards. Also known as 'ground lighting'. Often used for still-life photography of glassware and metallic objects to provide full lighting but without the flash highlights that would occur with front or side lighting.

A scanned banknote with **bas-relief** applied

base line *(typ)* The imaginary line on a page grid that indicates the base of a block of text. ➔ *grid (1)*

baseline *(typ)* The imaginary line, defined by the flat base of a lower case letter such as 'x', upon which the bases of all upper and lower case letters apparently rest.

baseline backup *(com)* ➔ *backup, global/baseline*

baseline grid *(typ)* Some page-layout applications have an underlying grid, usually invisible, to which the baselines of text can be 'locked' so that they line up across all columns of a page. ➔ *base line*

baseline shift *(typ)* The attribute applied to a character that moves it up or down from its baseline. ➔ *baseline*

base stock *(pap)* The main constituents from which paper is made.

basic size *(pap)* The standard size of a particular paper, against which other sizes are measured. For example, the basic size of cover papers is 20 x 26in. ➔ *basic weight/basis weight; paper sizes*

basic weight/basis weight *(pap)* The weight, in pounds, of a ream of paper (500 sheets) cut to a designated size (basic size). ➔ *basic size; paper sizes*

basil *(fin)* A binding material made from sheepskin and used as a poor-quality substitute for leather. ➔ *binding*

bas-relief *(gen)* An image that is embossed and which stands out in shallow relief from a flat background, designed to give the illusion of further depth.

bastard (1) *(pri)* Any aberration or abnormal element in the printing process.

bastard (2) *(pap)* Generally any non-standard size of paper. Also, specifically, an obsolete paper size of 33 x 20in. ➔ *basic size; paper sizes*

bastard (3) *(typ)* In typesetting, a character that is foreign to the font in which it is set. Also, in mechanical typography, a character that is smaller or larger than the body upon which it is cast. ➔ *font; body (1)*

bastard title *(gen)* ➔ *half title (2)*

batch mode/processing *(com)* The processing of data in automated batches, as distinct from data that is processed as it is input (interactive mode, or realtime). For example, a spellchecker runs in batch mode when applied to a block of text, but not when applied to an individual word. An example of batch processing is when you apply a Photoshop 'Action' to two or more files. → *interactive mode; realtime*

baud *(int)* (pron. *bord*); The number of signal changes transmitted per second during data transmission by modem. → *baud rate*

baud rate *(int)* The speed at which a modem transmits data, or the number of 'events' it can handle per second. Often used to describe the transmission speed of data itself, but since a single event can contain two or more bits, data speed is more correctly expressed in 'kilobits per second' (kbps). → *baud; bit; event*

Baumé scale *(pri)* A scale used to measure the density of liquids used in printing.

BBS *(int) abb.:* bulletin board service. → *bulletin board service; on-line service provider; sysop*

BCP *(com) abb.:* Bézier control point. → *Bézier curve*

beard *(typ)* In metal type, the space between the baseline of the x-height and the body of type, forming the 'shoulder'. Also called the 'bevel'.

bearers *(pri)* The rings on the end of the cylinders of printing presses that determine the plate-to-blanket pressure. → *blanket cylinder*

bearoff *(typ)* In conventional metal typesetting, the adjustment of the spacing of the type to correct the justification.

beating *(pap)* The process of converting raw pulp, or 'half-stuff', into paper pulp. → *half-stuff; stuff*

Beat-matching/mapping *(aud)* Matching the tempo of an audio loop to the tempo of the track into which it has been pasted. In most cases, this will alter the pitch of the sample, but some programs can now retain pitch information.

bed (1) *(pri)* The steel table of a letterpress machine on which the frame containing metal type ('forme') is placed. The expression 'put to bed' originally described the secured forme, although it is now generally used in printing to describe plates once they are secured and ready to print. → *put to bed*

bed (2) *(fin)* The flat metal surface of a guillotine, on which paper is cut. Also called a 'table'. → *guillotine; table (1)*

begin even *(typ)* Instruction to the typesetter to set the first line of copy 'full out' without indenting it.

bellows *(pho)* An extendable section of folding cloth on some photographic cameras that connects the lens to the part that holds the film. Such cameras are often referred to as 'bellows cameras' and are generally used with large-format film.

belly *(typ)* The front or 'nick' side of metal type.

below the line *(gen)* A term used in advertising to describe promotional items that fall outside a specific campaign.

Photoshop's Actions can **batch process**

A camera **bellows** attachment

B

belt press *(pri)* A printing press that performs the entire manufacturing process of a book, from paper roll to binding. ➔ *binding*

benday/Ben Day tints *(pre)* Originally a proprietary technique, named after Benjamin Day and introduced in 1901, of applying tints of a colour to artwork or printing plates using a pattern of dots. Nowadays the term is generally used to describe an effect rather than the technique employed to achieve the effect.

bender *(pap)* Paper or board stock that can be folded without breaking. ➔ *board (1)*

bestiary *(gen)* ➔ *grotesque (1)*

beta testing *(com)* Testing software prior to commercial release, typically by designated members of the public working under non-disclosure agreements, for the purpose of eliminating errors. ➔ *alpha test; beta version*

beta version *(com)* A version of a software program prior to commercial release, used for final checks for errors ('beta tests'). Beta versions are also frequently used for review purposes. ➔ *beta test; alpha version; release version*

bevel (1) *(gen)* A chamfered edge applied to type, buttons or selections to lend them a 3D effect. In 3D software, it can also mean to extrude a polygon along its Normal producing bevels around its perimeter.

bevel (2) *(typ)* On metal type, the sloping surface connecting the face to the shoulder. Also called the 'beard'.

bevel (3) *(pri)* The outer edge of a printing plate that is used to secure the plate to the press.

bevelled boards *(pap)* Strong, bevel-edged boards used mainly for binding large volumes. ➔ *boards; binding*

Bézier *(gen)* A method of creating curves from straight lines by adding control points to the line, which can then be dragged in and out to increase or decrease the curvature. Named after the mathematician who invented the underlying maths.

Bézier control handle/point *(com)* ➔ *Bézier curve*

Bézier curve *(com)* In drawing applications, a curved line between two control points. Each point is a tiny database, or 'vector', which stores information about the line, such as its thickness, colour, length and direction. Complex shapes can be applied to the curve by manipulating handles, which are dragged out from the control points. Bézier curves are used to define very precise shapes on a path. Most applications provide a 'pen tool' to draw such curves. ➔ *vector*

Bézier spline *(com)* ➔ *Bézier curve*

b/f (1) *(gen)* abb.: brought/bring forward. Any matter that has been moved forward from previous pages. ➔ *take over/take forward*

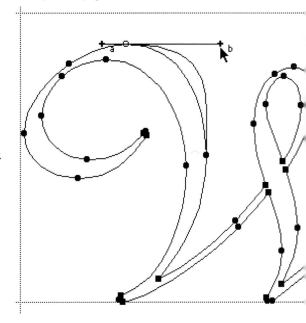

The points of a
Bézier curve

b/f (2) *(typ)* abb.: bold face. Shorthand for the instruction to set text in a bold face. → *bold (face)*

Bible paper *(pap)* Very thin paper that is both tough and opaque and is generally used for printing Bibles and prayer books. Also called 'India' paper.

bibliography *(gen)* A list of publications, generally included at the end of a book, but alternatively printed on the back ('verso') of the half title or title page ('biblio' page). A bibliography may list other titles by the author, or reference material on a particular subject. → *end/back matter; half title (1 & 2); title page*

bichromated colloids *(pri)* Any substance, such as gum arabic, used as the base for light-sensitive coatings when making litho plates. → *offset litho(graphy)*

bicycling *(pri)* The duplication and transportation of materials, such as film or artwork, to another printer to enable simultaneous production of a job.

bimetal(lic) plate *(pri)* A lithographic printing plate made from two different metals, one water-receptive, the other ink-receptive. Such plates allow the printing of long runs on high-speed presses. → *offset litho(graphy)*

bimetal varnish *(pri)* Varnish added to printing ink to toughen it when dry. Also called binding varnish.

bin *(aud)* A visual aid on video-editing software, where a virtual bin represents the container used to store clips or still images in the pre-digital film-making process. These image or audio clips can then be taken from the bin for use in the timeline.

binary *(com)* An arithmetical system that uses 2 as its base, meaning that it can only be represented by two possible values: a 1 or a 0, on or off, something or nothing, negative or positive, small or large, etc. All digital data, no matter how complex, is stored as a

The 0s and 1s of **binary** code

series of ones and zeros. In a digital sound recording, for example, an analog-to-digital convertor transforms audio information into a series of binary digits – or bits – that the computer can save, read and process. → *binary code; binary system; bit*

binary code *(com)* The computer code, made up of 1s and 0s, that is used to represent a character or instruction. For example, the binary code 01100010 represents a lower-case 'b'. → *binary; binary file; bit*

binary digit *(com)* → *bit*

binary file *(com)* A file in which data is described in binary code rather than text. Binary files typically hold pictures, sounds or a complete application program. → *binary; binary code; BinHex*

binary system *(com)* Numbering system that uses two digits, 0 and 1, as distinct from the decimal system of 0–9. → *binary; bit*

binder's board *(fin)* Board used as a stiffener for binding books, around which cloth or other materials are wrapped. → *boards; bookbinding; book cloth*

binder's cloth *(fin)* → *book cloth*

binder's creep *(fin)* The displacement of the leaves in the signatures of a book, requiring the inner pages of the folded signatures to have a slightly smaller trim size. Creep increases with paper thickness. Also called 'thrust', 'shingling' and 'pushout'. → *signature (1); wraparound (2)*

Binder's creep causes leaves to move

binder's die/brass *(fin)* A brass block used for blocking, or stamping, the cover of a book. → *block (2)*

binding *(fin)* The process of joining and securing the assembled leaves of a printed work, such as a book or brochure. There are many methods of binding, including mechanical methods such as plastic comb binding and ring binding, and more conventional methods such as smyth-sewn, side-sewn, section-sewn, saddle-sewn and adhesive binding. → *bookbinding*

binding edge *(fin)* → *spine*

binding margin *(pri)* → *back (edge) margin*

binding varnish *(pri)* → *bimetal varnish*

BinHex *(int)* Acronym for 'binary to hexadecimal', a file format that converts binary files to ASCII text, usually for transmission via e-mail. This is the safest way of sending document files – particularly to and from Macintosh computers – since some computer systems along the e-mail route may only accept standard ASCII text characters. Encoding and decoding BinHex may be done automatically by some e-mail software, but otherwise it must be done manually, usually with a file compression utility. → *ASCII; binary; e-mail*

BIOS *(com)* abb.: Basic Input/Output System. The code (usually residing on a chip placed on the motherboard of a computer) that handles basic hardware input and output operations, such as interactions with a keyboard or hard disk drive. → *I/O*

bit *(com)* Acronym for binary digit. The smallest piece of information a computer can use. A bit is expressed as one of two values: a 1 or a 0, on or off, something or nothing, negative or positive, small or large, etc. Each alphabet character requires eight bits (called a 'byte') to store it. → *binary; bit density; bit depth; bit map/bitmap; bit rate; byte*

From top to bottom, images at 2, 8 and 24-bit **bit depth**

bit density *(com)* The number of bits occupying a particular area or length – per inch of magnetic tape, for example. → *bit; bpi*

bit depth (1) *(com)* The number of bits assigned to each pixel on a monitor, scanner or image file. 1-bit, for example, will only produce black and white (as it is binary, the bit is either on/1 or off/0), whereas 8-bit will generate 256 greys or colours (256 is the maximum number of permutations of a string of eight 1s and 0s), and 24-bit will produce 16.7 million colours (256 x 256 x 256). → *binary; bit*

bit depth (2) *(aud)* Bit-depth refers to the word length, or number of bits, used to describe each sample in a piece of digital audio. The higher the bit-depth capability of a digital audio device, the greater the detail with which it will transfer, record, produce or reproduce sound. 16-bit is the standard for CD-quality audio and is considered to be sufficient for consumer devices. The recording industry standard is 24-bit, which can be saved and reproduced by DATs (Digital Audio Tapes) or computers with 24-bit soundcards and analog-to-digital convertors.

bit map/bitmap *(com)* Strictly speaking, any text character or image comprised of dots. A bit map is a 'map' of 'bits' that describes the complete collection of bits that represent the location and binary state of a corresponding set of items, such as pixels, which are required to form an image on a display monitor. ➔ *binary; bit; bitmapped font; bitmap graphic; pixel*

bitmap graphic *(com)* An image made up of dots or pixels, and usually generated by paint or image-editing applications, as distinct from the vector images of some drawing applications.

bitmapped font *(com)* A font in which the characters are made up of dots, or pixels, as distinct from an outline font, which is drawn from 'vectors'. Bitmapped fonts generally accompany PostScript 'Type 1'

fonts and are used to render the fonts' shape on screen (they are sometimes called 'screen' fonts). To draw the shape accurately on screen, your computer must have a bit map installed for each size (they are also called 'fixed-size' fonts), although this is not necessary if you have Mac OS X or ATM installed, because they use the outline, or 'printer' version of the font (the file that your printer uses in order to print it). TrueType fonts are 'outline' and thus do not require a bitmapped version. ➔ *bit map/bitmap; outline font; Type 1 font; vector*

bit rate *(com)* The speed at which data is transmitted across communications channels, measured in bits per second (bps). Modem speeds typically range from 2,400bps to 56,000bps, but higher speeds are measured in kilobits (kbps) or even megabits (mbps) per second – ISDN connections, for example, are usually either 65kbps or 128kbps. 'Bit rate' is sometimes erroneously referred to as 'baud rate'. ➔ *baud; baud rate; bit; bps; ISDN*

black art *(gen)* ➔ *base artwork*

black box *(pre)* A colloquial term for a piece of equipment that converts data or performs other automatic tasks, but which does not have a keyboard attached.

black letter *(typ)* A general term for an old style of typeface originally based on a broad-nib script, and variously called 'text letter', 'gothic' (UK), 'Old English' (US) or 'Fraktur' (Germany). ➔ *antiqua; English; Fraktur*

Looking closely at a **bit map** reveals pixels

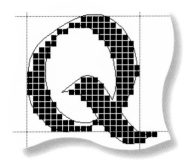

Berlin

An example of a **black letter** face

A **bitmapped font** is made up of pixels

black out *(pre)* → *black patch*

black patch *(pre)* A patch applied to camera-ready art which, at film negative stage, acts as a window into which a halftone image is stripped. → *camera-ready copy/art (CRC); halftone (1); stripping (1)*

black printer (1) *(pri)* The printing plate that prints black ink in four-colour process printing. Also called the 'key' plate.

black printer (2) *(pre)* The piece of film that will be used to make the black printing plate in four-colour process printing. → *black printer (1)*

blad *(gen)* Acronym for 'book layout and design', which originally referred to the first 32 pages of a forthcoming book printed as a sample for advance-selling to bookshops. Today the term describes any number or sequence of specimen pages printed as a publicity brochure. → *dummy (2)*

blade coater *(pap)* A unit for applying a coating to paper, which is then evenly distributed by means of a flexible blade. → *coated paper*

blanc fixe *(pap)* An artificial form of barium sulphate, which along with china clay, is added to paper pulp as a white filler.

blank (1) *(pap)* Thick card or other substrate used specifically for making posters and advertising displays.

blank (2) *(pri)* An unprinted sheet or page.

blank dummy *(gen)* → *dummy (2)*

blanker *(com)* → *screen saver; blanker*

blanket (1) *(pri)* In offset litho printing, the rubber-coated sheet that transfers the inked impression from printing plate to paper. In gravure printing, a similar rubber sheet covers the impression cylinder of a printing press. → *blanket cylinder; gravure; lithography; offset (1)*

blanket (2) *(pri)* A rubber sheet used to cover the 'flong' when casting a stereotype plate. → *flong; stereo(type)*

A page with **bleed** before and after cutting

blanket cylinder *(pri)* In offset litho printing, the cylinder to which the blanket is attached. The blanket transfers the inked image from plate to paper. → *blanket (1); offset litho(graphy)*

blanket piling *(pri)* The accumulation of paper fibres and other detritus on the surface of the blanket of an offset printing press, resulting in poor print quality. → *blanket (1); fluffing*

blanket smash *(pri)* Lack of ink on a printed sheet, caused either by insufficient pressure of blanket to paper, or by an area of blanket which is too thin. → *blanket (1)*

blanket-to-blanket press *(pri)* In offset printing, a configuration where a continuous web of paper is fed between two blanket cylinders, printing both sides at once. Also called a 'perfecting press'. → *blanket (1); blanket cylinder; web offset*

blanking interval *(com)* The split second when the beam of electrons in a video monitor switches off. This occurs each time the beam moves from the end of one horizontal line to the beginning of the next (the 'horizontal blanking interval'), and also when it moves from the last line at the bottom of the screen to the first line at the top (the 'vertical blanking interval'). → *monitor*

blank line *(gen)* → *white line*

bleach(ed)-out *(pho)* Originally, a weak, unfixed photographic print used as a base for an outline drawing (after inking, the remaining photograph would be bleached out leaving just the drawing), but latterly describing the effect of a high-key photograph. → *high key*

bled-off *(pri)* The areas of an image (or any other matter) printed beyond the edge of the page trim. → *bleed (1)*

bleed (1) *(pri)* The margin outside the trimmed area of a sheet which allows for tints, images or other matter to print beyond the edge of a page. If sheets are printed without bleed, it is generally not possible to print matter right up to the edge of the page. → *bled-off*

bleed (2) *(pri)* An aberration that occurs when the edge of an area of printed ink spreads into an adjacent area of a different colour ink.

bleed-offs *(pri)* → *bled-off*

blend(ing) *(com)* The merging of two or more colours, forming a gradual transition from one to the other. Most graphics applications offer the facility for creating blends from any mix and any percentage of process colours. The quality of the blend is limited by the number of shades of a single colour that it is possible to reproduce without visible 'banding'. Since this limit is determined by the PostScript maximum of 256 levels, banding may become more visible when the values of a single colour are very close. However, blending two or more colours reduces the risk of banding. → *banding; PostScript*

Blending mode *(com)* In Photoshop, individual layers can be blended with those underneath using Blending modes. Some examples of these mode are: *Normal, Behind, Clear, Dissolve, Multiply, Screen, Soft Light, Hard Light, Color Dodge, Color Burn, Darken, Lighten, Difference, Exclusion, Overlay, Saturation, Color* and *Luminosity*. Blending modes enact changes upon the original pixels in an image (sometimes called the base layer) by means of an applied blend colour (or 'paint' layer). This produces a resultant colour based on the original colour and on the nature of the blend. Many users find that blending mode results can be unpredictable and use trial and error to get the desired effects.

blessed folder *(com)* → *System Folder*

blind emboss/stamp *(pri)* An impression made from a relief surface such as a letterpress block or type, but without ink or foil, giving a bas-relief effect. → *bas-relief*

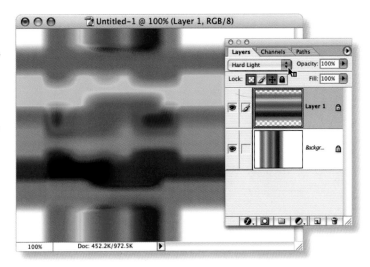

blind folio *(pri)* Page number used for reference or identification, but not actually printed on the page. Also called 'expressed folio'. → *folio (1)*

blind image *(pri)* An image that has printed badly – or not at all – because of excess moisture or other defects on the plate ('blinding'). → *blinding*

blinding *(pri)* The poor surface of an apparently sound printing plate, which creates a poorly printed image, or none at all. → *blind image*

blind P *(typ)* The character ¶, usually used as an invisible character in page layout and word processing applications to indicate a new paragraph. Also called a 'reverse P' or 'paragraph mark'.

blind stamping/blocking *(pri)* → *blind emboss/stamp*

blind tooling *(fin)* The process of embossing a design onto a book cover with heated tools, but without foil.

blister card/pack *(gen)* Packaging or displays in which the contents are mounted on card and protected by a transparent plastic bubble.

block (1) *(pri)* In traditional letterpress printing, an etched or engraved metal plate after it has been mounted.

Here the *Hard Light* **Blending mode** has been applied to the higher layer, altering the way the colours mix with those below

block (2) *(fin)* A metal stamp, usually made of brass, used to impress a design onto a book cover or jacket. Blocks are frequently used with metallic foils ('blocking foils'). The verb 'to block' means to emboss a book cover or jacket. ➔ *binder's die/brass; blocking; blocking foils; stamp (2)/ stamping*

block (3) *(com)* A place, or area, regarded as a single unit, where data is stored either temporarily in memory or on a storage medium such as a hard disk. ➔ *allocation block*

block book *(pri)* A book printed from page-size wooden blocks. Originally used before the invention of movable type. ➔ *block printing*

blocking *(fin)* The technique of impressing a design onto book covers or jackets.
➔ *block (2); gold blocking; ink blocking*

blocking foils *(fin)* Strictly speaking, a metal beaten to a thin 'leaf', which is then applied to a book cover by means of blocking. Nowadays, imitation foils made of plastic and coloured with metal powders are used. 'Gold blocking' is sometimes erroneously used to describe any blocking finish with a gold metallic foil, but more accurately describes blocking with actual gold metal. The same applies to other precious metals.
➔ *block (2); blocking; gold blocking*

blocking press *(fin)* A press that uses heated blocks to stamp designs onto book covers.
➔ *blocking*

block letter *(typ)* Originally, type characters cut from a wooden block and used for printing and embossing. Nowadays, the term is used to describe large, gothic sans serif letterforms.

block printing *(pri)* Printing using wooden blocks. The main printing method before the invention of movable type, block printing is still used for specialist work, such as printing wallpapers and fabrics. ➔ *relief printing*

The **Blue Book** is an enhanced CD format

Blooming letters were carved from wood

block stitching *(fin)* ➔ *wire stitch(ing)*

blooming letters *(typ)* Large display capitals engraved in wood, characterized by strokes formed by stalk, leaf and flower motifs. As distinct from 'floriated' initials; capitals set against a background of leaves and flowers.
➔ *floriated / floriated initials*

Blue Book *(com)* The document that specifies all parameters for Enhanced Music CD (CD Extra) interactive technology, a multi-session CD that contains audio tracks in one session and a data track in the other.
➔ *Enhanced Music CD*

Blue laser/Blu-Ray discs *(com)* Nine of the world's electronics giants, including Sanyo and Toshiba, have united behind an optical disc system called Blu-Ray. The DVD-sized rewritable discs are encoded by a blue laser, rather than a red one. Blue light has a shorter wavelength than red, which means that blue lasers can focus on smaller areas of disc and write more data into the same space. Current estimates put the capacity of Blu-Ray discs at between 12 GB and 27 GB, depending on whether they are single- or double-sided.

blueline (1) *(pre)* A low-quality proof used as a final check before platemaking. Originally, bluelines were made by the diazo, or dyeline, process, producing a blue-on-white image, hence the name. Nowadays, the term applies to any proof in which sensitized paper is exposed to the actual printing film. Bluelines are generally made from a composite of the black and cyan films rather than all four process colours, and are used for checking such things as page order and missing items, but not – obviously – for checking colour. ➔ *diazo(type)/diazo process; Ozalid; silverprint; Vandyke print*

blueline (2) *(gen)* Non-reproducible blue guidelines printed on paper and used as a grid to assist in laying out long documents such as books. ➔ *grid (1)*

blueline (3) *(pre)* A drawing in non-reproducible blue ink or pencil, used as a guide for constructing camera-ready art or illustrations. ➔ *camera-ready copy/art (CRC)*

blueline (4) *(pre)* A registration guide for assembling the individual printing film components, such as halftones, and 'stripping' them to film 'flats'. ➔ *flat (1); stripping*

blueline flat *(pre)* ➔ *blueline (4)*

blueprint *(pre)* ➔ *blueline (1)*

blues *(pre)* ➔ *blueline (1)*

blurb *(gen)* A colloquial term, originating in the USA in the early 20th century, for the description of a book and/or its author that is usually printed on the book jacket flaps or on promotional literature. ➔ *jacket flaps; puff*

Blur filter *(com)* The conventional blur effect filter, which is designed to detect noise around colour transitions and remove it. It does this by detecting pixels close to boundaries and averaging their values, effectively eliminating noise and random colour variations. *Blur More* is identical but applies the effect more strongly. Somewhat crude, the *Blur*

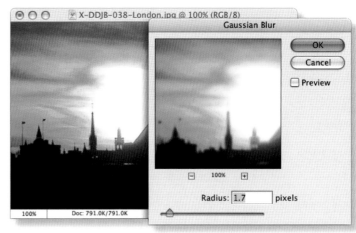

filter is now joined in many image-editing filter sets with more controllable filters such as the *Gaussian Blur* and *Smart Blur* filters.

Gaussian Blur is a Photoshop **Blur filter**

board (1) *(pap)* An imprecise term generally used to describe any heavy or thick paper or other substance. In the US this usually means anything thicker than 6mil (0.006in), while in the UK it is defined for customs duty purposes as being any paper exceeding 220gsm in weight. ➔ *boards; caliper (1); paperboard*

board (2) *(com)* ➔ *circuit board*

board covers *(fin)* An inexpensive binding style in which paper-covered boards are used instead of cloth or imitation cloth boards. ➔ *binding; boards*

boarded leather *(fin)* Binding leather that has been dampened and pressed between boards to enhance the natural grain. ➔ *boards*

board glazed *(pap)* A smooth, but not highly-glazed paper made by a process in which boards – rather than metal plates – are used to finish the surface. ➔ *board (1); boards*

board paper *(fin)* ➔ *endpapers*

boards *(pap)* A general term used to describe substances such as millboards and strawboards used for casing books, and also to describe certain types of printing card such as ivory and Bristol boards. ➔ *board (1); case (1)*

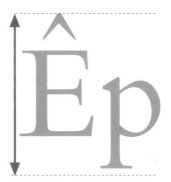

The full character
body height

bocasin *(fin)* A fine quality buckram.
➔ *buckram*

body (1) *(typ)* The shank of a piece of metal type.

body (2) *(gen)* The main part of a book, excluding end matter, covers, prelims, etc.
➔ *end/back matter; prelims/preliminary pages*

body (3) *(int)* One of the main structures of an HTML document, falling between the header and the footer. ➔ *footer (3); header; HTML*

body (4) *(pri)* An imprecise term describing the stiffness or softness of printing ink.

body copy/matter *(gen)* The matter forming the main part of a printed work, including text and images but excluding page headings and, sometimes, captions.
➔ *body (2)*

body height *(typ)* The full height of a font's characters, including any accents above and decenders below the baseline.

body paper/stock *(pap)* The substance forming the substrate of coated printing paper. ➔ *coated paper*

body size *(typ)* The size, in points, by which type is measured. Originally, this meant the body of the piece of metal on which the character sits, but in computer typography it means the size of a font, without leading. ➔ *body (1); point (1)*

body type *(typ)* The type used in setting the main text of a book. ➔ *body copy/matter*

bogus *(gen)* An arcane and redundant procedure describing copy for press advertisements which, having been received by the publisher in plate, block or film form, is then reset in type, which is immediately discarded without being used.

bold (face) *(typ)* A version of a font having a conspicuously heavier appearance or weight than the same design with a medium or light weight.

bolts *(fin)* The three edges ('head' bolts, 'fore-edge' bolts and 'tail' bolts) of a folded sheet, which will be trimmed before binding. The remaining folded edge is not called a bolt but the 'back' or 'last' fold.

bomb *(com)* ➔ *crash (1)*

bonding strength (1) *(pri)* The ability of a printing ink to resist various faults in printing, such as 'picking'. ➔ *picking*

bonding strength (2) *(pap)* The strength with which paper fibres bond together.

bond paper *(pap)* A standard grade of strong, durable and smooth writing paper, generally used for stationery printing. ➔ *bank paper*

book *(gen)* A general term describing a set of paper sheets that have been bound together. Various attempts have been made to define the term: it was once assumed in the UK that a book was any publication costing sixpence or more, while other countries define a book as being a publication with a specified minimum number of pages. A UNESCO conference once defined a book as being 'a non-periodical literary publication containing 49 or more pages, excluding the covers'.
➔ *bookbinding*

bookbinding *(fin)* The collecting and fastening together of the printed pages of a work and enclosing them within a cover. The main stages of binding a book are folding the printed sheets of paper, cutting the edges, rounding and backing, lining the backs, making and blocking (stamping) the cases, and, finally, securing the cases to the book block. ➔ *binding; blocking; book block; case (1); rounding and backing*

book block *(fin)* A book that has been folded, gathered and stitched, but not yet cased-in. ➔ *cased/casebound; casing-in*

book cloth *(fin)* A fabric made from dyed, coated calico and used to cover cased books. ➔ *cased/casebound*

book face *(typ)* Traditionally, a term for a particular typeface, the term is now used to describe any font suitable for setting the text of a book.

book jacket *(gen)* ➔ *dust jacket/wrapper; jacket flaps*

booklet *(gen)* Strictly speaking, a booklet is any publication larger than a pamphlet but containing no more than 24 pages. However, a booklet now tends to mean any publication of a few pages with less than permanent binding. ➔ *binding; pamphlet*

book make-up *(pre)* ➔ *make-up (1)*

Bookmark *(int)* A feature of some Web browsers that remembers frequently visited websites. The equivalent in Microsoft's Internet Explorer is called a 'Favorite'. ➔ *Favorite; Web browser*

book paper *(pap)* A generic term for any paper suitable for book printing.

bookplates *(gen)* Printed labels, usually pasted onto the inside front cover of a book, decreeing its ownership.

book proof *(pri)* Imposed page proofs, folded and trimmed but usually not stitched or bound, and assembled in book form. ➔ *imposition/impose*

book sizes *(fin)* Nowadays, book sizes are determined by the metric ISO paper sizes, which are used throughout the world, although not widely in the US. ➔ *American book sizes; British book sizes; ISO A-series paper sizes; paper sizes*

Boolean *(com)* Named after G. Boole, a 19th-century English mathematician, Boolean is used to describe a shorthand for logical computer operations, including those which link values, such as 'and' or 'not'. These are called 'Boolean operators'. The search of a database could be refined using Boolean operators – for example, 'book and recent or new but not published'. 'Boolean expressions' compare two values and come up with ('return') the result of either 'true' or 'false', represented by 1 and 0. In 3D applications, Boolean describes the joining or removing of one shape to/from another.

boom *(pho)* A device used in photography for supporting the camera or lights, consisting of a metal arm that pivots on a vertical stand.

boot blocks *(com)* Specially assigned areas of a disk or volume, which contain the information your computer system needs to start up. ➔ *block (3)*

boot disk *(com)* ➔ *startup disk*

boot/boot up/booting up *(com)* Short for 'bootstrapping', this describes the process of starting up a computer, which in turn involves loading the operating system into memory – in other words 'pulling it up by its bootstraps'. More commonly called 'startup' or 'starting up', the process is sometimes called a 'cold boot', as distinct from a 'warm boot' which refers to rebooting ('restarting') the computer once it is already switched on. Restarting a computer by physically switching off the power and then switching it back on is also called a cold boot. ➔ *startup*

border *(gen)* A decorative design or rule surrounding matter on a page. Sometimes called a 'frame'.

bosses *(fin)* In traditional bookbinding, the small raised ornaments made of metal and usually fixed at the corners of a book cover to protect against rubbing. ➔ *bookbinding*

'bot (robot) *(int)* → *robot*

bottomband *(fin)* A band placed at the bottom of the spine of a book. → *head/tail band*

bottoming *(pri)* A fault that occurs in relief printing when ink is transferred to the non-image areas of the plate or block, and is then printed on the sheet. → *relief printing*

bottom out *(gen)* Arranging text on a page so that it breaks in an appropriate place at the bottom of the page, to avoid aesthetic anomalies such as single words (orphans) and short lines (widows). → *bad break; orphan; widow (line)*

bottom printing *(pri)* Printing on the underside of translucent film or paper so that the design reads through the top.

bounce lighting *(pho)* The method of lighting a subject by reflected light – for example, off the walls, ceiling or other suitable reflector.

bound book *(fin)* Originally used to describe a book with boards attached to the book block but before it was covered with leather or cloth. Nowadays, the term generally describes any bound or cased book. → *boards; bookbinding; book block; cased/casebound*

bounding box *(com)* A rectangular box, available in certain graphics or drawing applications, which encloses an item so that it can be resized or moved. In 3D applications, the bounding box is parallel to the axes of the object. → *axis; box (2)*

bourgeois *(typ)* A largely defunct name for a type size, now standardized as 9 point. → *brevier; brilliant; point (1)*

bowl (1) *(typ)* The curved strokes of a type character, enclosing the counter. Also called a 'cup'. → *counter*

The **bowl** of the letter 'B'

bowl (2) *(typ)* The enclosed space in a text character, such as a b, g, o, q or p. → *bowl (1)*

box (1) *(gen)* A printed item surrounded or defined by a rule, border or background tint. → *box feature/story; box rule*

box (2) *(com)* A container of any shape into which text or pictures are placed in certain applications. → *bounding box*

box feature/story *(gen)* Matter printed separately from the main text (body) of a publication, and marked off by a box rule, border or tint. Also called a 'sidebar'. → *border; box rule; callout*

boxhead *(gen)* In tabulated matter, the heading of each column.

box rule *(gen)* A rectangular box defined on all four sides by a rule. → *box (1); box feature/story*

'B' paper sizes *(pap)* → *ISO A-series paper sizes*

bpi *(com)* abb.: bits per inch. → *bit density*

BPM *(aud)* abb.: beats per minute. A measure that can be applied to all music, but is most often associated with electronic rhythms and drumbeats. Most rhythm-based software or hardware offers a BPM setting to control the speed of the rhythms produced – more beats per minute means a 'faster' song. Knowing the BPM of songs also helps DJs to match beats when they are mixing tracks; this can be read on most electronic music using special hardware or software devices.

BPOP *(pri)* *abb.:* bulk packed on pallets. An instruction to the printer to deliver a job on 'pallets', wooden trays designed to be used with fork-lift trucks.

bps *(com)* *abb.:* bits per second. ➔ *bit rate*

brace *(typ)* A type character that is used to group phrases or lines of text. The brace at the start of the phrase or on the left side of a block of text is called the open brace ({), as distinct from the close brace (}) at the right side or end. Not to be confused with 'bracket' or 'parenthesis'. ➔ *brace end; bracket(s); parenthesis*

brace end *(typ)* A type character representing a horizontal brace. ➔ *brace; cock(end)*

bracket(s) *(typ)* A type character used in pairs (open and close) to enclose or separate text or numbers. Brackets are often used to enclose matter that is designated for later deletion. Not to be confused with 'brace' or 'parenthesis'. ➔ *brace; parenthesis*

bracketed type *(typ)* A type design in which the serifs are joined to the main stem in an unbroken curve. ➔ *serif*

bracketing *(pho)* In photography, a series of exposures of the same subject, each one varying progressively to either side of the estimated amount, in order to allow for uncertainties in exposure and processing.

brass *(fin)* An engraved plate used by bookbinders to block, or stamp, a design onto a book cover. ➔ *block (2)*

break (1) *(gen)* An interruption in the flow of text, such as at the end of a line, paragraph or page. ➔ *break-line*

break (2) *(pap)* Weakness in paper which causes a web to tear, thus interrupting printing. ➔ *breaking length; web (1)*

breakacross *(gen)* An image or tint that extends across the gutter onto both pages of a double-page spread. Also called 'crossover', or 'reader's spread'. ➔ *double-(page) spread; gutter margin; spread*

breaking length *(pap)* A measure of the tensile strength of a web of paper, defined by the length at which a suspended web will tear due to its own weight. ➔ *break (2); web (1)*

break-line *(typ)* The last line of a paragraph. ➔ *widow*

breakthrough *(pri)* Penetration of ink through the printed paper.

breve *(typ)* A symbol (˘) used to indicate the pronunciation of a short or unstressed vowel. ➔ *accent*

brevier *(typ)* A largely defunct name for a type size, now standardized as 8 point. ➔ *bourgeois; brilliant; point (1)*

bridge *(com)* A link between two or more networked devices. ➔ *gateway; network*

bright enamel *(pap)* Paper with a highly polished coating, usually on one side only.

brightness *(gen)* The relative lightness or darkness of a colour, usually measured as a percentage from 0% (black) all the way up to 100% (white). Brightness is one of the three dimensions of colour in the HSB colour system. ➔ *HSB; hue; saturation*

brightness range *(pho)* The range of tones in a photographic subject, from darkest to lightest.

brilliant *(typ)* A largely defunct name for a type size, now standardized as 4 point. ➔ *bourgeois; brevier; point (1)*

bring up *(pri)* To place material under a printing surface, thus raising it to the correct height for making an impression onto paper.

Bristol board *(pap)* A fine, laminated cardboard with a smooth surface, used for both printing and drawing. So-called because it is thought to have been originally made in Bristol. ➔ *boards*

British book sizes *(fin)* Modern book sizes
→ *American book sizes; book sizes*

Traditional British book sizes

Name	Size; in inches	in millimetres
Pott Octavo (Pott 8)	6¼ x 4	159 x 102
Foolscap Octavo (F'cap 8)	6¾ x 4¼	171 x 110
Crown Octavo (Cr. 8)	7½ x 5	191 x 127
Large Post Octavo (L. Post 8)	8¼ x 5¼	212 x 133
Demy Octavo (Dy 8)	8¾ x 5	220 x 127
Medium Octavo (Med. 8)	9 x 5¾	229 x 146
Royal Octavo (Roy. 8)	10 x 6¼	254 x 159
Super Royal Octavo (SuR 8)	10 x 6¾	254 x 171
Imperial Octavo (Imp 8)	11 x 7½	279 x 191
Foolscap Quarto (F'cap 4)	8½ x 6¾	216 x 171
Crown Quarto (Cr. 4)	10 x 7½	254 x 191
Large Post Quarto (L. Post 4)	10½ x 8¼	267 x 210
Demy Quarto (Dy 4)	11¼ x 8¾	286 x 220
Medium Quarto (Med. 4)	11½ x 9	292 x 229
Royal Quarto (Roy. 4)	12½ x 10	318 x 254
Foolscap Folio (F'cap Fol)	13½ x 8½	343 x 216

Broadcast Wave/B-Wave/BWF *(aud)* The European Broadcasting Union (EBU) has introduced 'a file format that contains the minimum information that is considered necessary for all broadcast applications'. Broadcast Wave (B-Wave, or BWF) is a 'higher level descriptor [that can] reference other files containing more complex sets of information'. To you and me, that's an audio file format that lets all other audio file formats exist within it.

broad fold *(fin)* Paper that has been folded with the direction of grain running along the shorter dimension.

broadside/broadsheet *(pri)* Originally, broadsides, or 'broadsheets', were sheets of paper printed on one side only and used for printing official notices. Nowadays the term is used to describe a variety of large-sheet jobs, which may be printed on one or both sides. Consequently, broadsheet is often used to describe a large-format newspaper, as distinct from the smaller tabloid size. → *tabloid*

broadside page *(pri)* A page in which the matter has been rotated 90° to print sideways.

brochure *(fin)* A short publication that has its pages stitched together but is otherwise unbound. The term derives from the French 'brocher', meaning 'to stitch'. → *pamphlet*

broken images *(pri)* The printing effect that results from damaged or worn plates.

bromide *(pho)* Photographic paper coated on the surface with an emulsion of light-sensitive silver bromide. Bromide paper is used for printing continuous tone photographs from negatives, and also extensively in the prepress industries, which describe a 'bromide' as an alternative high-quality output. It is used for generating camera-ready art from an imagesetter, thus distinguishing it from film output.
→ *camera-ready copy/art (CRC)*

bronzing (1) *(pri)* A gold or metallic effect produced by dusting a sheet of paper, on which a special ink has been printed, with a metallic powder.

bronzing (2) *(pri)* An undesirable 'blotching' effect in four-colour process printing that is caused by an imbalance of ink constituents.

brownline/brownprint *(pre)* → *blueline (1)*

browser (1)/Web browser *(int)* An application enabling you to view, or 'browse', World Wide Web pages across the Internet. The most widely used browsers are Microsoft's Internet Explorer, Apple's Safari and Netscape's Navigator and Communicator. Each displays pages according to standards but the result is not always identical. ➔ *HTML; Internet; World Wide Web (WWW)*

browser (2) *(com)* An application for cataloguing and viewing image, animation and sound files, so that it is easy to keep track of their whereabouts on your hard disk or archive media.

bruising *(pap)* An aberration in paper caused by too much pressure or heat during calendering, resulting in a mottled effect.
　➔ *calender*

brush-coated paper *(pap)* A highly opaque and stable but expensive coated paper.
　➔ *coated paper*

brush graining *(pri)* ➔ *graining*

B-Spline *(com)* A type of curve.

bubblejet printer *(com)* Canon's branding for their range of inkjet printers, derived from the way ink droplets are expelled onto the paper as bubbles. ➔ *inkjet printer*

buckle folder *(fin)* A folding machine in which the paper sheet is fed into an adjustable stop that causes the sheet to buckle. Two 'nip' rollers then fold the sheet along the buckle. Also called a 'plate folder'.
　➔ *combination folder; fold/folding; knife folder*

buckram *(fin)* A strong, coarse book cloth made of jute, linen or cotton that has been glazed and stiffened. ➔ *bocasin; book cloth*

buckskin *(fin)* ➔ *deerskin*

buffer *(com)* An area of computer memory set aside for the storage or processing of data while it is in transit. The buffer can either be in RAM or on a hard disk within your

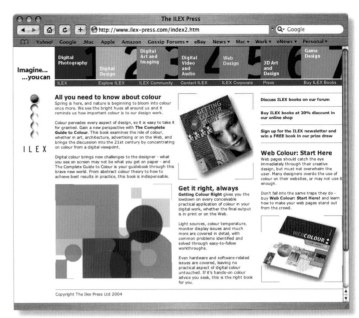

computer, and is sometimes called the 'cache'. Buffers are commonly used by output devices such as modems and printers, which are then able to process data more quickly, while at the same time freeing up your computer so that you can keep on working. Buffer can also refer to the temporary storage space in a digital camera where shots can be held before transfer to the memory card. ➔ *cache; memory; random access; spool/spooler/spooling*

buffing *(pri)* The final polishing of a printing plate before it is etched.

bug *(com)* A programming error in software that can cause it to behave erratically. Completely error-free software is difficult to produce due to the complexities of today's computer systems, but good software should be essentially bug free. One solution is for developers to issue patches, which can be downloaded and installed to fix problems that are not detected before launch. ➔ *patch; program*

built fraction *(gen)* A fraction constructed from a numerator, separator and denominator, as distinct from a 'case' fraction – one that is ready made. Also called 'piece' fractions.
　➔ *fraction*

Safari, Apple's
Web browser

bulk (1) *(fin)* The thickness of the assembled pages of a publication, minus its covers.
→ *bulking dummy*

bulk (2) *(pap)* The thickness of a given number of sheets of paper when put under a particular amount of pressure. Bulk can also refer to the thickness of a sheet of paper in relation to its weight.

bulk factor *(pap)* The number of sheets of paper that make up a thickness of one inch (2.5cm).

Applying a **bump map** gives texture

bulking dummy *(gen)* A blank book made with the exact number of pages and the same paper stock, and bound to the same specification as the final published edition. A bulking dummy may be used for various purposes, but most importantly for making marketing proposals and sales presentations, and for calculating the exact dimensions of the jacket. Also called a 'thickness copy'. → *dummy (2)*

bulldog *(pri)* A newspaper printer's colloquial term for the first edition of the day.

bull's eye *(pri)* → *hickie; hickey*

bullet *(typ)* A dot used to itemize lists or to emphasize passages of text.

bulleted list *(int)* An HTML style for webpages in which a bullet precedes each item on a list. → *bullet*

bulletin board service (BBS) *(int)* A facility, usually non-commercial, that enables you to use a modem and telephone line to share information and exchange files on specialist subjects with other like-minded computer users. As distinct from commercial online service providers, which offer a wider range of services.

bumped out (1) *(typ)* A line of characters to which extra space has been added so that it aligns with a specific, longer line. As distinct from 'justified' alignment, which applies to all lines in a block of text.
→ *alignment*

bumped out (2) *(typ)* Widely leaded text.
→ *leading*

bumping up/bump-up *(pri)* The preparation of halftone plates for printing, usually on a rotary press, where the original plates are made ready before stereos are cast.
→ *halftone (1); make-ready*

bump map *(com)* A bitmap image file, normally greyscale, most frequently used in 3D applications for modifying surfaces or applying textures. The grey values in the image are assigned height values, with black representing the troughs and white the peaks. Bump maps are used in the form of digital elevation models (DEMs) for generating cartographic relief maps.
→ *digital elevation model*

bundle (1) *(com)* In the Mac OS, a bundle is a resource that associates files with icons.
→ *operating system*

bundle (2) *(pap)* Two reams of paper, or 1000 sheets. → *ream*

bundling *(fin)* The tying together of signatures, prior to binding. Can also be used by computer resellers to describe closely related sale items, such as software and hardware, which are sold together as one package. → *binding; signature (1)*

B

bureau *(pre)* → *service bureau*

burin *(pri)* A tool used to engrave wood or metal.

burn (1) *(pre)* The process of using light to expose an image onto a printing plate.

burn (2) *(com)* The process of writing data to optical media such as a CD-R disc. So-called because the process involves literally burning small pits – the size of which determines a 0 or a 1 – into the surface of a platter. → *CD-R/CD-RW; optical disc/media*

burn (3) *(int)* To convert a file from an uncompressed to a compressed format, specifically for use with Internet Web browsers. → *browser (1); Internet*

burn (4) *(pho)* A method of obtaining darker areas in a photographic print by selectively increasing exposure to light in the relevant areas. The *Burn tool* in certain image-editing applications digitally simulates the mechanical technique. The opposite effect – lightening areas of an image – is called 'dodging'. → *dodge/dodging; masking (2)*

burning in *(pri)* In intaglio processes, fusing etching powder to the plate by heating it. → *intaglio*

burnish *(gen)* Generally, to polish or smooth a surface by rubbing it. In prepress, printing and finishing, this can mean a number of operations, such as increasing the dot size of a relief plate by rubbing it, reducing the cell size of a gravure plate, or brightening book edges. → *burnished edges; gravure*

burnished edges *(fin)* The polishing of the coloured edges of a book by applying wax and then rubbing with a burnishing tool. → *burnish; burnisher (1)*

burnisher (1) *(fin)* A hand-tool, sometimes made of stone, used for burnishing book edges. → *burnish; burnished edges*

burnisher (2) *(pri)* A metal tool used for removing rough spots from printing plates.

burn out *(pre)* The process of overexposing a printing plate so that very small dots are not reproduced.

burnout (mask) *(pre)* The process of masking images and copy after film assembly and prior to platemaking to eliminate unwanted portions, or to make space for new insertions. → *burn through*

burn through *(pre)* Exposure of film through a mask. → *burnout (mask)*

burst binding *(fin)* A device on a web press that enables glue to penetrate the pages during perfect binding. → *perfect binding*

bus (1) *(com)* A path along which information or data is passed in a computer, or between one device and another.

bus (2) *(com)* A common connection between a number of circuits.

butt lines *(pri)* → *lap lines*

button *(com)* An interface control, usually appearing in dialog boxes, which you click to designate, confirm or cancel an action. Default buttons are those that are usually emphasized by a heavy border and can be activated by the 'Enter' or 'Return' keys. → *dialog/dialog box*

by-line *(gen)* A label denoting the author of an article. → *credit/courtesy line*

byte *(com)* A unit of storage equivalent to 8 bits. It is possible to configure eight 0s and 1s in only 256 different permutations, so a byte can represent any value between 0 and 255 – the maximum number of ASCII characters, one byte being required for each. For example, the memory capacity of a RAM module is usually measured in megabytes (MB) while the storage capacity on a hard drive is usually measured in gigabytes (GB). → *ASCII; bit; nibble/nybble*

Selecting the Photoshop **Burn** tool

Mac OS X's 'OK' **button**

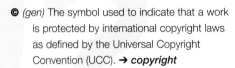

Cc

© *(gen)* The symbol used to indicate that a work is protected by international copyright laws as defined by the Universal Copyright Convention (UCC). ➔ *copyright*

c *(pre) abb.:* cyan ➔ *cyan (c)*

cache *(com)* (pron.: *'kash'*) A small area of memory (RAM) set aside for the temporary storage of frequently accessed data. This has the effect of speeding up some computer operations, since data accessed from RAM is processed much faster than that from disk. Cache can also be stored in a separate hardware chip, which comes soldered onto the motherboard of some computers and on some add-on circuit boards. ➔ *backside cache; buffer; random access memory (RAM)*

CAD *(com) abb.:* computer-aided design. Strictly speaking, any design carried out using a computer, but the term is generally used with reference to 3D design, such as product design or architecture, where a computer software application is used to construct and develop complex structures. ➔ *CAD/CAM; CAM*

CAD/CAM *(com) abb.:* computer-aided design and manufacture. The process of design and manufacture in which computers are used to assist and control the entire process from concept to finished product. ➔ *CAD; CAM*

CADD *(com) abb.:* computer-aided drafting and design. ➔ *CAD*

cake/pie diagram/chart *(gen)* An illustration that shows the divisions of a whole quantity as segments of a circle or ellipse.

Cakewalk DXi *(aud)* A plug-in interface for soft synths based on Microsoft's DirectX architecture, currently supported only by Cakewalk's SONAR audio production package. Allows routing of MIDI tracks, realtime control of synths, and so on.

calender *(pap)* A column of metal rollers at the end of the papermaking process, which applies pressure to the paper, thus closing the pores and giving the paper a smooth surface. ➔ *super-calender*

calender crush *(pap)* ➔ *bruising*

calendered paper *(pap)* Paper that has been finished in a calender, giving it a smoothness or gloss described as a 'machine finish', which, in turn, may be described as 'low' or 'high' depending on the degree of gloss. The varnish used to coat the paper is often also referred to as 'calendered varnish'. ➔ *calender; machine finish (MF)*

calf *(fin)* Smooth-finished bookbinding material made from calfskin. ➔ *bookbinding*

calibrate/calibration *(gen)* The process of adjusting a machine or piece of hardware to conform to a known scale or standard so that it performs more accurately. In graphic reproduction, it is important that the various devices and materials used in the production chain – including scanners, monitors, imagesetters and printing presses

A simple **cake/pie diagram/chart**

A monitor fitted with a colour **calibration** device

– conform to a consistent set of measures in order to achieve true fidelity, particularly where colour is concerned. Calibration of reproduction and display devices is generally carried out with a 'densitometer'.
→ *densitometer*

calibration bar *(pre)* → *colour bar*

caliper (1) *(pap)* The measure of the thickness of paper or board, expressed as millionths of a metre ('microns'), or thousandths of an inch ('mils'). → *board (1); caliper (2)*

caliper (2) *(pap)* An instrument used for measuring paper thickness. → *caliper (1)*

calligraphy *(typ)* The art of writing, based on handwriting from Roman times and embracing such scripts as half-uncial, Carolingian, humanistic and their derivatives. The word derives from the Greek word *kalligraphia,* which means 'beautiful writing'.

callout *(gen)* A piece of text separated from the main body of running text, sometimes emphasized by a box rule or other device, and often associated with an illustration.
→ *box feature/story; box rule*

calotype *(pho)* The earliest method of recording images onto sensitized film or paper, invented and patented by the Englishman William Fox Talbot in 1841.

CAM *(com) abb.:* computer-aided manufacture. Generally used in conjunction with CAD ('CAD/CAM'). → *CAD; CAD/CAM*

cameo (1) *(typ)* Typefaces in which the letterforms are reversed to show white on a dark background.

cameo (2) *(pap)* In America, a type of coated paper with a dull finish, suitable for printing halftones or engravings. The UK equivalent is 'matt art'. → *coated paper; halftone (1); matt art*

cameo (3) *(gen)* A small relief design, either stamped out of any suitable material or simulated by a computer program. Cameos were originally made from a hard stone such as onyx, and set onto a background of a different colour.

cameo binding *(fin)* A book cover that has been adorned with a stamped or inset cameo. → *cameo (3)*

camera *(pho)* A device in which light passes through a lens to record an image. The image can be recorded onto presensitized film or paper, or by means of electronic sensors (CCDs) that digitally 'write' the image to a storage device such as a memory card or hard disk. → *CCD; process camera; vertical camera*

camera angle *(pho)* A general term describing the viewpoint of the camera, but also specifically with reference to its angle from the horizontal. → *camera moves*

camera moves *(com)* A feature of 3D applications allowing you to perform typical film and video camera movements in animated sequences, such as 'pans', 'tilts', 'rolls', 'dolly shots' and 'tracking shots'.
→ *dolly (shot); pan(ning); roll (2); tilt; tracking (2)/tracking shot*

Camera RAW format *(pho)* A file format used by high-end digital cameras, that can be thought of as a high-quality digital negative. It contains the image data in uncompressed form.

camera-ready copy/art (CRC) *(gen)* Material, such as artwork, prepared and ready for photographic conversion to film in preparation for printing. Also called a 'mechanical', 'composite art' or 'paste-up'. ➜ *paste-up/pasteup*

camera shake *(pho)* The term describing usually undesirable movement of a camera at the moment a photograph is taken, resulting in a blurred or ghosted image.

cancel (1) *(pri)* A printed leaf of a publication that, containing errors, is cut out and removed from its section and replaced by another, appropriately amended. ➜ *section*

cancel (2)/abort *(com)* The button in dialog boxes allowing you to cancel the action that invoked the box. ➜ *dialog/dialog box*

cancelled numeral *(typ)* A numerical character, used in mathematics, crossed through with a diagonal stroke.

cancel-title *(pri)* A replacement title page, often showing a change of imprint, such as when a work printed for publication in one country is later prepared for publication in another.

The **cap height** of the letter 'E'

canon *(typ)* A former size of type, measuring about 48 points.

caoutchouc binding *(fin)* An early form of adhesive binding, in which many single leaves were bonded together by a rubber solution called caoutchouc. ➜ *adhesive binding*

cap (1) *(fin)* A paper covering used to protect a book block during binding. ➜ *binding; book block; capping up*

cap (2) *(typ)* abb.: capital (letter). ➜ *capital*

capacitor *(pho)* The electrical device in electronic photographic flash units that enables a charge to be built up and stored.

cap height *(typ)* The height of a capital letter, measured from its baseline. ➜ *baseline*

Camera RAW format allows a higher degree of post production

capital *(typ)* An upper-case letter such as A, B, C, etc. The term originates from the inscriptional letters at the top, or capital, of Roman columns. Also called 'majuscules'. → *small capitals/caps; uncials; upper case*

cap line (1) *(typ)* An imaginary horizontal line defining the tops of capital letters.

cap line (2) *(typ)* A line of text set entirely in capital letters.

capping up *(fin)* The wrapping of the body of a book with thin paper to protect the edges of the block while adding the covers, head and tail bands, etc. Can also be used to describe the process of making lower case letters into capitals. → *cap (1)*

caps and smalls *(typ)* Text in which the first character of each word is set in capitals, and the subsequent characters are set in small capitals. → *capital; even s. caps/ even smalls; small capitals/caps*

caption *(gen)* Strictly speaking, this is a headline printed above an illustration identifying its contents. Nowadays a caption is generally used to mean any descriptive text that accompanies illustrative matter, and should, more accurately, be described as a 'legend'. A caption may also be referred to as a 'cutline' (US). → *legend*

capture *(com)* The term describing what you do when you record an image by whatever means – taking a photograph or scanning a picture, for example. → *screen capture*

carbonless paper *(pap)* A chemically coated paper that produces duplicate copies of handwritten or typed documents onto another sheet without the use of carbon paper. Also called 'NCR' paper, representing either the company that developed it, National Cash Register Corp., or alternatively 'no carbon required'.

carbon print *(pho)* A photographic print made onto pigmented gelatine-coated material. Carbon prints were formerly known as 'charcoal' prints because charcoal powder was originally used as a black pigment. → *carbon tissue*

carbon tissue *(pri)* A semi-opaque, gelatine-coated paper which, when made light-sensitive by treating it with alkali dichromate, is used for various methods of photographic reproduction. These include conventional gravure printing and screen printing processes. → *carbon print; gravure; screen printing*

card *(com)* → *circuit board*

cardboard/card *(pap)* → *paperboard*

card fount/font *(typ)* A traditional term for the smallest complete size of a font design manufactured and sold by a typefounder. → *font*

cardinal numbers *(gen)* Numbers used in sequential counting, such as 1, 2, 3, as distinct from 'ordinal' numbers, which are used to indicate placement (such as first, second, third).

cardioid *(aud)* The heart-shaped pattern that applies to the way a cardioid microphone picks up sound: most from the front, less from the sides and very little from the rear. In other words, it is a directional pattern. Hypercardioid microphones also pick up sound from behind in a similar pattern.

caret/caret mark *(typ)* A term derived from the Latin 'is lacking' and represented by the symbol (⅄). Used in copy preparation and proof correction to indicate the location of text to be inserted.

caricature *(gen)* The depiction – as a photograph, model or drawing – of a person or object with exaggerated key features or characteristics. Generally executed for comic or satirical purposes.

carry forward/over *(gen)* ➔ *take over/take forward*

Cartesian coordinate system *(com)* A geometry system employed in 3D applications that uses numbers to locate a point on a plane in relation to an origin where one or more points intersect.

carton *(fin)* A container, generally designed to be flattened out when not in use.

cartouche *(gen)* A decorative device, usually in the form of a scroll with rolled up ends, which is used to enclose a title or illustration.

cartridge paper *(pap)* A strong, general-purpose white paper, which, when uncoated, may be used for drawing, envelopes, etc. Coated cartridge paper is commonly used as an all-round paper in offset printing. ➔ *offset litho(graphy); web offset*

cartridge, removable *(com)* Storage media protected by a plastic casing so that it can be transported from one drive to another. Strictly speaking, the term can apply to any removable media, whether magnetic or optical, but it generally excludes 'floppy' disks. ➔ *floppy disk*

cascade *(int)* A hierarchy of webpage style sheets, with each one forming the framework for the next. ➔ *cascading style sheet (CSS)*

cascading style sheet (CSS) *(int)* A specification sponsored by the World Wide Web Consortium for overcoming the limitations imposed by 'classic HTML'. Web designers ('authors') have increasingly sought tools that would enable them to control every element of page design more tightly. As a result, the Web authoring community has developed unwieldy workarounds that generate bulky HTML code, which, in turn, has resulted in longer downloads and browser incompatibilities. A CSS allows the designer to exercise greater control over typography and layout in much

the same way as a page-layout application. Several style sheets can be applied to a single page, thus 'cascading'. ➔ *GIF; HTML; World Wide Web*

case (1) *(fin)* The stiff cover of a book, usually made by machine and consisting of two boards, a paper 'hollow' and a suitable binding material such as cloth. ➔ *book cloth; cased/casebound*

case (2) *(typ)* A traditional type compositor's box or tray that is divided into small compartments for storing type. Cases were generally used in pairs, upper for capital letters and lower for small letters, thus spawning the terms 'upper case' and 'lower case' to describe such letters.

case (3) *(pri)* The base plate, which, when covered with wax, is used in electrotyping for creating the mould. ➔ *electro(type)*

casebound *(fin)* ➔ *cased/caseboard*

cased/casebound *(fin)* Books that have had a case attached to their sewn sections. Also called 'hardbound' or 'hardbacked'. ➔ *case (1)*

case fraction *(typ)* A ready-made fraction, as distinct from a 'split', 'built' or 'piece' fraction. Also called a 'true' fraction. ➔ *built fraction; fraction*

casein *(pap)* An adhesive obtained from curdled milk and used in the manufacture of coated papers. ➔ *coated paper*

case insensitive *(com)* The term used to indicate that upper or lower case characters input into a field, such as in a 'Find' dialog or e-mail address, are not significant and will therefore have no effect on determining the outcome of the request. ➔ *case sensitive*

case sensitive *(com)* The term used to indicate that upper or lower case characters input into a field, such as in a 'Find' dialog or e-mail address, are significant and will determine the outcome of the request. ➔ *case insensitive*

A book's **case** protects the block

casing-in *(fin)* The final stage in the production of cased books, when cases are attached to the sewn and trimmed book blocks. → *book block; case (1); cased/casebound*

cast (1) *(com)* The components of a presentation in some multimedia applications, such as graphics, animations, films and sounds.

cast (2) *(gen)* → *colour cast*

cast-coated paper *(pap)* A high-quality coated art paper with an exceptionally glossy finish, giving it an enamel appearance.

casting *(typ)* The traditional method of generating type characters by using machines which, fitted with a mould or 'matrice' (mat), would cast the type characters from hot molten metal. Type would either be cast as individual characters using a 'Monotype' machine, or as complete lines ('slugs') using a 'Linotype' machine. → *Linotype; Monotype*

cast-off *(typ)* The process of estimating the amount of space or number of pages that will be required to accommodate copy to be typeset. Traditionally, this was done either by comparing the character count to that of a printed sample of the font to be used, or by using the typefounder's copyfitting tables, which were produced for every font the foundry manufactured. Nowadays, page-layout and word-processing applications provide instant and accurate calculations of copy length. → *cast-up; character count; copyfitting (1)*

cast-up *(typ)* The process of calculating the amount of (traditional) typesetting that will be required to complete a job. In mechanical typesetting, the cast-up includes estimating the amount of white space required, for word spaces, extra leading and white lines, as well as the actual characters, since these would all require as much time in compositing terms and extra metal for casting the type. → *casting; cast-off; copyfitting (1)*

catadioptic lens *(pho)* → *mirror lens*

Cataloging-in-Publication (CIP) *(gen)* A classification used by The Library of Congress (US) and British Library (UK) for cataloguing books. Every book published is assigned a unique number, which is printed on the imprint page.

catch-letters *(gen)* → *catchword*

catchline *(gen)* A temporary heading, used for identification purposes, printed at the top of a galley proof. → *galley proof*

catch title *(gen)* → *signature title*

catch-up *(pri)* In offset lithography, printing on non-image areas due to insufficient dampening of the plate. Also called 'dry-up'. → *offset litho(graphy); scum/scumming*

catchword *(gen)* A word printed (or written, in the case of a manuscript) at the foot of each page, which is also the first word of text on the following page. Originally these served as an aid to compositors, printers and binders to ensure that pages were set, imposed and gathered in the correct order, but latterly their only practical use is as an aid to the reader. In dictionaries and encyclopedias, the word printed at the top of each page to indicate the first or last entry can be called a catchword. In cases where only the first three letters of each word are printed, these are called 'catch-letters'.

cathode ray tube (CRT) *(com)* The standard video display device consisting of a glass vacuum tube containing a cathode that projects a beam of electrons onto a sensitized flat surface at the far end of the vacuum tube.

cause-and-effect diagram *(gen)* A pictorial representation of the analysis of a process, identifying the cause of a problem or the solution to it, and the effect that may have on the process. Also called a 'fishbone' diagram.

C/C++ *(com)* A programming language widely used for compiling software programs, particularly for use on Macintosh computers. → *program*

CCD *(com) abb.:* charge-coupled device. A tiny light sensor ('photosite') sensitized by receiving an electrical charge prior to exposure. CCDs are used in flat-bed scanners and most digital cameras for converting light into picture data. → *camera; CMOS; digital camera*

CCD array *(com)* A collection of CCDs arranged in a line. → *CCD*

CCITT *(int) abb.:* Comité Consultatif Internationale Téléphonique et Télégraphique (Consultative Committee on International Telephony and Telegraphy). An organization sponsored by the United Nations, which sets worldwide communications standards, especially with regard to data and voice transmission and compression.

CD *(com) abb.:* compact disc. → *CD-I; CD-R/ CD-RW; CD-ROM; compact disc*

CD-DA *(com) abb.:* compact disc-digital audio. A storage technology that uses the CD format for storing high-quality digital audio. → *compact disc; Red Book*

CD Extra *(com)* → *Enhanced Music CD*

CD-I *(com) abb.:* compact disc-interactive. A compact disc technology similar to CD-ROM and originally intended for the consumer electronics market. Developed by Philips, CD-I discs require a special player but can be viewed on a regular television set. CD-I technology has been supplanted by the widespread acceptance of CD-ROM technology in both the consumer and business markets, and also by the introduction of the highly capacious DVD (digital versatile disc). → *CD-ROM; DVD; Green Book*

CD Plus *(com)* → *Enhanced Music CD*

CD-R/CD-RW *(com) abb.:* compact disc-recordable/compact disc-rewritable. Specially made CDs that can record data by means of a laser that burns microscopic holes ('pits') into a thin recording layer. CD-Rs can be read by most standard CD-ROM players, but are rather more fragile than mass-replicated CDs. Since they cannot be read by all CD players, they are generally used for storage purposes. → *burn (2); CD-ROM; compact disc; Orange Book; WORM*

CD-ROM *(com)* Acronym for compact disc-read-only memory. A CD technology developed for the storage and distribution of digital data for use on computers. Data is stored by means of tiny pits – the size of which determine a 0 or a 1 – burned into an encapsulated layer and read by a laser that distinguishes the pits from 'lands' (the spaces between the pits). Based on audio CD technology, CD-ROMs have a diameter of 12cm (5in) and come in two capacities: 74 minutes in duration, giving a data capacity of around 650Mb, or 63-minute discs giving a data capacity of 550Mb. Exact capacity can vary from one manufacturer to another. → *burn (2); CD-I; CD-R/CD-RW; compact disc; Yellow Book*

Placing a **CD-ROM** into a CD reader

CD-ROM/XA *(com) abb.:* compact disc-read-only memory/extended architecture. An extended version of the original CD-ROM standard, which enhances the real-time playback capability of time-based data. CD-ROM/XA is similar to CD-I technology but is intended for use with computer CD-ROM drives rather than with special players. A CD-ROM/XA drive will also read CD-ROM and CD-I discs. → *CD-I; CD-ROM; compact disc*

CEL *(com)* Not to be confused with Autodesk Animator Pro's native file format, CEL stands for 'Cool Edit Loop'. These files are loop tracks that have been compressed as MP3 data, and which contain Cool Edit-specific information on the number of beats used, tempo, key and stretch method (if applicable). While MP3 files usually contain a few samples'-worth of silence on either end – making them unsuitable for use as loops – Cool Edit eliminates this silence automatically from its CEL files.

cel (1) *(gen) abb.:* cellulose acetate.
→ *cellulose acetate*

cel (2) *(gen)* The name given to individual animated stages of a sequence in conventional animation. These are drawn on transparent acetate sheets, which are overlayed onto a static background. Each cel forms a 'frame' in the animation.
→ *animation; cellulose acetate; frame (2)*

cell (1) *(pri)* A term used in gravure printing to describe the tiny recessed pits in the cylinder or plate that carry the ink. In conventional gravure printing, tones are determined by the varying depth of each cell. → *gravure*

cell (2) *(com)* A single space or unit for entering data in rows and columns, such as in a spreadsheet.

cellophane *(pap)* Transparent cellulose acetate film that is both very thin and very flexible.
→ *cellulose acetate*

◇	A	B
1	YE 2003/4	January
2	34523	3044.35626
3	33246	2931.74603
4	9878	871.075838
5	123	10.8465608
6	67789	5977.86596
7	42345	3734.12698
8	78978	6964.5502₆

In this Excel example, **cell** B6 is selected

cell padding *(com)* The space separating cells in a table or spreadsheet. → *cell (1)*

cellulose *(pap)* A fibrous substance – originally obtained only from certain plants – but now obtained almost exclusively from wood. Used as the basic substance in papermaking.

cellulose acetate *(gen)* A synthetic translucent material that may be clear or coloured, and with a shiny or matt surface. Used in the preparation of artwork ('mechanicals') as well as in photography for adding colour light effects.

central processing unit (CPU) *(com)* Referring to either the main microchip that performs a computer's core calculating functions (in other words, its brains), or, just as frequently, the box in which the chip resides.

centre-aligned (1) *(typ)* → *centred*

centre-aligned (2) *(gen)* Two or more items – text or pictures – that are aligned along their central axes.

centred *(typ)* Unjustified type that is centred in its measure, as distinct from ranged (aligned) left or right. → *alignment; unjustified*

centred dot/point *(typ)* A period (full point) centred on the x-height of a piece of type.

centre fold/spread *(pri)* Facing pages in the centre of a section. Centre spreads are also called 'naturals'. ➜ *double-(page) spread; section (1)*

centre head *(gen)* ➜ *heading (2)*

centre notes *(gen)* Notes set between columns of text.

centre-stitching *(fin)* A binding that uses thread stitched through the centre fold, similar to wire saddle-stitching. ➜ *binding; saddle-stitched*

centre-weighted exposure *(pho)* In automatic 'through-the-lens' (TTL) metred cameras, TTL is the method of measuring exposure whereby the calculation is based on the tones in the centre of the picture.

CEPS *(pre)* (pron.: 'seps') Acronym for Colour Electronic Prepress System. A term describing the entire computer-based prepress process, from scanned image to final page film. CEPS is generally used to describe high-quality colour reproduction, as distinct from inferior 'desktop colour' reproduction. ➜ *desktop colour; OPI*

CERN *(int)* abb.: European Organization for Nuclear Research (formerly Conseil Européen pour la Recherche Nucléaire). The birthplace of the World Wide Web, now overseen by the World Wide Web Consortium, based in Switzerland. ➜ *World Wide Web*

cf *(gen)* abb.: confer. The Latin term for 'refer to' or 'compare', and used to point the reader to a footnote to text.

CGI (1) *(int)* abb.: Common Gateway Interface. ➜ *Common Gateway Interface*

CGI (2) *(com)* abb.: computer-generated image. A catch-all term for any image produced on a computer.

CGI scripts *(int)* The programming instructions used by Web developers to execute CGI features. ➜ *CGI (1)*

Venezia

An example of **chancery italic**

chain lines/marks *(pap)* Visible lines on laid paper, caused by the wire gauze on the 'dandy' roll, part of the 'fourdrinier' papermaking machine. ➜ *dandy roll; fourdrinier; laid paper*

chain stitch *(fin)* The binding stitch at the head and tail of a section, made before the next section is sewn. ➜ *section (2)*

chalking *(pri)* An aberration in printing resulting in loose, dusty ink on the surface of the paper. This is caused by rapid absorption of the ink by the paper, which consequently slows down the drying time.

chamfered edges *(fin)* The bevelling of the edges of heavy binding boards so that there is a neater turnover of the cover material. ➜ *bevelled boards*

chancery italic *(typ)* A style of handwriting on which italic type designs are based. These formal scripts were used in the 15th and 16th century for official documents and letters.

change bar *(gen)* When revising a technical publication, the change bar is a vertical rule in the margin beside the text, indicating that it differs from the original.

channel (1) *(com)* Part of an image as stored in the computer; similar to a layer. Commonly, a colour image will have a channel allocated to each primary colour (e.g. RGB) and sometimes one or more for masks or other effects. Channels can be viewed individually in image editing programs like Photoshop, where they appear as greyscale images representing the strength of the primary colour across the image.

channel (2) *(int)* A feature of Web technology whereby information is automatically transmitted to your Web browser, as distinct from having to request it yourself. ➜ *push (technology)*

channel service unit/data service unit (CSU/DSU) *(int)* ➜ *CSU/DSU*

*!?

chapter drop *(gen)* The distance beneath a chapter heading at which the text commences. ➔ *chapter heading*

chapter heading *(gen)* The display heading at the start of each chapter, traditionally set in a uniform font, size, style and location (on a right-hand page, for example).

character (1) *(typ)* Any single letter, number, punctuation mark or symbol. Characters were traditionally called 'sorts'. ➔ *character (2)*

character (2) *(com)* Any single letter, number, punctuation mark or symbol represented on a computer by 8 bits (1 byte), including invisible characters such as 'space', 'return' and 'tab'. ➔ *character (1)*

character attribute *(com)* ➔ *attribute (2)*

character count *(typ)* The total number of characters in a piece of copy to be set. ➔ *cast-off*

character, double *(typ)* ➔ *double character*

character format *(com)* ➔ *format (2)*

character generator (1) *(com)* A computer program that provides the code for generating a font. ➔ *program*

character generator (2) *(com)* The VDU of a phototypesetting machine or word processor that displays characters.

character image *(com)* The arrangement of bits making up a character in a font. ➔ *bit*

character key *(com)* Any keyboard key that, when pressed, generates an image ('keyboard event') on screen, as distinct from a 'modifier' key, such as the shift or control keys, which do nothing until a character key is pressed. ➔ *modifier key*

character origin *(typ)* The location on the baseline used as a reference point for drawing a character. ➔ *baseline*

character set *(typ)* The complete repertoire of letters, numbers and symbols in a font design. ➔ *ISO/Adobe character set*

character shape player (CSP) *(int)* Software inside a Web browser that enables you to view, or 'play back', the character shapes of embedded fonts in a 'PFR' (portable font resource). ➔ *Character Shape Recorder (CSR); font embedding; TrueDoc*

character shape recorder (CSR) *(int)* Software inside an 'authoring' (multimedia) application that enables you to define – or 'record' – the character shapes of a font for embedding in a 'PFR' (portable font resource). ➔ *Character Shape Player; font embedding; TrueDoc*

character space *(typ)* The distance between each character as determined by the font designer, and as distinct from 'kerning' and 'tracking', which are modifications of that distance. ➔ *character width; kerning; tracking (1)*

characters per inch (cpi) *(typ)* ➔ *cpi*

characters per line (cpl) *(typ)* ➔ *cpl*

characters per second (cps) *(typ)* ➔ *cps*

character/text mode *(int)* Those Web browsers that can display text data only and which cannot display graphics without the assistance of a 'helper' application. Even browsers with the capacity to display

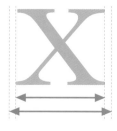

The shorter measure is **character width**

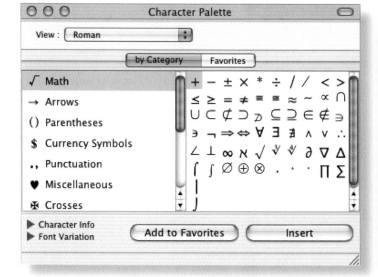

Apple Mac OS X's *Character Palette* showing a selection of **character keys**

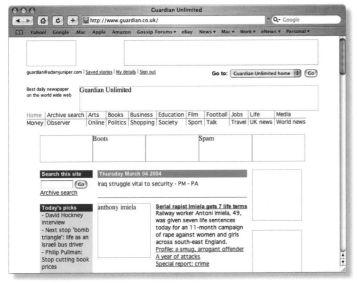

A webpage in **character mode**

The sphere is a **child object** to the cube

chat *(int)* A 'discussion' between two or more people typed live via an online Internet service. → *Internet*

chatterbots *(int)* Software 'helpers' that give advice and explain local etiquette on the Web in interactive environments, such as chat rooms. → *chat; World Wide Web*

checkbox *(com)* A small square button that can be 'toggled' on or off, indicating (by a check mark or cross) that the labelled item is selected or 'checked'. Unlike 'radio' buttons, of which only one can be selected from a group, any number of checkboxes can be selected.

chemical ghosting *(pri)* → *gloss ghosting*

chemical graining *(pri)* → *graining*

chemical pulp *(pap)* Pulp prepared from wood chips by treatment with chemicals to remove the non-cellulose material such as resin, ligneous matter and oils. Also called 'chemical wood', these pulps are used for making better grades of 'woodfree' paper. → *cellulose; mechanical (wood) pulp; woodfree paper*

chemical reversal *(pho)* Chemical treatment of a photographic image to convert it from negative to positive, or vice versa.

chemical transfer *(pri)* → *photomechanical transfer (PMT)*

chiaroscuro *(pri)* (pron.: *kee'ar'oskooro*); Italian for 'clear' (*chiaro*) and 'dark/obscure' (*oscuro*), the term describes single-colour wood engravings printed using a key block for the darkest tone, followed by a succession of tint blocks to add lighter shades or colours.

child object *(com)* An object linked hierarchically to another object (its 'parent'). For example, when a 'child' box is placed within a 'parent' box, and the latter is moved, the child – and all its 'grandchildren' – move with it, retaining their relative

graphics allow a preference for operating in character mode, or 'graphics off' mode, which some users prefer because pages load faster, and fewer bytes are downloaded. Web designers can add 'alternative' text in the HTML code so that viewers don't miss out. → *browser (1)/Web browser; World Wide Web*

character width *(typ)* The width of each character, determined from the origin of one to the origin of the next. → *character origin; character space*

charge-coupled device (CCD) *(pho)* → *CCD*

chart paper *(pap)* A strong, good-quality paper that is suitable for printing maps.

chase (1) *(pri)* In letterpress printing, a heavy rectangular metal frame into which type and illustration blocks are locked before it is placed on the bed of the press. → *form (2)/ forme*

chase (2) *(fin)* To make a groove or cut a design into a surface such as a block or book cover.

chased edges *(fin)* The wavy effect on gilded edges of a book, achieved by using heated tools known as goffering irons. Chased edges are also known as 'goffered' edges. → *gilt edges*

positions and orientation. This enables manipulation of complex structures, particularly in 3D applications. → *down tree; parent object*

china clay *(pap)* Also called 'kaolin', the substance used in papermaking to increase surface qualities such as gloss and smoothness. China clay has now largely been replaced by artificial sulphate of lime ('satin white'), which provides a smoother surface. → *satin white*

chip/microchip *(com)* The most essential computer component, consisting of a small piece of silicon impregnated with miniature electronic circuits. Chips provide the basis of computer processing functions.
→ *central processing unit (CPU); random access memory (RAM)*

chipboard *(pap)* Thin, cheap board made from recycled paper and used for edition-binding cases. → *case (1)*

choke *(pre)* One of the 'trapping' techniques (along with 'spread') used in print preparation for ensuring that two abutting areas of ink print without gaps. A choke traps a surrounding light background to a dark, inner foreground object by expanding the edge of the inner object so that the two colours overlap. Since the darker of the two adjacent colours defines the visible edge of the object, it is always preferable to extend the lighter colour into the darker. Traditionally, spreads and chokes were achieved by slightly overexposing the film so that the image areas expanded, and the piece of film used for the choke was alternatively termed a 'skinny'. Nowadays, software applications provide automatic trapping features. → *spread (2); trapping*

chopper fold *(fin)* → *right-angle fold*

chroma (1) *(aud)* Shortened form of chrominance, the technical name for the colour component of a video signal.

chroma (2) *(gen)* The intensity or purity of a colour, and so its degree of saturation. Technically it refers to the mixture of wavelengths in a light source, where a single wavelength is the maximum chroma and an even mixture of all wavelengths is the minimum.

chromolithography *(pri)* Obsolete lithographic printing process in which many colours were printed from separate litho stones.

chromo paper *(pap)* A smooth paper, more heavily coated than art paper – usually only on one side – which can be dull or glazed.
→ *art paper; coated paper*

chuck *(pri)* The core supporting a paper roll in a web-fed printing press. → *web (1)*

chute delivery *(pri)* A particular method of delivering printed material from a press.

Cibachrome *(pho)* A proprietary process for obtaining photographic colour prints directly from transparencies, developed by Agfa.

cicero *(typ)* A unit of the European Didot system for measuring the width ('measure') of a line of type and the depth of a page. One cicero equals 12 Didot points, or 4.511mm (3/16in). The unit is said to derive from the size of type cut for a 15th-century edition of Cicero's De Oratore. → *Didot point; point*

CIE *(gen)* abb.: Commission Internationale de l'Eclairage. An international organization that defined a visual colour model that forms the basis for colourimetric measurements of colour. → *CIE L*a*b* colour space*

CIE L*a*b* colour space *(com)* A three-dimensional colour model based on the system devised by CIE for measuring colour. L*a*b* colour is designed to maintain consistent colour regardless of the device used to create or output the image, such as a scanner, monitor or printer. L*a*b* colour consists of a luminance or lightness component (L) and two chromatic components: a (green to red) and b (blue to

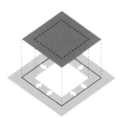

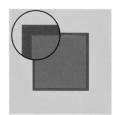

The yellow ink expanded to **choke** the blue

yellow). Lab color (without the asterisks) is the internal colour model used by Adobe Photoshop when converting from one colour mode to another, and 'Lab mode' is useful for working with Kodak PhotoCD images. → *CIE*

c.i.f. *(gen) abb.:* cost, insurance and freight. A shorthand for indicating that a price quoted for a job includes delivery to a location specified by the customer. → *f.o.b.*

Cinepak *(com)* A compression setting ('codec'), used by QuickTime that is best suited for sequences to be played from multimedia CD-ROM presentations, especially when slower computers or slower CD-ROM drives (such as 2x speed) may be used. Since CD ROM drives are now much faster, other, more modern codecs often provide better results. Equally Cinepak is not well suited to the slow data rates needed for web video. → *CD-ROM; codec (1)*

CIP *(gen) abb.:* Cataloging-in-Publication. → *Cataloging-in-Publication (CIP)*

circuit board *(com)* The support – made of fibreglass or pressboard – upon which chips and other electronic components are mounted. Components are usually linked to one another by connections that are stamped onto the board with metallic ink, and these are called 'printed circuit boards' (PC boards). The main board in a computer – bearing the CPU, ROM, and RAM chips – is called the 'motherboard' or 'logic board'. A board that plugs into an expansion slot is called an 'add-on board' (or card). A board that plugs into another board is called a 'daughterboard'. → *chip/ microchip; daughterboard*

circuit edges *(fin)* A book binding used typically for limp-backed Bibles and prayer books, in which projecting covers are turned over to protect the edges. → *Yapp binding*

circular *(gen)* Advertising matter printed as a single leaf or folded sheet.

circular screen *(pre)* An adjustable halftone screen that can be rotated to prevent undesirable 'moiré' patterns in colour reproduction. → *moiré*

circumflex *(typ)* A symbol (^) placed over a vowel in some languages to indicate a special quality such as a contraction. → *accent*

CISC *(com)* (pron.: 'sisk'); Acronym for Complex Instruction Set Computing. → *complex instruction set computing (CISC); microprocessor; RISC*

cissing *(pri)* A printing defect that occurs when wet ink (or varnish) recedes from the paper surface, leaving small uncoated areas.

CIX *(int)* (pron.: 'kicks'); Acronym for Commercial Internet Exchange, an alliance of Internet service providers (ISPs). → *Internet Service Provider (ISP)*

clamshell press *(pri)* A machine with two hinged platens such as are found on diecutting and heat-transfer equipment.

classified ad(vertisement) *(gen)* Small newspaper or magazine advertisement (thus sometimes called 'small ad'), appearing in a 'personals column', for example. Generally sold by the line or column inch. As distinct from 'display' advertisement, which will take up more space on a page, often contain graphics or images, and will cost more. → *advert(isement); display advertisement*

clay-coated paper *(pap)* → *art paper*

clean install *(com)* The process of installing completely new operating system software. A clean install will create new system software components rather than updating existing ones. If you perform a clean install, all the other components of your system that may have been loaded when you installed your applications and utility software will have to be reinstalled or copied separately – a time-consuming business. However, a clean install is sometimes necessary to 'flush out' unnecessary or corrupt files. → *operating system*

clean proof *(gen)* A galley or press proof that is free from errors. → *dirty proof; galley proof; press proof*

ClearType *(com)* A font technology, developed by Microsoft, designed for the smooth rendering of fonts on screen, particularly for use with electronic books ('eBooks') and other electronic forms. Readability is dramatically improved on colour LCD monitors, such as those used by laptops and high-quality flat-screen desktop displays.

cliché *(pri)* Originally a French term, now used elsewhere in Europe, for a stereotype ('stereo') or electrotype ('electro').
→ *electro(type); stereo(type)*

Click (track) *(aud)* Optional audible click in audio software that counts out the BPM (beats per minute) and time signature of a recording. It is not recorded as audio, and it can be switched on or off at any time.

clickable map/image *(int)* An invisible shape surrounding a graphic on a webpage that serves as a 'button' which, when clicked, will take you to another page or website.
→ *button; World Wide Web*

client *(com)* In a 'client/server' arrangement, such as on a network or on the Web, the client is the end-user (your computer). On the Web, your browser is a 'client program' which talks to Web servers. → *network; server; World Wide Web*

client pull *(int)* An instruction sent by a Web browser to a server to collect a particular set of data.

client-side *(com)* Processing done by you on your own computer rather than by a network server ('server-side'). → *server-side*

client-side image map *(int)* A means of navigating a webpage via a clickable image map, which includes the hyperlinks ('URLs') in the page itself, so that you can move around without intervention by the server.
→ *server-side image map*

clinometer *(pho)* Surveying device that measures slopes – useful for photographing subjects that may not be absolutely vertical, such as a painting.

clip art/clip media *(com)* Collections of (usually) royalty-free photographs, illustrations, design devices and other pre-created items, such as films, sounds and 3D wireframes. Clip art is available in three forms – on paper, which can be cut out and pasted on to camera-ready art, on computer disk, or, increasingly, via the Web. The quality of clip art collections can vary enormously, as can the licensing requirements, so you are advised to check both before purchasing. Clip art collections are sometimes referred to as 'copyright-free', but, since the publisher almost always retains ownership of the copyright of the material, this is not accurate. Your purchase of the material merely grants you the licence to use the images without payment of further fees, and does not assign the copyright to you. → *copyright-free; image resource; royalty-free*

Some items of
clip art

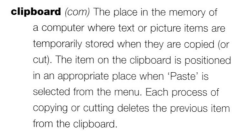

clipboard *(com)* The place in the memory of a computer where text or picture items are temporarily stored when they are copied (or cut). The item on the clipboard is positioned in an appropriate place when 'Paste' is selected from the menu. Each process of copying or cutting deletes the previous item from the clipboard.

clipping (1) *(gen)* Limiting an image or piece of art to within the bounds of a particular area.
→ *clipping path*

clipping (2) *(aud)* Unlike recording to magnetic tape, where a small amount of overdrive can produce a desirable fuzzy effect, any digital audio signal over 0 dB is in danger of clipping. This creates awful-sounding digital distortion and should be avoided by making sure the highest peak of your audio file does not exceed 0 dB.

clipping (3) *(pri)* The loss or removal of colour image data outside certain tonal limits. Converting an image from RGB to CMYK for print typically involves clipping of the most saturated greens and blues, because these colours cannot be reproduced in print.

clipping group *(com)* A stack of image layers that produce a resultant image or effect that is a net composite of the constituents. For example, where the base layer is a selection shape (say, an ellipse), the next layer a transparent texture (such as craquelure) and the top layer a pattern, the clipping group would produce a textured pattern in the shape of an ellipse.

clipping path *(com)* A Bézier outline that can be drawn around a subject or image element to determine which areas of an image should be considered transparent or 'clipped'. Using a clipping path, an object can be isolated from the remainder of the image, which is then rendered transparent, enabling background elements in an image composite to show through. A particular application is when cut-out images are to be placed on top of a tint background in a page layout. When a clipping path is created, it can be embedded into the image file, normally when saved to the EPS format. Clipping paths are generally created in an image-editing application such as Adobe Photoshop. → *Bézier curve; DCS*

clipping plane *(com)* In 3D applications, a plane beyond which an object is not visible. A view of the world has six clipping planes: top, bottom, left, right, hither and yon.

clip test *(pho)* A small piece cut from the end of an exposed roll of film, which is processed in advance to determine whether any adjustment may be necessary in processing.

An image showing a red **clipping path**

clock speed/rate *(com)* The speed at which a computer's central processing unit (CPU) can process instructions. This is regulated by the pulses of a quartz crystal, the frequency of which is measured in megahertz (millions of cycles per second). The more there are, the faster the computer. Clock speed determines the speed of such operations as screen redraw or RAM access. → *central processing unit (CPU)*

clogged *(pri)* → *filling in/up*

clone/cloning *(com)* In most image-editing packages, clone tools allow the user to sample pixels (picture elements) from one part of an image, such as a digital photograph, and use them to 'paint' over another area of the image. This process is often used for the removal of unwanted parts of an image or correcting problems, such as facial blemishes. In Photoshop, the tool is called the *Clone Stamp* tool (sometimes known as the *Rubber Stamp*).

close (1) *(fin)* → *closed section/signature*

close (2) *(typ)* The second of a pair of punctuation marks, as in brackets or quotation marks:])'.

closed file *(com)* A file that does not have an access path, thus preventing you from reading from or writing to it. → *access path*

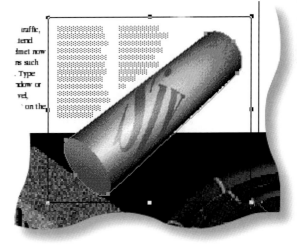

CLOSED FILE

closed h *(typ)* An italic 'h' in which the shorter stroke curves inwards, as in '*h*'.

closed section/signature *(fin)* A section or signature in which the bolts have been left uncut. ➔ *bolts; section (2); signature (1)*

close up *(typ)* An instruction to delete a space to bring characters closer together.

cloth boards *(fin)* A binding in which cloth covers stiff boards, as distinct from limp or flexible covers. ➔ *binding; boards*

cloth faced *(pap)* ➔ *linen faced*

cloth joints *(fin)* A binding in which cloth is used to reinforce the fold of an endpaper. ➔ *binding; endpapers*

cloth lined *(pap)* ➔ *linen faced*

Clouds filter/Render filter *(com)* Creates a cloudscape using random values between those of the foreground and background colours. Care is therefore needed in selecting sensible colours in order to create a realistic effect. When aiming to create a realistic sky, background and foreground colours are completely interchangeable. This filter does not depend on the currently active image, unlike the *Difference Clouds* filter, which subsequently blends the clouds with the underlying image.

cloverleaf/pretzel/propeller symbol *(com)* The symbol (⌘) used to identify the 'Command key', or 'Apple key' on Macintosh keyboards.

club line *(typ)* ➔ *orphan*

CLUT *(com)* Acronym for Colour LookUp Table. A preset table of colours (to a maximum of 256) that the operating system uses when in 8-bit mode. CLUTS are also attached to individual images saved in 8-bit 'indexed' mode. When an application converts a 24-bit image to 8-bit, it creates a table of up to 256 of the most frequently used colours in the image. If a colour in the original image does not appear in the table, the application chooses the closest one or simulates it by 'dithering' available colours in the table. ➔ *colour library; dithering (1); indexed colour; operating system*

CMC7 *(typ)* A font used for magnetic ink character recognition.

CMM *(com) abb.:* colour management module. ➔ *colour management module (CMM)*

CMOS (Complementary Metal-Oxide Semiconductor) *(pho)* An alternative sensor technology to the CCD, CMOS chips are used in high-resolution cameras from Canon and Kodak. ➔ *CCD; digital camera*

CMY *(gen) abb.:* cyan, magenta, yellow. The primary colours of the 'subtractive' colour model, created when you subtract red, green or blue from white light. In other words, if an object reflects green and blue light but absorbs, or subtracts, red, it will appear to you as cyan. Cyan, magenta and yellow are the basic printing process colours. ➔ *CMYK; colour model; RGB; subtractive colour mixing*

CMYK *(gen) abb.:* cyan, magenta, yellow and black (black is represented by the letter 'K', for 'key' plate) – the four printing process colours based on the subtractive colour model. In colour reproduction, most of the colours are achieved by cyan, magenta and yellow, the theory being that, when all three are combined, they produce black. However, this is rarely achievable and would be undesirable since too much ink would be used, causing problems with drying time, etc. For this reason, black is

The result of the
Clouds filter

62

CLOSED H

used to add density to darker areas, while to compensate, smaller amounts of the other colours are used (this also has cost benefits since black is cheaper than coloured inks). The degree of colour that is 'removed' is calculated by a technique known as 'undercolour removal' (UCR). → *CMY; colour model; RGB; UCR*

coated lens *(pho)* A photographic lens coated with a thin film that reduces 'flare' (undesirable scattered light). → *flare*

coated paper *(pap)* A general term describing papers that have had a mineral coating applied to the surface after the body paper was made, such as art, chromo and enamel papers. Coated paper is also known as 'surface paper'. → *art paper; blade coater; chromo paper; coating slip*

coating slip *(pap)* The name given to the solution of minerals, binders and other additives used to coat paper. → *coated paper*

cock (end) *(typ)* The middle part of a brace end, when constructed in three pieces. → *brace; brace end*

cockle *(pap)* A finish achieved by air-drying paper, producing papers such as onionskin.

cockled/cockling *(pap)* Paper that has become distorted due to uneven absorption of moisture, usually because of poor storage. This can sometimes be remedied by 'conditioning' the paper – drying it out with conditioned air.

cockroach *(typ)* A colloquial term for display text set entirely in lower case type.

cock-up figure/letter *(typ)* → *superior character*

cock-up initial *(typ)* → *raised cap(ital)*

code *(com)* The instructions in a piece of software that tell the computer what to do. Code can take various forms, from 'binary code' – a series of 1s and 0s – to programming languages and 'script' (code that is written in a sort of English so that the user can understand it). HTML is a programming code written for Web browsers, while typical scripting codes include 'lingo', which is written for Macromedia Director presentations, and AppleScript, which enables you to create shortcuts for common tasks on Macintosh computers. → *AppleScript; binary code; browser (1)/Web browser; compiler; HTML; interpreter; script (1)*

codec (1) *(com)* Acronym for compressor/ decompressor, the technique used to rapidly compress and decompress sequences of images, such as those used for QuickTime and AVI films. → *AVI; QuickTime*

codec (2) *(com)* An algorithm used as part of a program to decompress incoming data from a broadcast signal or DVD, or compress data during the export process.

codet *(pre)* → *colour bar*

co-edition *(gen)* A work, such as a book or multimedia title, that is to be published in another language or territory, either simultaneously or at a later date.

cold boot *(com)* → *boot/boot up/booting up*

cold composition *(typ)* A form of low-quality typesetting for camera-ready copy done on special (or even ordinary) mechanical 'golf ball' or 'daisy wheel' typewriters. Also called 'strike-on' composition or 'impact printing'. → *camera-ready copy/art (CRC); daisy wheel; golf ball*

cold-set ink *(pri)* A solid ink which, when used on a 'hot press' (one that has a heated cylinder), melts into a liquid, then solidifies on contact with the paper.

cold type *(typ)* Type supplied to the typesetting house as individual pieces, as distinct from type cast by 'hot metal' machines such as Monotype and Linotype. → *hot metal (type); Linotype; Monotype*

colinear *(com)* Two or more objects that are in line.

*!?

collate *(fin)* The process of sorting printed pages or signatures into their correct order. Also called 'conflate' (US). → *back(step) collation; back(step) mark; signature (1)*

collating mark *(pri)* → *back(step) mark*

Collision detection *(com)* The ability of a program to calculate the proximity of objects and prevent them from intersecting.

collotype *(pri)* A 'planographic', photo-mechanical printing process that uses a gelatine-coated plate onto which the image is photographically exposed without using a halftone screen, thus achieving continuous tones. Collotypes are typically used for short-run fine art edition prints. Also known as 'photogelatine printing'.
→ *planographic (printing)*

colophon *(gen)* A message traditionally inscribed at the end of a manuscript book, indicating the title, author's name, date of completion, dedication, etc. Nowadays, a colophon may be printed at the beginning or end of a book, giving production information such as the title, printer's name, date of printing and copyright.

Color-Key™ *(pre)* A proprietary dry proofing system developed by 3M. → *dry proof*

ColorMatch RGB *(com)* A smallish, and now somewhat outdated RGB colour space, originally designed by Radius to match the typical gamut of its high-quality monitors and provide a good match between screen and offset print.

ColorSync *(com)* Apple Computer's system-level implementation of ICC-based colour management.

colour (1) *(gen)* The visual interpretation of the various wavelengths of reflected or refracted light.

colour (2) *(typ)* In typography, the name used to describe the generally light or bold appearance of a particular typeface, regardless of its actual weight.

colour bar *(pre)* The colour device printed on the edge of colour proofs or in the trim area of press sheets, which enables the repro house and printer to check – by eye or with instruments – the fidelity of colour separations and the accuracy of printing. The colour bar helps to monitor such things as ink density, paper stability, dot gain, trapping and so on. Also called a 'codet' (US). → *colour separation; copyboard chart; trapping*

colour-blind emulsion *(pre)* Photographic emulsion that is sensitive only to blue, violet or ultraviolet light. → *contact film*

colour-blind film *(pre)* → *contact film*

colour break *(pre)* The edge between two areas of colour in an image.

colour burnout *(pri)* The undesirable change in the colour of printing inks due to chemical reactions, either when the ink is mixed or as it dries after printing.

colour calibrate *(gen)* → *calibrate/calibration*

colour cast *(pho)* A bias in a colour image, which can be either intentionally introduced or the undesirable consequence of a lighting problem. Intentional colour casts tend to be introduced to enhance an effect (such as accentuating the reds and oranges of a sunset) and can be done via an appropriate command in an image-editing application. Alternatively, they can be done at the proof stage to enhance the colour in an image. Undesirable casts are typically due to an imbalance between the lighting source and the response of the film (or that of the CCD in the case of a digital camera). Using daylight film under tungsten lighting causes an amber colour cast, while setting the colour balance of a digital camera for indoor scenes can give a flat blue cast outdoors.

colour chart *(pre)* A printed reference chart used in colour reproduction to select or match colour tints made from percentage variations of the four process colours.

The letter 'M' created as a single piece of **cold type**

An image suffering from a strong red **colour cast** can be corrected in Photoshop

For absolute accuracy, you should use one prepared by your chosen printer and printed on the actual paper that will be used for the job (a situation that is highly unlikely to occur in reality). →*colour picker (2); colour swatch; CMYK*

colour coder *(pre)* → *densitometer*

colour constancy *(gen)* The ability of the human eye and brain to perceive colours accurately under a variety of lighting conditions, compensating automatically for the difference in colour temperature. This phenomenon is also known as 'chromatic adaptation'.

colour correction *(pre)* The process of adjusting colour values in reproduction in order to achieve the desired result. Although this can occur at scanning or image-manipulation stage, colour correction is generally carried out after 'wet' proofing (proofs created using process colour inks) and, as a very limited last resort, on press.

colour depth *(com)* The number of bits required to define the colour of each pixel. For example, only one bit is required to display a black-and-white image (it is either

on or off), whereas an 8-bit image can display either 256 greys or 256 colours, and a 24-bit image can display 16.7 million colours – eight bits each for red, green and blue (256 x 256 x 256). → *bit; bit depth*

coloured edges/tops *(fin)* The edges or tops of books that have been coloured. Colour is usually applied by spray gun to the book blocks prior to binding. After colouring, wax may be applied to give the edges a gloss or, for the most glossy finish, the edges may be rubbed with a burnisher. Also called 'stained' edges. → *book block; burnished edges; burnisher (1)*

coloured link *(int)* → *active hyperlink*

coloured printings *(pap)* Low-grade (and thus cheap) paper, used primarily for covering low-cost publications.

colour filters *(pho)* Thin sheets of transparent material, such as glass or gelatine, which are placed over a camera lens to modify the quality of light or colours in an image. → *cellulose acetate*

COLOUR FILTERS

colour gamut *(com)* Gamut, or 'colour space', describes the full range of colours achievable by any single device on the reproduction chain. While the visible spectrum contains many millions of colours, not all of them are achievable by all devices and, even if the colour gamuts for different devices overlap, they will never match exactly – the 13.7 million colours that can, for example, be displayed on a monitor cannot all be printed on a commercial four-colour press. For this reason, various 'colour management systems' (CMS) have been devised to maintain consistency of colour gamuts across various devices. ➔ *colour management module (CMM); colour management system (CMS)*

colourimetry *(gen)* The technical term for the scientific measurement of colour.

colour library *(com)* An application support file that contains predefined colours. These may be the application's default colours, colours defined by you, or other predefined colour palettes or tables. ➔ *application (support) / file; CLUT; colour picker (1)*

colour management module (CMM)
(com) A profile for managing and matching colours accurately across different platforms and devices. CMMs conform to a colour management system (CMS) such as that defined by the International Color Consortium (ICC). CMMs interpret the ICC profiles that describe the RGB and CMYK colour spaces on your computer. There are usually existing ICC profiles that are installed onto your computer by ICC-compliant applications such as Adobe Photoshop, or you can create your own. The selected profile is then embedded in the image you are working on, so that it can later be used as a reference by other devices in the production process. You may find a variety of CMMs on your computer: those built into ICC-compliant applications (usually the best if you are

unsure of how to use CMMs); the Kodak Digital Science Color Management System (primarily for use with images using the Kodak Photo CD format); or CMMs specified by the computer operating system, such as Apple ColorSync and Microsoft ICM. ➔ *CMYK; colour management system (CMS); ICC profile; RGB*

colour management system (CMS) *(com)* abr. CMS. The name given to a method devised to provide accuracy and consistency of colour representation across all devices in the colour reproduction chain – scanners, monitors, printers, imagesetters and so on. Typical CMSs are those defined by the International Color Consortium (ICC), Kodak's Digital Science Color Management System, Apple's ColorSync and Microsoft's ICM. ➔ *colour gamut; colour management module (CMM); ICC*

colour model *(gen)* The method of defining or modifying colour. Although there are many proprietary colour models such as FO COLTONE, TRUMATCH, TOYO and DIC, the two generic models are those based on the way light is transmitted – the 'additive' and 'subtractive' colour models. The additive colour model is used in computer monitors, for example, and transmits varying proportions of red, green and blue (RGB) light, which we interpret as different colours. By combining the varying intensities of RGB light, we can simulate the range of colours found in nature and, when 100% values of all three are combined, we perceive white, whereas if there is no light we see nothing or, rather, black. The subtractive colour model is based on the absorption (i.e. subtraction) and reflection of light, and is used when printing cyan, magenta and yellow inks – if you subtract 100% values of either red, green or blue from white light, you create cyan, magenta or yellow. ➔ *additive colours; CMY; RGB; subtractive colour mixing*

The RGB **colour model** (top) and CMYK (below)

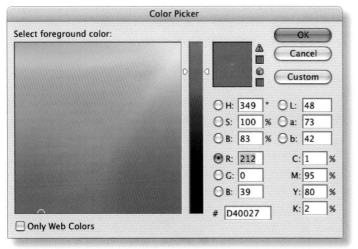

The Adobe
colour picker

colour negative film *(pho)* Photographic film in which the image, after it has been processed, is formed in negative colours, from which positive colour prints are then made. As distinct from colour transparency film, which is positive and is not generally used for making prints. Also referred to as 'colour negs'. ➔ *colour transparency (film)*

colour picker (1) *(com)* A colour model when displayed on a computer monitor. Colour pickers may be specific to an application such as Adobe Photoshop, a third-party colour model such as PANTONE, or to the operating system running on your computer. ➔ *colour model*

colour picker (2) *(gen)* A book of printed colour samples that are carefully defined and graded and from which you can select spot colours. Colour pickers generally conform to a colour model, such as PANTONE, so that you can be confident that the colour you choose will be faithfully reproduced by the printer; as distinct from a 'colour chart', which is generally used to select colours made up from process colour inks. ➔ *colour chart; colour model; colour swatch*

colour positives *(pre)* A set of positive printing films – usually one for each of the four separated process colours: cyan, magenta, yellow and black, although the film for a spot colour may also be described as a colour positive. ➔ *CMYK*

colour printing *(pri)* Printing in inks other than black. The major commercial printing processes today are offset lithography (either sheet- or web-fed) and web gravure. Screen printing is also widely used, although generally for more specialist work and in small print runs. Colour letterpress printing – the oldest method – has all but died out except for very specialist work. ➔ *gravure; offset litho(graphy); printing processes*

colour reversal film *(pho)* ➔ *colour transparency (film)*

colour rotation/sequence *(pri)* The order in which each colour is printed. In four-colour process printing, the order is usually yellow first, followed by magenta, cyan and finally black. This sequence is important, since it minimizes the chance of getting undesirable moiré patterns on halftone images, and also because it can affect the efficacy of ink 'trapping'. ➔ *CMYK; moiré*

colour scanner *(pre)* ➔ *scanner*

colour separation *(pre)* The process of dividing a multicoloured image into the four individual process colours – cyan, magenta, yellow and black (by using red, green and blue filters) so that the image can be reproduced on a printing press. Conventionally, this was done using the filters in a 'process' camera, but colour separations are now prepared digitally on a scanner or a computer. ➔ *scanner; CMYK*

colour separations *(pre)* The set of four films for each of the four process colours – cyan, magenta, yellow and black – generated as a result of the colour separation process.
→ *CMYK; colour positives; colour separation; printer*

colour space *(com)* Description of the full range of colours achievable by any single device in the reproduction chain, along with any tonal and colour deviations. The colour space models device behaviour. While the visible spectrum contains millions of colours, many of them are unachievable in digital imaging. Even though the colour gamuts of different devices overlap substantially, they are unlikely to match exactly. For example, the colours that can be displayed on a monitor cannot all be printed on a commercial four-colour press, and vice-versa; the press can print some colours that the monitor cannot display.

colour swatch *(gen)* A sample of a specific colour, taken either from a colour chart, colour picker or some other printed example, and used as a guide either for specification or reproduction of spot colours or process tints. → *colour chart; colour picker (2)*

colour table *(com)* A predefined table, or list, of colours used to determine a specific colour model, such as for converting an image to CMYK. A colour table, or 'CLUT', also describes the palette of colours used to display an image. → *CLUT; CMYK; colour management module (CMM); colour model; ICC profile*

colour temperature *(gen)* A measure of the composition of light. This is defined as the temperature to which a black object would need to be heated to produce a particular colour of light. The colour temperature is based on a scale that sets zero as absolute darkness and increases with an object's brightness. A tungsten lamp, for example, has a colour temperature of 2900K, while the temperature of direct sunlight is around 5000K and is considered the ideal viewing standard in the graphic arts.

colour transparency (film) *(pho)* A photographic image on transparent film generated, after processing, as a positive image. Colour transparencies are ideal as originals for colour separations for process colour printing, because they provide a greater range of colours than reflective prints. Colour transparency film is supplied for a variety of camera formats, typically 35mm, 2¼ in square, and 4 x 5in. Colour transparencies are also known variously as 'trannies', 'colour trannies', 'slides' (which generally refers to 35mm only) and 'colour reversal film'. → *colour negative film*

colour value *(gen)* The tonal value of a colour when related to a light-to-dark scale of pure greys. → *lightness*

colour wheel *(gen)* The complete spectrum of visible colours represented as a circular diagram and used as the basis of some colour pickers. The HSB (hue, saturation, brightness) colour model determines hue as the angular position on the colour wheel and saturation as the corresponding radial position.

CMYK **colour separations**

The **colour space** of a typical RGB display marked within the theoretical L*a*b space

The colour spectrum as a **colour wheel**

column (1) *(gen)* The vertical division of a page to organize text, captions and illustrations. A column is measured by its width, traditionally in 'ems' or 'picas', but increasingly in inches or millimetres.
➔ *em; grid (1); pica*

column (2) *(typ)* A vertical division in tabulated matter. ➔ *boxhead*

column/column-face rule *(gen)* A rule, usually light-faced (thin), used to separate vertical columns on a page.
➔ *column (1, 2)*

column inch/centimetre *(gen)* A measure of space signifying one column wide by one inch (or centimetre) deep, used most often for calculating the cost of display advertising in printed journals. ➔ *agate; agate line*

coma *(pho)* A photographic lens aberration that causes blurring at the edge of a picture.

comb binding *(fin)* ➔ *plastic comb/coil binding*

combination folder *(fin)* A folding machine that combines both buckle and knife methods of folding. ➔ *buckle folder; fold/folding; knife folder*

combination line and halftone *(pre)* A single plate, block or piece of film onto which both line and halftone matter have been merged. Also called 'line and halftone fit up'. ➔ *halftone (1); line and halftone*

combination plate *(pri)* A printing plate prepared from a number of separate film negatives or positives, either all at once or individually, requiring several exposures. Also called 'photo-composed plate'. ➔ *plate (1)*

come-and-go/coming and going *(pri)* An imposition scheme in which the top, or head, of the first page is laid to the top of the last page, and so on throughout the section. The signatures are then doubled up with the last head-to-head against the first, finally being separated at trimming stage. Frequently used in paperback book printing, this method allows two copies to be printed from one set of plates
➔ *imposition/impose; signature (1)*

comma *(typ)* A punctuation mark (,).

comma-delimit *(com)* To separate elements of data, such as records or fields in a database, using a comma. ➔ *tab-delimit*

command *(com)* An instruction to a computer, given by the operator, either by way of the mouse when selecting a menu item for example, or by the keyboard. ➔ *mouse*

command-line interface *(com)* A user interface in which instructions are given to the computer by means of a chain, or line, of commands via the keyboard only. For example, the MS-DOS (Microsoft Disc Operating System) interface may prompt you to select one item from a list of options, then another, and so on until you reach your goal. In the worst examples, you may not be presented with any options at all, but are simply expected to know the command. The opposite of GUI (graphical user interface). ➔ *graphical user interface (GUI); interface; MS-DOS*

comment *(int)* A remark in authoring applications and Web browsers – identified by a specific character such as an explanation point (in HTML) – which is ignored by the application or browser when the pages are viewed, but which can be read by anyone who has access to the code. ➔ *HTML*

commercial a *(int)* The type character @ used as an abbreviation for 'at', primarily in e-mail addresses to signify location ('you@yourdomain.com', for example).
➔ *e-mail*

commercial art *(gen)* A general term used to describe any art prepared for commercial reproduction, thus distinguishing it from fine art. This activity is nowadays more widely described as 'graphic design'. ➔ *art(work); graphic design*

*!?

commercial colour *(pre)* The term (sometimes used derogatorily) applied to colour images generated by desktop scanners as opposed to high-resolution reproduction scanners. → *scanner*

commercial register *(pri)* The degree of tolerance in the register of the inks in four-colour process printing, usually as defined by the customer.

Common Gateway Interface (CGI) *(int)* A programming technique for managing and transferring data between Web server software and other applications, such as databases. → *CGI (1)*

Common Ground *(int)* A 'portable document format' (pdf) for creating material to be viewed across the World Wide Web. Common Ground DP ('DigitalPaper') format documents retain all the formatting of text and graphics and can be shared by Macintosh, Windows and UNIX users. Like Adobe Acrobat PDF files, Common Ground DP documents can be indexed and searched, but, unlike Acrobat files which require you to have viewing software already installed on your computer, Common Ground DP documents contain a 'mini' viewer already embedded in the file.
→ *Acrobat; PDF; World Wide Web*

comp (1) *(pre)* abb.: comprehensive.
→ *comprehensive*

comp (2) *(typ)* abb.: compose, composing, composition. The process of setting type.
→ *compositor; typesetting*

compact disc *(com)* A digital storage technology, developed by Philips and Sony Corp., on which data is stored by means of tiny pits burned into the disc's surface, the presence of which determines a binary 0 or a 1.

compiler *(com)* Software that converts 'high-level' programming code ('source' code), such as that written in C++, into low-level 'machine code' ('object' code), a language that hardware will understand. This is necessary because the machine understands only binary code. For example, if you were to instruct your computer to add two numbers in binary code, it would look something like 1101 0011 0001 0011 1110, whereas a high-level language would allow you to write 'add 1 to 2'. → *binary code; C/C++; computer language; interpreter*

comping *(gen)* The process of preparing a 'comprehensive' (comp), or layout, and also of indicating areas of type in a comp. In the latter, text was traditionally indicated by pairs of ruled lines, but since layouts are now more frequently prepared on computer, text is indicated by 'greeked' (greyed-out) type or by 'dummy' text (often called 'Latin'), a meaningless language used to simulate real text. → *comprehensive; greek/greeking*

complementary colours *(gen)* Any pair of colours directly opposite each other on a colour wheel, which combine to form white (or black depending on the colour model: subtractive or additive).

Complementary Metal-Oxide Semiconductor (CMOS) *(pho)* → *CMOS*

complex instruction set computing (CISC) *(com)* A type of microprocessor used in some earlier computers. → *CISC; RISC*

complex object *(com)* In 3D applications, a grouped object comprised of several simple objects. → *child object; down tree; parent object*

Component Video *(com)* A QuickTime 'codec' (compression setting) that generates a 2:1 compression and, being limited to 16-bit colour depth, is best suited for archiving films. → *codec (1); QuickTime*

compose/composing *(typ)* → *comp (2)*

Complementary colours are found opposite each other on the colour wheel

A **complex object** from a 3D application

composing room *(typ)* The area in a printing plant specifically set aside for typesetting and make-up. ➔ *comp (2); make-up (1); typesetting*

composite *(aud)* A basic video signal that combines chrominance and luminance information into a single video stream.

composite art(work) *(gen)* A rarely used term for camera-ready art that combines several different elements, such as text and illustrations. Commonly used terms include 'mechanical', 'paste-up' or 'CRC' (camera-ready copy). ➔ *mechanical*

composite book *(gen)* A book made up of several different parts, such as the complete works of an individual author or collected works by several authors, bound into a single volume.

composite colour file *(com)* The low-resolution file that combines the four CMYK files of an image saved in the five-file DCS (desktop colour separation) format and which is used to preview the image and position it in layouts. Since the composite file is not the one used for separations, you should take care when using it with runaround text. If, for example, you define a path in QuarkXPress, that path will not be reflected in the four separation files and the runaround will not work as you planned. ➔ *CMYK; DCS*

The CMYK **composite colour files** separated in order from cyan (top) to Key/Black (bottom)

composite film *(pre)* ➔ *flat (1)*

composite video *(com)* A video 'bus', or signal, in which all the colour information is combined, such as in the 'video out' RCA jack on older VCRs (video cassette recorders). This results in loss of quality. On computer monitors, quality is maintained by keeping each of the RGB colour signals separate. ➔ *bus (1); RGB*

compositing/composing machine *(typ)* ➔ *hot metal (type)*

composition *(typ)* The setting of type. ➔ *comp (2); typesetting*

composition size(s) *(typ)* The traditional name for any size of type below 14pt, so-called because these were the sizes that could be set on a hot metal 'compositing' (typesetting) machine. ➔ *comp (2); hot metal (type); point (1); typesetting*

compositor *(typ)* The person who sets type – individual pieces of metal set by hand originally, but now by any method. An increasingly rare breed since the computer has all but eliminated this trade. Traditionally called a 'typographer' in the US, which, now that the designer has total control over typography, is probably a more appropriate description. In the days of metal type, the compositor would also make up and impose pages. Also called a 'typesetter', although this can also mean the machine upon which type is set. ➔ *comp (2)*

compound lens *(pho)* A photographic lens made up of two or more elements (lens pieces), enabling the lens to be optically adjusted.

compound printing *(pri)* Printing two or more colours in a single pass. To do so, different areas of the forme (in letterpress printing), or different sections of the inking system (in offset printing) are separately inked. ➔ *form (2)/ forme; printing processes*

*!?

comprehensive *(gen)* A preliminary rendition of a design, simulating the printed item, but to show intent rather than final detail. A typical comp will consist of illustrations, photographs and typeset text – not necessarily those that will actually be used, but which are close enough to convey the concept. Also variously called a 'mock-up', 'presentation visual', 'finished rough' or 'dummy'. ➔ *comping; dummy (2)*

compression (1) *(com)* The technique of rearranging data so that it either occupies less space on disk or transfers faster between devices or along communication lines. Different kinds of compression techniques are employed for different kinds of data – applications, for example, must not lose any data when compressed, whereas photographic images and films can tolerate a certain amount of data loss. Compression methods that do not result in data loss are referred to as 'lossless', whereas 'lossy' is used to describe methods in which some data is lost. Films and animations employ techniques known as 'codecs' (compression/decompression). There are many proprietary utilities for compressing data, while typical compression formats for images are LZW (lossless), JPEG and GIF (both lossy), the latter two being used commonly for files transmitted across the Internet. ➔ *codec (1); GIF (Graphics Interchange Format); Internet; JPEG; LZW; QuickTime*

compression (2) *(aud)* A compression wave is a graphical representation of how sound travels through the air. On a continuous waveform, the individual 'waves' are closer together at the point of origin, and this area of higher 'pressure' moves along the wave.

compressor (1) *(aud)* Compression packs a signal into a smaller dynamic space. Compressors work by lowering a signal's transient peaks – the higher the peaks, the more they are packed into a tighter space.

Modern pop production uses compressors heavily on vocals – not because modern vocalists are too powerful, but because compression makes quiet vocal passages seem much louder by evening out a performance, sometimes to the point of making it sound unnatural. A related device is the limiter, which sets a threshold on the dynamic level of signal it will allow through.

compressor (2) *(com)* ➔ *codec (1)*

CompuServe GIF *(int) abb.:* Graphic Interchange Format. ➔ *GIF (Graphics Interchange Format)*

computer *(com)* An electronic device that can process data (usually binary) according to a predetermined set of variable instructions called a 'program'. ➔ *binary; binary code; program*

computer graphics *(gen)* Strictly speaking, any graphic item generated on or output by a computer, such as page layouts, typography, illustrations, etc. However, the term is sometimes more specifically used to refer to a particular genre of computer-generated imagery, such as that which looks as though it were generated by computer.

computer input device *(com)* ➔ *input device*

computer language *(com)* The language, or code, devised to make computers work. These may be 'high level' – those used for writing application programs and written so that the user (or, at least, the programmer) can understand it, or 'low level' (usually binary) which only the computer can understand. ➔ *binary code; program*

computer output device *(com)* ➔ *output device*

computer terminal *(com)* ➔ *terminal*

computer-to-plate (CTP) *(pri) abb.:* computer-to-plate. The process of making printing plates directly from digital data, without the need for film. Also known as 'direct to plate'.

a a

Type, after (left) and before (right) being **condensed**

concatenate *(gen)* To string together two or more units of information. For example, 'Quick' and 'Time' becomes 'QuickTime' when concatenated, or a split file becomes one.

concave polygon *(com)* A polygon whose shape is concave – for example, a star shape.

concertina fold *(fin)* → *accordion/concertina fold*

condensed *(typ)* Of type designs, those faces whose height is greater than their width. Although a condensed style can be applied to computer-generated fonts by 'horizontal scaling', specifically designed condensed typefaces retain the correct relative proportions, or 'stress', between their horizontal and vertical strokes – a characteristic that is distorted and exaggerated by horizontal scaling.
→ *expanded/extended type; horizontal scaling; stress*

condenser (lens) *(pho)* A photographic lens that concentrates light into a beam. Used in enlargers and process cameras (a camera used for preparing film and plates for printing). → *process camera*

condenser microphone *(aud)* Ideal for percussive elements because they capture nuance better than dynamic microphones through the use of two charged plates of metal. They require a battery or other power source to operate.

conditioning *(pap)* A treatment given to paper either to dry it out or add moisture. This is done by subjecting the paper to streams of conditioned air in specially constructed chambers. Conditioning is particularly important in areas of the world where atmospheric conditions are extreme.
→ *cockled/cockling; humidified*

cones *(gen)* One of two forms of the eye's photoreceptors, found on the retina. Cones are sensitive to colour, while the other type, rods, respond only to intensity.

conflate *(fin)* → *collate*

conjugate *(pho)* The distance between the centre of the lens and either the subject or the sensor (depending which side).

conjugate leaves *(fin)* Any two leaves of a publication that are comprised of one piece of paper, such as the centre spread of a signature. → *signature (1)*

console *(com)* The part of a mechanical system – computer or otherwise – where instructions are given, either via switches or a keyboard.

constrain (1) *(com)* A facility in some applications to contain one or more item within another – for example, in a page-layout application, a picture box (the 'constrained item') within another picture box (the 'constraining box').

constrain (2) *(com)* In 3D applications, to restrict an item to a particular plane, axis or angle. → *axis*

constraining box/item *(com)* → *constrain (1)*

contact film *(pho)* Special 'continuous tone' film used to produce a same-size negative image from a film positive original, or vice versa, when the two are placed in direct contact with each other. Also called 'colour-blind film'. → *colour-blind emulsion*

contact (halftone) screen *(pre)* A sheet of film bearing a graded dot pattern, which, when placed in direct contact with photographic film or printing plates, converts continuous tone images, such as photographs or artwork, into 'halftones' (images made up of dots) that are suitable for printing. Originally, the screens were engraved on glass, but film-based contact screens give better definition. Now this method of generating halftone images has been supplanted by computers, which apply halftones to images digitally. → *halftone (1); halftone screen*

C

contact manager *(com)* → *database; database manager*

contact printing frame *(pre)* → *vacuum frame*

contact prints/contacts *(pho)* Photographic prints made by placing an original negative or positive film in direct contact with the bromide paper. → *bromide*

content *(int)* The information presented in a multimedia presentation or webpage, as distinct from the interface or code used to make it.

content provider *(int)* A provider of information on the Web, as distinct from a provider of a service, such as an ISP. → *Internet Service Provider (ISP)*

contents (page) *(gen)* The part of the 'prelims' (the front matter of a publication) that lists the content: divisions (chapters), the order in which they appear and their location (by page number). → *prelims/preliminary pages*

content-type *(int)* A MIME (Multipurpose Internet Mail Extensions) convention for identifying the type of data being transmitted over the Internet to such things as e-mail applications and Web browsers. → *e-mail; Internet; MIME*

contiguous *(com)* Adjacent, or next to; contiguous 'space' is particularly important in the context of memory (RAM) because an application requires the amount of memory allocated to it to be working as one chunk. While your computer may indicate that the amount of available memory is adequate to open a large application, you may find that, if you have opened and closed several applications during a session, the application will not run. This is because the memory has been gradually split into smaller chunks. In order to create enough 'contiguous' memory, you may need to restart your computer. Contiguous space is also important for storing files on disk, for while data files can be split up into many pieces and still be usable, the more fragments there are, the longer it takes the disk drive 'head' to find them. Therefore, files stored contiguously on disk will be accessed faster and will thus open more quickly. There are many commercial utilities for cleaning up the files on your hard disk and rearranging them (called 'optimizing' or 'defragmenting'). → *defragment(ing); RAM; reboot*

continuous feeder *(pri)* On an automatic sheetfed printing press, the mechanism that supplies the sheets of paper – and which can be replenished – without interrupting the printing process. → *sheet-fed (press)*

continuous fold *(fin)* A paper folding system that converts rolls of paper into 'accordion' folds. → *accordion/concertina fold*

continuous tone *(aud)* In digital audio, this refers to a tone that repeats the same cycle (high peak, then low peak) continuously until the source is switched off.

continuous tone (ct) *(pre)* An image that contains infinite continuous shades between the lightest and darkest tones, as distinct from a 'line' illustration, which has only one shade. Usually used to describe an image before it is either broken up by the dots of a halftone screen for printing or 'dithered' into a pattern of colours for viewing on low-resolution monitors. Also called 'contone'. → *halftone (1); dithering (1)*

continuous-tone image *(gen)* An image, most usually a photograph, in which there is a smooth progression of tones from black to white.

contone *(pre)* → *continuous tone*

contouring *(pri)* A defect in a printed image, by which varying tones are distinguished by visible steps rather than gradually.

contra italic *(typ)* A style of type that slants backwards, an example being Minion Contra Italic. → *backslanted type; italic*

The Mac OS X
Control Panel

An image at high (top)
and low (bottom)
contrast

contrast *(gen)* The degree of difference between adjacent tones in an image (or computer monitor) from the lightest to the darkest. 'High contrast' describes an image with light highlights and dark shadows, but with few shades in between, whereas a 'low contrast' image is one with even tones and few dark areas or highlights. ➔ *high key; low key*

contrast grade *(pho)* ➔ *grade*

contrast ratio *(pap)* The opacity of paper, 100% being totally opaque.

contre jour *(pho)* A photographic term that describes a picture taken with the camera lens pointing towards the light source.

control character *(com)* A non-printing character generated by the 'control key' (a 'modifier key' – one that is used in conjunction with another), which is used by some applications to perform a particular function. ➔ *modifier key*

Control Panel *(com)* A small application that enables you to configure system software or to customize various aspects of your computer, such as time, date, speaker volume, and so on.

control point *(com)* In 'vector'-based (drawing) applications, a little knob, or point, in a 'path' (line), which enables you to adjust its shape or characteristics by means of Bézier control handles. ➔ *Bézier control handle/point; vector*

controlling dimension *(gen)* One of the dimensions – either height or width – of an image, that is used as the basis for its enlargement or reduction in size.

convection drying *(pri)* After printing, the process of drying the ink by circulating warm air around the paper.

convergence (1) *(com)* In colour monitors, the adjustment of the three RGB beams so that they come together in the right place on the screen. ➔ *monitor; RGB*

convergence (2) *(pho)* The distortion of parallel lines, especially in architecture, caused by the angle of view and the lens.

converter *(pri)* A type of offset litho printing press that can be converted to print either two colours on one side of a sheet or a single colour on both sides in one pass. ➔ *offset litho(graphy)*

converting *(fin)* The final operation, after printing, which completes the print job. This includes finishing processes such as folding, laminating, gluing, box manufacture, and so on.

convex polygon *(com)* A polygon whose shape is convex – for example, a regular hexagon shape.

cookie *(int)* A small piece of information deposited in your web browser (and thus on your hard disk) by a website, storing such things as custom page settings or even personal information. Think of a cookie as a sort of luggage 'claim-check', whereby you drop your bag off and get a ticket. When you return with the ticket, you get your bag back. Cookies store their data on your computer and can only be retrieved by the site that sent them, so their security risk is very low. ➔ *World Wide Web*

cool colours *(gen)* A relative (and subjective) term used to describe colours with a blue or green bias.

coordinates *(com)* Numerical values that define locations in 2D or 3D space.

Coplanar *(com)* When points or polygons lie on the same plane.

copperplate printing *(pri)* An intaglio printing process used in short-run printing, which produces a very sharp, black image. ➔ *intaglio*

coprocessor *(com)* A microprocessor chip that sits alongside your computer's main processing unit (CPU), and which carries out specific specialized functions, such as speeding up graphics display or handling data-intensive tasks such as math calculations. A coprocessor may sometimes be described by its specific function – for example, 'floating point unit' ('FPU') or 'math coprocessor', both of which carry out math calculations. ➔ *central processing unit (CPU)*

copy (1) *(gen)* Any manuscript, typescript, transparency or computer disk that is to be used for reproduction. Also called 'original'.

copy (2) *(com)* The facility in virtually all computer software to copy a selected item, which places it on the 'clipboard' so that it can be 'pasted' elsewhere. As distinct from 'cut', which deletes the item while at the same time copying it. ➔ *clipboard; cut (7); cut and paste; paste*

copyboard *(pre)* ➔ *vacuum frame*

copyboard chart *(pho)* In photography, a colour control strip that is placed beside the subject as an aid to colour fidelity for subsequent processing and reproduction. Copyboard charts are particularly used for ensuring accurate colour reproduction of fine art subjects.

copydot (technique) *(pre)* ➔ *dot-for-dot (2)*

copyfitting (1) *(typ)* Calculating the amount of space typeset copy will occupy when set in a specific font, size and measure. ➔ *cast-off; cast-up*

copyfitting (2) *(typ)* Modifying typeset copy so that it will fit into a given space. This may be done by variously cutting or adding words, increasing or decreasing character or word space, horizontal scaling, etc.

copyholder *(pre)* A person who reads the original copy out loud while another checks and corrects the galley proof. ➔ *galley proof*

copy-protected *(com)* Software that has been produced in such a way as to prevent its unauthorized use. This is normally achieved either by software 'encryption' (embedding it with a unique serial number) or – where very expensive software is concerned – by protecting it with a hardware 'dongle', a device that must be plugged into your computer in order for the application to work. ➔ *dongle; encryption*

copyright *(gen)* The right of a person who creates an original work to protect that work by controlling how and where it may be reproduced. This does not necessarily mean that ownership of the work itself automatically signifies ownership of copyright (or vice versa) – ownership of copyright is transferred only if the creator of the work assigns it in writing. While certain aspects of copyright are broadly controlled by international agreement, as defined by the Universal Copyright Convention (UCC), there are, however, some differences from country to country, particularly when it comes to the period, or 'term', for which a work is protected (in most countries, this is 50 years after its creator's death). In the United States, the Pan American agreement decrees that ownership of an 'intellectual property' (the legal description of copyright ownership) be established by registration, whereas in the United Kingdom it exists automatically by virtue of the creation of the work. There is often confusion between copyright in a work and the 'right' to publish it – ownership of the right to publish a work in one country may not extend to other countries, nor does it necessarily signify ownership of copyright. Equally, the author of a book, for example, may own copyright in the text, whereas copyright on the design of the book may be owned by its designer or publisher. ➔ *copyright notice (line); license*

copyright-free *(gen)* A misnomer used to describe ready-made resources such as clip art. In fact, resources described as such are rarely, if ever, 'copyright-free'. It is generally only the licence to use the material that is granted by purchase. The correct description would normally be 'royalty-free' – that is, material that you can use under licence and which is free from payment of further fees. ➔ *clip art/clip media; copyright; image resource; royalty-free*

copyright notice/line *(gen)* The indication of ownership of copyright in a work ('form of notice'), particularly one that is reproduced, as required by the Universal Copyright Convention. This states that all the first and subsequent editions of a work bear the word 'Copyright' or the symbol '©' (most publishers include both), the year of publication (or first publication if it is a straight reprint) and the name of the owner of the copyright in the work. Thus a notice would appear: 'Copyright © 2005 A.N. Author'. ➔ *copyright*

copywriting *(gen)* The creation of copy specifically for advertising and promotional purposes.

The **corner radius** of a rounded rectangle

corner marks *(pre)* Marks in the corner of an image or page that usually indicate its final size after trimming or cropping, but which can also be used as a guide for positioning or for registration during make-up or printing. Also called 'crop marks', 'trim marks' or 'cut marks'. ➔ *make-up (1); register marks/registration marks*

corner radius *(gen)* In a round-cornered rectangle, the dimension of the radius of the curve.

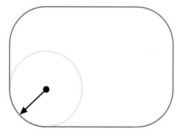

corners (1) *(typ)* The traditional term for the material used for constructing corners in ruled frames or connecting ornamental borders.

corners (2) *(fin)* Triangular pieces of material or leather that cover the corners of half- or three-quarter bound books.

corona wire *(com)* Thin wires through which an electrical charge is passed to fuse toner particles in laser printers and photocopiers. ➔ *laser printer*

corporate identity *(gen)* All aspects of an company's image and identity, generally imposed throughout its communication, promotion and distribution material, both internally as well as externally. Also called 'house style'. ➔ *image (2)*

corrigendum/corrigenda *(gen)* A leaf inserted into a publication after printing to indicate errors that were noticed subsequent to printing. Also called 'erratum/errata'. ➔ *erratum/errata (slip)*

corrugated board *(pap)* A paper board with a fluted surface.

corruption, file *(com)* → *file recovery*

COSM (Composite Object Sound Modelling) *(aud)* Roland Corporation's technology for digitally reproducing the sounds from analog equipment, such as instruments, amplifiers, guitar pickups, effects and even room reverberation.

cosmetics *(gen)* Sometimes used to describe the overall appearance of an image, such as colour, contrast, sharpness, etc.

couch *(pap)* To lift sheets onto board or felt for drying during the papermaking process. The name derives from the board itself, called 'couch'.

counter *(typ)* The enclosed or partially closed area of a type character, such as the centre of an 'O' or the space between the vertical strokes of a 'U'.

counter-etch *(pri)* The application of acid solution to a litho plate so that it becomes receptive to ink. → *lithography*

counter-mark *(pap)* A watermark, often the papermaker's logo or initials, placed in the second half of a sheet of paper, opposite the normal watermark. → *watermark (1)*

cove *(pho)* → *scoop*

cover *(fin)* Paper, board, cloth, leather or other material to which the body of a book is secured by glue, thread or other means. The cover of a machine bound book is called a 'case'. → *body (2); case (1)*

cover board *(pap)* The material resulting from pasting together two or more pieces of cover paper, and used to cover books. → *cover; cover paper*

covering *(fin)* The process by which a cover is fixed to the spine or by which the endpapers of a book are pasted to the cover. → *body (2); casing-in; endpapers*

cover paper *(pap)* Strong, thick paper used to cover booklets and brochures. → *cover*

cover title *(fin)* The title of a book as stamped or printed on its spine. → *spine*

'C' paper sizes *(pap)* → *ISO A-series paper sizes*

cpi *(typ) abb.:* characters per inch. The number of type characters per inch in copyfitting. → *alphabet length; copyfitting (1)*

cpl *(typ) abb.:* characters per line. The number of type characters per line in copyfitting. → *alphabet length; copyfitting (2)*

CP/M *(com) abb.:* Control Program for Micrcomputers. One of the oldest computer operating systems. → *operating system*

c print/c-type *(pho)* Any reflective photographic colour print, originating from the Tripack colour print material developed by Kodak.

cps *(com) abb.:* characters per second. The output speed of a printing machine, such as an inkjet or dot-matrix printer, or the number of characters transmitted by a modem in each second. → *dot-matrix printer; inkjet printer; modem*

CPU *(com) abb.:* central processing unit. → *chip/microchip; coprocessor*

crash (1) *(com)* The colloquial term for an error in system or application software that results in a failure by the computer to respond to input from the mouse or keyboard. Recovery from this state is unlikely – if not impossible – and rebooting, or restarting, the computer is the only course of action, resulting in the loss of unsaved work. A crash may be apparent in a number of ways, such as a 'freeze' in which the pointer does not move; a 'hang', in which the pointer moves but there is no other response to mouse clicks or keyboard commands; or a 'system error' dialog.

A book bound using **crash (3)**

crash (2) *(pri)* To number a multipart set of forms on carbonless paper by printing, with a letterpress machine, the top sheet of each made-up set so that the number appears on the other sheets in the set.

crash (3) *(fin)* A loose-weave cloth, such as muslin, used for binding casebound books, or for strengthening the joints.
→ *casebound; joint*

crash finish *(pap)* A paper with a coarse, linen-like surface.

crawl *(aud)* A titling effect where text moves sideways from one edge of the screen to another (usually right to left).

crawling *(pri)* An imperfection in printing, which occurs when thick ink overprints wet ink.

CRC *(gen) abb.:* camera-ready copy.
→ *camera-ready copy/art (CRC)*

crease *(fin)* → *score (1)*

creasing (1) *(fin)* An indented line impressed into paper or board to make it easier to fold – when making hinges for book covers, for example.

creasing (2) *(pap)* The undesirable effect, seen as deep creases, which results from printing on paper that has been stored incorrectly – for example, at the wrong humidity.

creator code signature *(com)* A four-letter code assigned to identify the application that created documents generated by applications written for use on Macintosh computers, especially those using older versions of Mac OS. Each creator 'signature' is normally registered with Apple Computer so that each is unique – 'QXP3', for example, identifies QuarkXPress 3, while Adobe Photoshop's creator code is '8BIM'.
→ *type (2)*

credit/courtesy line *(gen)* A line of text accompanying an illustration or photograph to identify its creator or owner, and/or the organization that supplied it. → *by-line*

creep *(fin)* The displacement of the leaves in each signature of a book, due to the effect of folding. Creep increases with paper thickness. Also known as 'thrust', 'shingling' and 'pushout'. → *shingle/shingling; wraparound (2)*

crimping *(pap)* → *creasing (1)*

crocking *(pri)* The undesirable effect caused when printed ink smudges, or dry ink rubs off.

Cromacheck *(pri)* A proprietary off-press proofing system from Du Pont that uses plastic laminates.

Cromalin *(pre)* A proprietary dry-proofing system from Du Pont that uses toners on light-sensitive paper. Also known as an 'off-press proof' or 'prepress proof'.
→ *MatchPrint*

Cronak process *(pri)* The chemical treatment of zinc plates to improve tonal reproduction.

crop *(gen)* To trim or mask an image so that it fits a given area, or to discard unwanted portions of an image.

crop marks *(gen)* → *corner marks*

cropped *(fin)* A book with overtrimmed margins.

cropping *(gen)* The process of removing unwanted areas of an image, leaving behind the most significant elements.

cross fade *(aud)* An audio transition where sound from one track fades out while sound or video from another fades in, creating a smooth mix from one to the other.

cross front *(pho)* A camera in which the lens can be moved laterally in relation to the film.

cross-grain *(fin)* → *against the grain*

cross-grained morocco *(fin)* A goatskin binding material embellished with artificially produced diagonal lines. → *morocco*

crosshair/crossbar pointer *(com)* The shape that the pointer or cursor may adopt when you select a tool, to draw a box in a drawing application, for example. → *pointer*

C

cross hatch *(gen)* A line drawing style in which tonal variations are achieved by two or more groups of parallel fine lines, each group being drawn at a different angle to the others.

crosshead *(gen)* → *heading (2)*

cross-head *(gen)* A subsection or paragraph heading, distinguished by font, weight or size, which sits on a line of its own and usually marks a subdivision of a chapter. As distinct from a 'cut-in head', which is set within the text. Also known as a 'centre head'. → *cut-in head; sub-head/ sub-heading*

cross-laminated *(pap)* Paper consisting of several sheets, or coatings applied to substrates, in which each layer is laid or applied at right angles to the previous one.

crossline screen *(pre)* A film screen engraved with two sets of parallel lines that cross each other at right angles, forming transparent squares. Used for making halftones. → *halftone screen*

crossmarks *(pri)* → *register marks/ registration marks*

crossover *(gen)* → *breakacross*

cross-platform *(com)* The term applied to software, multimedia titles, or anything else (such as CDs or DVDs) that will work on more than one computer platform – that is, it will run on different operating systems, such as Mac OS and Microsoft Windows. → *operating system*

cross-rendering *(gen)* To render colours from one colour space to another, usually for proofing or soft-proofing purposes, simulating one device on another.

cross-section *(gen)* An illustration of an object, which shows it as if sliced through with a knife, thus exposing interior detail or workings. → *cut-away*

cross-stemmed w *(typ)* A design of the character 'W' in which the centre strokes cross rather than meet at the top.

crown *(pap)* → *paper sizes*

crowner *(gen)* A store display item used for publicizing a book or product. Crowners are placed on top of, or next to, the product itself. → *streamer*

crown octavo *(pap)* → *paper sizes*

crow quill *(gen)* A very fine ink pen, deriving from the days when scribes used the cut quill of a crow to write with.

CRT *(aud)* abb: cathode ray tube. → *cathode ray tube (CRT)*

crystallization *(pri)* The process of ink drying too quickly and repelling overprinting inks, causing poor trapping. → *trapping*

CSP *(int) abb.:* character shape player. → *character shape player (CSP)*

CSR *(int) abb.:* character shape recorder. → *character shape recorder (CSR)*

CSS *(int) abb.:* cascading style sheet. → *cascading style sheet (CSS)*

CSS2 *(int)* The second CSS specification, most notable for its introduction of absolute positioning and media types. → *cascading style sheet (CSS); CSS3*

CSS3 *(int)* The third specification for CSS, which breaks the markup language into more manageable modules. → *cascading style sheet (CSS); CSS2*

CSU/DSU *(int) abb.:* channel service unit/data service unit. A hardware device that translates data between a network and a telephone line. → *network*

ct (1) *(pre) abb.:* continuous tone. → *continuous tone (ct)*

ct (2) *(pre)* A file format used by Scitex prepress systems for storing continuous tone scanned images. → *continuous tone (ct); prepress*

c/t *(pho) abb.:* colour transparency. → *colour transparency (film)*

CTP *(pri) abb.:* computer-to-plate → *ablation plate; computer-to-plate (CTP)*

An example of a **cross hatch** line drawing

A **cross-section** illustration

cubic mapping *(com)* In 3D applications, the technique of applying one copy of a texture map (or image) to each of the six sides of a cube. → *cylindrical mapping; texture mapping/surface mapping*

culture *(gen)* → *corporate identity*

cup *(typ)* → *bowl (1)*

cure (1) *(pap)* To condition paper to the correct temperature and humidity in preparation for printing.

cure (2) *(pri)* The process of drying ink sufficiently to prevent 'set-off' (undesirable transfer of ink from the front of one sheet to the back of the next). → *set-off*

curl *(pap)* The measurement of the degree to which the edges of a sheet of paper will curl, particularly those used in wet or damp processes.

curly quotes *(typ)* → *smart quotes*

currency symbol *(typ)* → *monetary symbol/ currency symbol*

cursive *(typ)* A 'running script', or lettering that is formed without raising pen from paper. This style of writing developed into a script that was used, up until the early 16th century, for diplomatic and administrative documents and which, in turn, inspired the first italic typefaces. → *italic*

cursor *(com)* The name for the blinking marker that indicates the current working position in a document. This is usually the point in a line of text at which the next character will appear when you strike a key on the keyboard. The cursor may be represented by a small vertical line or block and is not to be confused with the 'pointer' – the marker indicating the current position of the mouse. → *pointer*

curtain coater *(pri)* A machine used for coating flat sheets of paperboard with an even coating of solution such as adhesive.

curved plate *(pri)* A plate used on a rotary press that curves around the plate cylinder. → *plate (1); rotary press*

curved screen *(pri)* In screen printing, a mesh screen used for printing onto objects with a curved surface. → *cylindrical printer; screen printing*

curve point *(com)* → *symmetrical point*

curves *(com)* A tool for precise control of tonal relationships in image-editing applications, such as Photoshop. The curve graphically represents the relationship between input and output tonal levels in the image as a whole or in an individual channel.

cushion *(pap)* The compressible property of paper. A paper will lack cushion if its fibres are 'dead'. → *dead*

cut (1) *(pri)* A contraction of 'woodcut', nowadays used to describe any print made from a relief block, etching or engraving.

cut (2) *(pri)* A metal relief plate from which an image is printed.

cut (3) *(gen)* An instruction to editors to delete copy.

cut (4) *(pri)* To dilute ink, lacquer or varnish with solvents.

cut (5) *(pre)* To reduce ('etch') the dot size in halftone film. → *halftone screen*

cut (6) *(fin)* To trim the edges of a book. → *cut edges*

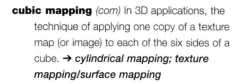

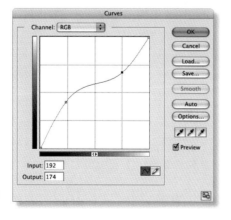

A one dollar image with **cubic mapping** applied

The Photoshop **Curves** dialog box

cut (7) *(com)* In virtually all applications, a feature that allows you to remove an item from a location in a document, at the same time copying it to the 'clipboard' so that it can be 'pasted' elsewhere. As distinct from 'copy', which places the item on the clipboard while leaving the original where it is. → *clipboard; copy (2); cut and paste;*

cut ahead *(pap)* Paper that has been cut so that the watermarks do not fall in the same position on each sheet. As distinct from 'cut to register', in which they do. → *cut to register; watermark (1)*

cut and paste *(com)* The process of removing an item from a document ('cutting' the item, which places it on the 'clipboard') and then placing it elsewhere ('pasting' it), either in the same document or another.
→ *clipboard; copy (2); cut (7)*

cut-away *(gen)* An illustration of an object, in which part of its outer 'shell' has been removed to show the inner workings or detail. → *cross-section*

cut back binding *(fin)* An alternative name for adhesive or unsewn binding, so-called because the folded and gathered sheets are trimmed at the back. → *adhesive binding*

cut dummy *(pre)* Cut proofs of illustrations or pages, assembled in sequence to act as a guide for the make-up of pages.

cut edges *(fin)* All three edges of a book that have been cut so that they are all flush.
→ *cut (6)*

cut flush *(fin)* A book with its cover trimmed to the same size as the pages. Also known as 'flush boards' or 'trimmed flush', or, if stiffened, 'stiffened and cut flush'.

cut-in head *(gen)* A paragraph or section heading, distinguished by font, weight or size, which is set within the text. As distinct from a 'cross-head', which sits on a line of its own. → *cross-head; sub-head/sub-heading*

cut-in side notes *(gen)* Notes to a text that are indented into the main body of the text.
→ *marginal notes*

cutmarks *(pri)* → *corner marks*

cutout (1) *(gen)* A halftone image in which the background has been removed to provide a freeform image. Also known as an 'outline halftone' or 'silhouette halftone'. → *halftone*

cutout (2) *(fin)* A display card or book cover into which a pattern or hole has been cut.

cut score *(fin)* Partial slitting of paper that acts as an aid in creasing.

cut sheets *(pap)* Paper that has been trimmed into sheets.

cut-size paper *(pap)* A general term for paper that has been trimmed into sheets of small sizes, usually 8½in x 11in, and used for printing and photocopying.

cutline *(gen)* → *caption*

cut-marks *(gen)* → *corner marks*

cutter *(fin)* → *guillotine*

cutting and creasing *(fin)* The process – usually carried out on a cylinder press – of cutting special shapes into or out of board, such as in packaging and book covers, and then creasing it in preparation for folding.
→ *cylinder press; diecutting*

cutting cylinder *(fin)* A cylinder on a rotary press bearing a knife to cut the paper web into sheets.

cutting edge *(gen)* At the forefront; pioneering; innovative. Also referred to as 'state of the art'.

cut to register *(pap)* Paper that has been cut so that the watermarks fall in the same position on each sheet. As distinct from 'cut ahead' in which they do not. → *cut ahead; watermark*

CV (Control Voltage) *(aud)* MIDI's analog predecessor, which was used to control or direct communications between analog synthesizer modules using small bursts of voltage.

A **cut-away** illustration created in a 3D tool

A **cutout** photograph showing a white background

cwt *(pap) abb.:* hundredweight. In the US, this is a measure of weight of 100lb/45.4kg (technically called a 'short' hundredweight), and is sometimes used when specifying the cost of paper; in the UK, it is 112lb/50.8kg (a 'long' hundredweight). A 'metric' hundred weight is 50kg.

cyan (c) *(gen)* With magenta and yellow, one of the three subtractive primaries, and one of the three process colours used in four-colour printing. Sometimes referred to as 'process blue'. → *magenta (m); yellow (y)*

cyan printer *(pre)* The plate or film used to print cyan ink in four-colour process printing.

cyberspace *(int)* The virtual environment in which communication takes place, particularly on the Internet, but also general telecommunication links and computer networks. → *virtual reality*

cylinder *(pri)* Any roller or drum used on a papermaking machine or rotary printing press. → *rotary press*

cylinder machine *(pap)* A papermaking machine, mostly used for making boards, in which pulp is deposited on the surface of a gauze-covered cylinder. Also known as a 'vat' machine. → *fourdrinier*

cylinder press *(pri)* A rotary press in which the sheet to be printed is wrapped around a cylinder and brought into contact with the printing surface, which is laid flat. Cylinder presses are mainly used for specialized work, such as diecutting. → *diecutting*

cylindrical (map) projection *(gen)* A map projection in which all lines of longitude ('meridians') run parallel with each other and at right angles to the lines of latitude ('parallels'). Cylindrical projections are highly distorted at the Polar extremities but, when wrapped around a sphere, appear normal and are thus ideal for use with 3D applications. Cylindrical projections are widely used for navigation purposes and thus for navigational graphics. 'Gall' and 'Mercator' are typical cylindrical projections, named after the men who devised them.

cylindrical mapping *(com)* In 3D applications, the technique of applying a texture map (image) to a cylindrical 3D object, such as applying the label on to a bottle. → *cubic mapping; texture mapping/surface mapping*

cylindrical printer *(pri)* A screen printing device for printing onto cylindrical objects, such as bottles. → *curved screen; screen printing*

Cyrillic alphabet *(typ)* The characters used for writing and printing the Russian and Bulgarian languages. → *Latin (1)*

An image subject to **cylindrical mapping**

Dd

DAC *(aud) abb.:* digital-to-analog convertor. The component in any digital audio device, such as a CD player or your PC, which converts the digital stream of bits into analog (changes in voltage that your speakers turn back into soundwaves). In cheap soundcards, the DAC can be noisy or hissy. As a result, it is better to have a sophisticated 16-bit card than a cheap 24-bit one. An A/D convertor turns analog data into a stream of bits. Home studio, USB-based A/D convertors are cheap and commonplace, operating at up to 96 kHz and 24-bits.

Daemon *(int)* Special networking software, used mostly on computers running the UNIX operating system, which handles requests from users, such as e-mail, the World Wide Web and other Internet services. **→ e-mail; Internet; operating system; UNIX; World Wide Web**

dagger *(typ)* A 'reference mark' (†) used in text to refer the reader to a footnote. A dagger is also sometimes used next to a name to signify that the person is deceased. Also known as an 'obelisk' or 'obelus'. **→ double dagger; reference mark**

daguerrotype *(pho)* The first practical method of creating and fixing a photographic image. Invented by Louis J.M. Daguerre in 1833, the process involved exposing a silvered copper plate to iodine or bromine vapour, which made it light-sensitive.

Dahlgren *(pri)* A proprietary dampening system used in litho printing to reduce levels of moisture. **→ lithography**

daisy-chain *(com)* The linking together, in a line, of computer hardware devices. Typically, USB-connected devices such as desktop printers and scanners are daisy-chained to the computer. **→ network**

daisy wheel *(typ)* The printing head on some impact printing devices, such as typewriters, on which each character sits on individual 'petals' arranged around the wheel. **→ cold composition**

dampening *(pri)* In litho printing, the necessary process of moistening the non-image areas of a printing plate to repel ink. **→ lithography**

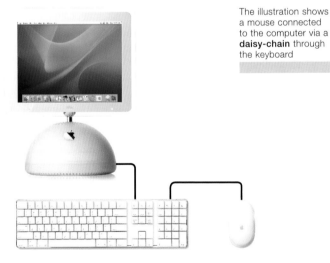

The illustration shows a mouse connected to the computer via a **daisy-chain** through the keyboard

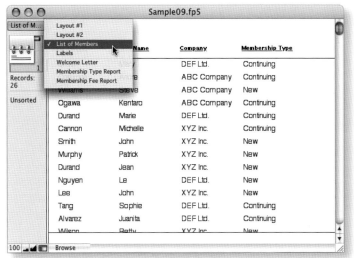

FileMaker Pro is a popular **database**

Darkfield lighting was used in this image

dampening fountain *(pri)* A tray on a litho press that holds water for moistening the plate. Also known as a 'water pan'. → *dampening; lithography*

dandy roll *(pap)* A wire cylinder on a papermaking machine that impresses a watermark and laid lines into the paper while it is still wet. → *chain lines/marks; fourdrinier; laid paper*

dark field illumination *(pre)* A method of checking the quality of halftone dots on a piece of film by holding the film at an angle against a dark background.

darkfield lighting *(pho)* A lighting technique used in photomicrography in which the subject is lit by a cone of light from below, with the background appearing black. → *photomicrography*

dark reaction *(pre)* A slow chemical change that occurs in photo-sensitized materials when stored in a dark place over time.

darkslide *(pho)* A sheet of lightproof material used in film holders to protect the film from exposure until it is mounted on the camera.

dash *(typ)* Strictly speaking, a dash can be any short rule, plain or decorative, but is usually used to describe an em dash (—) or en dash (–), as distinct from a hyphen (-). → *em dash/rule; en dash/rule; hyphen*

DAT *(com) abb.:* digital audio tape. → *back up/ backing up (1); digital audio tape (DAT); random access*

data *(com)* Although strictly speaking the plural of 'datum', meaning a piece of information, 'data' is nowadays used as a singular noun to describe – particularly in the context of computers – more or less anything that can be stored or processed, whether it be a single bit, a chunk of text, an image or audio.

data bank *(com)* Any place or hardware device where large amounts of data are stored for ready access.

database *(com)* Information stored on a computer in a systematic fashion and thus retrievable. This generally means files in which you can store any amount of data in separate but consistent categories (called 'fields') for each type of information, such as names, addresses and telephone numbers. The electronic version of a card index system (each card is called a 'record'), databases are constructed with applications called 'database managers', which allow you to organize information any way you like. → *database manager; field; record*

database engine *(com)* → *database manager*

database management system (DBMS) *(com)* → *database manager*

database manager *(com)* An application for constructing databases, allowing you to define, enter, search, sort and output information. Database managers can be 'flat-file', in which information can be created and accessed only in a single, self-contained database, or 'relational', in which information can be shared and exchanged across two or more separate databases. Other database managers are those in which the fields are predefined (but unmodifiable) for a specific purpose, such as 'contact managers' (electronic address books). Database managers are also known

as 'database engines', 'database management systems' (DBMS) or even just 'database'. → *database; flat-file database; relational database*

data bits *(com)* An expression used in data transmission to distinguish bits containing the data being transmitted from bits giving instructions on how the data is to be transmitted. → *bit; Transmission Control Protocol (TCP)*

data blocks *(com)* → *block (3)*

data bus *(com)* The path, or circuitry, along which data is transmitted by a processor, as distinct from the circuitry used by the processor to handle memory. → *bus (1); memory*

data compression *(com)* → *compression (1)*

data encryption *(com)* → *encryption*

data file *(com)* → *document (1)*

data fork *(com)* The part of a document file on computers running Mac OS (especially pre OS X), which contains user-created data, such as text or graphics, as distinct from the 'resource fork', which contains resources like icons and sounds. A document file may consist only of a data fork or it may contain a resource fork as well, whereas an application always has a resource fork and may have a data fork. → *resource fork*

Data Interchange Format (DIF) *(com)* A file format used by database and spreadsheet applications for exporting records. DIF files preserve field names and content but not formatting. → *database; field; file format; formatting; spreadsheet*

data processing *(com)* The systematic processing of information, whether it be sorting text or batch processing images.

data transfer rate *(com)* Strictly speaking, the speed at which data is transferred from one device to another, but generally referring to the transfer from a disk drive into computer memory and usually measured in megabytes per second. → *interleave ratio; megabyte (Mb/Mbyte/meg); memory*

dateline *(gen)* In newspapers and periodicals, a line of type that is placed above an item, giving the date and place of its creation and the assumed date when writing copy – i.e. 'today'.

datum *(com)* A piece of information. Its plural, 'data', is nowadays commonly used as a singular noun in place of 'datum'. → *data*

daughterboard *(com)* A circuit board that plugs into another board, such as the 'motherboard' (the board containing the main circuitry and processors of a computer). → *circuit board; motherboard*

DAW (digital audio workstation) *(aud)* This refers to a digital recording device that can be used alone to record, mix and master tracks of audio, often offering various built-in effects.

daylight film *(pho)* Colour photographic film balanced for use in daylight or in conditions where the light source provides a colour temperature of 5400K, such as electronic flash.

dazzle *(typ)* A colloquial term describing the visual effect caused by exaggerated differences between widths of strokes in a letterform.

DBMS *(com) abb.:* database management system. → *database manager*

DCA *(com) abb.:* document content architecture → *document content architecture (DCA); file format*

DCS *(com) abb.:* Desktop Color Separation. → *composite colour file; Desktop Color Separation (DCS); EPS; OPI*

DATA BITS

The separate files that make up a **DCS**

DDCP *(pre)* abb.: direct digital colour proof → *direct digital colour proof (DDCP); inkjet printer*

DDES *(int)* abb.: Digital Data Exchange Standard. → *ANSI; Digital Data Exchange Standard; interface; ISO (1)*

dead *(pap)* The description of paper fibres that have lost their resilience and strength during the papermaking process, probably due to excessive beating. → *cushion*

deadline *(gen)* The final date by which a job or process must be completed.

dead matter *(pre)* Nowadays, any matter that is left over or not used during the entire printing process, but originally referring specifically to typeset matter.

debug(ging) *(com)* To hunt out and correct programming errors in computer software. → *bug*

decal *(pri)* A design, printed on special paper, which can be transferred onto another surface by applying pressure ('duplex decal'; 'adhesive decal'), or heat and pressure ('heat-release decal'), or by soaking it in water so that it slides off the paper ('simplex decal'). → *dry transfer lettering; duplex board/paper*

decibel (dB) *(aud)* A measurement used to describe the sound pressure level or intensity of sound. One decibel is the smallest change in sound level that the human ear can detect. It is based on a logarithmic scale – a 10dB increase at any point indicates a doubling in sound pressure level.

decimal point *(typ)* A full point, or period, placed after a whole number and before the numerator in decimal fractions. This is commonly shown as, for example, '2.1', but may also be shown as '2·1' (UK) or '2,1' (Europe). → *numerator*

decimal tab *(typ)* A tab alignment option in some word processing and page-layout applications, which allows you to align numeric values by their decimal points, one above the other. → *decimal point*

deckle (1)/deckle strap *(pap)* The edging frame or strap on a papermaking mould or machine, which confines or controls the pulp. → *deckle (2); deckle edge*

deckle (2) *(pap)* A term sometimes used to describe the width of a web of paper on a papermaking machine. → *deckle (1)/deckle strap*

deckle edge *(pap)* The rough, uneven edge of untrimmed handmade paper. Deckle edge effects are also applied mechanically to machine-made paper. → *deckle (1)/deckle strap*

decompressor *(com)* → *codec (1)*

decryption *(com)* The process of removing the protection given to data or a document by encryption. Usually, the same software used to encrypt data must be used to decrypt it. → *encryption*

dedicated *(gen)* Any system, software or piece of equipment designed to execute a specific task and not otherwise adaptable. Also known as a 'proprietary system'.

dedicated flash *(pho)* A flash unit that is integrated with a camera's built-in automatic light metering system.

deep-etched plate *(pri)* → *deep-etch(ing)*

deep-etch(ing) *(pri)* A process in lithographic printing that involves etching away the printing areas of the plate so that they are slightly recessed below the surface. This technique prolongs the life of the plate and is thus used for printing long runs. Also known as 'positive reversal process'. → *deep-etch halftone*

deep-etch halftone *(pre)* A halftone image from which the highlight dots have been removed so that clean areas of plain paper are visible. Traditionally, this was done either on the printing plate or on the film, but it is now more common to control halftone dot coverage digitally on computer. Also known as 'drop-out halftone', it should not be confused with 'deeply-etched halftone'.
→ *deeply-etched halftone; drop-out/ dropped out halftone; halftone (1)*

deep gold *(fin)* Top-quality gold leaf, used for 'tooling' on handbound books, unlike the cheaper 'pale-gold' leaf used for gilding the edges of books. → *tooling*

deep line cut *(pri)* A method of improving trapping in screen printing. → *trapping*

deeply-etched halftone *(pri)* In lithographic printing, the technique of etching a halftone image to extra depth on the plate, but without removing the highlights. This technique is used for holding detail when printing on coarse paper. Not to be confused with 'deep-etch halftone'.
→ *deep-etch halftone*

deerskin *(fin)* A bookbinding leather originally used to cover wooden book boards.

default *(com)* The settings of a hardware device or software program determined at the time of manufacture or release. These settings remain in effect until you change them, and your changes are stored – when applied to software – in a 'preferences' file. Also known as 'presets' and 'factory settings'.

definition *(gen)* The overall quality or clarity of an image, determined by the combined subjective effect of graininess (or resolution in a digital image) and sharpness.
→ *resolution (1)*

deflection *(pri)* A condition in flexographic printing by which the 'fountain' and 'anilox' rolls bow slightly. Although this is normal, excessive bending may result in uneven printing. → *anilox system*

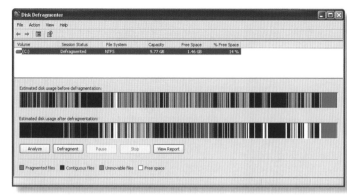

defragment(ing) *(com)* The technique of joining together pieces of 'fragmented' files – those which, due to a shortage of contiguous storage space on the disk, have been split into smaller pieces – so that they are easier for the drive heads to access, thus speeding up disk operations. The process is also known as 'optimizing'.
→ *contiguous; optimize/optimizing*

degauss(ing) *(com)* The technique of removing, or neutralizing, any magnetic field that may have built up over time in a colour monitor. Magnetism can distort the fidelity of colour display. Since most modern monitors perform a degauss automatically, this process is usually only necessary on older monitors.

degradability *(int)* The term applied to Web browsers that support new advances in HTML technologies while at the same time serving browsers based on previous versions of the technologies. → *HTML*

degradation *(aud)* Loss in quality due to repeated use. This occurs mostly in analog recording, where some detail and quality is lost with each step of the recording process; in other words, every modification of the audio piece requires a new generation of tape, each of which introduces distortion and other noise.

degradé/degradee *(gen)* A graded halftone tint which, by varying the dot size, gradually changes from one edge to the other.
→ *halftone (1); vignette*

The Windows XP **Defragment** tool

A close-up of a halftone, or **degradé**

deinking *(pap)* The technique of removing ink and other additives from used paper so that it can be recycled.

de-interlace *(aud)* Each 'frame' in a video clip actually contains two 'fields' of alternating vertical lines, which are combined together (or interlaced) to create the frame. In motion this isn't highly noticeable, but if a still image is taken from the video clip, the lines or a slight blur will often become visible. De-interlacing is the process of combining the two fields into a single frame without these effects.

delamination *(pri)* The separation of the layers in multi-ply (layer) papers and boards. This is sometimes caused during printing by incorrect ink 'tack' (stickiness). ➔ *tack*

delay *(aud)* An audio effect that gives the illusion of one or multiple distinct echoes, and which can be adjusted to achieve a variety of effects. It also refers to the amount of delay carefully applied to sound emerging from the rear speaker in surround-sound systems, which gives it a slight separation from a corresponding front-end sound, creating the illusion of space.

dele *(gen)* The name used to describe the symbol ('ᐟ'), representing the letter 'd' for the Latin 'deleatur') indicating matter that is to be deleted.

delete *(gen)* ➔ *dele*

delimit *(com)* To separate items of information, such as words, lines of text, or – in databases, for example – fields and records. This is done by placing a character ('delimiter') at the end ('limit') of each item. Commonly used characters are generated by the 'tab' and 'comma' keys (to separate fields) and the 'return' key (to separate records). Files formatted thus are described as 'delimited'. ➔ *database; field; record*

delimited *(com)* ➔ *delimit*

delimiter *(com)* ➔ *delimit*

Delineated lines used to highlight elements in line artwork

delineate *(gen)* To emphasize certain outlines in line drawings or artwork by making them heavier.

delivery *(gen)* The process of handing over any part of a process or job to another, or to the method of final output.

DEM *(com) abb.:* digital elevation model.
➔ *digital elevation model; mapping resource; relief map*

demand printing *(pri)* A method of printing in which the copies are produced as and when they are needed. The document is generally stored electronically and produced on some kind of electronic device, such as a laser or inkjet printer. Demand printing allows frequent modification or updating of documents and eliminates the need for storing bulky quantities of inventory. Also known as 'on-demand printing'. ➔ *inkjet printer; laser printer*

demographic edition *(gen)* An edition of a journal, such as a newspaper or magazine, which has its content – both editorial and advertising – modified to suit a specific geographic area or consumer group.

dendritic growths *(pap)* Small, treelike growths in paper, caused by oxidization of minute particles of metal that were not removed during making.

denominator *(typ)* The number below the line ('separator') in a fraction. ➔ *fraction; numerator; separator*

dense *(gen)* An image that is too dark.

densitometer *(pre)* A precision instrument used to measure the optical density and other properties of colour and light in positive or negative transparencies, printing film, reflection copy or computer monitors. Also called a 'colour coder'. ➔ *calibrate/ calibration*

density (1) *(typ)* The general amount and compactness of text set within a given are

This image has a high **density**

density (2) *(gen)* The darkness of tone or colour in any image. In a transparency, this refers to the amount of light that can pass through it, thus determining the darkness of shadows and the saturation of colour. A printed highlight cannot be any lighter in colour than the colour of the paper it is printed on, while the shadows cannot be any darker than the quality and volume of ink that the printing process will allow.

density (3) *(pap)* The weight to volume ratio of paper.

density range *(gen)* The maximum range of tones in an image, measured as the difference between the maximum and minimum densities (the darkest and lightest tones). → *density (2)*

deprecated *(int)* The term applied to versions of code technology that are gradually being replaced or eradicated. → *hypertext markup language (HTML)*

depth *(pri)* The difference in height between the printing and non-printing surfaces of printing plates.

depth of field *(pho)* The subjective range – in front of or behind the point of focus – in a photograph in which the subject remains acceptably sharp or focused. Depth of field

is controlled by the lens aperture; the smaller the aperture, the greater the depth of field or sharpness. → *aperture; focal length; focus*

depth of focus *(pho)* The distance through which the film plane can be moved from the point of focus and still record an acceptably sharp image. → *depth of field; focal length; focus*

depth of strike *(typ)* The depth from the face of a piece of metal type to the base of the counter.

desaturate *(gen)* To reduce the strength or purity of colour in an image, thus making it greyer. → *saturation*

desaturated colour *(gen)* Colour that contains a greater amount of grey in proportion to the hue. → *desaturate; saturation*

descender *(typ)* The part of a lower case character that extends below the baseline of the x-height, as in the letters p, q, j, g, y. → *ascender*

descreen(ing) *(com)* The technique of removing a halftone dot pattern from an image to avoid an undesirable 'moiré' pattern, which may occur when a new halftone screen is applied. This can be achieved in image-editing applications using

The top image has a longer **depth of field** than the lower one

The **descender** of a lowercase 'p'

An image before (left) and after (right) it has been **desaturated**

DENSITY

built-in 'filters' (effects) to blur the image slightly and then sharpen it. However, you can achieve better results with dedicated image-enhancement applications, which do this automatically using sophisticated 'interpolation' methods. → *halftone (1); interpolate/interpolation; moiré*

deselect *(com)* To deactivate an active item, such as a picture box or highlighted text, usually by clicking outside or away from the item.

desensitize *(pri)* Chemical treatment of a lithographic plate to make the non-image areas water-receptive so that they repel ink. The chemical solution used is called an 'etch'. → *etch*

designation marks *(pri)* Initial letters (usually corresponding to a book title) that were traditionally printed near the 'signature' letter of each section, for identification prior to binding. → *section (2); signature (1)*

design motif *(gen)* → *motif*

desk copy *(gen)* A copy of a book that is given to teachers and lecturers so that it may become required reading for students, thus increasing sales. Also known as 'inspection copies'.

desktop *(com)* The general environment of a 'graphical user interface' (GUI), imitating, as far as is practical, a real desk, with folders, files and even a wastebasket for throwing things away. → *graphical user interface (GUI)*

Desktop Color Separation (DCS) *(com)* A file format used for outputting image files to colour separation. DCS files combine a low-resolution image for displaying on screen with high-resolution EPS format data for colour separations. There are two versions of DCS format files: DCS 1.0 and DCS 2.0. DCS 1.0 files comprise five files: a single low-resolution composite file for placing in a layout, plus four high-resolution separation files, one each for cyan, magenta, yellow and black. The DCS 2.0 format allows you to save spot colours with the image, which you can choose to save as a single file (which saves space) or as multiple files as in DCS 1.0. Clipping paths can also be saved with both DCS 1.0 and DCS 2.0.

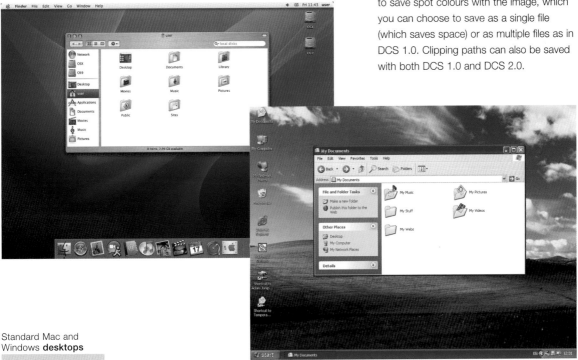

Standard Mac and Windows **desktops**

D

desktop colour *(com)* Colour images prepared or generated using a desktop system, where an original is scanned by a desktop scanner, adjusted on a desktop computer, and positioned and output using a page-layout application. The term is often used – not necessarily derogatorily – to indicate colour reproduction of an inferior quality to that produced on a high-end CEPS system. → *CEPS; desktop scanner; desktop (publishing) system*

desktop computer *(com)* Those personal computers that not only perform all the necessary functions of desktop publishing, but will also fit on a real desktop. As opposed to a portable, tower or rack system. → *desktop publishing (DTP)*

desktop publishing (DTP) *(gen)* The entire computer-based process of generating text, laying it out on a page with images, and then printing the result – in other words, publishing it. The term was originally coined when the first personal 'desktop' computers to use GUIs (the Apple Lisa and Macintosh) were introduced. It gained credence with the arrival of the laser printer, PostScript and the first release of Adobe PageMaker. Early on the potential of desktop computers in the professional design and graphic arts industries was viewed with scepticism by professional designers, feeling it indicated amateurism. → *desktop computer; graphic design; Macintosh*

desktop (publishing) system *(com)* A collection of standard desktop hardware devices and off-the-shelf software applications capable of handling the entire desktop publishing process. As distinct from specialist equipment, such as drum scanners, used in high-end prepress systems. → *desktop computer; desktop publishing (DTP)*

desktop scanner *(com)* A small device for scanning images and text, which forms part of a desktop system. Although such scanners are becoming increasingly more sophisticated and capable, the quality of image generated by them cannot yet match that produced by a high-end 'drum' scanner. → *drum scanner; scanner*

destructive editing *(aud)* This refers to editing (effects or other processing) that is applied directly to the data of an original digital audio file, the result of which may then be saved, overwriting the original file. Non-destructive editing takes place when effects are applied to one or more audio files within a software program (such as a virtual mixer), the result of which may be rendered to a new file while keeping the original files unchanged.

detail *(gen)* The degree to which individual features of an image are defined.

detail/layout paper *(pap)* Thin, translucent paper with a hard surface used for layouts and 'comps' (rough drawings). → *comprehensive*

Deutsche Industrie-Norm (DIN) *(gen)* A code of standards established in Germany and used widely throughout the world to standardize such things as size, weight and other properties of particular materials and manufactured items – for example, computer connectors and photographic film speed – so that they are universally compatible.

develop *(pho)* To make visible a latent image on exposed photographic film or paper. → *developer*

developer *(pho)* A solution containing a chemical ('developing agent') that reveals an image on exposed photographic film or paper.

developing agent *(pho)* → *developer*

developing ink *(pre)* A greasy liquid applied to lithographic plates to protect the ink-receptive image areas while the plate is etched and gummed.

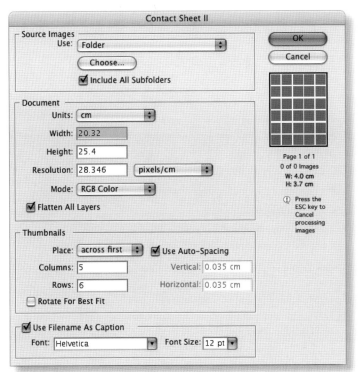

A **dialog box** in
Adobe Photoshop

developing tank *(pho)* A light-fast container used for developing photographic film or paper. → *developer*

development *(pri)* Removing the unhardened coating from the surface of an exposed lithographic plate.

device (1) *(com)* An alternative term for any piece of hardware, but usually used to describe a piece of equipment that is peripheral to the computer itself (a 'peripheral device'). → *external device*

device (2) *(gen)* A trademark or design printed in a book, identifying the printer or publisher. Also called a 'printer's mark'.

device independent *(com)* Any software that controls the preparation or output of pages or images regardless of the hardware device on which they are prepared or output. PostScript, for example, is a device-independent 'page description language' (software that describes to a printer how the content of a page is to be arranged when it is output).

DHTML *(int)* → *Dynamic HTML*

diacritical mark *(typ)* A sign denoting the particular value or pronunciation of a character. → *accent*

diaeresis/dieresis *(typ)* A pair of dots placed over the second of two vowels to indicate that it must be pronounced as a separate syllable, as in 'naïve'. → *umlaut*

dialog/dialog box *(com)* A window that appears onscreen, requesting information or a decision before you can proceed further. → *alert box*

dial-up *(int)* A connection to the Internet or to a network made by dialling a telephone number for access.

diamond *(typ)* A former size of type, measuring about 4.5 points.

diaphragm *(pho)* An adjustable opening, or 'aperture', behind a camera lens, which controls the amount of light that reaches the film. The aperture opening is calibrated on the camera lens by 'f-stop' numbers. Also called an 'iris diaphragm'. → *f-stop*

diapositive *(pho)* A photographic transparency in which the image is positive.

diarylide yellow *(pri)* A pigment used in yellow process inks.

diazo(type)/diazo process *(pre)* abb.: diazonium. A method of photographic printing from a transparent or translucent original, in which a light-sensitive coating is applied to a paper, cloth, plastic or metal surface. This is then exposed to blue or ultraviolet light and the image developed by ammonia vapour. The resulting print may be blue (referred to as 'blues', 'bluelines' or 'blueprints'), brown ('browns', 'brownlines' or 'Vandykes') or black. Also known variously as 'ozalids', 'dyelines', 'diazoprints', 'direct-positives' and 'whiteprints', diazos are widely used in prepress stages for checking imposed film ('flats') as well as by architectural and engineering draughtsmen. The process is also used for preparing presensitized litho plates. → *blueline (1); Ozalid*

DIC Color Guide *(pri)* A proprietary colour system of Dainippon Ink and Chemicals used primarily for printing projects in Japan.

dichroic filter *(pho)* A filter that permits certain wavelengths of light to pass through while preventing others.

dichroic fog *(pho)* An aberration in processed film, appearing as a red or green cloud and caused by an imbalance of chemicals in the developer.

dictionary *(com)* A file found in some applications, which provides the facility for checking words and documents for correct spelling. → *auxiliary dictionary; exception dictionary*

Didot point *(typ)* The unit of type measurement used in Continental Europe, devised by François Didot in 1775. A Didot point measures 0.343mm (0.0148in), compared to the Anglo-American point of 0.35mm (0.013837in). Twelve Didot points are referred to as a 'cicero' or 'Didot pica'. → *cicero; pica; point (1)*

die (1) *(pri)* An engraved stamp used for impressing an embossed design onto paper. → *emboss(ing)*

die (2) *(fin)* A pattern or design of sharp blades, which, when mounted on a press, are used to cut shapes out of paper or board. → *diecutting*

diecutting *(fin)* A process in which paper or board is cut to a particular shape or design using a 'die' on a 'die press'. → *cutting and creasing; die (2); die press*

dielectric printing *(pri)* A non-impact printing method in which toner is applied to electrically charged paper. Also known as 'electrographic printing'. → *electrostatic printing*

die press *(pri)* A machine that uses a 'die' to cut or emboss a shape into paper or board. → *die (1); die (2)*

diesis *(typ)* → *double dagger*

die stamping *(pri)* A printing technique that uses a 'die' to emboss a relief image onto a surface. Ink or metallic foil is generally used to add colour, but if not the surface is said to be 'blind-stamped'. Also known as 'relief stamping'. → *die (1)*

DIF *(com) abb.:* Data Interchange Format.

differential letterspacing *(typ)* The spacing of each letter according to its individual width. → *letterspacing/letterfit*

diffraction *(pho)* The scattering of lightwaves as they strike the edge of an opaque surface. In the conventional preparation of halftones, this can affect dot formations. → *halftone (1)*

diffuse *(pho)* A softened effect in a photograph, created by scattered light and giving an object the appearance of, for example, being viewed through translucent glass.

A **diffuse** photographic effect

diffuse highlight *(pre)* An area of highlight on a halftone image that bears the smallest printable dot. → *halftone (1)*

diffuser *(pho)* Any material that scatters transmitted light, thus increasing the area of the light source. → *diffuse*

diffusion *(gen)* The scattering of light resulting in a softening of the light and of any shadows cast. Diffusion occurs in nature through mist and cloud-cover, and can also be simulated using diffusion sheets and soft-boxes.

diffusion transfer *(pre)* → *photomechanical transfer (PMT)*

digit (1) *(typ)* Any numeral from 0 to 9. → *bit*

digit (2) *(typ)* A printer's symbol ('ornament') depicting a hand with a pointing finger. Also known as a 'hand', 'fist' or 'index'. → *ornament*

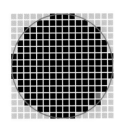

A matrix of **digital dots** in a halftone

digital *(com)* Anything operated by or created from information or signals represented by binary digits, such as a digital recording. As distinct from analog, in which information is represented by a physical variable (in a recording, this may be via the grooves in a vinyl platter). → *bit*

digital audio tape (DAT) *(com)* A magnetic medium used to store large amounts of data. Used for either backing up or archiving data, DAT tapes are 'linear' – that is, they run from beginning to end – and thus cannot be used for 'primary' storage like a hard disk, because the data cannot be accessed at random.

digital camera *(pho)* A photographic device that captures and records images in binary form on a small light-sensitive sensor rather than on film. Digital cameras are available for all types of photography, from point-and-shoot to professional studio and outdoor work, and now outsell conventional cameras. → *CCD; CMOS (Complementary Metal Oxide Semiconductor)*

digital data *(com)* Information stored or transmitted as a series of 1s and 0s ('bits'). Since values are fixed (so-called 'discrete values'), digital data is more reliable than analog, because the latter is susceptible to sometimes uncontrollable physical variations. → *bit, discrete value*

Digital Data Exchange Standard *(com)* An ANSI/ISO approved standard that allows equipment produced by different manufacturers to communicate ('interface') with each other.

digital device *(com)* Any piece of equipment that operates by means of instructions or signals represented by binary digits, such as a computer. → *bit; digital*

digital dot *(com)* A dot generated by a digital computer or device. Digital dots are all of the same size whereas halftone dots vary, so, in digitally generated halftones several dots – up to 256 (on a 16 x 16 matrix) – are required to make up each halftone dot. → *bit; halftone (1)*

digital elevation model *(com)* A collection of regularly spaced elevation data from which 3D models of the earth's surface can be generated. DEMs are used extensively by cartographers to produce shaded relief maps using special software.

digital photography *(pho)* The process either of capturing an image with digital equipment or of manipulating photographic images on a computer, or both. In either case, the term describes photographs that are recorded or manipulated in binary form rather than on film. → *bit; digital camera*

Digital Subscriber Loop (DSL) *(int)* → *ADSL*

digital-to-analog convertor (DAC) *(aud)* → *DAC*

digital video effect (DVE) *(aud)* → *DVE*

Digital Video Interactive (DVI) *(com)* A computer chip developed by Intel that compresses and decompresses video images.

digitize *(com)* To convert anything – for example, text, images or sound – into binary form so that it can be digitally processed, manipulated, stored and reconstructed. In other words, transforming analog to digital. → *bit; digital*

digitizer *(com)* Strictly speaking, any hardware device such as a scanner or camera that converts drawn or photographed images into binary code so that you can work with them on your computer. However, the term is generally used more specifically with reference to 'digitizing tablets'. → *digitizing tablet/pad*

digitizing tablet/pad *(com)* A hardware device consisting of a flat, rectangular pad, which allows you to input images into your computer by drawing on it with a 'stylus' (a penlike instrument) as though you were working on paper. Also called a 'graphics tablet/pad'. ➔ *stylus*

digraph *(gen)* A pair of letters representing one sound, such as 'ph' in photo and 'sh' in sheet. ➔ *diphthong*

dimensional stability *(pap)* The resistance of a substance to changes that may affect its physical dimensions. For example, the dimensions of a sheet of paper may be affected by moisture.

dimensions *(gen)* In describing the size of 3D objects, the standard dimensions are length, width and height.

DIMM *(com)* abb.: dual-inline memory module. ➔ *dual-inline memory module (DIMM)*

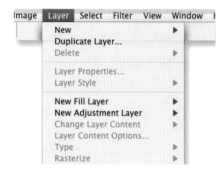

dimmed command *(com)* The condition of an item in a menu or dialog box when it is disabled or unavailable for use. The disabled item is displayed as grey or in a paler colour than its active counterpart, and is thus 'dimmed'. Also known as a 'greyed' command. ➔ *dialog/dialog box; menu*

dimmed icon *(com)* The condition of an icon that indicates that a file or folder is open or that a disk is unmounted (not available, as in an ejected disk). Also known as a 'greyed' or 'ghosted' icon. ➔ *icon*

DIN *(gen)* abb.: Deutsche Industrie-Norm. ➔ *Deutsche Industrie-Norm; ISO (1)*

dingbat *(typ)* The modern name for fonts of decorative symbols, traditionally called printer's 'flowers', 'ornaments' or 'arabesques'. ➔ *arabesque; flower; ornament;*

dinky *(pap)* A half roll ('web') of paper. ➔ *web (1)*

dinky dash *(gen)* ➔ *jim-dash*

diopter *(pho)* The measurement of the refractive properties of a lens, such as those used for close-up photography. A concave lens is measured in negative diopters, a convex lens in positive diopters. ➔ *lens*

diorama *(gen)* A small-scale model of a scene, such as a film set.

DIP *(com)* abb.: dual in-line package. ➔ *chip/microchip; circuit board; dual in-line package (DIP)*

diphthong *(typ)* The symbol which represents two vowels that are pronounced as a single syllable – for example, Œ and Æ. ➔ *digraph*

diploma paper *(pap)* A high-quality paper specifically made for printing official documents, certificates and so on.

DIP SIMM *(com)* A 'high profile' (taller) SIMM chip. ➔ *SIMM*

DIP switch *(com)* Small switches on some hardware devices that are used to select an operating mode, giving the device a unique identity number when connected to others. ➔ *SCSI ID (number)*

direct access *(com)* Access to an item by means of a single direct path. For example, your computer has direct access when connected to another by means of a continuous, dedicated telephone line rather than via modems and regular telephone lines. ➔ *modem*

DirectConnect *(aud)* A data interface that allows up to 32 separate channels from a soft synth or sampler to be independently routed and mixed in the sound editing package Pro Tools. Developed by Digidesign for the Macintosh computer.

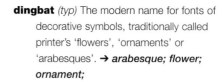

Examples of popular **dingbats**

The grey options are **dimmed commands**

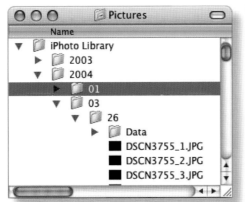

Mac OS showing a **directory structure**

direct cost *(gen)* The cost of a project related directly to that job, excluding normal overhead costs of the business (indirect costs). For example, a photograph commissioned for a specific job is a direct cost, whereas the cost of heating your office while you brief the photographer is an overhead cost. → *overhead cost*

direct digital colour proof (DDCP) *(pre)* Any colour proof made directly from digital data without using separation films, such as those produced on an inkjet printer. → *inkjet printer*

direct entry *(com)* Any matter that is entered into a computer directly, such as via a keyboard, rather than input by some other means, such as via a scanner.

direct halftone *(pre)* A halftone negative or positive produced by exposing the original directly through a halftone screen onto film. → *direct screening*

directional *(gen)* The words in an image caption, such as 'above' and 'below', which direct the reader to the relevant picture.

direct litho(graphy) *(pri)* A lithographic printing process in which the printing plate is brought into direct contact with the paper, as distinct from 'offset' lithography, in which the printing image is transferred via a 'blanket cylinder' to the paper. Also known as 'di litho'. → *offset litho(graphy)*

direct mail *(gen)* Advertising matter sent directly through the mail to prospective customers.

directory (1) *(com)* A more technical term for 'folder', normally used in reference to folders in Web servers or Windows computers.

directory (2) *(com)* An invisible catalog of information about all of the files on a disk. The 'volume directory' contains general information about the disk, whereas the 'file directory' logs specific information such as the files' physical location on the disk, so they are vital system files. → *directory structure; file; folder (1); volume (1)*

directory structure *(com)* The underlying hierarchical structure of all the files on a hard disk. → *directory (2)*

direct positive *(pre)* → *photodirect*

direct reading *(pho)* The common term for taking a meter reading directly using light reflected from a subject.

direct screening *(pre)* A method of creating colour halftone film separations directly from an original, without the need for continuous tone negatives. → *continuous tone*

DirectShow *(com)* Old Microsoft multimedia technology for film sequences (formerly called 'ActiveMovie'), for playback on the Windows operating system from the Web, CD-ROM and DVD-ROM. → *CD-ROM; DVD-ROM; Windows*

DirectSound *(aud)* (PC) Microsoft-developed driver for Windows 98 onwards, which is often regarded as causing problems with certain soundcards at low buffer settings. If you are experiencing audio glitches or dropouts, this may be the problem. Alternatively, you may need to change your latency time or buffer settings to compensate.

direct to plate *(pri)* → *computer-to-plate (CTP)*

dirty proof *(gen)* A proof that is heavily corrected. → *clean proof; foul proof; galley proof; press proof*

D

dis/diss *(typ) abb.:* distribute. The returning of all matter used in a print job to its original owner or source. The term originally related specifically to traditional metal type composition, when individual letters and spaces were returned to their correct places in the case so that they could be re-used.

disc *(com)* A circular platter on which digital data is stored in the form of minute pits (the size of which represents a 0 or a 1). These are 'burned' by a laser into a shiny metallic layer encapsulated in the disc. The data is optically 'read' by reflecting a laser beam, which distinguishes the pits from 'lands' (the spaces between the pits), off the disc. Usually referred to as CDs and DVDs (both of which have many variants), optical discs are widely used for audio and video recording as well as for data storage. Optical discs, particularly DVDs, are capable of holding large amounts of data and are more resilient to damage than magnetic media. Not to be confused with a 'disk', which is much the same thing, but uses magnetic rather than optical techniques to store data. There is a third type of disc, which combines both techniques and is called a 'magneto-optical disc' (MO). ➔ *CD; disk; DVD; magneto-optical disc (MO/MOD)*

discrete value *(gen)* A value that is individually distinct and varies only by whole, defined units, as distinct from a value that is infinitely variable ('non-discrete value').

discretionary hyphen *(com)* A manually inserted character which, in some applications, indicates where a word can be broken if necessary so that text will fit comfortably on a line. The hyphen will print only if the word needs to be broken.
➔ *hyphen*

disk *(com)* A circular platter with a magnetic surface on which computer data is stored. Data is written to and read from the disk by a mechanism called a 'disk drive'. Disks may be rigid ('hard disk') or flexible ('floppy disk'), and may reside on a disk drive installed inside your computer ('internal disk drive'), in a device connected to your computer ('external disk drive') or in a cartridge that can be transported between disk drives ('removable disk'). A disk drive may contain several 'platters', but is referred to in the singular – 'disk'. Not to be confused with 'disc', which uses optical rather than magnetic techniques to store data. There is also a third type of disc, which combines both techniques and is called a 'magneto-optical disc' (MO). ➔ *disc; magneto-optical disc (MO/MOD)*

disk crash *(com)* A colloquialism describing the operating failure of a hard disk drive, preventing you from accessing data. This may be brought about by corruption of the disk's 'format' (the way information is arranged on the disk), dirt or dust on the disk's surface, or failure of a mechanical part in the drive. If the former, repairs can sometimes be made with a disk maintenance utility, but in the latter case repair is unlikely and may result in complete loss of all your data. You should always regard a disk crash as being inevitable – not a question of 'if' but 'when' – and back up your data regularly. ➔ *crash (1); formatting; hard disk*

disk image *(com)* A single file that represents an entire volume such as a floppy disk, hard disk, or CD-ROM and which, when opened ('mounted'), can be used as though it were a separate disk. Disk images are typically used for making copies of 'installer' disks and also for creating partitions for recording data to CD-R discs. Also called 'software partitions' or 'file partitions'. Not to be confused with an 'image file', which is a picture file stored on disk. ➔ *image file; partition(ing)*

display *(com)* A common word for your computer system's monitor. There are a number of display technologies prevalent in the marketplace. CRT (Cathode Ray Tubes)

An image converted to black and white with no **dithering** (middle) and diffusion dithering (bottom)

Two copies of an original full-colour image reduced to a lower bit depth using both a set **dither** pattern (left) and the more 'varied' diffusion technique

are gradually making way for flat panel displays, in the form of LCD where computer monitors and smaller televisions are concerned, and gas plasma for larger presentation devices. These newer technologies are slowly overcoming problems with angle of viewing and colour reliability. ➔ *CRT; LCD (1); monitor*

display advertisement *(gen)* Advertising matter positioned in a prominent position in printed publications and designed to a quality that will attract immediate attention. As distinct from 'small', or 'classified' advertisements. ➔ *advert(isement); classified ad*

display board *(pap)* A heavy, coated, coloured board with a dull finish.

display matter/type *(typ)* Larger-size fonts, usually 14pt or more, used mainly for headings. As distinct from smaller sizes used for continuous text, captions and so on. ➔ *display size(s)*

display size(s) *(typ)* Traditionally, any size of type above 14pt. ➔ *composition size(s)*

dissolve *(aud)* A video transition where the video from one track fades out to be replaced by the video from another track fading in.

dissonance *(gen)* The spatial tension between elements in a typographic design.

distortion *(aud)* Whenever the output of audio sound does not exactly match the input, distortion has been introduced into the signal whether it is audible or not. This also refers to a desirable effect brought about by applying an extreme amount of overdrive

to a sound, but it cannot be done 'naturally' on a computer as it can on a guitar amplifier. As such, many digital filters are available to digitally emulate a wide variety of distortion effects.

distortion copy *(pre)* Any matter for print that has been deliberately distorted prior to production in order to compensate for naturally occurring dimensional changes, such as shrinkage, which may occur during the process.

distributed rendering *(com)* The process of rendering chunks of one or more files, such as a 3D film, simultaneously on one or more computers. This saves considerable time since large renderings can take several hours – even days – to complete.

distribution/distributing roller *(pri)* A cylinder (or series of cylinders) on a printing press that distributes ink to the plate, smoothing it as it does so.

dithering (1) *(com)* A technique of 'interpolation' that calculates the average value of adjacent pixels. This technique is used either to add extra pixels to an image – to smooth an edge, for example, as in 'anti-aliasing' – or to reduce the number of colours or greys in an image by replacing them with average values that conform to a predetermined palette of colours. Dithering is also used by some printing devices to simulate colours or tones. ➔ *anti-aliasing; CLUT; continuous tone; indexed colour; interpolate/interpolation; re-sampling*

D

dithering (2) *(aud)* Intelligent reduction of the bit rate of an audio file by adding small amounts of white noise (noise that covers the entire frequency spectrum). Apogee UV22HR dithering is a standard dithering process adopted by Cubase SX and other audio production software.

dithering (3) *(gen)* A technique by which a large range of colours can be simulated by mingling pixels. A complex pattern of intermingling adjacent pixels of two colours gives the illusion of a third colour, although this makes the image appear grainy.

ditto/prime marks *(typ)* The symbol (") indicating that the text matter directly above it is repeated. Alternatively used as a symbol for inches or seconds.

diurnal *(gen)* A newspaper or journal that is published daily.

diverging/divergent lens *(pho)* A camera lens that causes light rays to bend outwards from the optical axis. Also called a 'negative element'.

DLS *(aud) abb.:* downloadable sample format. An accessible audio sample file format.

D-max *(pho) abb.:* maximum density. As can be achieved in a photographic original or by a photomechanical system. ➔ *D-min*

D-min *(pho) abb.:* minimum density. As can be achieved in a photographic original or by a photomechanical system. ➔ *D-max*

DNS *(int) abb.:* Domain Name Service ➔ *Domain Name Service (DNS)*

dock *(com)* To connect one device – usually a computer – to another.

doctor blade (1) *(pri)* A long, thin, flexible steel blade used variously to remove or apply ink or coating before or after printing. For example, a doctor blade is used in gravure printing to wipe excess ink from the surface of the printing cylinder. ➔ *cylinder; gravure*

doctor blade (2) *(pap)* The flexible blade used to keep cylinders clean during papermaking.

doctor(ing) *(pri)* To alter the constituents of printing ink in order to improve the quality of a printed job.

document (1) *(com)* Any file created or modified on a computer by means of application software, such as a letter written in a word processing application or a design created in a page-layout application. A document file is generated on your hard disk the first time you 'save' something. Each time you save changes to your document, the original is updated rather than created anew. To create a new version of the same document, use the 'Save as...' command. Also known as a 'data file'.

document (2) *(int)* The entire contents of a single HTML file. HTML documents are generally referred to as 'webpages', since this is how they are rendered for display by browsers. ➔ *browser (1)/Web browser; HTML; World Wide Web*

documentary (photography) *(pho)* A term applied to film or still photography using images which, undistorted by interpretation, accurately describe real events.

document-based queries *(int)* A method of sending information from your browser to a Web server, such as when you click on a 'search' button to look something up. ➔ *document (2); World Wide Web*

document content architecture (DCA) *(com)* A file format used for transferring partially formatted text documents between applications.

document exchange format (DXF) *(com)* ➔ *DXF*

document heading *(int)* An HTML-style ('tag') that defines text headings in a range of predetermined sizes and weights (originally levels 1 to 6), so that you can add emphasis to a line of text. ➔ *HTML*

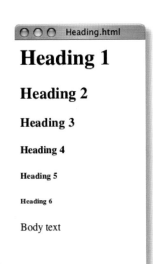

Heading 1

Heading 2

Heading 3

Heading 4

Heading 5

Heading 6

Body text

Apple's Safari Web browser rendering the six **document heading** styles of the HTML format

document root *(int)* The place on a Web server where all the HTML files, images and other components for a particular website are located. → *HTML; server; World Wide Web*

document transfer rate *(int)* The speed, measured in documents per minute, at which webpages are transmitted to your computer once you have requested them. → *document (2)*

Document Type Definition (DTD) *(int)* A formal SGML specification for a document, which lays out structural elements and markup definitions.

dodge/dodging *(pho)* A method of obtaining lighter areas in a photographic print by the selective use of masking (hiding relevant areas from light). The dodge 'tool' in certain image-editing applications digitally simulates the mechanical technique. The opposite effect – darkening areas of an image – is called 'burning'. → *burn (4); masking (2)*

dog-ear(ed) *(pap)* Corners of a page that are misfolded, worn or battered with use.

dogleg *(gen)* Colloquial term for a leader line that changes direction towards its point of reference. → *leader line/leader rule*

dolly (shot) *(pho)* A rolling trolley that supports a camera tripod, used in both still and film photography but more often the latter. A dolly is also used in 3D applications for a movement control in which the 'camera' moves around in 3D space as though gliding on the surface of an imaginary sphere, with the subject at its centre. This should not be confused with 'panning', where the camera rotates at a fixed point to view a scene, or 'tracking', where the camera moves past the subject in a parallel plane. → *camera moves; pan(ning); tracking (2)*

Domain Name Service (DNS) *(int)* In basic terms, the address of a website. Such an address is actually a number that conforms to the numerical Internet Protocol (IP) addresses used by computers for information exchange. However, names are easier to remember. Domain names include at least two parts: the 'subdomain', typically a company or organization, or even your own name, and the 'high-level domain', which usually follows the last dot, (as in '.com' for commercial sites, '.org' for non-profit sites, '.gov' for governmental sites, and '.edu' for educational sites). The top-level domain name may also indicate a country code for sites outside the United States (although a site without a country code does not necessarily mean it is inside the US), such as '.uk' for the United Kingdom, '.de' for Germany, '.fr' for France, and so on. Other, more recent, top-level domain names include .web and .biz. → *Internet; World Wide Web*

dongle *(com)* A hardware 'key' that plugs into a computer port to enable its associated software to run. Once a common method of copy-protecting software, dongles now generally accompany only very expensive, high-end applications.

*!?

D

Doppler effect *(aud)* When the source of a sound is moving towards the listener, the pitch of the sound will seem higher; and when it is moving away, the pitch will seem lower. This is the result of shifts in frequency brought about by a compression of the sound waves on approach, and a stretching of the sound waves on moving away, as can be observed by standing near a passing train. Measuring the rate at which the pitch changes would allow you to estimate the speed of the train.

DOS *(com)* abb.: Disc Operating System. → *MS-DOS*

dot *(com)* A term that can mean one of three things: halftone dot (the basic element of a halftone image), machine dot (the dots produced by a laser printer or imagesetter) or scan dot (strictly speaking, pixels, which comprise a scanned bitmapped image). Each is differentiated by being expressed in lpi (lines per inch) for a halftone dot, dpi (dots per inch) for a machine dot and ppi (pixels per inch) for a scan dot – although the latter is sometimes expressed erroneously – in dpi. Thus, since the term 'dot' is used to describe both halftone and machine dots, scan dots should always be referred to as pixels. → *halftone dot; machine dot; pixel; scan dot*

dot and tickle *(gen)* A colloquial expression for an illustration technique in which an image is composed out of small, stippled dots using a fine pen.

dot area *(pre)* The pattern of a halftone and the area it occupies – that is, not just the dots themselves but also the spaces in between.

dot etching *(pre)* The conventional process of using chemicals to reduce the size of halftone dots on negative or positive film, in order to modify the tonal values of a halftone image. → *hard dot; soft dot*

dot-for-dot (1) *(pri)* Printing colour work in perfect register.

dot-for-dot (2) *(pre)* A method of generating printing film by photographing a previously screened or printed halftone image. On fine-screened images, the usual allowable maximum limit of enlargement or reduction is around 10 per cent. Also called 'copydot' technique. → *screened print*

dot formation *(pre)* The pattern of dots produced by halftone images printed in two or more colours. → *dot pattern*

dot gain *(pre)* The tendency, during the reproduction chain from original to printed image, of halftone dots to grow in size, either photographically in prepress stages, or in ink during printing. This often leads to inaccurate results, but if the dot gain characteristics of a particular printing press are known, compensation can be made during reproduction. A dot-gain scale is usually included on proofs to check this occurrence, and is specified as a percentage of the size of the dot. Dot gain is the opposite of dot loss.

dot leader *(typ)* A leader line comprised of dots, generally used to guide the eye in tabulated matter, lists and so on. → *leader line*

dot-matrix printer *(com)* A simple but inexpensive printer that uses a grid of metal pins to create the printed image, with hammers hitting the correct combination of pins to make the shape of a type character.

dot pattern *(pre)* The pattern created by halftone dots after all colours are printed. A halftone image printed in register and with the correct halftone screen angles will produce a 'rosette' pattern, whereas incorrectly angled halftone screens will produce a pattern known as 'moiré'. → *dot formation; moiré; rosette(s); screen angle*

dot range *(pre)* The difference in size between the largest and smallest printable dots of a halftone image. → *halftone (1)*

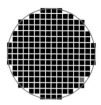

A halftone **dot** made from a 16x16 matrix

An image and halftone screen **dot pattern**

A series of different **dot shapes,** from the top: round, diamond, elliptical, square, cross line and line

An image at 300, 150, 72 and 36 **dpi**

dot shape *(pre)* The shape of the dot in a halftone screen. Although traditional halftones use round dots (which actually look square in the midtones), some applications or output devices allow you to choose between round, square, linear (not actually dots, but lines) and elliptical dot shapes. Elliptical dots are less prone to dot gain than round dots, while linear screens are used for visual effect rather than as any particular benefit to the reproduction of an image. → *halftone (1)*

dot slur(ring) *(pri)* The 'skidding', or elongated smudging of a halftone dot caused by excessive movement between plate and paper during printing. → *halftone (1)*

dots per inch (dpi) *(com)* A unit of measurement used to represent the resolution of devices such as printers and imagesetters. Is also commonly used to describe resolution, on computer monitors and images, which should more properly be expressed in pixels per inch (ppi). The closer the dots or pixels the better the quality. Typical resolutions are 72ppi for a monitor, 300dpi for a LaserWriter and 2450dpi (or more) for an imagesetter. → *pixels per inch (ppi); resolution (1)*

dot spread *(pri)* → *dot gain*

dot/stripe pitch *(com)* The distance between the dots or pixels (actually, holes or slits in a screen mesh) on your monitor: the closer the dots, the finer the display of image. → *pixel; resolution (1)*

dot value *(pre)* The size of halftone dots in an image or tint, expressed as a percentage of the solid colour. → *dot range; halftone (1)*

double burn/print down *(pre)* To use two or more film negatives to expose an image onto a sensitized plate – often using one for line work and a second for halftones.

double character *(typ)* Two metal type letters on a single type body such as a ligature or diphthong. → *ligature*

double-click *(com)* The action of clicking the mouse button twice in rapid succession. Double-clicking while the pointer is positioned in an appropriate place is a short-cut to performing functions such as opening documents or highlighting words in text. → *mouse*

double coated paper *(pap)* Paper that is coated on both sides. → *coated paper*

double column *(typ)* → *half-measure*

double dagger *(typ)* The mark '‡' used to indicate notes to a text. Also called a 'diesis' or 'double obelisk'. → *dagger*

double digest fold *(fin)* A basic fold to make a signature in web printing. → *signature (1); web (printing) press*

double-dot halftone *(pre)* Two halftone films made from a single original image, one exposed to accommodate midtones, the other to reproduce highlights and shadows. When combined, they produce a printed image with a greater tonal range than would be possible with a single exposure. → *duotone; halftone (1)*

double etch *(pre)* The two-step preparation of a gravure plate used, for example, to etch line work separately from tone images. → *gravure*

double image *(pri)* A printing aberration caused by additional or duplicated halftone dots.

double-(page) spread *(gen)* Generally used to describe any two facing pages of a document or publication. Strictly speaking, however, a double-page spread ('truck' or 'double truck') occurs when text or images cross the gutter to occupy the two centre pages of a section. Otherwise it should be more accurately described as a 'false double'. ➔ *centre fold/spread*

double pica *(typ)* A former type size of about 22pt, now 24pt (2 x 12pt picas). ➔ *pica*

double rule *(gen)* The term used to distinguish two lines of different thickness (in traditional typesetting, made from brass) from two lines of the same thickness called a 'parallel rule'. ➔ *parallel rule*

double-thick cover stock *(pap)* Two sheets of thick paper stock laminated together.

double title page *(gen)* A book in which the title page occupies a double-page spread. Strictly speaking, a 'title page' is a single, right-hand page. ➔ *title page*

double tone ink *(pri)* A printing ink that produces a secondary tone as it dries, creating the illusion of two-colour printing in a single pass.

double truck *(gen)* ➔ *double-(page) spread*

doubling *(pri)* A printing aberration causing a faint duplication of a halftone image.

doublures *(fin)* The decorative lining of the inside face of the boards of a handbound book.

Dow etch *(pri)* A proprietary process for etching photoengraved plates.

download *(int)* To transfer data from a remote computer – such as an Internet server – to your own. The opposite of upload. ➔ *server; upload*

downloadable font *(com)* A font that can – or must – be loaded into the memory of your printer, as distinct from one that is already resident in its ROM or hard disk. Since printers usually come with very few preinstalled fonts, this often means that all the fonts you use must be downloadable. PostScript Type 1 fonts come in two parts: screen font and printer font, and the latter is frequently described as a 'downloadable font'. ➔ *Type 1 font*

downsample/downsampling *(com)* ➔ *resample*

down stroke *(typ)* The most pronounced vertical or near vertical stroke in a type character, originally the downward stroke of a pen in calligraphy.

down time *(gen)* A period of time in which a person, machine or device is idle, for whatever reason.

down tree *(com)* In some applications, particularly 3D, the hierarchy in which all objects are children to other objects. ➔ *child object*

DP file *(int) abb.:* DigitalPaper file. ➔ *Common Ground*

dpi *(com) abb.:* dots per inch. ➔ *dots per inch (dpi)*

dpsi/dpi2 *(gen) abb.:* dots per square inch. ➔ *dots per inch (dpi)*

draft (US), draught (UK) *(gen)* The initial stage of a manuscript, text or illustration that will subsequently be refined, rewritten or edited. A draft design is variously called a 'rough', 'visual', or 'scamp'. When a manuscript is eventually ready for typesetting, it is called a 'final draft'. ➔ *rough*

drag *(com)* Carrying out an action by holding down the mouse button while you move the mouse (moving the pointer on screen) and then releasing the mouse button to complete the action. Dragging is most commonly used to perform such tasks as selecting and moving items, selecting pull-down menu commands and selecting text.

DOUBLE IMAGE

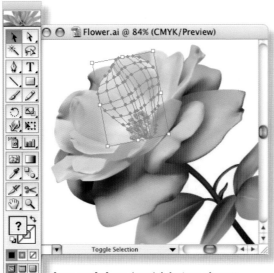

Adobe Illustrator is a
drawing application

drag-and-drop *(com)* A feature of some
operating systems and applications that
enables you to select an item and move or
copy it to another location simply by
'dragging' it with the mouse button held
down and then 'dropping' it in the desired
location by releasing the mouse button.

DRAM *(com)* Acronym for dynamic RAM
(random access memory), pronounced
'dee-ram'. Memory that is active only while
supplied by an electric current, and is thus
lost when power is turned off. Generally
referred to as simply 'RAM'. The more
expensive static RAM ('SRAM') does not
lose its memory in the absence of power.
DRAM comes in the form of chips that plug
into the motherboard of your computer.
→ *RAM*

draw (1) *(pri)* A printing aberration in which
halftone dots appear larger near the tail end
of a printed sheet, caused by misregister.
→ *halftone (1)*

draw (2) *(fin)* To gather together all the
signatures of a publication prior to binding.
→ *F and Gs/F/Gs*

draw(ing) application *(com)* Drawing
applications can be defined as those that
are object-oriented (they use 'vectors' to
mathematically define lines and shapes), as
distinct from painting applications that use
pixels to make images ('bitmapped
graphics'). Some applications combine
both. → *paint(ing) application*

drawdown *(pri)* The technique of assessing the
colour of a printing ink by thinly spreading a
small amount on a sample of the paper on
which it is to be finally printed.

drawn on (cover) *(fin)* A paper or board book
cover that is glued to the spine of a sewn or
adhesive bound book.

dressing *(pri)* Part of the make-ready process
whereby printing cylinders are packed to
change the degree of impression or, by a
fractional amount, the 'print length' of the
final image. → *make-ready*

driers *(pri)* Various substances, usually metallic
salts, added to printing ink to speed up the
drying process.

drill *(fin)* A coarse cloth used for binding books.

drill(ing) *(fin)* Boring holes in paper or binding
using a rotating 'die'. → *die (2)*

drive head *(com)* The part of any kind of disk
drive that extracts ('reads') data from, and
deposits ('writes') data to, a disk or tape.
In hard drives, one read/write head is
positioned above each side of every disk
platter (a hard drive may consist of several
platters). These move on rails, or swinging
arms, over the surface of the platter, which
rotates at high speed. → *hard disk*

driver/device driver *(com)* A small piece
of software that tells a computer how to
handle or operate a piece of hardware,
such as a printer, scanner or disk drive.
Depending on its function, a driver may be

D

located with the operating system software and therefore loaded at startup, or it may form a 'plug-in' to an application (as do some scanner drivers, for example). → *operating system; plug-in*

driving out *(typ)* A conventional metal typesetting term, referring to arranging the spaces in a line of type to fill the measure.

drop (1) *(gen)* A space, or margin, usually at the top of a page or column, before the printed image starts. A 'chapter drop' indicates the place on a page where text starts at the beginning of a chapter. → *drop down*

drop (2) *(gen)* The maximum number of text lines or image depth in a column, as is constrained by the page grid.

drop cap(ital)/letter/dropped initial *(typ)* A large initial character at the beginning of a piece of text or paragraph, which is inset into the lines of type around it. → *hanging cap(ital); two-line letters*

drop down *(gen)* The point at which text matter starts beneath a chapter heading. Also called 'chapter drop'. → *drop (1)*

drop-down menu *(com)* The menu that appears when you click on a title in the menu bar along the top of your screen. Also called 'pop-down menu' or 'pull-down menu'. → *menu bar; menu title*

drop folios *(gen)* Page numbers positioned at the foot of each page, usually referred to simply as 'folios'. → *folio (1)*

droplet *(com)* A Mac OS file created with AppleScript, which executes a sequence of actions when an item is dropped onto its icon. You can define droplets to automate tasks such as turning on file sharing. → *AppleScript*

drop letter *(typ)* → *drop cap(ital)/letter/ dropped initial*

drop-off *(com)* The effect of a value decreasing as the distance from a reference point increases. In lights the intensity may be set to drop off, the further from the light you get.

dropout (1) *(pre)* The use of masks or filters to prevent unwanted areas of an image from appearing on final negative or positive film.

dropout blue/colour *(pre)* The use of blue pencils or other markers to construct camera-ready art or write instructions on artwork, used because blue does not reproduce when photographed with certain types of photographic film used in prepress work. Also called 'nonrepro blue', 'fade out blue' or 'face out blue'. → *dropout ink*

drop-out/dropped-out halftone *(pre)* Removal of dot formations from a halftone negative or positive, so that the highlights print as clear white. → *halftone (1)*

dropout ink *(pre)* Any coloured ink that is visible to the human eye but not 'seen' by a scanner or reprographic film. Dropout inks are used to print forms and layout grids, for example. → *dropout blue/ colour*

dropout (mask) *(pre)* The use of masks, filters or other means during reproduction to prevent highlight dots or a specific item from appearing on final negative or positive film.

dropped head *(gen)* A chapter title that is set lower than the top of a full page of text.

dropped initial *(typ)* → *drop cap(ital)/letter/ dropped initial*

dropped-out type *(typ)* Type that is reversed out of its background to read, for example, as white on a colour. Also called 'reversed-out' or 'knocked-out' type.

dropping out *(pre)* A repro house or output bureau term for replacing a low-resolution 'FPO' scan with a high-resolution scan prior to final film output. → *FPO*

drop shadow *(gen)* A shadow projected onto the surface behind an image or character, designed to lift the image or character off the surface.

drop shadow effect *(gen)* Produces a shadow beneath a selection conforming to the selection outline, and is available as a filter, plug-in or layer feature. Depending on

The **drop** indicates the maximum number of lines

The **drop down** is the space between a chapter heading and the first line of text

A **dropped head** is lower than the normal page drop

the filter, the shadow can usually be moved relative to the selection, given variable opacity or even tilted. With tilting, a drop shadow can be applied to a selection (say, a person) and will mimic a sunlight shadow.

drop tone *(pre)* → *line conversion (technique)*

drum (1) *(pri)* An alternative term for the cylinder of a printing press or papermaking machine. → *cylinder*

drum (2) *(pri)* A roller that distributes ink on a printing press.

drum (3) *(pre)* The glass or plastic cylinder in an electronic scanner onto which originals, such as transparencies, are mounted for scanning. → *drum scanner*

drum scanner *(pre)* Originals are mounted onto a rotating glass or plastic cylinder and are scanned by a laser for eventual output as colour-separated printing film. The term distinguishes high-end scanners from inferior flatbed or 'desktop' varieties. → *desktop scanner; scanner*

dry-back *(pri)* Changes in certain characteristics, such as colour or density, of a printing ink after drying.

dry finish *(pap)* Paper or board with a rough, uncoated surface.

drying in *(pri)* Loss of detail in a screen-printed image, caused by ink drying and clogging the screen mesh.

dry litho *(pri)* A lithographic printing technique in which the non-printing areas of the plate are etched to leave a relief printing area, thus avoiding the need for water. Dry litho is a variation of the 'letterset' printing technique. → *letterset*

dry mounting *(gen)* To mount items such as photographs onto board using heat-sensitive adhesive tissue.

dry offset *(pri)* → *letterset*

dry printing *(pri)* Multicolour printing in which each successive ink colour is allowed to dry before the next is applied.

dry proof *(pre)* Any colour proof made without printing ink, such as a Cromalin or Matchprint, but particularly proofs produced digitally – from a laser printer, for example. → *Color-Key™; Cromalin; Dylux; MatchPrint; off-press proofing*

dry signal *(aud)* This refers to an audio signal with no effects applied to it. → *wet signal*

dry stripping *(pre)* The assembly ('stripping') of film negatives or positives after they have been processed and dried.

dry transfer lettering *(gen)* Lettering and other designs that are transferred to artwork by releasing them from the back of a plastic sheet by rubbing the front of the sheet. Also called 'rub-ons', 'rub-downs' and 'rub-offs'.

dry trapping *(pri)* The property of a printed ink, once dry, to accept a wet overprinted ink. → *trapping*

dry-up *(pri)* → *catch-up*

DSL *(int) abb.:* Digital Subscriber Loop. → *ADSL; ISDN*

DSP (1) *(com) abb.:* Digital switch port. → *port*

DSP (2) *(com) abb.:* Digital signal processor.

DSP Digital Signal Processing (effects) *(aud)* Group of processes that applies spacial, time and other dimensions to a signal.

DTD *(int) abb.:* Document Type Definition. → *document (2); Document Type Definition (DTD); SGML*

DTP *(gen) abb.:* Desktop publishing. → *desktop publishing (DTP)*

dual-inline memory module (DIMM) *(com)* A standard type of computer memory ('RAM') chip. → *memory; RAM; SIMM*

dual in-line package (DIP) *(com)* The particular way in which some chips are mounted – with two parallel rows of pins – so that they can be plugged into a computer circuit board.

D

dual roll stand *(pri)* A structure supporting two rolls ('webs') of paper, which are simultaneously fed through a press to streamline production. ➔ *web (1)*

duck foot quotes *(typ)* Quotation marks (« ») used in French and German text. Also called 'guillemets'.

duct *(pri)* The reservoir in a printing press where ink is distributed to the inking system used by the press. Also called an 'ink fountain'. ➔ *fountain*

ductor roller *(pri)* A roller on a printing press that carries water or ink from the 'fountain' roller to either the 'dampening' or 'distributing' roller.

dull finish *(pap)* Paper with a matt surface. ➔ *coated paper*

dull seal *(pap)* Paper with an adhesive backing.

dumb quotes *(typ)* Used to describe 'prime' marks when they are used, erroneously, as quotation marks or apostrophes. In some computer or application configurations, prime marks appear by default when the 'quote' key is typed, unless preferences are set to substitute true quotation marks (called 'smart' or 'curly' quotes). ➔ *primes/ prime marks; smart quotes*

dumb terminal *(com)* A display device and keyboard that does not possess any computing power on its own, but which is networked to a server on which it relies for intelligent processing. ➔ *Telnet; terminal*

dummy (1) *(gen)* ➔ *bulking dummy*

dummy (2) *(gen)* A mock-up of a design, such as a pack or illustrated book, showing the position of headings, text, captions, illustrations and other details. ➔ *bulking dummy; comprehensive*

dumpbin *(gen)* A free-standing container used to display goods – particularly paperback books – in a self-service retail outlet. Dumpbins are generally supplied to the outlet by the manufacturer or publisher of the goods. ➔ *header card*

duodecimo *(pap)* ➔ *twelvemo/12 mo*

duotone *(pre)* A monochromatic image combining two halftones with different tonal ranges made from the same original, so that when printed in different tones of the same colour (usually black, thus sometimes described as a 'double-black duotone'), a wider tonal range is reproduced than is possible with a single colour. Special effects can be achieved by using the same technique printed with different coloured inks. The term is sometimes used erroneously to describe a 'duplex halftone' or 'false duotone' (a duplicate halftone printed in two colours). ➔ *duplex halftone*

A cyan and magenta **duotone**

dupe *(gen)* A duplicate of anything, although generally used to describe a copy of an original transparency.

duplex *(gen)* Literally, 'two-in-one', such as simultaneous two-way communication over telecommunication lines, a single press with two units, or a single sheet of paper made from two different coloured sheets. ➔ *duplex board/paper; duplex halftone; half duplex; simplex*

duplex board/paper *(pap)* Two sheets of paper or board of different qualities or colours, which have been brought together and combined, usually by lamination, but sometimes while the paper is still in the wet state on the papermaking machine. ➔ *duplex; twin-wire paper*

duplex halftone *(pre)* Two exact duplicate halftone negatives (or positives) made from the same original, but printed in two different colours. Sometimes incorrectly described as a 'duotone' when a 'false duotone' is the correct definition. ➔ *duotone; duplex*

DUAL-INLINE MEMORY MODULE (DIMM)

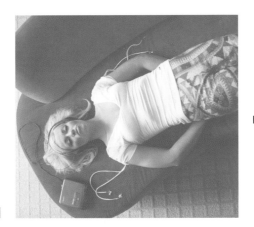

Cyan and magenta
duplex halftone

duplicate/dupe film *(pre)* A direct, same-size copy of a film original, made by contact exposure from one to the other.

duplo *(pre)* A scanning technique in which two colour separations are exposed onto a single piece of film.

dusting *(pri)* A build-up of debris (such as paper particles) in offset printing onto the non-image areas of the blanket. Also known as 'powdering', although this also describes a printing fault in which the substrate and ink separate after printing. ➔ *powdering*

dust jacket/wrapper *(gen)* The printed paper cover bearing a design, folded around, but not attached to a bound book, and in which it is sold. Originally employed to protect the binding but now used as a marketing aid. Also called 'book jacket' and 'book wrapper'.

Dutch paper *(pap)* Any deckle-edged paper manufactured in the Netherlands. ➔ *deckle edge*

DVD *(com) abb.:* digital versatile disc. A high-capacity (up to 17.08 gigabytes of data) storage disc similar to a CD-ROM, onto which data is 'written' by means of tiny 'pits' burned into the disc's surface by a laser, but which uses a shorter wavelength so that the pits can be closer together. There are four capacities of DVD, some of which are double-sided, others with two layers of information on each side: DVD5 (which holds 4.7Gb of data), DVD9 (8.5Gb), DVD10 (9.4Gb) and DVD18 (17.08Gb). There is a variety of recordable formats available. ➔ *CD-ROM; DVD-A; DVD-R/DVD+R/ DVD-RW/DVD+RW; DVD-ROM; DVD-Video*

DVD-A *(aud) abb.:* digital versatile disc-audio. Similar to an audio CD but with a capacity of 17Gb – enough for around 32 hours of music. All DVD formats are vulnerable to damage and dirt, but recordable options are now affordable, either standalone or as part of a standard PC or Mac package. Dedicated DVD-A players are needed to get the full dynamic range from DVD-A discs. Sampling rate: 44.1 kHz–192 kHz. Frequency range: 16 Hz–20 kHz. Dynamic range: 144 dB. Capacity: 4.5 GB approx.

DVD-R/DVD+R/DVD-RW/DVD+RW *(com)* Abbreviations for the incompatible recording formats available for DVD. DVD-R and +R can be recorded once and played on most (but by no means all) DVD players, whereas the RW formats are only readable by newer players. The dash and plus are significant, and you must select the correct kind for your DVD burner, or it will not work. DVD-RAM is a further re-recordable alternative, championed by Panasonic. ➔ *CD-R/ CD-RW; DVD; DVD-A; DVD-ROM; DVD-Video*

DVD-ROM *(com) abb.:* digital versatile disc-read only memory. ➔ *CD-ROM; DVD; DVD-A; DVD-R/DVD+R/DVD-RW/DVD+RW; DVD-Video*

DVD-Video *(com) abb.:* digital versatile disc-video. A high-capacity DVD used for storing feature-length films for playing back via set-top boxes plugged into a TV. The DVD players contain an 'MPEG' decoder that enables many playback features – a choice of camera angles, for example. It supports 16:9 anamorphic widescreen, but not new HDTV standards. ➔ *DVD; DVD-Audio; DVD-R/DVD+R/DVD-RW/DVD+RW; DVD-ROM; MPEG*

D

DVE *(aud) abb.:* digital video effect. A special effect or transition enabled by non-linear, digital video processing, often employing complex motion controlled through motion paths.

DVI *(com) abb.:* Digital Video Interactive.
→ *Digital Video Interactive (DVI)*

Dvorak keyboard *(com)* A keyboard layout on which the more frequently typed keys are positioned most comfortably in relationship to your dominant typing fingers. An alternative layout to the familiar and widely used 'QWERTY' arrangement found on typewriters and computer keyboards. → *qwerty*

DWD *(aud)* The native format for DiamondWare Sound Toolkit, which is meant for games and multimedia and is supported by some other software, such as Cool Edit Pro.

dwell *(pri)* The brief moment of time when a printing surface makes contact with paper and an impression is made. → *kiss impression*

DXF *(com) abb.:* document exchange format. A standard file format developed by Autodesk – originally for its AutoCAD application – for storing 3D and CAD files. → *CAD*

dye-based ink *(pri)* Inks, the colours of which are obtained from aniline dyes, used mainly for flexographic printing and for screen printing on to textiles. In the latter, dye-based inks are sometimes called 'dye pastes'. → *aniline; flexography/flex*

dye cloud *(pho)* A fault in developed photographic film resulting in a zone of bleached colour in one of the emulsion layers.

dye diffusion *(pri)* → *dye sub(limation)*

dyeline *(pre)* → *diazo(type)/diazo process*

dye-sensitization *(pho)* In the manufacture of photographic film, the standard process of adding dyes to emulsion in order to control its light-sensitivity, used particularly to make black-and-white film panchromatic.
→ *panchromatic*

dye sub(limation) *(pri)* A printing process in which vapourized ink dyes are bonded to a substrate by heat, producing near photographic-quality proofs. Dye sublimation allows digital printing of large images onto a range of materials and is thus particularly suitable for fashion, architectural and other large-format display items, since size is no limitation and runs can be as low as a single item. Also known as 'dye diffusion'.

Dylux *(pre)* The proprietary name for a photo-sensitive dry proof paper, developed by Du Pont, which does not require chemical processing. → *dry proof*

dynamic HTML (DHTML) *(int)* A development of HTML that employs CSS and JavaScript to add enhanced features such as basic animations and highlighted buttons to webpages without the need for a browser plug-in. DHTML is built into version 4.0 or later generations of Web browsers.

dynamic microphone *(aud)* As opposed to a condenser microphone, this type of microphone uses a vibrating diaphragm and a magnetic field to alter sound into electrical impulses.

dynamic RAM *(com)* → *DRAM*

dynamic range *(aud)* This is the range of volume, measured in decibels, at which an audio system can perform without introducing noise (at low levels) or distortion (at high levels) and is related to bandwidth.

DVE

Ee

E13B *(typ)* The name of the font of numerals and symbols that is used for magnetic ink character recognition (MICR). → *MICR*

ear *(gen)* The advertising spaces either side of the front-page title line of a newspaper.

easel-binder *(fin)* A 3D display stand with ring binding, used for making presentations.

easing *(com)* The gradual acceleration ('easing in') or deceleration ('easing out') of an animation sequence between key frames.

echo *(aud)* A secondary sound that is heard by the listener after the original sound that produced it. This can happen naturally, if the sound bounces off a surface, or it can be introduced into an audio recording through the use of effects. For example, 'slap-back' echo was an effect often used on Elvis' vocals.

e-commerce *(int)* Commercial transactions conducted electronically over a network or the Internet. → *e-mail*

ECW *(aud) abb.:* effects controls window. An Adobe Premiere Pro dialog enabling fine control of the settings and motion of a digital effect.

edge acuity *(pri)* The maintenance of a sharp edge on a printed image. An even ink spread encourages acuity.

edge gilding *(fin)* The process of applying a gold edge to a page border. As distinct from 'gilt edges', in which the trimmed book edges are covered with gold leaf. → *gild; gilt edges; red under gilt edges*

edge lighting *(pho)* Light that hits the subject from behind and slightly to one side, creating flare or a bright rim lighting effect around the edges of the subject.

edges *(fin)* The cut edges of a book block.

edge staining *(fin)* The application of colour to any trimmed edge/edges of a book block. → *sprinkled edges*

edit *(gen)* To commission, manage, sanction, amend or correct material, whether text or images.

edit line *(aud)* In a video-editing application, the line on the timeline showing the position of the current frame during playback or editing.

Adobe Premiere Pro's **ECW** here shown in use with a realtime preview of 'Sequence 01' to its right.

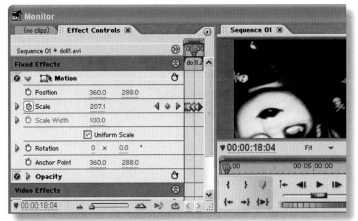

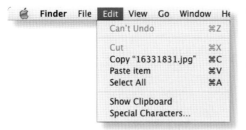

Edit menu *(com)* A standard menu in most applications (in the Mac OS, one of the three standard menus alongside the 'Apple' and 'File' menus), containing commands for such actions as cut, copy and paste.
→ *File menu*

edition *(gen)* The complete number of copies of a publication printed and published at one time, either for the first time ('first edition'), or after some change has been made ('revised edition', 'second edition' and so on). → *issue (2)*

edition binding *(fin)* Sometimes used to describe a 'casebound' (hardback) book. Also called 'publisher's binding'. → *cased/casebound*

EDO *(com)* abb.: extended data output → *extended data output (EDO); RAM*

effect *(aud)* This can refer to modification of an audio signal, or to modification of a digital image on your computer.

e.g. *(gen)* abb.: *exempli gratia.* A Latin term meaning 'for example'.

eggshell finish *(pap)* A smooth – but not glossy – surface on particular types of coated paper and board.

Egyptian *(typ)* The generic term for a group of display typefaces with heavy slab serifs and little contrast in the thickness of strokes.

eight-bit/8-bit *(com)* This refers to the allocation of eight data 'bits' to each pixel on display monitors or digital images, producing a display or image of 256 greys or colours. → *bit*

eighteenmo/18mo *(gen)* A traditional 36-page section comprising 18 folded pages. Also called 'octodecimo'.

eight sheet *(gen)* A standard poster format – 153 x 203cm (60 x 80in).

Ekta Space PS 5, J. Holmes *(pho)* A freely downloadable archive-quality working space designed to cover just the colour gamut of Ektachrome transparency film, ensuring little or no colour is clipped during transformation from the input space.

electric etching *(pri)* An alternative to acid, this method uses electricity to remove the unwanted areas of a copper plate.
→ *etch; etching*

electrographic printing/electrography *(pri)* → *dielectric printing*

electronic commerce *(int)* → *e-commerce*

electronic design *(gen)* Any design activity that takes place with the aid of electronic devices, such as computers. Also known as 'e-design'. → *CAD*

electronic engraving machine *(pri)* A method of making a line and tone printing plate without photographic processing or chemical etching. An electronically controlled stylus cuts or burns away the unwanted surface.

electronic imaging *(pre)* A system of manipulating, retouching and assembling scanned, digital images prior to output as film.

electronic mail *(int)* → *e-mail*

electronic publishing *(gen)* → *desktop publishing (DTP)*

electroplating *(pri)* A method of applying a thin metal coating to a different metal surface, such as a gravure cylinder.

Most applications have an **Edit menu** with similar options

An example of an **Egyptian** typeface

EDIT MENU

electrostatic copying *(pri)* A method of copying an image using an electrically charged, photo-sensitive drum or plate that temporarily retains the original image before transferring it to paper using an imaging agent ('toner'). → *electrostatic printing*

electrostatic printing *(pri)* A method of 'inkless printing' using an electrically charged, photo-sensitive drum or plate that temporarily retains the original image before transferring it to paper using an imaging agent ('toner'). Typically used for large-format printing.

electro(type) *(pri)* A method of making a duplicate of a letterpress plate by pressing a mould into its surface, and then by electrochemical plating, applying a shell of copper to the mould. The mould is then removed and tin plated on the back, before being filled with a backing, such as molten lead or liquid plastic.

element (1) *(com)* Any object in a drawing application such as text, a shape or an image.

element (2) *(int)* The items comprising a webpage – for example, text, graphics and animations.

elephant face *(typ)* A bold, fat typeface.

elephant folio *(pap)* A traditional book size, approximately 14 x 23 inches.

elephant hide *(fin)* A durable binding material made from fabricated parchment.

elevation *(gen)* The drawn vertical projection of an object, typically front, side or end.

ELF *(com)* abb.: extremely low frequency; → *extremely low frequency (ELF); radiation shield/screen*

elhi books *(gen)* Acronym for Elementary and High school books. A term used by the US educational book trade.

ellipse *(gen)* An oval shape that corresponds to the oblique view of a circular plane.

Ellipse/Oval tool *(com)* In graphics applications, particularly those used for painting, drawing and page make-up, a tool that enables you to draw ellipses and circles. → *ellipse*

ellipsis (1) *(typ)* A sequence of three dots (...) used within text to indicate a pause, or that part of a phrase or sentence has been left out. An ellipsis can be generated by a single keystroke combination. → *ellipsis (2)*

ellipsis (2) *(com)* In menus and dialog boxes, three dots following a command and indicating that additional information is required before the command can be carried out. → *ellipsis (1)*

elliptical dot (screen) *(pre)* A halftone screen in which the dots are elliptical in shape, these being less prone to 'dot gain' whilst at the same time providing a greater range of midtones. → *dot gain; dot shape*

em *(typ)* Traditionally, the width occupied by a capital M, which, usually being a square, gave rise to a linear measurement equal to the point size of the type being set; thus a 9-point em is 9 points wide. A 12-point em is generally called a pica, or pica em, and measures 4.22mm (0.166in). Half an em is called an en. → *en; pica*

e-mail *(int)* Acronym for electronic mail. Messages sent from your computer to someone else with a computer, either locally (through a network) or transmitted over the Internet. This is usually done via a remote computer ('server'), which stores messages in the recipient's 'mailbox' until they are collected. → *Internet; MIME; server; spam/spamming*

embedded program *(int)* A command or link written within text or lines of code on webpages. → *World Wide Web*

embedded style sheet *(int)* A collection of instructions in a digital file (usually HTML) defining fonts, colours and layout, which overrides the default settings when displayed on a different computer. → *style sheet*

E

EM QUAD

emblem book *(gen)* A type of book, revived in the 16th century, that first appeared in the medieval period and comprised a series of moral epigrams or mottos illustrated by woodcuts or engravings.

emboss(ing) *(fin)* Relief printing or stamping in which dies are used to impress a design into the surface of paper, cloth or leather so that the letters or images are raised above the surface. Also called 'waffling'. → *die (1)*

embossed binding *(fin)* Traditional book binding of leather or cloth where an image was impressed using a heated die (and counter die) with the image in relief. Added gilding and lettering were added later.

embossed finish *(pap)* A type of paper on which a textured surface has been applied during manufacture.

embossing cylinder *(pap)* A roller on a papermaking machine that has an etched or milled surface texture, which is used to produce embossed finish paper.
→ *embossed finish*

embossing plate *(pap)* An intaglio plate with a surface texture that is used to emboss a sheet of paper. → *embossed finish*

embroidered binding *(fin)* An intricate needlework design usually worked in coloured silks or gold thread on a canvas, silk or velvet surface. Popular in the 16th and 17th centuries, they were sometimes adorned with pearls, sequins and with clasps made from precious metal.

em dash/rule *(typ)* A dash the width of an em (—), the actual width depending on the size of type being set. → *dash; em; en dash/rule; hyphen*

emerald *(typ)* A traditional size of type of about 6.5 point, between the nonpareil and the minion, and also known as a 'minionette'.
→ *minion, nonpareil*

Mac OS emulating RISC OS (with which it has some similarities)

em quad *(typ)* An em space, which is the size of a square of the type size being set. Traditionally called a 'mutt' or 'mutton'.
→ *em; quad (2)*

em space *(typ)* A space the width of the point size of the type being set. → *em; quad (2)*

emulation *(com)* To simulate otherwise incompatible software or hardware in order to make it compatible – running Microsoft Windows on a Macintosh computer, for example.

emulsion *(pho)* The light-sensitive coating of a photographic material, which, when exposed and processed, reveals the image.

emulsion side *(pre)* The side of the substrate of a photographic film on which the light-sensitive emulsion resides, identifiable as the matte side of the film. When, in photomechanical reproduction (duplicating film, for example), the emulsion side of one piece of film is placed in direct contact with the emulsion side of another (or a plate when printing down), a sharp image is guaranteed. Normally, the emulsion on positive film is on the back of the film ('emulsion down'), whilst on negative film it is on the front ('emulsion up'). → *right reading; wrong reading*

EM SPACE

emulsion speed *(pho)* A rating given to photographic film so that an exposure can be calculated; also called 'film speed'. The slower the speed, the finer the emulsion, thus the better the quality of the photographic image. The trade-off is that the slower the speed, the more light that is required to expose the image. Film speed is defined by ASA or DIN standards. ➔ *ASA; Deutsche Industrie-Norm (DIN)*

en *(typ)* Half an em. ➔ *em*

enamel *(pap)* A coating that provides a glossy surface to paper.

encapsulated PostScript (EPS) *(com)* A standard graphics file format used primarily for storing 'object-orientated', or 'vector', graphics files generated by 'drawing' applications such as Adobe Illustrator and Macromedia FreeHand. An EPS file usually has two parts: one containing the PostScript code that tells the printer how to print the image, the other an on-screen preview which can be in PICT, TIFF or JPEG formats. Although used mainly for storing vector-based graphics, the EPS format is sometimes used to store bitmapped images, particularly those used for desktop colour separation ('DCS'). These EPS files are encoded as either 'ASCII' – a text-based description of an image – or 'binary', which uses numbers rather than text to store data. Bitmapped EPS files to be printed from a Windows-based system use ASCII encoding, whereas those to be printed on the Mac OS are usually saved with binary encoding.

encode (1) *(com)* The conversion of data to a machine-readable form.

encode (2) *(aud)* The process of exporting video to a particular format, usually involving some form of compression.

encryption *(com)* Complex algorithms that scramble data in order to protect information from unauthorized access. Encrypted files usually require a password, 'key' or code to 'unlock' the data. ➔ *decryption*

encyclopedia *(gen)* A reference book, with the entries usually in alphabetical order, which summarizes human knowledge, sometimes of a specific subject. The Roman writer Pliny (AD 23–79) compiled one of the earliest examples. ➔ *glossary (1)*

end a break *(typ)* In traditional typesetting, the instruction to a compositor to fill out the last line of a paragraph with quad spaces. ➔ *full out*

en dash/rule *(typ)* A dash half the width of an em (–), the actual width depending on the size of type being set. ➔ *dash; em dash/ rule; hyphen*

end cap *(com)* In drawing applications, the method in which the end of a line is rendered. In 3D applications, it refers to the closing of an open end left by a lathe, sweep or extrude operation. ➔ *mitred/ mitre (2)*

end even *(typ)* An instruction to end a paragraph or section of copy with a full line of text.

end-leaves/leaf *(fin)* ➔ *endpapers*

end/back matter *(gen)* The final pages of a book, following the main body, usually containing glossary and index. Also known as 'back matter', 'end matter', 'postlims', 'endlims', or 'subsidiaries'. ➔ *prelims/ preliminary pages*

Here straight and rounded **end caps** have been selected using Adobe Illustrator

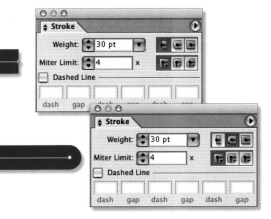

end-of-line decisions *(typ)* The capability of an application to make decisions about word hyphenation when justifying lines of text. ➔ *hyphenation and justification (H&Js/H/Js)*

endoscope *(pho)* A device for photographing normally inaccessible places, such as internal organs of the body.

endpapers *(fin)* Lining paper at each end of a book. Endpapers are attached to the inner sides of the boards and to the first and last page of the book block, helping to secure the book to its case. Also called 'lining papers'. ➔ *book block*

end time *(com)* The point at which an animation playback ends.

engine-sized *(pap)* A process of sizing paper to make it more impervious to ink and moisture. A rosin or starch is added to the pulp during the papermaking process. ➔ *rosin*

English *(typ)* A traditional size of type of about 14 point, used with reference to any font, even if it were a foreign language font ('English Greek', for example). Before 1800, all black-letter typefaces were also referred to as 'English', so a 14-point black-letter type would have been described as 'English-English'. ➔ *black letter*

English finish *(pap)* A book paper that has been 'super-calendered' to achieve a very smooth finish.

engraved face *(typ)* A typeface characterized by a pattern of lines or cross-hatching.

engraving (1) *(pri)* A block or plate made from wood or metal into which a design or lettering has been cut, engraved or etched. ➔ *intaglio*

engraving (2) *(pri)* A print taken from an engraved plate or block. ➔ *intaglio*

Enhanced Music CD *(com)* Also known as CD Extra (formerly 'CD Plus'), this is the standard for interactive CDs defined in the 'Blue Book', which specifies that the discs consist of two parts ('sessions'), the first containing pure audio tracks, the second containing data. Although the audio tracks of Enhanced Music CDs can be played on audio CD players, the data session will not be played. ➔ *Blue Book; CD-DA*

Enhanced Screen Quality font (ESQ) *(com)* Specially 'hinted' TrueType fonts for enhanced viewing on computers running Windows.

enlargement *(gen)* A reproduction that is greater than 100% of its original size. ➔ *halftone blowup*

enlarger *(pho)* A photographic device that enables the projection of a film negative (or positive) onto a sheet of paper with a light-sensitive emulsion.

en quad *(typ)* A space the size of half an em, or half the square of the type size being set. ➔ *em; em quad; quad (2)*

en space *(typ)* A space the width of half the point size of the type being set. ➔ *en*

Enter key *(com)* On keyboards, the key that confirms an entry or command or may force a carriage return. On some computer systems, the Enter key duplicates much of the function of the Return key. In some applications, it may also have a specific function. ➔ *Return key*

entrelac *(fin)* A traditional design used to decorate book covers, it comprises ribbons or interlaced strapwork derived from Islamic arabesques.

entrelac initial *(typ)* A traditional decorative initial that is incorporated into a larger design or tracery and appears at the start of a chapter. ➔ *floriated/floriated initial*

envelope *(aud)* The envelope of a sound refers to its attack (the initial stab of sound), its sustain (the main body of the sound), its decay (the gradual lowering of volume, if any) and its release (the final point at which the sound dies). Many software programs introduce various other elements into an

Endpapers help to bind a book block to the case

artificial envelope control function, but in most cases, adjusting the envelope of a sound makes it seem much less natural to the human ear.

environment map *(com)* In 3D applications, a 2D image (PICT or BMP, for example) that is reflected onto the surface of a 3D object.

Envoy *(int)* A 'portable document format' (PDF) created by Novell for the exchange of formatted documents across the Internet. ➔ *Internet; PDF*

EO *(com) abb.:* erasable optical. ➔ *CD-R/ CD-RW; erasable optical (media); magneto-optical disc (MO/MOD); WORM*

EOT *(com) abb.:* Embedded Open Type font. A font format developed by Microsoft that enables fonts to be delivered over the Web. ➔ *OpenType*

EP *(gen) abb.:* electronic publishing. ➔ *electronic publishing*

ephemeris (1) *(gen)* A diary, calendar or almanac.

ephemeris (2) *(gen)* A popular title for periodicals of the 17th and 18th centuries.

ephemeris (3) *(gen)* A star map and almanac of astronomical information.

epigraph *(gen)* A brief synopsis of content, to be found on the first page of each chapter of a book; or a brief text or quotation found within the prelims of a book.

epitome *(gen)* A condensed version of a text pared down to its essential elements, as in a compendium.

EPS *(com) abb.:* encapsulated PostScript; ➔ *ASCII; binary; DCS; encapsulated PostScript (EPS); vector*

equalisation (EQ) *(aud)* This refers to a process whereby the amplitude of certain sound frequencies is adjusted either to make it more 'realistic', or to make it stand out in or fit into a mix. It is also common for various frequencies to be enhanced when playing back songs, particularly in a club environment, so as to achieve a bass boost,

for example. A graphic equaliser allows adjustment of a limited number of frequencies, while a parametric equaliser allows adjustment of any frequencies in the sound as well as its bandwidth.

equalize/equalization *(com)* The process of digitally enhancing an image by increasing its tonal range.

equivalent weight *(pap)* Papers of the same weight per unit of measurement – gsm (grammes per square metre) – regardless of their sheet size. ➔ *paper substance*

erasable optical (media) *(com)* Storage media that can be written to as well as read from, commonly referred to as either 'WORM' (write once read many) or 'CD-RW' (compact disc-rewritable) media. ➔ *CD-R/CD-RW*

erase *(com)* An option in some dialog boxes to erase the selected disk, thus deleting everything on it.

ergonomics *(gen)* A design science that studies the efficiency and comfortable interaction between the human form and its working environment, sometimes referred to as 'human engineering'.

An **environment map** reflected in a 3D sphere

An image before (top) and after (bottom) **equalization**

*!?

erratum/errata (slip) *(gen)* A list in a publication that corrects errors in the text or illustrations. This may be printed in the publication itself or inserted into it as an 'errata slip' after the publication is printed.
→ *corrigendum/corrigenda*

error-checking *(com)* A means of ensuring the integrity of data. This can occur either when the data is input – via a keyboard, for example (a spellchecker is a type of error-check) – or when it is transmitted via a device such as a modem.

error code *(com)* A number that sometimes accompanies error messages to give some indication of the nature of the problem.
→ *error message*

error correction (protocol) *(com)* A method of checking the integrity of data transmission (usually by modem). A 'parity' error check is a typical method, in which seven bits of data are transmitted, followed by an eighth that indicates whether the sum of the previous seven is either odd or even. If a discrepancy occurs, the data will be retransmitted.

error diffusion *(com)* In digital scanning, the enhancement of an image by averaging the difference between adjacent pixels. In graphics applications, this technique is more commonly referred to as 'anti-aliasing', which, in turn, uses a technique known as 'interpolation'. → *anti-aliasing; interpolate/interpolation; resample*

error message *(com)* A message box that automatically appears if you have attempted to do something that your computer or an application won't permit or cannot do, or, at worst, if your computer crashes.
→ *error code*

ES *(pap)* abb.: engine-sized. → *engine-sized*

Esc(ape) key *(com)* A keyboard key, the function of which depends on the operating system or application you are using, but generally used to cancel something you are doing.

esparto *(pap)* A paper made from a variety of soft-fibred long grass (esparto) found in Spain and North Africa.

ESQ *(com)* abb.: Enhanced Screen Quality.
→ *Enhanced Screen Quality font (ESQ)*

establishing shot *(com)* A scene from an animation or film/video sequence showing the wider environment in which the action is about to take place. For example, the shot of an entire room before zooming in to a detail, such as the remains of an unfinished meal.

et al *(gen)* A Latin phrase *et alii*, meaning 'and others'.

etch *(pre)* To dissolve away an area of printing plate to produce either a relief image or intaglio image (depending on the printing method) or, on film, to reduce the size of halftone dots. The term is also used to describe the process of desensitizing the non-image areas on a litho plate (which are protected by a 'ground') to make them receptive to water instead of ink.
→ *desensitize*

etching *(pri)* A type of fine art print taken from etched plates. → *etch*

etch proof *(pre)* → *repro (2)*

E-text *(int)* A 'text-only' file transmitted via the Internet.

Ethernet *(com)* A hardware connection standard used on local area networks (LAN), which offers fast data transfer.
→ *LAN; network*

Etruscan binding *(fin)* A method of decorating calf skin bindings in the style of ancient Etruscan vases.

An **Ethernet** cable

ERRATUM/ERRATA (SLIP)

et seq (gen) abb.: et sequens. Latin phrase for 'and the following', referring to the following pages.

eucalyptus fibre (pap) An ingredient in papermaking taken from the eucalyptus tree. It has largely replaced esparto (a type of grass). → *esparto*

even folios (gen) Left-hand pages (verso) that are numbered evenly: 2, 4, 6, etc.

even pages (gen) The left-hand pages in a publication – usually those with even numbers.

even s. caps/even smalls (typ) Text set as small capitals without an initial full capital at the beginning of the word or sentence. → *caps and smalls; small capitals/caps*

event (com) Anything that a computer may need to respond to, such as a mouse click or a disk insertion.

event-driven (com) Description of an application in which responses are based on events generated by the user. → *event*

event-handling mechanism (com) A facility, built into the operating system software, that allows other software programs to respond to circumstances or commands as they occur. → *operating system*

Different applications handle their **exception dictionaries** in different ways. InDesign CS integrates it with the spelling dictionary.

even working (pri) A work printed in any number of sections of equal size, such as 16, 32 or 48 pages.

excelsior (typ) A traditional size of type of about 4 points, or half the size of 'brevier' (8 points). → *brevier*

exception dictionary (com) In an application's hyphenation or spell-checking dictionary, a list of user-defined words or word breaks that are exceptions to the default settings. → *auxiliary dictionary; dictionary*

excerpt (gen) An extract of text reproduced from a published work.

existing light (pho) Alternative name for available light; the term describes all natural and environmental light sources (those not specifically for the purpose of photography).

ex libris (gen) A Latin phrase meaning 'among the books of', which, printed on a bookplate (a panel pasted into the front of a book) and followed by a person's name, indicates ownership of the book.

exotic (typ) A traditional term used to describe a typeface with characters of a language not based on Roman letterforms – Hebrew or Arabic, for example. → *latin (1)*

expandable cloth (fin) A type of flexible cloth used in bookbinding.

expanded/extended type (typ) Any typeface design with a flattened, stretched out appearance, usually specifically designed to retain the correct relative proportions, or 'stress', between the horizontal and vertical strokes, thus avoiding the anomalies that occur as the result of type distortion features of a computer application ('horizontal scaling'). → *condensed*

expansion card/board (com) A circuit board added to a computer, which allows you to extend its capabilities – an accelerator card, for example. → *circuit board*

Dictionary

Target: User Dictionary   Done
Language: English: UK
Dictionary List: Added Words
Word: con~~ver~~sa~~tion.   Hyphenate
Add
Remove

*!?

E

expansion slot *(com)* The place in a computer where additional circuit boards can be plugged in. → *circuit board; expansion card/board*

expediting changes *(gen)* → *rush changes*

expertosis *(gen)* An appropriate term, coined in previous editions of *The Macintosh Bible* (Peachpit Press), which describes the prevalent phenomenon of the inability of some experts to understand the needs and limitations of people who are not themselves expert.

expert set *(typ)* A font that contains additional characters to the standard set of typefaces, providing such things as ligatures, small caps, ornaments, true fractions and swash characters.

expert system *(gen)* → *artificial intelligence (AI)*

explicit *(gen)* Derived from the Latin *explitus ex liber*, meaning 'it is unrolled to the end', and referring to an inscription at the end of a manuscript roll – usually a repeat of the title, place or date of publication. When applied to a book, it is often the printer's name.

exploded view *(gen)* An illustration of an object displaying its component parts separately – as though it were exploded – but arranged in such a way as to indicate their relationships within the whole object when assembled. → *ghosting (2)*

Explorer *(int)* A cross-platform Web browser produced by Microsoft. → *browser (1)/ Web browser; Netscape*

export *(com)* A feature provided by many applications to allow you to save a file in an appropriate format so that it can be used by another application or in a different operating system. For example, an illustration created in a drawing application may be exported as an EPS file so that it can be used in a page-layout application. → *import; import/export filter*

exposure *(pho)* The amount of light that is permitted to reach a photo-sensitive material, such as photographic film, so that an image is recorded. This is usually a combination of the length of time and the intensity at which the light shines upon the material.

exposure latitude *(pho)* A range of exposure settings appropriate for a given photographic film.

exposure metre *(pho)* A device, used in photography to calculate the correct exposure, which measures the light generated by, reflected off, or falling on, a subject. Also called a 'light metre'.

exposure setting *(pho)* On a camera, the combination of shutter speed and amount of aperture (lens opening).

expressed folio *(gen)* → *blind folio*

expurgated edition *(gen)* A book that has been edited to remove matter that is considered to be offensive.

extended character set *(typ)* The characters available in a font other than those that appear on the keyboard, such as accents, symbols, etc., and which are accessed by combinations of key strokes. → *character set*

extended data output (EDO) *(com)* A RAM chip with fast access time. → *RAM*

Extensible Markup Language (XML) *(int)* An evolution of HTML (the underlying language used on webpages), offering more sophisticated and rigorous control. XML allows the creation of user-defined tags, which expands the amount of information that can be provided about the data held in documents. → *Extensible Style Language (XSL)*

Extensible Music Format (XMF) *(aud)* A music-specific evolution of XML (Extensible Markup Language), XMF is a metadata file type and contains MIDI files, rich media files, samples and so on. → *Extensible Markup Language (XML)*

An **exploded view** shows how individual components fit together

expanded type

Helvetica shown as **expanded type**

Name	Version	Developer	Get Info String
ServerPrefs.framework	10.2.3	Apple	High Level AppleFileServer Framework
SetupAssistant.framework	1.3.0	Apple	Copyright Apple Computer, Inc. 2002
SetupAssistantIA.framework	10.3.0	Apple	Copyright Apple Computer, Inc. 2002
SetupAssistantSupport.framework	10.3.0	Apple	Copyright Apple Computer, Inc. 2001
SherlockCore.framework	1.1	Apple	Sherlock Core Framework
SoftwareUpdate.framework	1.6	Apple	Software Update ...ple Computer Inc.
SpeechDictionary.framework	3.2	Apple	Not Available
SpeechObjects.framework	1.2	Apple	Implements NSSp...cognition classes.
SPSupport.framework	4.0.2	Apple	SPSupport framework 0.0.1d1
StuffIt.framework	StuffIt	Third ...veloper	StuffItFramework,..., Aladdin Systems
SyncConduit.framework	1.4	Apple	© 2002-2003 Apple
SyncEngine.framework	1.2	Apple	© 2002-2003 Apple
SyncServices.framework	1.2	Apple	© 2002-2003 Apple
System.framework	7.0	Apple	Not Available
SystemConfiguration.framework	1.7.1	Apple	Not Available
SystemUIPlugin.framework	1.1	Apple	SystemUIPlugin v...ple Computer, Inc.

Contextual Menu
Fonts
Frameworks
Kernel Extensions
Preference Files
Preference Panes
Services
Screen Saver

Hide Detail   Number of Items: 144   Number Enabled: 144   Number Disabled: 0

Detail Information

Name: StuffIt.framework
Kind: Document
Size: 295.7 K
Project Name: Aladdin_StuffItExpander
Source Version: 7040000

Version: StuffIt
Build Version: 33
Release Status:
Created: Fri, Oct 4, 2002, 1:23 am
Modified: Tue, Feb 24, 2004, 10:26

Where: /Library/Frameworks/StuffIt.framework

Reveal in Finder

X Overload is an **extension manager**

Extensible Style Language (XSL) *(int)* A style sheet similar to the CSS (cascading style sheets) used for HTML. With XML, content and presentation are separate; with XSL, tags indicate how content should be displayed. An XML document has to be formatted before it can be read, and the formatting is usually accomplished with XSL style sheets. Style sheets consist of formatting rules for how particular XML tags affect the display of a document on a computer screen or a printed page. → *Extensible Markup Language (XML)*

extension (1) *(com)* A file that adds functions to a computer or application. Operating system extensions include such items as hardware 'drivers', which control devices like printers and monitors, whereas application extensions (usually called 'plug-ins') can include any kind of enhancement, from mundane file-handling operations (such as importing and exporting documents) to more exciting special effects. → *driver/ device driver; plug-in*

extension (2) *(pho)* A tube attached to a camera to increase magnification of the subject.

extension cover *(fin)* A paperback cover that extends beyond the trimmed page size.

extension/init conflict *(com)* A problem caused by some extensions being incompatible with other extensions, system files, or applications, and which may cause your computer to crash or behave erratically. There are several utilities available that test and resolve extension problems. → *extension (1); extension/init manager; init*

extension/init manager *(com)* Utility software that enables you to manage extensions – for example, to turn off the ones you don't need (extensions use up memory) – or to test them for incompatibilities. → *extension (1); init*

extension rings *(pho)* An adapter that fits into an SLR between the sensor and the lens, allowing focusing on closer objects.

external command (XCMD) *(com)* Specially written extensions to the scripting language of certain authoring applications, enabling the program to perform specialized commands. → *external function (XFCN)*

external device *(com)* Any item of hardware that is connected to a computer but resides externally – a disk drive, for example, may reside internally or externally. → *device (1); peripheral device*

external (disk) drive *(com)* Any disk drive connected to a computer that does not reside inside the computer's case. → *external device*

external function (XFCN) *(com)* Specially written extensions to the scripting language of certain authoring applications, enabling the program to perform specialized functions. → *external command (XCMD)*

external reference *(com)* A resource that resides in a location outside of the application using it. → *resource (1)*

E

extra bound *(fin)* A handbound book characterized by lavish tooling and superior finishing details and construction.

extra calf *(fin)* An extra bound book with finest calf rather than morocco covering. → *extra bound; morocco*

extra cloth *(fin)* A coloured material with a plain finish used for bookbinding.

Extract *(com)* A process in many image-editing applications whereby a selected part of an image is removed from areas round it. Typically, a subject is 'extracted' from the background.

extracts *(gen)* Quotations found within a text, from another work, and which are usually indented or set in a smaller font, or both.

extranet *(int)* The part of an organization's internal computer network or intranet that is available to outside users – for example, information services for customers.
→ *intranet*

extrapolate *(com)* Creating new values for a parameter based on the values that have gone before.

extremely low frequency (ELF) *(com)* The electromagnetic radiation generated by certain types of electrical current, which some research indicates may be potentially carcinogenic (cancer-causing) in the event of sustained exposure. Computer monitors, particularly CRT models, emit ELF radiation in various quantities, depending on factors such as size, although modern monitors filter out the radiation. The sides and back of a monitor emit greater amounts of radiation than the screen. VLF (very low frequency) radiation is also emitted, but is easier to filter and considered to be less harmful than ELF.

extrude *(com)* The process of duplicating the cross-section of a 2D object, placing it in a 3D space at a distance from the original and creating a surface that joins the two together. For example, two circles that become a tube.

extruders *(typ)* A typographic term used to describe ascenders and descenders.
→ *ascender; descender*

Eyedropper tool *(com)* A tool used to sample colour values from a clip or image so that it can be duplicated and used in another operation.

eye point *(com)* In a 3D world, the position of the viewer relative to the view.

A selection of **Eyedropper** tools

Selecting edges with an **Extract** tool

Fabriano *(pap)* A handmade paper named after the home of Italy's earliest papermill (13th century).

face *(typ)* Traditionally, the printing surface of any metal type character, but nowadays used as a series or family name for fonts with similar characteristics, such as 'modern face' or 'old face'. ➜ *font; typeface*

face material *(pap)* Any material suitable for use as pressure-sensitive transfers or decals.

face out/fade out blue *(pre)* ➜ *dropout blue/colour*

facet edge *(pri)* The impression left on a sheet of paper by the edge of a printing plate such as an engraved plate. Also called a 'plate mark'.

facsimile *(gen)* ➜ *fax*

facsimile edition *(gen)* The re-publishing of an out-of-print book, where each page is photographically copied from the original, with no new material.

facsimile halftone *(pre)* The removal of the dots from the highlight areas of a halftone to obtain a more natural reproduction of pencil or crayon drawings. Synonymous with 'highlight halftone'. ➜ *highlight halftone; specular highlight*

factory settings *(com)* ➜ *default*

factotum *(typ)* A traditional type ornament that provides a space to contain any capital letter, normally an initial cap at the beginning of a chapter.

fade *(com)* A common transition. In a fade-in, the image starts at black and increases in colour until it reaches regular levels. In a fade-out, the image gets darker until it fades to black.

fadeback *(pre)* ➜ *ghosting (1)*

fade out blue *(pre)* ➜ *dropout blue/colour*

fader *(aud)* A slider or knob control on a mixer that adjusts the sound level of a given track, or the entire mix. A 'flying fader' on a hardware mixer is a motorized slider control whose levels can be recalled later on, and it will reset itself. This is a standard feature on all virtual mixer software.

fall off *(com)* In a 3D environment, the degree to which light loses intensity away from its source.

false bands *(fin)* A method of simulating a flexibly sewn book by padding out a hollow backed book with strips of leather or card.

false double *(gen)* ➜ *double-(page) spread*

false duotone *(pre)* ➜ *duplex halftone*

family *(typ)* A series type design such as Goudy Old Style, Goudy Catalogue, Goudy Handtooled, etc., with all the variations of weight (light, roman, bold, etc.) and their italic styles, as distinct from a typeface or font, which describes each single variation. ➜ *font; typeface*

Myriad Pro Light Condensed
Myriad Pro Light Condensed Italic
Myriad Pro Condensed
Myriad Pro Condensed Italic
Myriad Pro Semibold Condensed
Myriad Pro Semibold Condensed Italic
Myriad Pro Bold Condensed
Myriad Pro Bold Condensed Italic
Myriad Pro Black Condensed
Myriad Pro Black Condensed Italic
Myriad Pro Light
Myriad Pro Light Italic
Myriad Pro
Myriad Pro Italic
Myriad Pro Semibold
Myriad Pro Semibold Italic
Myriad Pro Bold
Myriad Pro Bold Italic
Myriad Pro Black
Myriad Pro Black Italic

The Myriad Pro font
family

fan binding *(fin)* A superior style of decorative binding made in France and Italy in the latter part of the 17th century. It featured an intricately tooled fan motif with four quarter fans repeated at the corners.

F and Cs/F/Cs *(fin)* → *folded and collated/gathered (F/Cs, F&Cs, F/Gs, F&Gs)*

F and Gs/F/Gs *(fin)* → *folded and collated/gathered (F/Cs, F&Cs, F/Gs, F&Gs)*

fanfare *(fin)* A style of decorative cover with a design featuring a complex pattern of interlaced ribbons with foliage and flora, which borders a central compartment. The name derives from a book, *Les Fanfares et Corveés Abbadesques des Roule-Bontemps*, published in the early 17th century.

fan fold *(fin)* → *accordion/concertina fold*

FAQs *(com) abb.:* frequently asked questions. A list, often posted on webpages or in promotional literature, of answers to the most commonly asked questions by purchasers of software or hardware, or users of Internet services.

fart box *(typ)* → *text retrieval terminal*

fascicule *(gen)* A single, incomplete edition of a publication issued in instalments, such as a 'partwork'. → *partwork*

fashion board *(pap)* Board lined with cartridge, used for preparing artwork.

fast emulsion/film *(pho)* → *emulsion speed*

FAT *(com) abb.:* file allocation table. → *file allocation table (FAT)*

fat face *(typ)* Any type design with extreme contrast in the widths of thin and thick strokes, such as 'Poster Bodoni'.

fat matter *(typ)* A traditional term for typeset copy that is easy to set because it includes a large degree of spacing. Dense – thus difficult – copy is known as 'lean matter'.

Favorite *(int)* A feature of Microsoft's 'Internet Explorer' Web browser that remembers frequently visited websites. The equivalent in Netscape's 'Navigator' is called 'Bookmarks'. → *Web browser*

fax *(gen)* Acronym for 'facsimile'. The electronic transmission of copy from one location to another using regular telephone lines. Fax cards and modems can be connected to your computer to enable you to send and receive faxes direct, without the need for a separate fax machine.

FDHD *(com) abb.:* floppy disk high density. → *floppy disk*

feather(ing) *(gen)* The gradual fading away of the edge of an image or part of an image to blend with the background. Feathering tools are a feature of image-editing and painting applications. → *vignette*

featherweight paper *(pap)* A type of paper with a rough surface but tremendous bulk. One hundred sheets of 100gsm provide a bulk of 23mm.

fecit *(gen)* Latin for 'he has made it', an inscription on an engraving or drawing that is sometimes added to the artist's name.

feet *(typ)* The area at the base of a piece of metal type.

feet/foot margin *(gen)* The white space at the bottom of a page, between the main body and page trim.

feint ruling *(pri)* Thin lines that act as a writing guide, typically on the pages of account books and school exercise books, ruled by a special machine.

felt finish *(pap)* A finish applied during papermaking as the sheet is dried on a special felt.

felting *(pap)* On a moving wire of a fourdrinier, the process of binding the fibres of pulp together.

fat

Poster Bodoni is a **fat face** font

The edge of this map demonstrates **feathering**

felts *(pap)* The material, usually cotton or coarse woven wool, that is used to couch wet waterleaf paper (unsized paper). → *couch; waterleaf*

felt side *(pap)* The side of a sheet of paper facing away from the wire mesh during papermaking. Also called 'top side' or 'right side'. → *wire side*

ferrotype *(pho)* A photographic print made on a thin metal plate.

festoon *(pap)* A method of storing rolls of paper prior to splicing on a web press. It also has the effect of stretching the paper and removing the curl from the roll.

fibre *(pap)* The raw material (usually wood) used for making the pulp for paper.

fibre cut *(pap)* A defect that occurs during the papermaking process, caused when a bundle of fibres catches as it travels through the calender, resulting in a short, straight slice in the web.

fibre optic cable *(com)* A conduit used for high-speed data transmission. Made of glass or plastic fibres, it carries data transmitted as pulses of light.

fibre puffing *(pap)* The degrading or roughening of the surface of a coated paper, which can occur during heatset drying.

field *(com)* In documents and dialog boxes, the term generally describing any self-contained area into which data is entered. In some applications such as databases and spreadsheets, a field is generally interactive with another field in the same (or another) record, or the same field in another record. → *database; DIF; spreadsheet*

field camera *(pho)* Traditional folding design of a view camera that is sufficiently portable for carrying on location.

field curvature *(pho)* A lens aberration in which the plane of sharpest focus is curved rather than the flat surface needed at the film plane.

figure (1) *(typ)* A number, as distinct from a letter.

figure (2) *(gen)* The traditional description of an illustration on a page of text. → *plate (2)*

figure number *(gen)* The reference number identifying an illustration. → *figure (2)*

figure space *(com)* In some applications, a space equivalent to the width of a '0' in a given font.

file *(com)* A collection of data that is stored as an individual item on a disk or hard drive. A file can be a document, folder, application or resource. → *file format*

file allocation table (FAT) *(com)* A method used by computer operating systems to keep track of files stored on a hard disk. → *file tag*

file compression *(com)* A technique of consolidating data within a file so that it occupies less space and is faster to transmit over telecommunication lines. → *compression (1)*

file corruption *(com)* → *file recovery*

file dependency *(com)* A file that depends upon the contents of another in order to function. → *file*

F

file extension *(com)* The abbreviated suffix at the end of a filename that describes either its type (such as EPS or JPG) or origin (the application that created it, such as QXP for QuarkXPress files). A file extension usually comprises three letters (although Windows XP, Macintosh and UNIX systems may use more) and is separated from the filename by a full point. Extensions are compulsory and essentially automatic in Windows, but not on Apple computers, so Mac users should add them if they want their files to be recognised by PCs.

file format *(com)* The way a program arranges data that so that it can be stored or displayed on a computer. This can range from the file format used uniquely by a particular application, to those that are used by many different software programs. In order to help you work on a job that requires the use of several applications, or to work with other people who may be using different applications to yours, file formats tend to be standardized. Common file formats are TIFF and JPEG for bitmapped image files, EPS for object-oriented image files and ASCII for text files.
→ *ASCII; EPS; JPEG; TIFF/TIF*

file fragmentation *(com)* → *fragmented*

File menu *(com)* One of three standard menus appearing in the menu bar of most applications, where you invoke commands that allow you to create, open, save, print and close files. → *file*

filename *(com)* The name given to a file. In older Macintosh systems, filenames were limited to 31 characters in length, whereas Windows filenames can be up to 255 characters. Historically the safest file-naming convention is that of MS DOS, which consists of '8.3' (eight characters followed by a three-character suffix – all capitals). The suffix, or file extension, describes the file type. Windows filenames cannot contain any of the following characters: / \ | : * ? " $. When naming Macintosh files, it is best to avoid : and \ since these can interfere with some program functions.

file recovery *(com)* The process of resurrecting a file after you have deleted it or when it has become corrupted. The data comprising a file remains on a disk even if it has been deleted – only its name is in fact erased (from the invisible directory that keeps track of all the files on a disk). Until the space the data occupies is used by your computer for something else, it is sometimes possible to recover it with the aid of one of the many utilities available for this purpose. Recovering corrupted files is harder than recovering deleted ones. Although there are some applications that do this, there is no better safeguard than making very regular back-up copies of your files as you work on them.

file server *(com)* A computer that serves a network of other computers and provides central storage of files and programs.
→ *network*

file tag *(com)* Information relating to data stored on a disk, which, with the appropriate software, enables you to recover deleted files. 'File tag' should not be confused with the term 'tag', since that is the formal name for a markup language formatting command, such as that used for HTML.

The Apple Stickies
File menu

file transfer *(com)* The transmission of a file from one computer to another, either over a network or over telecommunication lines, using a modem. → *modem; network*

File Transfer Protocol (FTP) *(int)* A system for transmitting files between computers across the Internet or a network. Although Web browsers have FTP capabilities, dedicated FTP applications provide greater flexibility.

file type *(com)* In the Mac OS, the four-letter code that is assigned to every file when it is created and which identifies its kind or format, such as 'APPL' for an application, 'TEXT' for text files, and so on. Special software such as ResEdit is generally required to identify the file type. → *file*

fill *(com)* In graphics applications, the contents, such as colour, tone or pattern, applied to the inside of a closed path or shape, including type characters. → *path (2)*

fill character *(com)* The character inserted between specified tab stops in some applications. → *tab stop*

filler *(pap)* A material used to improve the opacity, brightness and printing surface of a paper. China clay, calcium carbonate and other white mineral pigments are commonly used. Filler can also be used as an economic method of increasing bulk.

Though you can use OS X's connect tool, Captain FTP is a popular **File Transfer Protocol** application

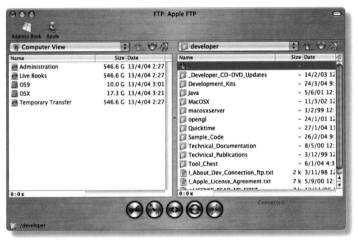

fillet (1) *(fin)* Straight lines embossed onto the cover of a book, used as decoration.

fillet (2) *(com)* In 3D software, a curved surface that is created between two adjoining or intersecting surfaces (usually NURBS), or a curved segment that joins two lines.

fill-in flash *(pho)* A technique that uses the on-camera flash or an external flash in combination with natural or ambient light to reveal detail in the scene and reduce shadows.

filling in/up *(pri)* A printing fault in which ink fills the spaces between halftone dots or the counters of type to produce undesirable small areas of solid colour. Also known as 'clogging'.

film (1) *(gen)* The term used to describe many synthetic materials, transparent or otherwise, but most often cellulose acetate. → *cel (1)*

film (2) *(pho)* A cellulose acetate base material that is coated with light-sensitive emulsion so that images can be recorded photographically. Photographic film can be colour or black and white, line or tone, negative or positive. → *cel (1); film (1)*

film assembly *(pre)* → *assembly*

film base *(pho)* A transparent substrate used as a carrier for such things as light-sensitive photographic emulsion.

film coating *(pap)* A lightweight film applied to paper. Also called 'wash coating'.

film format *(pho)* Standard measurements for sheet and roll photographic film, corresponding to usual film widths and standard camera sizes. Typical formats are 35mm, 5 x 4 inches and 10 x 8 inches.

film lamination/laminating *(fin)* A thin, protective plastic film that is bonded to a printed paper under pressure and heat. Laminates can have both a glossy or matt(e) finish.

F

FILM LAMINATION/LAMINATING

film negative *(pho)* A photographic image in which highlights and shadows are transposed. It is used in printing to make plates or film positives, and in photography to make prints.

film plane *(pho)* → *focal plane*

film positive *(pre)* A record of an image on clear film, emulating the original. Used for film assembly and for making printing plates. → *flat (1)*

filmsetting *(pre)* A term originally used to describe typesetting output onto photographic paper or film from a film matrix, when it was also called 'phototypesetting' or 'photocomposition'. Now extended to include, by virtue of the output medium being photographically based, computer typesetting produced on an imagesetter. → *typesetting*

film speed *(pho)* → *emulsion speed*

Filmstrip *(com)* A Macintosh file format created from PICT files, used, for example, to create high-speed animated buttons in multimedia presentations.

filter (1) *(pho)* A thin sheet of transparent material placed over a camera lens or light source to modify the quality or colour of the light passing through.

filter (2) *(com)* In computer software, a filter can be, strictly speaking, any component that provides the basic building blocks for processing data. However, the term is more commonly used to describe particular functions within an application, such as importing and exporting data in different file formats or for applying special effects to images. → *import/export filter*

filter (3) *(com)* → *import/export filter*

filter (4) *(pre)* The coloured glass, tinted gelatine, or cellulose acetate sheets used in conventional colour separation to absorb specific wavelengths of light so that the red, green and blue components of an original can be separated to provide the cyan, magenta, yellow and black films used in process printing.

filter factor *(pho)* The amount of compensation required for a photographic exposure if a filter is used. → *filter (3)*

final film *(pre)* The positive or negative film used to create the 'flats' from which printing plates are made, after all corrections have been made and in which the halftone dots are 'hard', as distinct from the 'soft' dots on film used for making corrections. → *flat (2); hard dot; soft dot*

final render(ing) *(com)* The final computer generation of a scene, after you've finally finished tweaking and agonizing (in low resolution). Usually involves the application of the final surface texture, lighting and effects to a 3D object, scene or animation. High-quality renders, particularly of animated scenes, require considerable computer processing power, so banks of linked computers are sometimes used to speed up the process using a technique called 'distributed rendering'. → *distributed rendering; render(ing)*

The Photoshop Elements **Filters** palette

A sky enhanced by a photographic **filter**

The

The 'e' shown here is a **finial letter** character

final size *(gen)* The size at which an image or piece of artwork will be printed.

Finder *(com)* On Macintosh computers, one of the three fundamental components (the others are the System file and the hardware ROM chips) that provides the desktop, file and disk management, and the facility to launch and use other applications.

fine etch *(pre)* A technique of adjusting the middle tones and highlights of a halftone plate after it has been 'rough etched'. → *rough etch*

fine-line copy *(pre)* Very thin lines in an original image that has been halftoned screened, and are thus difficult to reproduce.

fine rule *(gen)* A rule, traditionally of hairline thickness. In graphics applications, this can mean a rule of any thickness between 0.20–0.50 points, but it is generally defined as 0.25 points. → *hairline rule*

fine whites *(pap)* Offcuts of unprinted paper found at the papermaker, printer or bindery.

finger(ed)/fingering *(int)* A means of showing or revealing information about a user or group of users on the Internet. For example, you can finger an electronic mailbox to determine whether there are any unread messages, or a server for information about the state of the ISP's network.

finial letter *(typ)* A type character designed to be used only as the last letter in a word or line, usually incorporating some kind of decorative flourish ('swash'). → *swash characters*

finish *(pap)* The surface of a paper, usually one that is coated or embossed.

finished art(work) *(gen)* Any illustrative matter prepared specifically for reproduction. Artwork that includes or is comprised entirely of text is usually described as 'camera-ready art' or 'mechanical'. → *camera-ready copy/art (CRC); mechanical*

finished page area *(gen)* The area on a computer layout or printed sheet that will form the page after the sheet is trimmed. Once printed, the finished page area is delineated by corner marks ('trim' or 'crop' marks). → *trimmed page size (tps)/ trimmed size*

finished rough *(gen)* → *comprehensive*

finishing *(fin)* All operations that take place after printing, such as collating, folding, gathering, trimming, binding and packing.

firewall *(int)* A software security system that protects websites and networks from unauthorized access, such as unwanted junk mail.

FireWire (IEEE 1394) *(com)* A type of port connection, developed by Apple Computer and Sony, that allows for high-speed transfer of data between a computer and peripheral devices. Known officially as IEEE-1394 or, for reasons best known to themselves, as iLink by Sony, this method of transfer – quick enough for digital video – is employed by some high-resolution cameras. Like USB, it is also capable of providing power to external devices, such as portable hard drives, but FireWire, and the faster FireWire 800, can carry much more data.

firmware *(com)* Any permanent software incorporated into a hardware chip (usually a 'ROM' chip). On Macintosh computers, part of the operating system is built into a hardware ROM chip. → *ROM*

first edition *(gen)* The first time that a book is printed and published. It can also refer to additional printings from the same plates, so long as no changes have been made.

first generation copy *(gen)* A duplicate of an item, such as a photograph, made directly from the original, as distinct from a copy made from another copy of the original. → *duplicate/dupe film*

first impression *(gen)* → *first edition*

fishbone diagram *(gen)* → *cause-and-effect diagram*

F

fish-eye lens *(pho)* A camera lens with an extremely wide angle of view, producing a distorted image with an exaggerated apparent curve. → *wide-angle lens*

fist *(typ)* → *digit (2)*

fit (1) *(typ)* → *letterspacing/letterfit*

fit (2) *(pre)* The alignment and register of the ink colours of individual components on a printed page, as distinct from the register of the ink colours on an entire printed sheet. Errors of fit (described as 'out of fit') occur during film assembly, whereas errors of register occur when printing.

fix *(pho)* The process of making permanent the image on a film or paper after it has been developed. The term is also used to describe the chemical solution used in the process (fixative). → *developer*

fixed-focus lens *(pho)* A photographic lens with no variable focus adjustment. A feature of very cheap cameras.

fixed-size font *(com)* An alternative term for 'bitmapped' or 'screen' fonts – i.e. those that are designed to be viewed only on screen and not used for printing. → *bitmapped font*

fixed word spacing *(typ)* A constant space between words when text is set unjustified, as distinct from the variable spacing that is necessary to set justified text. → *justification; unjustified*

Fkey *(com)* A contraction of 'function keys'. Fkeys have nothing to do with special function keys on some keyboards ('F1', 'F2', etc.) but are the keyboard equivalents for basic functions such as copying and pasting. → *function keys; keyboard equivalent/shortcut*

fl *(gen) abb.:* floruit dates. → *floruit dates (fl)*

flag (1) *(gen)* → *masthead (2)*

flag (2) *(pri)* A tab inserted into a stack or reel of printed paper to indicate either a fault that must be examined or a change of edition.

flag (3) *(com)* Certain attributes of files, such as locked, invisible, busy, and so on.

flag (4) *(pho)* A matt black sheet placed between a lamp and a camera lens to reduce flare.

flame *(int)* Abusive messages sent via e-mail or posted to newsgroups. → *e-mail; flamewar; newsgroup; spam/spamming; troll/trolling*

flamewar *(int)* An ongoing reciprocal series of abusive newsgroup postings or e-mail messages against individuals and/or groups. → *e-mail; flame; newsgroup; spam/ spamming; troll/trolling*

flange *(aud)* Flanging is an extreme audio-phasing effect that was originally done by using the same track on two reel-to-reel tapes, and then slowing one of them down. It can be emulated digitally and all of the parameters can be set to change at predetermined intervals.

flare *(pho)* Scattered light that degrades the quality of a photographic image, usually caused by too much light being reflected. In some situations, flare can be used for beneficial effect and is even provided as a feature in some computer applications – the 'Lens Flare' filter in Adobe Photoshop, for example. → *coated lens*

A Photoshop Lens **Flare** effect

Flash (1) *(com)* Macromedia's application for creating vector graphics and animations for Web presentations. Flash generates small files, which are correspondingly quick to download and, being vector, are scalable to any dimension without an increase in the file size.

flash (2) *(pho)* A split-second, intense burst of artificially generated light used in photography to light a subject.

flash drying *(pri)* A method of drying ink on a very high-speed web press. The ink contains solvents that are burned off at the very high temperatures involved.

flat backed
binding style

Comparative
flatness

flash exposure *(pre)* In conventional halftone processing, a process of improving the tonal reproduction range of a halftone film negative by means of an additional exposure. This reinforces the dots in dark areas, which may otherwise run together and print solid. **→ main exposure**

flash synchronization *(pho)* A camera system in which the peak output from the flash unit occurs when the shutter is fully open.

flat (1) *(pre)* An assembly of composite imposed film, used to expose plates in preparation for printing. Also called 'composite film'. **→ final film**

flat (2) *(gen)* Said of any image – original or printed – which lacks sufficient colour or contrast, for whatever reason.

flat back(ed) (book) *(fin)* A binding style of either limp or cased books in which the 'rounding' is omitted, and the book thus has a square, or flat, spine. As distinct from a case binding that is rounded and backed. Also called 'square back'. **→ rounding and backing/rounded and backed**

flatbed *(pri)* A type of printing press on which the paper sheets sit on a horizontal surface, used for proofing.

flatbed cutter *(fin)* A device used for trimming the edges of books.

flatbed cylinder press *(pri)* A type of printing press on which the paper sheets are moved backwards and forwards beneath the impression cylinder.

flatbed rotary *(pri)* A type of printing press on which the paper is held on a reel ('web') but receives the impression from a flatbed plate.

flatbed scanner *(pre)* **→ desktop scanner**

flatbed web press *(pri)* **→ flatbed rotary**

flat colour *(pri)* A uniform colour of consistent hue. In printing, this usually means a specially mixed colour that is printed apart from any other colours. **→ mechanical tint; screen tint/tone**

flat copy *(pre)* Original artwork submitted for scanning. To enable superior-quality drum scanning, many 'flat copy' originals are now supplied unmounted or are created on flexible material.

flat etch *(pre)* Overall chemical reduction of the size of dots in a film halftone. **→ rough etch**

flat field noise *(com)* In a QuickTime sequence, the slight differences in areas of consecutive frames that should be identical.

flat-file database *(com)* A database application in which each file or collection of records is self-contained and cannot exchange information with another file. As distinct from a 'relational' database in which information in separate files is interchangeable. **→ database; database manager; record; relational database**

flat lighting *(pho)* Lighting that is usually low in contrast and low in shadows.

flatness *(com)* The number of straight lines or segments, in object-oriented drawing applications, which make up the curves in an image to be printed on a PostScript printer. The lower the number, the smoother the curve, although the difference between values of zero and three are barely discernible to the eye. Values higher than ten may result in visibly flattened curves, particularly when printed at low resolutions. **→ object-oriented; PostScript**

flat plan *(gen)* A diagrammatic thumbnail scheme of the pages of a publication, used to determine the distribution of colour and layouts before any design takes place. Also called a 'flow chart'.

flat proofs *(pre)* In colour printing, proofs made from each individual colour plate.

flat pull *(pre)* **→ rough proof/pull**

flat screen/panel (display) *(com)* A flat panel computer display that generates the image using technologies such as liquid crystal or gas plasma rather than using a bulky cathode ray tube (CRT).

F

flat stitching *(fin)* A method of stitching a flat backed book from the side, through all the pages. → *side-stitch/stab*

flat-tint halftone *(pre)* A halftone image printed over a flat tint of colour.

fleurons *(typ)* → *flower*

flexible binding *(fin)* A method of binding without the use of cover boards, with the back of the endpapers being pasted directly onto the cover, which may be made of leather or some other material.

flexible glue *(fin)* A type of glue that does not dry completely and is used for fixing the book block to the case.

flexible sewing *(fin)* A technique for sewing the sections of a book onto raised bands or cords. The thread is passed around each cord, providing a very strong binding that can usually be opened flat.

flexicover *(fin)* A durable cover material that strengthens a paperback book.

flexography/flexo *(pri)* A relief printing process that uses flexible rubber or plastic plates. Used mainly for printing onto various kinds of packaging, and sometimes newspapers, where it may be referred to as 'anilox' printing. → *anilox system; matrix (2)*

flex space width *(com)* In some page-layout applications, the ability to modify the width of an en space.

flicker *(com)* A vibrating image on a computer monitor, usually caused by a slow refresh rate. Also known as a 'strobe' effect. → *refresh rate*

flier *(gen)* An advertising insert loosely bound into a book.

flimsy *(gen)* A thin, translucent paper used for layouts. → *layout*

flip/flop *(gen)* The mirror-image reversal of an item from left to right (horizontal flip) or top to bottom (vertical flip). Also called 'reverse image'.

flipping *(com)* A method of texture mapping onto a 3D object that is a mirror image of the one being placed, specified across an axis of choice.

floating accents *(typ)* In metal setting, any accent that is cast separately from a type character. → *accent*

floating fleurons *(typ)* Decorative type elements used to make up panels with a pattern or border.

floating palette *(com)* A palette that is available all the time and which can be positioned anywhere on your screen by dragging its title bar.

A **flat-tint halftone**

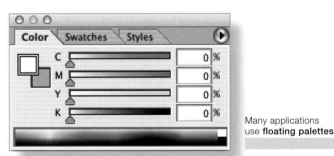

Many applications use **floating palettes**

FLAT STITCHING

The Mac OS **floppy disk** icon

floriated lettering

Type **flowers** originally decorated page borders

floating-point unit (FPU) *(com)*
→ *coprocessor*

flocculation *(pap)* A term used in papermaking when suspended particles in pulp join to form a mass.

flocking *(fin)* A method of creating a vaguely 3D texture by blowing fibres over an adhesive ink surface.

flong *(pri)* A papiermâché-like sheet used for making the moulds in which the 'stereotypes' used in rotary letterpress printing are cast. → *stereo(type)*

floppy disk *(com)* A flexible circular platter coated with a magnetic medium and housed in a plastic case, on which computer data is stored. Floppy disks are typically 3.5in diameter and may be single-sided, double-sided or high density (holding 1.4MB). Also called 'diskettes', floppy disks are becoming less viable as a storage medium and will eventually disappear, because computers are increasingly being built without floppy disk drives. → *disk drive*

floptical *(com)* A contraction of 'floppy' and 'optical'. A floptical is a 'magneto-optical' (MO) disc of the same size as a common 3.5in 'floppy' disk, but contains much more data – up to 230MB, compared with 1.4MB on a floppy. → *magneto-optical disc*

floret *(fin)* A tool used by bookbinders to impress a floral motif. → *flower*

floriated/floriated initial *(typ)* Decorative ornaments such as a border or initial letter featuring floral designs. → *blooming letters; entrelac; flower*

florin *(typ)* → *long s*

floruit dates (fl) *(gen)* A term used to indicate an approximation, when exact historical dates are not known.

flow chart (1) *(gen)* A diagrammatic representation of a process.

flow chart (2) *(gen)* → *flat plan*

flow control *(com)* A method of organizing the flow of data as it is transmitted via a modem or across a network.

flower *(typ)* Type ornaments and arabesques originally used to embellish page borders, but now encompassing any decorative font and usually called a 'dingbat'. Also known as 'fleurons' or 'florets'. → *arabesque; dingbat; ornament*

fluff(ing) *(pap)* An aberration in printing caused by the release of fibres from the surface of paper. Also known as 'fuzz' or 'linting'. → *blanket piling; picking*

flush *(typ)* → *justification; unjustified*

flush boards *(fin)* → *cut flush*

flush cover/boards *(fin)* A book cover trimmed to the same size as the pages within. Also called 'flush work' and, if the covers are 'limp' (soft), 'limp flush'.

flush left/right *(typ)* → *unjustified*

flush paragraphs *(typ)* Paragraphs in which the first word is not indented, but aligns with the left edge of the text. → *full out*

flush work *(fin)* → *flush cover/boards*

fluted board *(pap)* → *corrugated board*

flyer *(gen)* A cheaply produced printed circular, usually a single sheet, used for promotional purposes.

fly fold *(fin)* A sheet that has been folded once, making a four-page leaflet.

flying *(pri)* A spray of fine ink droplets generated by the ink rollers on a press running at a high speed. Also called 'ink fly'. → *misting*

flying paster *(pri)* The facility on a web press to replace one reel of paper with another without stopping the press. Also called 'autopaster'. → *web (1)*

fly leaf *(fin)* The portion of an endpaper which is not stuck down to the case. → *endpapers; paste-downs*

fly-title *(gen)* A subsidiary title page often separating distinct portions of a book. Also called a 'half title' page. ➔ *half title; title page*

FM screening *(pre)* abb.: frequency modulated screening; ➔ *amplitude modulated screening; frequency modulated screening (FM screening); halftone (1); stochastic screening;*

f-number/f-stop *(pho)* The calibration of the aperture size of a photographic lens. This is the ratio of the focal length ('f' = focal) to the diameter of the aperture. The numbers are marked on the equipment – for example, a camera lens normally calibrated in a standard series would include the following numbers: f1, f1.4, f2, f2.8, f4, f5.6, f8, f11, f16, f22, f32 and so on, and this sets the aperture size. The maximum amount of light that can be transmitted through a lens determines the 'speed' of a lens – a lens with a minimum aperture of, say f1, is a 'fast lens' (it lets in more light), whereas a lens with a minimum aperture of f3.5 is described as a 'slow lens'. ➔ *aperture; diaphragm*

f.o.b. *(gen)* abb.: free on board. A term indicating that the price quoted for a job does not include a delivery charge. ➔ *c.i.f.*

focal length *(pho)* The distance between the centre of a lens and its point of focus. ➔ *angle of view (2); f-number/f-stop*

focal plane *(pho)* The plane at which a camera lens forms a sharp image. Also called the 'film plane', the point at which the image is recorded.

focal plane shutter *(pho)* A camera shutter located close to the focal plane, in that two blinds form an adjustable gap that moves across the film, thus determining the exposure.

focal point *(gen)* The part of a design with the most impact, therefore the first point of contact.

focal range *(pho)* The range over which a camera or lens is able to focus on a subject (for example, 0.5m to Infinity).

FOCOLTONE *(gen)* A colour-matching system in which all of the colours can be created by printing the specified process colour percentages. ➔ *process colour*

focus *(pho)* The optical state where the light rays converge on the film or CCD to produce the sharpest possible image. Also used to describe the general degree of sharpness of a photographic image, ranging from 'in-focus' (sharp) to 'out-of-focus' (blurred).

fog (1) *(pho)* A grey tone that degrades part or all of a photographic image, whether on film or paper, caused by uncontrolled exposure of the material to light. ➔ *dichroic fog*

fog (2) *(com)* The simulated fog or haze effect generated by a 3D application.

foil (1) *(fin)* ➔ *blocking foils*

foil (2) *(pre)* Clear, stable film used as a backing for film assembly.

folded and collated/gathered (F/Cs, F&Cs, F/Gs, F&Gs) *(fin)* Sheets of a publication that, after printing, are folded, collated and then gathered in preparation for binding.

folder (1) *(com)* The pictorial representation of a directory, being a place provided by computer operating systems where you can organize your documents, applications, and other folders (when one folder is inside another, it is said to be 'nested'). Folders form the basis for the organization of all data on your computer. ➔ *directory (1)*

folder (2) *(fin)* A machine that creases and scores printed sheets during 'finishing'. ➔ *finishing*

folder bar *(com)* The bar above the scrolling list in many dialog boxes, which, when clicked, reveals a list of the folder hierarchy. ➔ *dialog/dialog box; folder (1)*

The top image is taken at a 28mm **focal length** while the lower is 85mm

Folder icons as they look on Macs and PCs

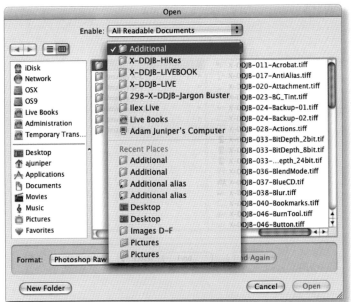

The menu springing from the **folder bar**

Fold outs are primarily used for extended diagrams or illustrations

folder/folding dummy *(fin)* A mock-up showing the sheet folded exactly as it will be in production.

fold/folding *(fin)* The folding of a single flat sheet to create a desired effect (accordion, French, gatefold, parallel, right-angle, etc.), or the folding of a printed signature/section of a multipage publication prior to gathering, stitching, trimming and binding.

folding endurance *(pap)* The number of times that a sheet can be folded before it breaks at the line of fold.

folding plate *(fin)* An oversize book illustration that has been folded so that it fits within the trim size before being bound in. → **gatefold; plate (2)**

fold marks *(gen)* Lines, usually dashed, indicating where a finished document should be folded.

fold out *(fin)* In a publication, a page that extends when unfolded to a size greater than the page size. The fold-out page must be imposed so that the fold occurs within the area of the trim size so that it is not trimmed off during finishing. Also called 'throw out' (or 'thrown out'), and 'pull out'. → **gatefold; thrown clear**

fold to paper *(fin)* Folding paper so that all edges – rather than just the printed page elements – align. Also called 'paper to paper'. → **fold to print**

fold to print *(fin)* Folding paper so that printed page elements align, regardless of the alignment of the edges of the paper. Also called 'type to type'. → **fold to paper**

foliation *(gen)* The rare practice in book publishing of numbering the leaves rather than each page, so that each alternate page is numbered consecutively. From the Latin 'foliatus', or 'leaved'. → **leaf (1)**

folio (1) *(gen)* Strictly speaking, the number of a leaf of a book when it is not numbered as two separate pages. However, a folio generally describes the number as printed on each page. → **foliation**

folio (2) *(gen)* The size of a book that is formed when each sheet containing its pages is folded only once, thus making four pages half the size of the sheet. A folio-size book generally describes any large-format book.

folio lap *(fin)* The area of excess paper that is allowed for machine-handling in the bindery. It will eventually be trimmed off.

follow copy *(gen)* An instruction to a typesetter to follow the exact spelling and punctuation of a manuscript, even if unorthodox, rather than the defined house style.

follow focus *(pho)* A camera focusing technique used when shooting a moving subject, during which the focusing ring is turned at exactly the rate necessary to maintain constant focus.

follow on *(gen)* → **run on (2)**

FON *(com)* A bitmap font format used on Windows computers.

FOND *(com)* Acronym for font family descriptor. On Macintosh computers, it refers to the log of an entire font family (all the sizes and styles of a typeface).

F

font *(typ)* Set of characters sharing the same typeface, which are stored by your computer and made available to applications where text is edited. There are two varieties of font; vector fonts like TrueType, which can be printed at any size with no loss of quality, and bitmapped fonts, which cannot be scaled.

font downloading *(com)* The process by which a font file is downloaded, or sent to a printer. A font may be available in the printer's built-in ROM chips, on its hard disk, manually downloaded into its RAM, or automatically downloaded by the printer driver when it is needed.

font embedding *(int)* The technology that allows you to specify a font on a webpage so it can be viewed by a browser running on any computer. These are not embedded in the HTML code but are special files displayed with tags similar to those used for images and objects. Netscape was the first to use this feature, called 'Dynamic Fonts', which uses Bitstream's 'TrueDoc' technology. This allows the designer to 'record' font shapes, then store them in a 'Portable Font Resource' (PFR) file, which is downloaded in the background and finally 'played back'. Internet Explorer includes 'Font Embedding', using a font format called 'OpenType', which was developed by both Microsoft and Adobe. → *OpenType; WEFT (2)*

font family *(typ)* The complete set of characters of a typeface design in all its sizes and styles. A typical font family contains four individual fonts: roman, italic, bold and bold italic. As distinct from a 'typeface' or 'font'. Also known as 'type family'. → *font; typeface*

font file *(com)* The file of a bitmapped or screen font, usually residing in a suitcase. → *bitmapped font; suitcase file*

font ID conflict *(com)* A problem that may occur on some computer systems when the identity numbers of two or more fonts are the same. It causes anomalies such as displaying or printing different fonts from the ones specified. In the early days of Macintosh computers, Apple imposed a limit of 128 identity numbers for all PostScript fonts that were installed on a Mac, which meant that there were inevitable conflicts if more than 128 fonts were installed. Nowadays there are a number of font utilities that resolve ID conflicts, and Adobe Systems Inc. maintains a register of unique font ID numbers and names for PostScript Type 1 fonts. → *FOND; Type 1 font*

font ID (number) *(com)* → *font ID conflict*

font substitution *(com)* A facility of some printers to substitute outline fonts for the basic system bitmapped fonts. On Macintosh computers, for example, Helvetica is substituted for Geneva, and Courier for Monaco.

font usage *(com)* A feature of some applications, which lists all the fonts used in a document.

foolscap *(pap)* A former standard size of printing paper measuring 13½ x 17in (343 x 432mm).

foot *(gen)* The margin at the bottom of a page or the bottom edge of a book.

footer (1) *(com)* The facility in some applications, particularly word processing programs, to automatically place text and numbers at the foot of each page.

footer (2) *(gen)* A running headline that appears at the bottom of a page, also called a 'running foot'. → *running head(ing)/ headline*

footer (3) *(int)* The concluding part of an HTML document, containing information such as the date, version, etc.

footline *(gen)* The last line of text to appear on a page, often containing the folio.

Arial Black

The Mac OS
font file icon

footnotes *(gen)* Explanatory notes printed at the foot of a page or at the end of a book.

footprint *(com)* The exact space on a surface occupied by an object or piece of hardware.

forced justification *(com)* In some page-layout applications, an option to stretch the last line of a justified text block to the full column width, regardless of the number of words or characters. → *hyphenation and justification (H&Js, H/Js)*

fore-edge *(gen)* The outer edge or margin of a book opposite to, and parallel with, the back, spine or binding edge.

fore-edge margin *(gen)* The outer margin of a page in a book or publication, sometimes called the 'outside margin'.

fore-edge painting *(fin)* The traditional decoration of the edge of a block of pages, visible only when the book is closed. It also describes the painting of the fore-edge of individual pages, which are visible only when the book is open. Also called 'painted edges'. → *sprinkled edges*

foreground *(gen)* The area or objects between the point of view and the main subject. → *foreground application*

foreground application *(com)* When working on a computer, the application that is currently active.

A typical Web **form**

foreign file *(com)* A document created in a different application or computer system to the one you are using.

foreword *(gen)* Introductory remarks about a work or its author.

form (1) *(int)* Fillable spaces (fields) on a webpage, which provide a means of collecting information and receiving feedback from people who visit the website. They are often used to buy an item, register a product, answer a questionnaire or access a database.

form (2)/forme *(pri)* One side of a printed signature, consisting of a number of imposed pages, usually in smaller or greater multiples of eight. The term derives from the 'forme' used in letterpress printing, i.e. type matter and illustration blocks 'locked up' in a 'chase' ready for printing. → *chase (1); section (2); signature (1)*

format (1) *(com)* To attribute type characteristics such as font, size, weight, tracking and leading to individual characters or words. → *style sheet*

format (2) *(com)* To attribute characteristics such as font, size, weight, tracking, leading, indents, hyphenation and justification and tabs to complete paragraphs. → *style sheet*

format (3) *(gen)* The size or orientation of a book or page or, in photography, the size of film. → *landscape format; portrait, upright format*

format (4) *(com)* → *file format*

formation *(pap)* The structure of paper, principally its fibre distribution.

formatting *(com)* The process of preparing a new disk so that it can be used with a computer for organizing and storing data. When a disk is formatted, sectors, tracks and empty directories are created. → *disk crash; initialize*

for position only (FPO) *(gen)* A term used to indicate that items positioned on a layout are of inappropriate quality for reproduction and are displayed only as a guide for positioning in lieu of the properly prepared version.

forty eight sheet *(gen)* A standard poster size: 305 x 1220cm (120 x 480in).

forum *(int)* An online service that enables users to post messages, to which other users may add or respond. These message 'threads' are usually organized around special interests, such as software user groups or popular cultural themes. → *newsgroup; UseNet*

Forward Delete key *(com)* A key, found on some keyboards, that deletes characters to the right of the text insertion point rather than to the left, as is the case with the standard Delete key.

forwarding *(fin)* In case binding, the stages in the bookmaking process after sewing but before the case is covered.

forward kinematics *(com)* Traditional animation is based on forward kinematics, where, for example, to make a character reach for an object, the upper arm is rotated first, followed by the forearm and then the hand.

forward slash *(typ)* → *slash*

foul proof *(gen)* A printed proof containing many revisions or corrections. → *dirty proof*

founder's/foundry type *(typ)* Metal characters used in hand-setting, as distinct from machine-set metal type.

foundry proof *(pri)* A letterpress proof pulled prior to sending the forme to the foundry.

fount *(typ)* An old-fashioned term for the word 'font', originating from the word 'foundry'.

fountain *(pri)* The reservoir containing either ink or dampening solution on a litho press. → *dampening fountain; ink fountain*

Original image (left) and **4-bit** version (right)

four-bit/4-bit *(com)* The allocation of four bits of memory to each pixel, giving an image or screen display of 16 greys or colours (a row of four bits can be written in 16 different combinations: 0000, 0001, 1001, 0110, etc). → *bit; eight-bit/8-bit*

four-colour process *(gen)* Any printing process that reproduces full-colour images which have been separated into the three basic 'process' colours: cyan, magenta and yellow, with the fourth colour, black, added for extra density. → *colour separation; process colour printing; three-colour (1) (process) reproduction*

fourdrinier *(pap)* A papermaking machine used to make paper in a continuous roll ('web'). Liquid pulp is drained through a moving wire, leaving a web of damp paper, which is then dried on steam-heated cylinders before further processing. → *chain lines/marks; dandy roll; laid paper; web (1)*

four-up *(fin)* The printing of four 16-page sections that are gathered, glued and covered as one unit, after which they are separated. → *two-up*

fovea *(gen)* The spot in the centre of the retina with the greatest concentration of photoreceptors, hence giving the sharpest vision.

foxed *(pap)* The deterioration of old paper, characterized by brown discolouration and spotting, usually caused by damp.

FPO *(gen)* abb.: for position only; → *for position only (FPO)*

FPS *(com)* abb.: frames per second. → *frames per second (FPS)*

FPU *(com) abb.:* floating-point unit.
→ *coprocessor*

fraction *(typ)* A type character (a 'case' or 'true' fraction), or assembly of type characters (a 'piece' or 'built' fraction), which denotes part of a whole number, such as ½. → *built fraction; case fraction*

fragment(ed) *(com)* The state of files stored on a hard disk over time when they become split into non-contiguous chunks, leaving only small areas of free space into which new data can be written. The consequence of this is that new files are divided into smaller pieces so that they will fit onto the disk: thus both the disk and the files on it are said to be 'fragmented'. The result can be a dramatic increase in the time it takes to access data, since any files being accessed may be spread over several areas of the disk. Many applications are available to 'defragment' disks by rearranging the files contiguously. → *defragment(ing); optimize/optimizing*

Fraktur *(typ)* A German black letter type.

frame (1) *(int)* On the Web, a means of displaying more than one page at a time within a single window – the window is divided into separate areas ('frames'), each

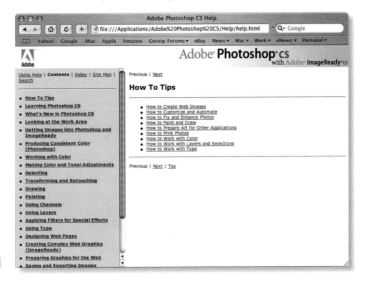

one displaying a different page. Confusingly, although a window displaying frames may contain several pages, it is nevertheless described as a singular page. A common use of frames is to display a menu that remains static while other parts of the webpage – displayed in the same window – contain information that can, for example, be 'scrolled'. → *scroll (2); World Wide Web (WWW)*

frame (2) *(aud)* A single still picture from a film or animation sequence.

frame (3) *(gen)* → *border*

frame (4) *(int)* On the Web, a means of displaying more than one page at a time within a single window. The window is divided into separate areas (frames), each one displaying a separate page.

frame (5) *(com)* An individual still image extracted from a television or video signal, comprising both interlace fields.

frame-based *(com)* Applications that require you to create text or picture boxes in a document before text or pictures can be added. QuarkXPress is an example of a frame-based application.

𝔉𝔯𝔞𝔨𝔱𝔲𝔯

The black letter type
Fraktur

A page made up of
three **frames**

frame grab(bing) *(com)* The capture of a single still frame from a video sequence.

frame rate *(aud)* Usually measured in frames per second (FPS), this is the rate or resolution at which video or animation plays. The common frame-rate for sequences used for computer display is 12–15 frames per second (FPS); in film, it is 24FPS; NTSC video, 30fps; and PAL video, 25fps. → *refresh rate*

frames per second (FPS) *(com)* The number of individual still images that are required to make each second of an animation or film sequence. → *frame (3); frame rate*

free-form deformation *(com)* In some 3D applications, a method of distorting the shape of a 3D object.

Freeform tool *(com)* In graphics applications, any tool that allows you to draw shapes 'freehand'.

freehand tool *(com)* → *Freeform tool*

free line fall *(typ)* → *unjustified*

free link *(com)* In a 3D environment, the ability of a child object to move independently of its parent while also moving when its parent moves. → *child object; parent object*

FreeMIDI and MAS *(aud)* (Mac) Two standards developed by MOTU (Mark of the Unicorn) for its Digital Performer audio production software. MAS (MOTU Audio System) allows audio routing from a soft synth into Performer's mixing environment, while FreeMIDI allows you to mix MIDI tracks from a soft synth within Performer.

free sheet (1) *(pap)* A paper that contains no groundwood, made from wood pulp treated with a caustic solution to remove impurities. → *woodfree paper*

free sheet (2) *(gen)* A newspaper that is distributed without charge to the reader. → *woodfree paper*

free space *(com)* A memory block that is available for allocation – in other words, space on a disk that is free and ready for writing data to. → *memory; block (3)*

free-standing insert (FSI) *(gen)* A self-contained item, usually in multiples of four pages, inserted into a publication such as a newspaper. → *insert (1)*

freeware *(com)* Any piece of software that is declared by its author to be available for use without charge. This differs from shareware ('try before you buy') and public domain (totally copyright-free) → *shareware*

freeze *(com)* → *bomb*

French calf *(pri)* A calfskin material used to cover 'nap' (high-quality) rollers on a litho printing machine. → *nap roller*

French dash *(typ)* → *swelled dash/rule*

French fillet *(fin)* A border comprising three lines, made up from a fine double line and a single line, used on 16th-century French bindings.

French fold *(fin)* A sheet that has been printed on one side only and then folded twice to form an uncut four-page section.

French folio *(pap)* A type of smooth, thin paper used for press make ready.

French groove *(fin)* → *French joints*

French joints *(fin)* A method of bookbinding in which the cover boards are inset a little way in from the spine and the covering material pressed into the gap that is left. It is a particularly useful technique when thick cover boards and heavy covering material are used. Also called a 'French groove', 'grooved joints' or 'sunk joints'.

French morocco *(fin)* Made from sheepskin grained to resemble genuine morocco, this is used in bookbinding as a cheaper alternative → *morocco*

French rule *(gen)* An ornamental rule with a diamond shape at its centre.

The **Freeform tool** is tucked behind the Pen tool in Photoshop CS

French sewing/stitch *(fin)* As well as describing the standard method of machine sewing, 'French stitch' is also a method of binding a ready-bound item into another publication.

French shell *(pap)* A type of marbled paper used in 18th-century France. ➔ *marbling*

frequency *(aud)* Measured in Hz or kHz, it refers to the number of complete sound waves – or cycles – that pass a certain point during one second; the higher the frequency, the higher the pitch. The frequency spectrum refers to all possible sounds, and the audible frequency spectrum is from about 20 Hz to about 20 kHz (20,000 Hz), although this can vary somewhat from person to person.

frequency modulated screening (FM screening) *(pre)* A method of screening an image for reproduction, which uses a random pattern of dots to reproduce a continuous tone image. Also known as 'stochastic screening'.

frequently asked questions (FAQs) *(com)* A method of delivering technical support to users of software, hardware and the Internet – and, increasingly, users of virtually any product or service – by means of a database of answers to the most commonly asked questions.

fresnel factor *(com)* In a 3D environment, the brightening of the edge of an object by increasing the intensity of reflection along the edge, giving a more realistic visual effect. ➔ *fresnel lens*

fresnel lens *(pho)* A lens used to concentrate the beam of a spotlight.

fringe (1) *(pre)* The edge around a 'soft' halftone dot, which may not be dense enough to prevent light passing through during final film-making, thus potentially altering the dot size. Also called a 'dot fringe' or 'halo'. ➔ *soft dot*

The poor selection of the foreground character has left an obvious **fringe**

fringe (2) *(com)* In image-editing, an unwanted border effect to a selection, where the pixels combine some of the colours inside the selection and some from the background.

frisket *(gen)* Paper or transparent material used as a stencil by airbrush artists to mask an area of an image.

frontal light *(pho)* Light that hits the subject from behind the camera, creating bright, high-contrast images, but with flat shadows and less relief.

front end (1) *(com)* In a networked system where your computer is connected to a server, the software used to gain access and interact with the server (the 'back end'). A Web browser is one such front end.

front end (system) (2) *(com)* The collection of hardware devices, such as keyboards and scanners, on which data is input. So-called to distinguish it from the collection of devices upon which data is output, such as imagesetters and printers.

F

front-facing polygons *(com)* In a 3D environment, those polygons whose normals (direction of render) point towards the camera or viewer.

front (jacket) flap *(gen)* → *jacket flaps*

frontispiece *(gen)* Traditionally, an illustration printed separately and then pasted onto the page opposite the title page of a book. Nowadays, any illustration printed opposite the title page.

front matter *(gen)* → *prelims/preliminary pages*

front projection *(pho)* The technique of projecting an image by using a two-way mirror placed between camera and subject, which enables the superimposition of additional images. → *back projection*

frothing *(pap)* The cause of a potential imperfection found in the process of coating paper, in which tiny areas of paper remain uncoated.

FSI *(gen)* abb.: free-standing insert. → *free-standing insert (FSI)*

f-stop *(pho)* → *f-number/f-stop*

FTP *(int)* abb.: File Transfer Protocol → *File Transfer Protocol (FTP)*

fugitive colour *(pri)* An unstable ink colour that may change or fade when exposed to certain conditions of light or atmosphere.

full bleed *(pri)* A printed sheet on which an image extends to all four edges. → *bleed (1)*

full bound *(fin)* A hardback binding in which the whole case is covered with the same material – for example, full leather or full cloth. Also called 'whole bound'. → *half bound/binding; quarter bound/binding*

full colour *(gen)* Synonymous with 'four colour', the term usually used to describe process colour reproduction. → *process colour printing*

full edition *(gen)* A complete, original edition of a work, applied only if an abridged edition has previously been published.

full face *(typ)* A headline type, always in capitals. Also called 'titling'.

full gilt *(fin)* A book with all edges gilded. → *gild*

full on the body *(typ)* A font of capital letters that covers the maximum area of the body. → *full face*

full out *(typ)* An instruction to set text to the full measure, without indents. → *justification; unjustified*

full point *(typ)* A full stop or period.

full-scale black *(pre)* A black separation film that reproduces the full tonal range of black in an image rather than just the darker areas, which is more common. → *skeleton black*

full shadow *(typ)* A type design with a heavy outline. → *shadow font*

full space *(typ)* In letterpress printing, a spacer between two lines of type.

full-text indexing *(com)* The facility to search and find a 'string' (contiguously connected text characters, which may occur within an entire text file.

full word wrap *(typ)* An instruction to avoid word breaks by taking the whole word at the end of each line to the next line. → *hyphenation & justification (H&Js, H/Js); word wrap*

fuming ghosting *(pri)* → *gloss ghosting*

function keys *(com)* A set of keys on some keyboards which can be assigned specific functions to carry out a sequence of mouse and keyboard actions, such as those defined by a 'macro' program. Not to be confused with Fkeys, which execute default commands. → *Fkey*

furnish *(pap)* The materials used in papermaking.

FYI *(gen)* abb.: for your information.

An example of a **full bound** book

Full bleed ensures the image prints right to the edge of the trimmed page

Gg

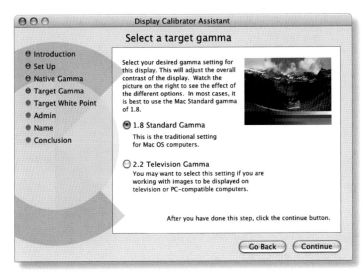

Selecting **gamma** in a Mac OS

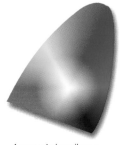

A **gamut** describes a range of colours

G *(com) abb.:* gigabyte → *gigabyte (GB/G/gig)*

gain *(aud)* The level of an audio signal. A volume control, for example, adjusts the output gain of your audio system.

Gall (map) projection *(gen)* → *cylindrical (map) projection*

galley proof *(gen)* A proof of typeset text before it is integrated into a page design, deriving from the days when metal type was proofed from a long, shallow, three-sided metal tray called a 'galley'. Also called a 'slip proof', referring to the broad strip of paper on which a galley proof is printed. → *catchline*

gamma *(com)* A measure of contrast in a digital image. Most often used when describing the behaviour of computer monitors (in which 'input' is the signal applied and 'output' is the measured brightness) but can also apply to photographic film, paper or processing techniques. → *gamma correction*

gamma correction *(com)* Modification of the midtones of an image by compressing or expanding the range, thus altering contrast. Also known as 'tone correction'. → *gamma*

gamut *(gen)* The full range of colours available within a particular colour space: the range that can be captured by an input device, reproduced by an output device or described in a working colour space (which may be larger than that of any real-world device). → *colour space*

GAN *(com) abb.:* global area network. → *global area network (GAN); wide area network*

gang shooting *(pre)* To make one item out of several by photographing them all together, such as making a single negative from several original images. → *gang up (2)*

gang up (1) *(pri)* To print two or more pages or jobs on the same sheet.

gang up (2) *(pre)* To place several originals (usually of the same proportions) together for scanning or some other means of reproduction. → *gang shooting*

gas plasma monitor *(com)* A computer display panel comprising a large matrix of tiny glass cells, each filled with a combination of gases. The simple structure means that gas plasma displays can be made in large sizes, typically ranging from 30 to 50 inches. ➔ *monitor*

gatefold *(fin)* A sheet folded into three equal segments by first dividing the sheet with two parallel creases and then folding both the outer segments across the middle of the sheet in overlapping layers. Also called a 'wallet fold'. ➔ *fold out*

gateway *(com)* A device or program used to connect disparate computer networks. ➔ *network; bridge; router*

gathering (1) *(fin)* Assembling and placing the signatures of a book in the correct order prior to binding. ➔ *folded and collated/gathered (F/Cs, F&Cs, F/Gs, F&Gs); signature (1)*

gathering (2) *(fin)* An alternative term for a quire or signature. ➔ *quire; signature (1)*

Gaussian Blur filter *(com)* Blur filter that applies a weighted average (based on the bell-shaped curve of the Gaussian distribution) when identifying and softening boundaries. It also introduces low-frequency detail and a mild 'mistiness' to the image, which is ideal for covering (blending out) discrete image information, such as noise and artefacts. A useful tool for applying variable degrees of blur and a more controllable tool than conventional blur filters. It can be accessed through the *Filter > Blur > Gaussian Blur* menu in Photoshop.

GB *(com) abb.:* gigabyte. ➔ *gigabyte (GB/G/gig)*

GCR *(pri) abb.:* grey component replacement. A colour separation technique in which black ink is used (instead of overlapping combinations of cyan, magenta and yellow) to create a proportion of both grey shades and the neutral (equal C, M and Y) part of

colours. This technique reduces ink use, and avoids color variations and trapping problems during printing but can lead to 'thin' or grey-looking looking shadow areas.

gear marks *(pri)* Regular, alternating light and dark marks, appearing as bands in solids and halftones, parallel to the gripper edge of a printed sheet. Gear marks are always uniformly spaced. ➔ *gripper edge*

gear streaks *(pri)* Unwanted, equally spaced parallel streaks on a printed sheet.

gel *(pri)* A contraction of 'gelation', meaning the drying of printing ink by evaporation or penetration.

gelatine filter *(pho)* Coloured filters made from dyed gelatine, normally placed over a camera lens to add a colour bias (or some other effect) to a shot with no significant impact on the optical quality of the final image.

gelatine process *(pri)* A process of duplication using gelatine to transfer an image in gravure printing.

gem *(typ)* An obsolete name for a size of type, approximately equivalent to 4 point.

generation *(gen)* A single stage of a reproduction process.

generative music *(aud)* A computerized system of producing music or interesting sounds whereby a software program uses a soundcard to randomly generate sound, restricted only by some previously set musical parameters and probabilities.

generic *(com)* Hardware devices, such as disk drives and printers, whose mechanisms are common to other brands.

Geneva *(com)* A Macintosh system font that is a bitmapped screen font similar to Helvetica. Like Chicago, it can't be deleted.

A selection of images that have undergone **GCR**, showing (from top) the CMY components, the full image and the key component only

An illustration using
ghosting

geometry *(com)* What 3D objects are made out of, or rather described by. Geometry types include polygons, NURBS and Bézier patches.

get in (1) *(typ)* An instruction to fit copy into less space than was initially estimated, or to gain extra space for copy by setting it close.

get in (2) *(typ)* In conventional typesetting, adding footnotes, headings, etc., to a galley of type matter, performed before actual page make-up.

getup *(gen)* A US term for the general format of a book, covering such aspects as general design, layout, and printing and binding.

ghost *(pri)* A printing defect whereby unwanted faint impressions of an image, text, etc. appear on printed sheets.

ghost icon *(com)* → *dimmed icon*

ghosting (1) *(gen)* To decrease the tonal values in the background of an image so that the main subject stands out more clearly. Also known as 'fadeback'. → *vignette*

ghosting (2) *(gen)* An illustration technique in which the outer layers of an object are faded to reveal its inner parts, which would not normally be visible. The technique is used particularly in technical illustration, to show parts of an engine covered by its casing, for example. → *exploded view*

GIF (Graphics Interchange Format) *(com)* Acronym for Graphics Interchange Format. One of the main bitmapped image formats used on the Internet. The GIF format supports up to 256 colours with two specifications: GIF87a and, more recently, GIF89a, the latter providing additional features such as the use of transparent backgrounds. The GIF format uses a 'lossless' compression technique, which handles areas of similar colour well, and allows animation. It is therefore the most common format for graphics and logos on the Internet, but JPEG is generally preferred for photographs.

GIF89a *(int)* → *transparent GIF*

gigabyte (GB/G/gig) *(com)* One gigabyte is equal to 1024 megabytes. → *kilobyte (KB/Kbyte); megabyte (MB/Mbyte/meg); terabyte*

giggering *(fin)* The technique of polishing the interior of a blind impression on a leather binding using a small hand tool.

gigo *(com)* Acronym for 'garbage in – garbage out'; the principle that input of a poor quality produces equally poor output, particularly when it comes to computer programming.

gild *(fin)* The application of gold leaf, or sometimes another metallic leaf, to the trimmed edges of a book. → *edge gilding*

gilding rolls *(fin)* Brass rolls, usually with ornamental designs, used for gold tooling.

gilt after rounding *(fin)* → *gilt solid*

gilt edges *(fin)* Trimmed book edges covered with gold leaf, as distinct from 'edge gilding' in which page borders are gilded. → *edge gilding*

gilt solid *(fin)* Book edges that have been rounded, then gilded. A process used only for expensive hand-finished bindings. Also known as 'gilt after rounding'. → *gild*

gilt top (g.t., g.t.e., t.e.g.) *(fin)* A book in which only the top is gilded.

gimbal lock *(com)* In 3D applications, a situation in which an object cannot be rotated around one or more axes.

glassine *(pap)* A semi-transparent glossy paper, used to protect photographic negatives and occasionally for book jackets.

glazed *(pap)* Paper with a very high gloss or 'polished' finish. → *super-calendered paper*

glazed morocco *(fin)* A fine goatskin leather used for covering books. Its polished finish is achieved by 'calendering' (passing between metal rollers). → *calender*

G

GLAZED MOROCCO

global area network (GAN) *(com)* A worldwide network of computers, similar to the Internet but linking 'wide area networks' (WANs).

global renaming *(int)* Software that updates all occurrences of a name throughout a website when one instance of that name is altered. ➔ *World Wide Web*

gloss (1) *(pap)* The amount of light reflected by the surface of paper ('reflectance'). Machine-finishing under pressure through rollers can give a slight gloss.

gloss (2) *(gen)* An occasional word or words of explanation in the text or margin of a text. ➔ *illuminated (2)*

glossary (1) *(gen)* An alphabetical listing of unfamiliar terms related to a particular subject – usually technical – with an accompanying explanation. This book is one such example.

glossary (2) *(com)* In some word-processing applications, a keyboard shortcut to insert frequently used words. Also known as 'indexing'.

gloss finishing *(fin)* Application of a film, varnish or lacquer to a printed sheet. Often used for book jackets and paperback covers to offer protection and also because it can give colour a greater 'depth', or density. ➔ *spot varnishing; varnish*

gloss ghosting *(pri)* An unwanted condition that sometimes occurs during sheet-fed printing, when ink from freshly printed sheets interacts with printed matter on the reverse of the sheet or on adjacent sheets, resulting in unwanted faint images. Also known as 'fuming ghosting' or 'chemical ghosting'.

gloss ink *(pri)* Printing ink usually consisting of a varnish or synthetic resin base and drying oils. Such ink dries quickly, and does not penetrate far into the paper and is thus normally used on coated and low-absorbency papers.

glow *(com)* A material parameter used to create external glows on objects. The glow usually extends beyond the object surface by a defined amount.

glued back only *(fin)* A book having a paper cover attached by adhesive on the back only, the sides being left loose.

glued down to ends *(fin)* A limp cover pasted to the first and last leaves of a book.

glue flap *(fin)* An overlapping flap or other area to which glue is applied to fasten folded containers or cartons.

gluing up *(fin)* A stage in the bookbinding process in which glue is used to supplement the structural integrity afforded by the sewing process, prior to rounding and backing. ➔ *pasting*

glyph (1) *(gen)* A sculptured character (from the Greek *glupho* meaning 'to carve'), but commonly used to describe a symbol that is intended to convey a message without the need for text, and is therefore understood by speakers of any language. Examples include a skull and crossbones to indicate 'danger' and a shattered glass for 'fragile'. ➔ *pictogram/pictograph*

glyph (2) *(typ)* An individual letter-shape, specific to a particular font and weight.

glyphic *(typ)* A type design derived from carved rather than scripted letters (from the French 'glyphe' meaning 'carve').

goffered edges *(fin)* ➔ *chased edges*

gold *(fin)* The precious metal traditionally used to decorate bindings and occasionally to illuminate lavish manuscripts. Normally supplied and used in leaf form. ➔ *gold leaf*

gold blocking *(fin)* The technique by which a design in gold leaf is stamped into the cover of a book by a heated die under pressure. Also known as 'gold tooling', although this originally referred to the process when it was carried out by hand. ➔ *ink blocking*

Some examples of **glyphs**

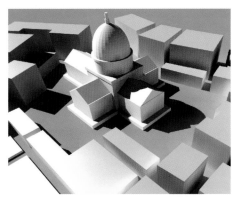

A scene rendered with **Gouraud shading**

The **grabber hand** is used to move items

Options for Photoshop's **Gradient** tool

goldenrod *(pre)* A yellowish light proof paper used for preparing 'flats' (an assembly of composite film). Original negatives or positives are attached to the paper into which masks have been cut. ➔ *flat (1)*

golden section *(gen)* A formula for dividing a line or an area into theoretically harmonious proportions. If a line is divided unequally, the relationship of the whole section to the larger section should be the same as that of the larger section to the smaller.

gold leaf *(fin)* A gold material – to which very small amounts of silver and copper have been added – which is rolled and beaten to an extremely thin foil. The manufacture of gold leaf is a painstaking craft still practised by hand, although machines capable of producing it have been developed. Gold leaf is the preferred material for the hand decoration of book covers and is not used widely for commercial bookbinding even though it is more durable than cheaper synthetic varieties.

golf ball *(typ)* A circular, interchangeable font matrix used on mechanical typewriters. ➔ *cold composition*

gopher *(int)* A software 'protocol', developed at the University of Minnesota, which provides a means of accessing information across the Internet using older services such as WAIS and Telnet. ➔ *Telnet; WAIS*

gothic *(typ)* ➔ *black letter*

gouache *(gen)* A watercolour paint in which the pigments are bound with gum arabic and made opaque by the addition of substances such as white lead, bone ash or chalk.

Gouraud shading *(com)* In 3D applications, a method of rendering by manipulating colours and shades selectively along the lines of certain vertices, which are then averaged across each polygon face in order to create a realistic light and shade effect.

grabber hand/tool *(com)* In some applications, the tool that enables you either to reposition a picture inside its box, or to move a page around in its window.

gradation/gradient *(com)* The smooth transition from one colour or tone to another. Photoshop and other programs include a Gradient Tool to create these transitions automatically.

grade *(pho)* The classification of photographic printing paper by the degree to which it affects the contrast of an image. Although not all makes are the same, the most common range from 0 (the lowest contrast, for use with high-contrast negatives) to 5 (the highest contrast, for use with low-contrast negatives). ➔ *contrast*

Gradient tool *(com)* Tool permitting the creation of a gradual blend between two or more colours within a selection. There are several different types of gradient fills offered, and those of Photoshop are typical: *Linear*, *Radial*, *Angular*, *Diamond* and *Reflected*. A selection of gradient presets are usually provided, but user-defined options can be used to create custom gradients.

graduation *(gen)* The smooth blending of one tone or colour into another, or from transparent to coloured in a tint. A graduated lens filter, for instance, might be dark on one side, fading to clear at the other.

grain (1) *(pap)* The prevailing direction and pattern of fibres in manufactured paper.

G

grain (2) *(pho)* The density of tiny light-sensitive silver bromide crystals – or the overlapping clusters of crystals – in a photographic emulsion. The finer the grain, the better the detail. Sometimes used in a coarse form for graphic effect either traditionally or recreated digitally.

grain (3) *(pri)* The rough property of the surface of some lithographic plates, which enables them to hold moisture. ➔ *lithography*

grain direction *(pap)* The alignment of paper grain in relation to the process it is being used for, such as in printing or bookbinding. In printing, the grain is described as being 'grain-long' if it runs in the same direction as the long dimension of the paper, and 'grain-short' if it runs with the short dimension.
➔ *machine direction*

grained leather *(fin)* Fine leather used in bookbinding, which has either had its natural grain or texture enhanced, or has had an artificial grain pressed onto its surface.

graininess *(pho)* The granulated effect present in a negative, print or slide. The degree to which it is visible depends on such things as film speed (it increases with faster films) and enlargement.

graining *(pri)* The treating of the surface of a lithographic plate in order to make it more receptive to moisture. Graining is achieved mechanically by various abrasion methods, or by the use of chemicals.

graining boards *(fin)* Wooden boards or copper plates used to impart various textures to bookbinding leather. Graining boards have a pattern cut into their surface, and are pressed onto the leather.

grammes per square metre (g/m², gsm) *(pap)* A unit of measurement used in the specification of paper (mostly in Europe), indicating its substance based on weight, regardless of the sheet size. Also called 'grammage'.

granite finish *(pap)* A type of paper manufactured from multicoloured fibres, giving a grained finish resembling granite.

graphic (1) *(typ)* A type design derived from drawn rather than scripted letter forms.

graphic (2) *(gen)* A general term describing any illustration or drawn design.

graphical user interface (GUI) *(com)* The concept of some computer operating systems, such as the Mac OS and Windows, which allows you to interact with the computer by means of pointing at graphic symbols (icons) with a mouse rather than by typing coded commands. Also known as 'WIMPs' or 'pointing interface'.
➔ *command-line interface; desktop; interface*

graphic arts *(gen)* The general term encompassing the entire craft of reproduction by means of any of the many printing processes. As distinct from 'graphic design' – providing a graphic solution to a specific problem and the implementation of that solution by whatever means.
➔ *graphic design*

graphic design *(gen)* Strictly speaking – and in its literal sense – graphic design is the arrangement and combination of shapes and forms based on 2D processes such as

An image with digitally simulated **grain**

typography, photography, illustration, video, motion picture, multimedia and various print methods. It does not necessarily exclude 3D design, since graphic design is utilized in many 3D contexts. In its less literal sense, graphic design embodies the profession of visual communication in as much as this forms an integral part of any marketing concept or strategy. Traditionally called 'commercial art', there are many alternative names such as 'graphic arts' or 'graphic communication', but it should not be confused with 'desktop publishing'.
→ *graphic arts*

Graphics *(com)* A QuickTime compression codec for use with still images with limited colour depth. Also called 'Apple Graphics'.
→ *codec (1); QuickTime*

Graphics Interchange Format (GIF) *(com)*
→ *GIF (Graphics Interchange Format)*

graphics tablet/pad *(com)* → *digitizing tablet/pad*

graticule *(gen)* A grid system of lines used to provide reference points on an image, particularly the lines of latitude ('parallels') and longitude ('meridians') on a map.

gravure *(pri)* An 'intaglio' printing process in which the image areas to be printed are recessed below the non-printing surface of the printing plate. These recesses (cells) are filled with a liquid ink and the paper draws the ink from the cells. → *intaglio*

Using **greeking** to hide the images

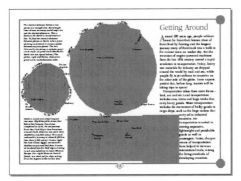

gravure screen *(pri)* A film marked with a grid of parallel horizontal and vertical lines, used for photographically defining the edges of gravure cells.

great primer *(typ)* An old name for a size of type, now standardized as 18 point.

Greek alphabet *(typ)* The characters and names of the Greek alphabet.

greek/greeking *(gen)* An indication – in a layout – of type or pictures by substituting rules or a grey tint for the actual letters or images. This is common practice when preparing rough visuals or scamps. Some computer applications provide greeking as a feature to speed up the process of screen redraw or proofing. → *comprehensive; dummy (1)*

greeking sheet *(gen)* A self-adhesive sheet of fake text, used in layouts to create a facsimile of body copy. → *greek/greeking*

Green Book *(com)* The document that specifies all parameters for CD-I technology.
→ *CD-I*

grey balance (1) *(pri)* The appropriate levels of yellow, magenta and cyan, which produce a neutral grey.

grey balance (2) *(gen)* A property of an RGB colour space such that equal levels of red, green and blue will always create a neutral grey. Working spaces are always grey-balanced.

grey component replacement (GCR) *(pre)* A colour separation technique in which black ink is used instead of overlapping combinations of cyan, magenta and yellow to create grey shades. This technique avoids colour variations and trapping problems during printing.

greyed command *(com)* → *dimmed command*

greyed icon *(com)* → *dimmed icon*

grey level *(com)* → *greyscale (2)*

greyness *(pri)* A quality of yellow, magenta and cyan process colour inks relating to the degree of contamination. An increase in the greyness value indicates a decrease in purity or saturation.

greyscale (1) *(pho)* A tonal scale printed in steps from white to black and used for controlling the quality of both colour and black-and-white photographic processing, and also for assessing quality in a halftone print. A greyscale (also called a 'step wedge', 'halftone step scale' or a 'step tablet') is sometimes printed on the edge of a sheet.

greyscale (2) *(com)* The rendering of an image in a range of greys from white to black. In a digital image and on a monitor, this usually means that an image is rendered with eight 'bits' assigned to each pixel, giving a maximum of 256 levels of grey. Monochrome monitors (rarely used nowadays) can display only black pixels, in which case greys are achieved by varying the number and positioning of black pixels using a technique called 'dithering'.
→ *8-bit; bit; dither(ing) (1)*

grid (1) *(gen)* A structure used for designing publications with multiple pages, such as books and magazines, to aid consistency throughout the publication. The grid usually shows such things as column widths, picture areas and trim sizes.

grid (2) *(com)* In some applications, a user-definable background pattern of equidistant vertical and horizontal lines to which elements such as guides, rules, type and boxes can be locked, or 'snapped', thus providing greater positional accuracy.
→ *baseline grid; guides*

gripper edge *(pri)* The edge of a sheet of paper, which is held by the grippers of a printing press. Also known as the 'feeding edge'. The opposite of the leaf edge.
→ *gripper margin; leaf edge*

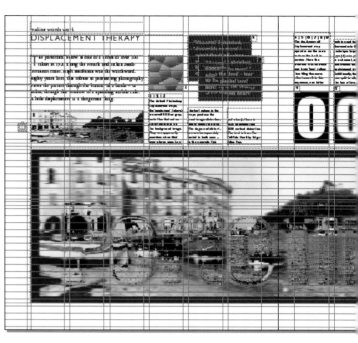

A typical page layout showing the **grid**

gripper margin *(pri)* The extra space on a sheet of paper where it is held by the grippers of a printing press, and which is later trimmed off. → *gripper edge*

gripper(s) *(pri)* The metal, finger-like clamps on the impression cylinder of a printing press, which hold a sheet of paper and guide it through the press. → *gripper edge; gripper margin*

groove *(typ)* A channel running along the bottom surface of a shank of metal type, in the same plane as the set (width).

grooved boards *(fin)* Book boards that have grooves in the back edges.

grooved joints *(fin)* → *French groove*

grotesque (1) *(gen)* An ornate graphic decoration involving combinations of somewhat surreal human, animal and plant images. Sometimes called a 'bestiary'.

grotesque (2) *(typ)* A term sometimes used to describe collectively sans serif display typefaces, such as Gill and Futura. Also known as 'grots'.

ground *(pri)* → *etch*

ground light *(pho)* A studio light that sits on the floor and is pointed upwards, usually to illuminate a background.

ground lighting *(pho)* → *base lighting*

ground plane *(com)* A reference plane oriented on the x–z axis in some 3D applications, providing a reference for the ground.

groundwood *(pap)* → *mechanical (wood) pulp*

group *(com)* A feature of some applications in which several items can be combined so that all the items can be moved around together, or so that a single command can be applied to all the items in the group. Reverting a group back to individual items is called 'ungrouping'.

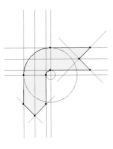

The lower **group** is treated as a single object, making editing work easier

GSM *(com) abb.:* global system for mobile communications. A telecommunication standard used increasingly throughout the world.

guarding-in *(fin)* → *guards*

guards *(fin)* Narrow strips of paper or linen onto which single plates are pasted before being sewn in with the sections of a book. This process is known as 'guarding' or 'guarding-in'.

GUI *(com)* (pron.: 'gooey') ; *abb.:* graphical user interface. → *graphical user interface (GUI)*

guides *(com)* Existing in many applications, these are non-printing horizontal and vertical lines that can be placed at inconsistent intervals and which help you to position items with greater accuracy. → *grid (2)*

The pink lines shown here are non-printing **guides**

guillemets *(typ)* → *duck foot quotes*

guillotine *(fin)* A machine in the print finishing line, which accurately cuts several sheets of paper at once. These sheets may be either flat, or folded and stitched. Also called a 'cutter'.

gum (1) *(pri)* A water-based solution containing gum arabic or cellulose gum, which is used to desensitize the non-image areas on litho plates to make those areas ink repellent.

gum (2) *(gen)* A general term describing any organic resinous binding agent incorporated into inks, varnishes, etc., or used as a binding medium (usually gum arabic) for water-based paints such as gouache.

gum blinding *(pri)* An aberration that occurs in litho printing when ink fails to adhere to an image area. → *etch*

gusseting *(fin)* Small, unwanted creases at the top of the inner pages of a closed signature. → *signature (1)*

gutter *(gen)* Strictly speaking, this means the spaces on a sheet of paper imposed for printing, which, when cut, will form the fore-edges of the pages. More commonly, however, the term describes the margin ('back margin') down the centre of a double-page spread, or the vertical space between adjacent columns on a page. → *gutter bleed*

gutter bleed *(gen)* An image allowed to extend into the fold of a publication, or to extend unbroken across the central margins of a double-page spread. → *gutter*

gutter margin *(pri)* → *gutter*

gutting *(gen)* A colloquial expression describing the practice of extracting key phrases or 'soundbites' from reviews of a publication, and subsequently printing them on the cover for promotional purposes.

gyro stabilizer *(pho)* An electrically powered camera support that incorporates a gyroscope to cushion the camera against vibrations. Used for such occasions as photographing from helicopters, cars and other vehicles.

Gzip *(com)* File compression technology used mainly on UNIX computers.

Hh

hairline register *(pri)* The maximum permissible deviation (0.003in/0.08mm) between printed colours in four-colour process printing

hairline rule *(gen)* Traditionally, the thinnest line that it is possible to print. In applications that provide it as a size option for rules, it is usually 0.25 point wide. ➔ *rule*

hairlines *(typ)* Very thin strokes in a type design.

hairspace *(typ)* In traditional typesetting, a very narrow space between type characters.

halation *(pho)* In the highlights of a photographic image, an unwanted spread of light beyond its natural boundary, caused by overexposure or (in platemaking) poor plate contact during exposure.

half-bound/binding *(fin)* A hardback binding in which the back and corners are covered in one material and the remainder of the sides in another. For example, a leather back and corners, with cloth sides.
➔ *corners (2); full-bound; quarter-bound/binding; three-quarter bound*

half cloth *(fin)* A half-bound book with a cloth-covered spine and corners, and paper-covered boards. ➔ *half-bound/binding*

half-diamond indentation *(typ)* A style of typesetting in which successive lines are indented at both ends, causing each line to be shorter than the last. Also known as 'in pendentive' setting.

half duplex *(int)* Communication between two devices over telecommunication lines, but in one direction at a time. ➔ *duplex*

half-leather *(fin)* A half bound book with a leather-covered spine and corners, and paper- or cloth-covered boards. ➔ *half-bound*

half-measure *(typ)* A double column of text on a page.

halfscale black *(pri)* ➔ *skeleton black*

half sheet *(pri)* A sheet, half the size of the normal ('normal' being the size of sheet required for the job). For example, if a job constitutes 144 pages in total, printing in 32-page sheets, a half sheet will be required to complete the job (32 x 4 = 128 + 16 = 144). ➔ *work and turn*

half-stuff *(pap)* Wet pulp in its raw state, before any of the other ingredients necessary in the papermaking process have been added.
➔ *beating; stuff*

half title (1) *(gen)* The title of a book as printed on the recto (right-hand page) of the leaf preceding the title page, usually the first page of a book. ➔ *recto; title page*

half title (2) *(gen)* The page on which the half title appears. Sometimes called a 'bastard title'. ➔ *title page*

Half-bound books usually have leather corners and spine, with cloth front and back

A close-up
halftone pattern

An example of
half-uncial style letters

A frame being adjusted
by its **handles**

halftone (1) *(pre)* The reprographic technique, developed in the 1880s, of reproducing a continuous tone image on a printing press by breaking it up into a pattern of equally spaced dots of varying size. This determines tones or shades – the larger the dots, the darker the shade. ➔ *continuous tone (ct)*

halftone (2) *(pre)* Any image reproduced by the halftone process. ➔ *halftone (1)*

halftone blowup *(pre)* An enlargement of a halftone image in which the screen dot pattern becomes coarsened. ➔ *halftone (1)*

halftone cell *(pre)* A halftone dot generated on a laser printer or imagesetter, comprised of a group of 'machine dots' in a grid space. ➔ *halftone dot; machine dot*

halftone dot *(pri)* The basic element of a printed image, where a continuous tone original is reproduced ('screened') by breaking it up into patterns of equally spaced dots of varying sizes to simulate the tonal values. Colour images are reproduced by overprinting halftone patterns in each of the primary colours. ➔ *separations*

halftone gravure *(pri)* A gravure printing plate in which the cylinder cells vary in surface area as well as depth, the latter of which is the norm. ➔ *gravure*

halftone screen *(pre)* Conventionally, a sheet of glass or film cross-hatched with opaque lines, used to convert a continuous tone image into halftone dots so that it can be printed. Computer applications generate a halftone screen digitally without the need for a physical halftone screen, by generating each halftone dot as an individual 'cell', itself made up of 'printer' dots. Also called a 'crossline screen' or 'contact screen'. ➔ *contact (halftone) screen; crossline screen; halftone (1); screen ruling*

halftone tint *(pre)* A printed area of even tone, achieved by uniform halftone dots. Tints are specified in percentages of the solid colour. Also called a 'screen tint'.

half-uncial *(typ)* A style of letters, composed of the mixed uncial and cursive letters used in medieval Europe as a book hand. Also called 'semi-uncial'. ➔ *cursive; uncials*

half-up *(gen)* A specification for artwork to be prepared at one-and-a-half times the size at which it will be reproduced. Artwork that is prepared half-up will need to be reduced by one third (66.6% of its original size) to print as intended. Also called 'one-and-a-half-up'. ➔ *twice up*

halo *(pre)* ➔ *fringe (2)*

hand *(typ)* ➔ *digit (2)*

hand composition *(typ)* The manual setting of metal type. ➔ *composition; typesetting*

handles (1) *(com)* In applications in which you 'draw' items such as lines, shapes, text boxes and picture boxes, the small black squares positioned at each corner (and sometimes in other places as well), which enable you to resize those items.

handles (2) *(com)* → *Bézier curve*

handmade paper *(pap)* Fine-quality, grain-free paper used for fine art prints, limited edition printing, etc.

handshake *(com)* The procedure of two networked computers, or other devices, introducing themselves to each other when initial contact is made, in order to establish data transmission protocols. → *protocol; XON/XOFF*

hang *(com)* → *crash*

hanging cap(ital) *(typ)* A large initial character of a piece of text that extends into the margin to the left of the paragraph.

hanging indent *(typ)* Typeset text in which the first line of each paragraph is set to the full width of the column and the remaining lines are indented to the right of the first line. Also called 'reverse indent' or 'hanging paragraph'.

hanging paragraph *(typ)* → *hanging indent*

hanging punctuation *(typ)* Punctuation marks that fall outside the column measure of a piece of text.

hard copy *(gen)* A physical copy of something, such as matter prepared for printing and used for revision or checking, or a printout of a computer document. As distinct from a 'soft' copy: a digital version. → *soft copy (1)*

hard cover edition, hardbound edition *(gen)* An edition of a book that is cased in boards, distinguishing it from a paperback edition, in which form it may also exist. → *cased/casebound*

hard cut *(aud)* A cut from one film or video clip to another, without any transition to soften the shift.

hard disk *(com)* A physical data storage drive, which stores data magnetically. Typically fixed inside the computer system, though more mechanically robust portable hard disks are a common way to carry large files around. → *drive head*

By duplicating an image layer and applying the **Hard Light** mode, you can strengthen an image's colour (as in the right of this image)

hard dot *(pre)* The dot on a halftone film produced either directly from a scanner or as final film and which, having dense, hard edges, can be only minimally retouched or etched. As distinct from a soft dot, which will allow a larger amount of etching. → *final film; soft dot*

hard-grain morocco *(fin)* A fine, supple goatskin leather used for bookbinding. Graining boards are used to give it a deep grain. → *graining boards*

hard hyphen *(typ)* A hyphen that will not permit the hyphenated word to break at the end of a line. → *hyphen*

Hard Light *(com)* A blending mode that creates an effect similar to directing a bright light at the subject. Depending on the base colour, the paint colour will be multiplied or screened. Base colour is lightened if the paint colour is light, and darkened if the paint colour is dark. Contrast tends to be emphasized and highlights exaggerated. Somewhat similar to Overlay but with a more pronounced effect.

hard sized *(pap)* A description of paper containing the maximum amount of size. Also called 'double sized'. → *size*

hardware *(com)* Any physical piece of equipment, generally in a computer environment, thus distinguishing it from firmware (programs built into hardware) and software (programs). → *firmware; software*

HANDLES

harmonic *(aud)* No two instruments produce exactly the same waveforms (or middle A would sound identical on all instruments) because they produce additional frequencies called partials. When the frequency of a partial is a complete multiple of the original pitch, it is called a 'harmonic'.

haze *(gen)* The scattering of light by particles in the atmosphere, usually caused by fine dust, high humidity or pollution. Haze makes a scene paler with distance, and softens the hard edges of sunlight.

HDTV *(com)* abb.: high-definition television.

head (1) *(gen)* → *head margin*

head (2) *(int)* → *header*

head (3) *(com)* → *read/write head*

headcap *(fin)* A small fold of leather at the head and tail of the spine on a hand bound book. Also called a 'French headcap'.

head crash *(com)* The failure of a disk drive, caused by one of its read/write heads coming into contact with, and damaging, the surface of a platter. → *platter; read/write head*

header *(com)* A label that identifies a file, document or page, occurring at its top, or 'head'. In an e-mail message or newsgroup posting, for example, it may contain such information as the route the message took to get to you, the recipient's e-mail address, and the name of the newsreader or mail program.

A **head band** strengthens a book's binding

header card *(gen)* An advertising card placed above a 'dumpbin', to draw attention to the items placed there. → *dumpbin*

header file *(int)* Files that contain information identifying incoming data transmitted via the Internet.

heading (1) *(int)* A formatting term used in HTML, which determines the size at which text will be displayed in a WWW browser. There are six sizes available, usually referred to as H1, H2, H3, H4, H5 and H6.

heading (2) *(gen)* The title at the beginning of a chapter or subdivision of text. A heading that appears in the body of the text is called a 'crosshead' or 'centre head'.

heading (3) *(com)* Local y-axis rotation. Part of the HPB rotation system (Heading Pitch Bank).

headless paragraph *(gen)* A paragraph set apart from other text, but without a separate heading.

headline (1) *(gen)* A line of type at the top of a page, specifying the title of the book, a chapter contained within it, the subject of the page or the page number. The convention is for the book title to be printed on left-hand (verso) pages with chapter titles on right-hand (recto) pages. Also called a 'page head'. If headlines are repeated throughout a book or chapter, they are referred to as 'running headlines', 'running heads', 'running titles' or 'topical heads'. Headlines and running heads placed at the bottom of pages are called 'footers' or 'running feet'.

headline (2) *(gen)* The title of the lead story in a newspaper or magazine article.

head margin *(gen)* The space between the first line of text matter and the top of the trimmed page.

head-piece *(gen)* The traditional term for a decorative device or motif, printed in the space above the beginning of a chapter.

head/tail band *(fin)* A narrow band of coloured silk or cotton cord, which is glued to the top (head band) and/or bottom (tail band) of the spine of a cased book, enhancing the strength and appearance of the binding.

head to head/foot/tail *(pre)* In page imposition, the placement of the heads and tails of pages on each side of a sheet to suit the requirements of printing and binding.

head trim *(fin)* A small amount of paper trimmed off the page above the head margin.

heap *(com)* A part of RAM set aside exclusively for use on demand by a computer operating system or applications. → *application memory (heap); RAM; system heap*

heat sealing *(fin)* A technique in which two materials, usually plastic, are fused together under heat and pressure.

heat-set ink *(pri)* Inks designed to dry quickly to enable faster printing, based on synthetic resins and volatile petroleum oils. Immediately after printing, the web of paper is heated and then cooled to dry rapidly and harden the ink.

heavy (face) *(typ)* An alternative term for bold type or, sometimes, type even heavier than bold. → *bold (face)*

height map *(com)* An image used to displace or deform geometry.

Helio-Klischograph *(pri)* A system used to engrave gravure printing cylinders, in which an image is electronically scanned and transmitted to a diamond-headed cutting tool that engraves the cells onto the cylinder. → *gravure*

help *(com)* A feature of operating systems and other software, which provides online explanations and advice.

helper application *(int)* Applications that assist Web browsers in delivering or displaying information such as film or sound files. → *plug-in; Web browser*

hemp *(pap)* A fibrous plant, the products of which are used in papermaking.

heraldic colours *(gen)* A standard system of representing the basic colours of heraldry by means of monochrome shading, hatching, etc. Used when colour printing is impractical or unwarranted.

hertz (Hz) *(com)* A measurement of frequency. One hertz is one cycle, or occurrence, per second.

Hexachrome *(pri)* A printing process developed by PANTONE based on six inks rather than the traditional CMYK four. In true Hexachrome, orange and green are the extra colours. Hexachrome should not be confused with other six-colour print processes, such as 'six-colour' inkjet printers that have extra cyan and magenta inks.

hex(adecimal) *(gen)* The use of the number 16 as the basis of a counting system as distinct from decimal (base ten) or binary (base two). The figures are represented by the numbers 1 to 0, followed by A to F. Thus decimal 9 is still hex 9, whereas decimal 10 becomes hex A, decimal 16 becomes hex 10, decimal 26 becomes hex 1A and so on.

hickie/hickey *(pri)* A common printing defect, visible as a spot of ink surrounded by a halo, caused by a speck of dirt forcing the paper away from the printing plate. Also called a 'bull's eye'.

hidden surface removal *(com)* A rendering method, usually wireframe, which prevents surfaces that cannot be seen from the given view from being drawn.

hierarchical file system (HFS) *(com)* The method used by the Mac OS to organize and store files and folders, so that they can be accessed by any program. Files are organized inside folders, which may, in turn, be inside other folders, thus creating a hierarchy.

hierarchical menu *(com)* A menu containing items that, when selected, generate their own menus (called 'submenus'). The presence of a submenu is normally indicated by a triangular symbol to the right of the menu item. → *hierachical file system (HFS)*

In the character to the left, **hinting** has been used to clarify the letter's shape

The **hinges** are the points at which the book block adjoins the cover

A **high-key** image

hierarchical structure *(com)* The technique of arranging information in a graded order, which establishes priorities and therefore helps find a path that leads them to what they want. Used extensively in networking and databases. ➔ *hierarchical file system (HFS)*

HiFi color *(aud)* Any process that increases the colour range (gamut) of an output device, usually by adding extra inks to the standard CMYK set. The three main HiFi systems are the Kuppers approach (CMYK + RGB), PANTONE Hexachrome (CMYK + orange and green) and MaxCMY (CMYK + extra CMY).

high density *(com)* A term that, particularly in relation to all things digital, invariably means more – thus better.

high-fidelity (hi-fi) *(aud)* This refers to the quality of audio; in other words, how closely an audio system reproduces the original sound.

high key *(pho)* A photographic image exposed or processed to produce overall light tones. ➔ *bleach(ed)-out; contrast; low key*

high-level domain *(int)* ➔ *Domain Name Service*

high-level language *(com)* Any programming language that is based as closely as possible on English rather than machine code. ➔ *machine code*

highlight (1) *(gen)* The lightest tone of an image, the opposite of shadow.

highlight (2) *(com)* To mark an item, such as a section of text, icon or menu command, to indicate that it is selected or active.

highlight dots *(pre)* The smallest dots on a halftone film image. ➔ *halftone (1)*

highlight halftone *(pre)* A halftone image in which the dots in the highlight areas have been etched out. ➔ *halftone (1)*

high mill finish *(pap)* A paper finish achieved by calendering, with a surface midway

between 'machine-finished' (MF) and 'super-calendered'. ➔ *machine finish (MF); super-calender*

high-profile *(gen)* Any item that stands apart or visibly proud of its surroundings. The opposite of low-profile. ➔ *low-profile*

hinged *(fin)* Separate sheets that have had a narrow fold applied to their inner edges, prior to insertion in a book, so that they lie flatter when the book is opened, and turn more easily.

hinges *(fin)* The points at which the main body (the book block) of a book adjoins the covers, forming the channels between the two halves of the endpapers.

hints/hinting *(com)* Information contained within outline fonts. Hinting modifies character shapes to enhance them when displayed or printed at low resolutions. Hinting is unimportant when fonts are printed at high resolution, such as on imagesetters.

histogram *(com)* A graphic representation of data, usually in the form of solid vertical or horizontal bars. Some image-editing applications use histograms to graph the

An example of a decorative, **historiated letter**

The two **histograms** reveal the tonal range

number of pixels at each brightness level in a digital image, thus giving a rapid idea of the tonal range of the image so that you can determine if there is enough detail to make corrections.

historiated letters *(typ)* Decorative initial capital letters, incorporating miniature drawings that illustrate events or themes in the accompanying text.

history (list) *(int)* A list of visited webpages logged by your browser during a session on the Internet. The history provides a means of speedy access to pages already visited during that session. ➔ *World Wide Web (WWW)*

hither plane *(com)* ➔ *clipping plane*

H&Js/HJs *(com) abb.:* hyphenation and justification. ➔ *hyphenation and justification (H&Js, H/Js)*

holdout *(pap)* The resistance of certain glazed papers to the penetration of printing ink.

holiday *(fin)* A traditional term to describe an area of a surface that failed to be pasted in the pasting unit.

holing out *(fin)* The punching or drilling of holes through the boards of a handbound book.

holland *(fin)* A fine-woven cloth, occasionally used for bookbinding purposes. Cloth of this type originated in Holland, hence its name.

hollow *(fin)* The strip of brown paper placed in the centre of a case to stiffen the spine, which allows the book to be opened easily.

hollow back *(fin)* The space at the back of a cased book between the case and the book block. Also called 'open back'.

hologram *(gen)* An image created by lasers to give an illusion of three dimensions, used commonly in security printing, but also as a novelty. ➔ *laser*

holograph *(gen)* A work written entirely in the author's own handwriting.

holster book *(gen)* A traditional name for a long, narrow note book, designed to fit in the pocket.

home page *(int)* On the World Wide Web, the term originally applied to the page that your own browser automatically linked to when you launched it. It is now commonly used to describe the main page or contents page on any particular site, which provides links to all the other pages on the site.

honing *(pri)* The technique of mechanically removing parts of the image area on a printing plate.

hooked/hooking *(fin)* Single leaf illustrations printed on sheets that are slightly wider than the accompanying text pages, thus allowing for an inner fold, or hinge, which fits around the section like a hook. ➔ *guards*

hook in *(typ)* The traditional term for setting words in brackets on the line below the main text when there is insufficient room in the specified measure.

hooks *(typ)* An old term for brackets.

horizontal scaling *(typ)* A feature of some applications to condense or expand type. Horizontal scaling retains the exact attributes of the source font but distorts its appearance. While the feature can sometimes be used advantageously, it can also produce ugly typography, in which cases the specially designed condensed or expanded versions of the font may look more aesthetic.

A **hollow back** is oftened found on cased books

Horizontal scaling

host *(int)* A networked computer that provides services to anyone who can access it, such as for e-mail, file transfer and access to the Web.

hostname *(int)* The name that identifies the computer hosting a website. → *Domain Name Service (DNS)*

HotJava *(int)* A Web browser, developed by Sun Microsystems, which is built in the Java programming language. → *Java; Web browser*

hotlist *(int)* A theme-related list on a webpage, which provides links to other pages or sites dedicated to that theme.

hot-melt adhesive *(fin)* An adhesive used in bookbinding.

hot metal (type) *(typ)* The general term given to type set on a 'compositing' machine, now largely obsolete, which casts type from molten metal either as single characters (as per Monotype) or as complete lines (as per Linotype). → *cold type; composition size(s); Linotype; Monotype; typesetting*

hot-pressed (HP) *(pap)* A type of fine paper whose surface has been given a glazed finish by the use of hot metal plates.

hot-press lettering *(typ)* A technique in which foil letters are impressed upon board, using heat and pressure.

hot-rolled *(pap)* Paper that has been glazed by steam-heated calenders. → *calender*

hot-shoe *(pho)* An accessory fitting found on most digital and film SLR cameras and some compact models, normally used to control an external flash unit.

hotspot/hot spot *(com)* The specific place on the mouse pointer icon that activates the item on which it is placed. → *pointer*

house corrections *(gen)* Corrections to proofs made by the publisher or printer, as distinct from those made by the author.

house organ *(gen)* A publication produced to give information about a company, distributed internally to employees, and sometimes to customers.

house style *(gen)* → *corporate identity*

H.P. *(pap)* abb.: hot-pressed. → *hot-pressed (HP)*

HSB *(gen)* abb.: Hue, Saturation, Brightness. The three dimensions of colour, and the standard colour model used to adjust colour in many image-editing applications. Sometimes also known as Hue, Saturation, Lightness (HSL). Hue is the pure colour, Saturation is the strength of the colour and the Lightness (or brightness) ranges from near black to near white.

HTML *(int)* abb.: hypertext markup language. The text-based language used to format documents published on the World Wide Web, and which can be viewed with a Web browser. → *PDL; Web browser*

HTML table *(int)* A grid on a webpage consisting of rows and columns of cells, allowing precise positioning of text, pictures, film clips or any other element. A table can be nested within another table. Tables offer a way of giving the appearance of multi-column layouts.

http *(int)* abb.: hypertext transfer protocol. A common protocol for information transfer over the Internet. → *HTML; URL; Web browser*

httpd *(int)* abb.: hypertext transfer protocol daemon. A collection of programs on a Web server that provide services, such as handling requests. → *request*

https *(int)* abb.: hypertext transfer protocol secure. Synonymous with 'http', but providing a secure link for such things as commercial transactions (online shopping with credit cards) or when accessing password-protected information.

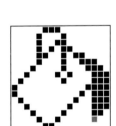

The **HSB** colour model, with Brightness represented left to right, Saturation up/down and Hues in the third dimension

The red pixel marks the cursor's **hotspot**

hue *(gen)* Pure spectral colour that distinguishes a colour from others. Red is a different hue from blue and, although light red and dark red may contain varying amounts of white or black, they may be the same hue. Hue is one of the three dimensions of colour in the HSB colour system. → *brightness; chroma (2); HSB; saturation*

Hue, Saturation, Brightness (HSB) *(gen)* → *HSB*

human engineering *(gen)* → *ergonomics*

humidified *(pap)* A term for paper that has undergone an artificial maturing process in order to alter its working properties. → *conditioning*

hygrometer *(pap)* An instrument used to test the moisture content of paper. Also called a 'hygroscope' (US).

hyperfocal distance *(pho)* The closest distance at which a lens records a subject sharply when focused at infinity, varying with aperture.

hyperlink *(int)* A contraction of 'hypertext link'. An embedded link to other documents on the Internet, usually identified by being underlined or highlighted in a different colour. Clicking on or selecting a hyperlink takes you to another document, part of a document or website. → *active hyperlink; hypertext*

hypermedia *(int)* The combination of graphics, text, film, sound and other elements accessible via hypertext links in an online document or webpage. → *hyperlink*

hypertext *(int)* A programming concept that links any single word or group of words to an unlimited number of others, typically on a webpage that has an embedded link to other documents or websites. Hypertext links are usually underlined and/or a different colour to the rest of the text, and are activated by clicking on them. → *hyperlink*

hypertext markup language (HTML) *(int)* → *HTML*

hypertext transfer protocol *(int)* A text-based set of rules by which files on the World Wide Web are transferred, defining the commands that Web browsers use to communicate with Web servers. The vast majority of World Wide Web addresses, or 'URL's', are prefixed with 'http://'. → *http*

hypertext transfer protocol secure (https) *(int)* → *https*

hyphen *(typ)* A dash (-) used to divide broken words or to link two words. → *dash; em dash/rule; en dash/rule; hyphenate*

hyphenate *(typ)* To break a word at the end of a line of text, usually between syllables, or to create a compound form from two or more words using a hyphen. → *hyphen*

hyphenation and justification (H&Js, H/Js) *(com)* The process of distributing space in a line of type to achieve the desired measure in justified text. Many computer applications provide features for doing this automatically using built-in dictionaries or H&J rules, or from criteria defined by you. → *automatic hyphenation; hyphenation exceptions; hyphenation zone; hyphenless justification; justification*

hyphenation exceptions *(com)* A feature of some applications that allows you to modify, add or delete words that are exceptions to its built-in hyphenation rules. → *hyphenation and justification (H&Js, H/Js)*

hyphenation zone *(com)* A feature of some applications allowing you to define a zone at the right of the column in which type is being set, in which words can be hyphenated. → *hyphenation and justification (H&Js, H/Js)*

hyphenless justification *(typ)* A justification method in which lines of text are aligned by means of word and letter spacing, without breaking words with hyphens at the end of lines. → *hyphenation and justification (H&Js, H/Js)*

hypo *(pho)* abb.: hyposulphate (although actually sodium thiosulphate). A photographic processing chemical.

IAB *(int) abb.:* Internet Architecture Board. The ruling council that makes decisions about Internet standards and related topics. → *ISOC*

IAC *(com) abb.:* interapplication communication. → *interapplication communication (IAC)*

I-beam pointer *(com)* The shape of the pointer when it is used to edit or select text. As distinct from the 'insertion point' or 'cursor', which indicates the point at which text will be inserted by the next keystroke. Also called the 'Text tool'. → *cursor; insertion point; pointer*

ibid *(gen) abb.: ibidem.* Latin for 'in the same place', used in the notes of a publication to mean a repeated reference.

IBM *(com) abb.:* International Business Machines, a major manufacturer of computing hardware. → *IBM PC*

IBM PC *(com) abb.:* IBM personal computer, usually describing a PC made by IBM but also often used as a generic term for any PC that is 'IBM compatible' (usually meaning one that runs a Microsoft operating system), thus distinguishing them from other computers, such as the Apple 'Macintosh' series. → *IBM; Macintosh; MS-DOS; Windows*

ICC *(com) abb.:* International Colour Consortium. An organization responsible for defining cross-application colour standards. → *colour management system (CMS)*

ICC profile *(com) abb.:* International Colour Consortium profile → *colour management module (CMM)* Consortium profile → *icon*

(gen) An on-screen graphical representation of an object, such as a disk, file, folder or tool, used to make identification and selection easier.

ICR *(com) abb.:* intelligent character recognition. A sophisticated form of optical character recognition (OCR), which recognizes not only a character's shape (like OCR) but also its typeface and point size (unlike OCR). → *OCR*

id *(gen) abb.: idem.* A Latin term meaning 'the same person', used in footnotes and bibliographies to indicate subsequent references to an author previously mentioned.

ideal format *(pho)* A particular size of photographic film measuring 2.3 x 2.7in (60 x 70mm).

ideogram *(gen)* A symbol used to indicate a concept or emotion. → *isotype*

ID number *(com)* Acronym for 'identity' number. A number given to a device, file or message to distinguish it from others. For example, an ID number is required by peripheral devices in a SCSI chain, or may sometimes be given in error alert boxes to indicate the likely cause of the error. → *SCSI ID (number)*

ID selector *(int)* A style sheet rule for a webpage element. → *style sheet*

i.e. *(gen) abb.: id est.* Latin for 'that is'.

IETF *(int) abb.:* Internet Engineering Task Force. A suborganization of the Internet

Bluetooth Icon

CDR Icon

Folder Icon

Document Icon.txt

JPEG Icon

PDF Icon

Font File Icon

A selection of Mac OS **icons**

i.e. *(gen)* abb.: *id est*. Latin for 'that is'.

IETF *(int)* abb.: Internet Engineering Task Force. A suborganization of the Internet Architecture Board (IAB), comprising a group of volunteers who investigate and help solve Internet-related problems and make recommendations to appropriate Internet committees.

illuminate/illuminated (1) *(gen)* A term describing the technique of embellishing letters, pages and manuscripts by using gold, silver and colours. Common in medieval times.

illuminated (2) *(gen)* A colloquial term for the 'glosses' (explanations placed between lines) in a translated Greek or Latin text. ➔ *gloss (2)*

illustrated *(gen)* A description applied to any printed item, particularly books, that contains reproductions of images as well as text. Although tables, graphs and other such data were once represented purely as text and thus not normally considered to be illustrations, even these are now deemed to be illustrations.

illustration (1) *(gen)* Any drawing, painting, diagram, photograph or other image reproduced in a publication to explain or supplement the text.

illustration (2) *(gen)* A term sometimes used specifically to distinguish a drawn image from a photograph.

IMA *(com)* abb.: Interactive Multimedia Association, a 'lossy' audio compression technology. ➔ *lossless/lossy*

image (1) *(gen)* In graphics, the description of any picture created by any method and used for any purpose. In reproduction, an image is printed in one pass through a press, whether it be a single picture or a complete imposed group of pages (in this context, individual pictures are called 'subjects'). ➔ *image area (2); subject*

image (2) *(gen)* The overall 'look' of an organization or product, which affects its character, reputation and marketing potential. ➔ *corporate identity*

image area (1) *(gen)* The area within which a particular image or group of images is to fit, sometimes including text.

image area (2) *(pri)* The ink-carrying area of a printing plate. ➔ *image (1)*

image-editing application/image editor *(com)* A computer application for manipulating images – for example, images captured with a scanner or digital camera. Image-editing applications are pixel-based ('bitmapped' as opposed to 'vector'), and provide features for preparing images for process colour printing (such as colour separations), as well as tools for painting and 'filters' for applying special effects. Also called 'image-manipulation program' or 'paint program'.

image file *(com)* Any digital file in which a graphic image or photograph is stored, as distinct from other data such as in a text file, database file or 3D file. Image files can be saved in a variety of formats, depending on which application created them, but are typically TIFF, GIF, JPEG, PICT, BMP or

Photoshop is a widely used **image-editing application**

EPS. Confusingly, the data format in which some images are stored is actually text (as in an EPS graphic, which is saved in 'ASCII' text format), but the file is still an image file. Not to be confused with a 'disk image', which refers to the contents of a volume stored in a single file. → *ASCII; EPS*

image fit *(pre)* → *fit (2)*

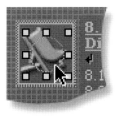

Image resources can range from photos to mapping resources

image library *(gen)* A source of original transparencies and pictures that can be used for virtually any purpose on payment of a fee, which usually varies according to usage. A picture used in an advertisement will invariably cost a great deal more than if the same picture were to be used inside a school textbook. Many libraries specialize in various subjects, such as garden plants, wildlife and fine art. Regarding the latter, the library may own the copyright in the photograph of a painting, but the ownership of copyright in the painting itself may belong elsewhere. → *copyright; image resource*

An example of an **image map**

image map *(int)* An image that contains a series of embedded links to other documents or websites. These links are activated when clicked on in the appropriate area of the image. For example, an image of a globe may incorporate an embedded link for each visible country and this, when clicked, will take the user to a document giving more information about that country. → *clickable map/image*

image master *(typ)* A film-based font used in filmsetting. → *filmsetting*

image resource *(com)* A source of ready-made material such as royalty-free image libraries, clip art and mapping resources, distributed digitally on various media such as CD-ROM and the Web, as distinct from 'image libraries', which supply original transparencies and pictures. → *clip art/clip media; image library; mapping resource; royalty-free*

imagesetter *(pre)* A high-resolution output device used to generate reproduction-quality copy for printing, either as film negatives or positives, or on photographic bromide paper for use as camera-ready artwork. → *RIP (1)*

image size *(gen)* A description of the dimensions of an image. Depending on the type of image being measured, this can be in terms of linear dimensions, resolution or digital file size.

image slicing *(int)* The practice of dividing up a digital image into rectangular areas or slices, which can then be optimized or animated independently.

image twist *(pri)* A crooked printed image, resulting in misregister, caused by the plate being mounted out of alignment.

imaging device *(pre)* A general term describing any dedicated piece of equipment that either captures an image from an original, such as a scanner or camera, or one that generates an image from a previously captured original, such as a contact printing frame or imagesetter.

imbrication *(gen)* A patterned design featuring overlapping leaves or scales arranged in the manner of roof tiles. From the Latin *imbricare*, meaning 'cover with rain tiles'.

I

imitation art (paper) *(pap)* A type of glazed, super-calendered coated paper. Also called 'machine coated' paper. ➔ *super-calender; water finish*

imitation cloth *(pap)* Book-covering material, actually made from paper, cloth or similar substances, finished and embossed to resemble real cloth.

imitation leather *(pap)* Book-covering material, actually made from paper, cloth or similar substances, finished and embossed to resemble real leather.

imitation parchment *(pap)* A strong, semi-transparent paper that is reasonably resistant to grease and water.

imitation watermark *(pap)* A mark resembling a watermark, but which is in fact made by stamping the paper very hard between a male die and a polished steel plate. ➔ *impressed watermark; watermark (1)*

impact printing *(pri)* ➔ *cold composition*

imperfection *(fin)* A book that has been incorrectly bound.

imperial *(pap)* A size of printing and drawing paper in the UK, which measures 22 x 30in (559 x 762mm).

import *(com)* To bring text, pictures or other data into a document. ➔ *export*

import/export filter *(com)* In some applications, a feature for translating a file from the host format to that of another, and vice-versa. ➔ *export; filter (1); import*

imposed proof *(pri)* A printed proof of imposed pages prior to the final print run. Also called a 'sheet proof'.

imposition/impose *(pre)* The arrangement of pages in the sequence and position in which they will appear on the printed sheet, with appropriate margins for folding and trimming, before platemaking and printing. ➔ *come-and-go/coming and going*

impressed watermark *(pap)* A mark made by pressing a rubber stereo onto a web of paper. Since this mark can be applied at any time after paper making, it does not have the security value of a genuine watermark. Also called a 'press mark'. ➔ *imitation watermark; watermark (1)*

impression *(pri)* All the copies of a publication or job printed at one time.

impression cylinder *(pri)* The cylinder on a rotary press, which holds the paper as it is brought into contact with the type, plates, offset roller or blanket cylinder. Also called a 'back cylinder'.

imprimatur *(gen)* Latin for 'let it be printed', at one time used to show that permission to print a publication had been granted by the appropriate authority.

imprint *(gen)* Either the name of the printer and the place of printing – a legal requirement in many countries if the work is to be published – usually appearing on the back of the title page or on the last page of a book ('printer's imprint'). Also refers to the name of the publisher, usually printed on the title page of a book ('publisher's imprint').

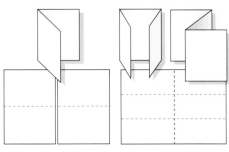

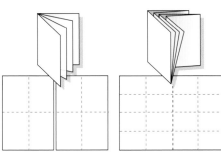

Some alternative **imposition** layouts

IMITATION ART (PAPER)

imprint page *(gen)* The page of a book usually appearing on the back of the title page (title verso), which carries details of the edition, such as the printer's imprint, copyright owner, ISBN, catalogue number, etc. → *imprint*

impulse outlet *(gen)* Describes a small product stand or rack that is placed in a retail situation other than the one where it may normally be expected (a book in a bookshop, for example), intended to attract 'impulse buyers'. Typical locations include supermarkets and airports. Also called 'rack-jobbing distribution' (US).

in boards *(fin)* The term describing a book that is trimmed after the boards have been attached.

in-camera (1) *(pho)* Photographic processing that takes place inside the camera, such as with Polaroid products.

in-camera (2) *(pho)* Photographic effects created inside the camera at the time of the shoot, as opposed to effects being applied later, such as during film processing or digitally with an image-manipulation application.

incident light reading *(pho)* Measurement of the light source that illuminates subject, in order to determine the exposure of a photograph, thus ignoring the subject's own characteristics.

Creating an **index colour** file

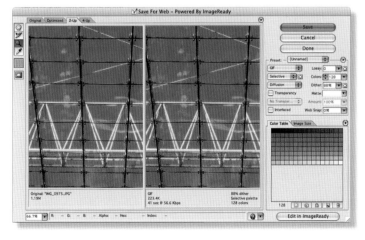

incipit *(gen)* A Latin term meaning 'it begins', followed by the first few words of the text, used to identify (usually very old) manuscripts published without a title page.

incremental leading *(typ)* The value given to line spacing equalling the largest character on the line plus or minus a user-defined value. → *leading*

incunabula *(gen)* Books printed before 1500.

incut notes *(gen)* → *cut-in side notes*

indent(ed) *(typ)* A line of type set to a narrower measure than the column measure, usually the distance of the start or end of the line from the left or right edges of the column.

indention *(typ)* A little-used alternative term for 'indented' – setting a line or lines of type to a narrower measure or at a greater distance from the left margin.

Indeo *(com)* A video compression codec developed by Intel. → *codec (1)*

indeterminate colour *(pre)* A trapping term to describe an area of colour comprised of many colours, such as a picture. → *trapping*

index (1) *(typ)* → *digit (2)*

index (2) *(gen)* The part of a publication that gives an alphabetical listing of selected words mentioned in the publication, with appropriate page numbers.

index (3) *(gen)* → *glossary (2)*

index board *(pap)* A card, usually in a range of colours, used typically to separate sections in a mechanically bound book or in an index guide. → *index guide; mechanical binding*

indexed colour *(com)* An image 'mode' of a maximum of 256 colours, which is used in some applications such as Adobe Photoshop to reduce the file size of 'RGB' images so that they can be used in multimedia presentations or webpages. This is achieved by using an indexed table of colours ('a colour lookup table') to which the colours in an image are matched. If a colour

INDEXED COLOUR

colours in a pattern called 'dithering'. → **CLUT; dithering (1); eight-bit**

index guide *(gen)* The marked divisions in a filing system, giving rapid access to sections that are categorized alphabetically or by subject. → *index board*

indexing (1) *(gen)* The preparation of an ordered list of words, subjects or categories, which forms an 'index', an alphabetical listing of selected words and an indication of where they can be found in a volume, document or file. → *index (2)*

indexing (2) *(gen)* Cutting or stepping the edges of pages or fixing reference tabs in order to mark major divisions within the work, such as the start of a new initial letter in a dictionary or encyclopedia. → *tab index; thumb index*

index letter/number *(gen)* A reference character or number used to connect an illustration to its caption or relevant text.

index page *(int)* The first page of any website, which is selected automatically by the browser if it is named 'index.htm' or 'index.html'; usually the homepage.

India ink/Indian ink *(gen)* A deep black ink used primarily by artists, illustrators or draughtsmen, and commonly used to prepare artwork for reproduction.

India paper *(pap)* → *Bible paper*

indicia *(gen)* A term meaning, literally, 'distinguishing marks', as required by the post office for bulk mailings.

indirect letterpress *(pri)* → *letterpress*

inedited (1) *(gen)* A work published as it was written, to which no editorial changes have been made.

inedited (2) *(gen)* A term describing any unpublished work, in particular those of an author who is dead.

inferior character *(typ)* Letters or numbers set smaller than the text and on or below the baseline – for example, H_2O. In many computer applications, inferior characters are called 'subscript'. → *superior character*

information agent *(int)* A generic type of computer program that automatically searches the World Wide Web, gathering and cataloguing information. → *robot; search engine; spider*

information service *(int)* → *bulletin board service (BBS)*

infra *(gen)* → *vide*

infra-red drying *(pri)* The use of infra-red radiation to rapidly dry ink, particularly appropriate on a high-speed web press.

inheritance *(com)* The hierarchical relationship between objects in object-oriented programming. For example, a characteristic inherited by one HTML element (a 'child') from another HTML element (its 'parent').

init *(com)* Abbreviation for initialization program. A small utility program ('extension') that runs automatically when your computer starts up and which modifies the way in which it operates. Some inits perform transparent tasks, such as enabling peripheral devices to work, while others may be 'control panel' programs, which allow you to configure or customize their functions. → *Control Panel; extension (1)*

initial cap(ital) *(typ)* The first letter of a piece of text that may be enlarged and set as a drop, hanging or raised cap, often at the beginning of a chapter. → *entrelac initial; floriated/floriated initial*

initialize *(com)* To clear the directory on a disk and create a new one so that new data can be stored. When a hard disk is initialized, its directory is emptied of file information, but the data itself remains (although it is invisible) until written over by the new files. When a floppy disk is initialized, the disk is formatted at the same time, thus any files

INDEX GUIDE

invisible) until written over by the new files. When a floppy disk is initialized, the disk is formatted at the same time, thus any files stored on it are deleted as well as the directory. ➔ *formatting*

ink *(pri)* A fluid comprised of solvents and oils in which is suspended a finely ground pigment of plant dyes, minerals or synthetic dyes that provide colour. There are many different types of inks for the various printing processes. ➔ *medium (1)*

ink abrasion *(pri)* The abrasive action of certain inks on printing plates, particularly over long print runs.

ink blocking *(fin)* The technique in which the title or a design is stamped into the cover of a book with an inked block. ➔ *blocking; gold blocking*

ink coverage *(pri)* The measure of the area that a given amount of printing ink is capable of covering satisfactorily.

ink distribution rollers *(pri)* Rollers on a printing press, whose action is to manage the printing ink from the ink duct until it reaches the plate in a fine, even film. Also called 'inkers'.

ink drier *(pri)* A chemical agent that is added to printing inks to assist and speed the drying process.

ink duct *(pri)* ➔ *duct*

inked art *(gen)* The state of camera-ready art, which is prepared first in pencil and then completed in ink.

ink fly *(pri)* ➔ *flying*

ink fountain *(pri)* ➔ *duct*

inking system *(pri)* The arrangement of ducts and rollers on a printing press, which control automatic distribution and delivery of ink to a substrate. Also called 'inking mechanism'.

inkjet printer *(com)* A printing device that creates an image by spraying tiny jets of ink onto a paper surface at high speed. ➔ *bubblejet printer; demand printing; direct digital colour proof (DDCP)*

inkless printing *(com)* ➔ *electrostatic printing*

ink limits *(pri)* The maximum permissible amount of ink that can be laid down on paper in commercial printing. Expressed as a percentage, it can range from 240 per cent for newsprint to 360 per cent for high-quality art books. Exceeding ink limits can cause drying problems, set-off or even cause the web to tear on a web press. Also known as 'total area coverage'.

ink penetration *(pri)* The degree to which ink penetrates a substrate, more acute during the moment of impression than after it, important if smudging or 'set-off' is to be avoided. ➔ *set-off*

ink receptivity *(pap)* The degree to which a substrate such as paper will absorb printing ink. ➔ *ink penetration*

ink spread *(pri)* In offset litho, the increase in the areas of each printed image or text character, caused by the spread of ink during printing, as it is transferred from plate to blanket and then to paper. When the size of a halftone dot is affected, it is called 'physical dot gain'. ➔ *dot gain; ink squash; physical dot gain*

ink squash *(pri)* The spread of ink beyond the details of an image, caused by excessive ink or pressure. ➔ *ink spread*

ink strength *(pri)* A term describing the degree of colour intensity of a printing ink.

ink transfer *(pri)* The critical part of the printing process, which determines the thickness of the ink film on the plate or blanket and thus the amount of ink transferred to paper. ➔ *tack*

ink transparency *(pri)* The degree to which a substrate will show through a printed ink.

inlaying *(fin)* A traditional method of decorating a book cover by insetting additional pieces of very thin leather or other material of contrasting colours into the surface. Books bound this way are said to be 'inlaid bindings'. ➔ *mosaic binding; onlaying*

in-line *(gen)* The description of a system or process in which specific components form part of a continuous sequence, such as the converting units attached to the press in a web printing system, or a scanner attached to an imagesetter, or an image that displays among text on a webpage. ➔ *online/ on-line*

in-line converting/finishing *(fin)* Any post-print process, such as trimming and folding, that is performed as part of a continuous automated process immediately after printing, common in web printing.
➔ *converting; offline converting/finishing*

in-line image *(int)* On webpages, an image that is displayed among text in the same browser window, rather than in a separate window or via a 'helper application'.
➔ *helper application*

inline lettering *(typ)* Any type design incorporating a white line. The line follows the outline of the character, and is drawn inside its shape. Also called a 'white-lined black letter'.

inline style *(int)* A style applied directly to elements on a webpage rather than by an embedded style sheet or an external, linked style sheet. ➔ *embedded style sheet*

in pendentive *(typ)* A style of typesetting in which successive lines are indented at both ends, causing each line to be shorter than the last until only one word occupies the last line, the whole piece forming a triangle. Also called 'half-diamond indentation'.

in-plant proofing *(gen)* The term describing proof corrections – made by a proofreader employed by the printing company – that may not be shown to the client.

in print *(gen)* A publishing trade phrase describing a book that is available from the publisher, as opposed to 'out of print', one that isn't. ➔ *out of print (o.p.)*

in pro(portion) *(gen)* Two or more subjects for reproduction that are to be enlarged or reduced in proportion to each other, or alternatively an illustration whose dimensions are to be enlarged or reduced in proportion to each other.

input *(com)* Generally, anything that is put in or taken into something else, but usually used with reference to entering data into a computer by whatever means.

input device *(com)* Any item of hardware capable of entering data into a computer – e.g. a keyboard or a scanner. ➔ *device (1)*

input resolution *(com)* The degree of definition by which an image is 'captured', thus determining the final quality of output. Final output quality depends on three aspects of input: scan resolution, the size of the original image as compared with its final size (in which case, resolution of the scanner may also be significant) and resolution of the output device. To calculate input resolution, multiply the eventual halftone screen frequency by two and then multiply that answer by the ratio of the final image size to its original dimensions. For example, if the image is to be printed with a halftone screen of 150 lines per inch, multiply 150 x 2 to get 300. If the image has an original size of 2 x 3 inches but will be printed at a size of 6 x 9 inches, it has a ratio of 3 (9 ÷ 3). So, 300 x 3 = 900: the input resolution, in dots per inch, for scanning the image. ➔ *output resolution; scan dot*

An example of
inline lettering

in quires *(fin)* A general term applied to printed sheets, especially those lying flat, before they are folded and gathered for binding. Also called 'in sheets'. → *quires/quire stock*

insert (1) *(gen)* Part of a publication that is printed separately, perhaps using different coloured inks or on different paper, but which is bound into that publication. Also called an 'inset'. When printed pages are wrapped around the outside of a publication or section, this is called an 'outsert' or 'outset'. → *free-standing insert (FSI); saddleback book*

An application **install** program

An **insert** might comprise a colour section in a black-and-white book

insert (2) *(aud)* An insert jack on a mixer is a port that sends sound to be processed through an external effects unit, which then sends the processed sound back through the same port.

insert (3) *(fin)* A piece of paper, board or printed item placed loose between the pages of a book. Also called 'loose inserts' or 'throw ins'.

insertion point *(com)* The point in a document or dialog box at which the next character or action typed on the keyboard will appear. It is indicated by a blinking vertical line ('text insertion bar'), which can be positioned in the appropriate place by using the I-beam pointer and clicking. → *I-beam pointer*

inset *(fin)* → *insert (1)*

insides *(pap)* In a ream of paper (500 sheets), the term given to the 450 sheets (18 'quires') sandwiched between two outer quires ('outsides'). → *outsides; quire (1); ream*

install *(com)* To add any item of software to a computer so that it can be used. This is invariably achieved by means of an 'installer' program, which puts files in their appropriate places. Installers are also updating programs.

intaglio *(pri)* A printing process in which the image to be printed is recessed below the surface of the plate, such as in commercial gravure printing or fine art etching. → *gravure*

integrated circuit *(com)* The electronic circuit embedded in a microchip.

Integrated Services Digital Network (ISDN) *(int)* → *ISDN*

intellectual property *(gen)* → *copyright*

intensification *(pho)* A technique for chemically adjusting the density of developed photographic emulsion. The chemicals are known as 'intensifiers'.

interactive *(com)* Any activity that involves an immediate and reciprocal action between a person and a machine (driving a car, for example), but more commonly describing dialog between a computer and its user. → *interactive mode*

interactive mode *(com)* The ability of an application to process data as it is input, as distinct from that which is processed in batches (batch mode). For example, spelling is checked as it is input rather than later as a batch. Also called 'real-time' processing. → *interactive; real-time*

interapplication communication (IAC) *(com)* A protocol used by software developers to allow data to be shared and exchanged between applications.

intercharacter space *(typ)* → *character space*

interface *(com)* The physical relationship between human beings, systems and machines – in other words, the point of interaction or connection. The involvement of humans is called a 'human interface' or 'user interface'. Also used to describe the screen design that links the user with the computer program or website. → *command-line interface; GUI*

interlaced GIF *(int)* A 'GIF89a' format image in which the image reveals increasing detail as it downloads to a webpage. → *GIF; GIF 89a; transparent GIF*

interlacing/interlaced *(int)* A technique of displaying an image on a webpage, in which the image reveals increasing detail as it downloads. Interlacing is usually offered as an option when saving images in GIF, PNG and JPEG ('progressive') formats in image-editing applications. → *interlaced GIF; PNG; progressive JPEG*

interleaved *(pri)* Sheets of paper placed between newly printed sheets in order to prevent ink transfer or set-off. Also called 'slip-sheeting'.

interleave ratio *(com)* The ratio between the numbers and the order of track sectors on a disk. Sectors that are numbered consecutively have a ratio of 1:1, while a ratio of 3:1 means that the numbers run consecutively only in every third sector. This indicates how many times a disk needs to rotate so that all data in a single track is read; a computer with a slow data transfer rate requires a disk to spin more often so that it has time to absorb all of the data in a track. The fastest ratio is 1:1 because all the data in a track will be read in a single revolution of the disk. Also called 'sector interleave factor'. → *data transfer rate*

interleaving/interleaved *(com)* The technique of displaying an image on screen – using a Web browser, for example – so that it is revealed as a whole in increasing layers of detail rather than bit by bit from the top down. The image appears gradually, starting with slices that are eventually filled in when all the pixels appear. → *progressive JPEG*

interlinear spacing *(typ)* → *leading*

interlock *(typ)* To reduce the space between type characters so that they overlap.

intermediate *(gen)* A copy of an original from which other copies can be made. → *interneg(ative)*

intermediate code *(com)* A representation of computer code, which lies somewhere between code that can be read by you or I (such as HTML source code) and machine-readable binary code (1s and 0s). Java bytecode is one such example. → *HTML; Java; machine code*

internal modem *(com)* A modem that is installed inside a computer. → *modem*

International Colour Consortium (ICC) *(com)* → *ICC*

International Standard Book Number *(gen)* A unique ten-figure serial number allocated to and appearing on every book published, which identifies the language in which it is published, its publisher, its title and a check control number. ISBNs are often represented as a bar code.

Internaut *(int)* A colloquialism for someone who travels ('surfs') the Internet.

interneg(ative) *(pho)* A photographic negative used as the intermediate step when making a copy from a transparency or flat original. Also called 'intermediary'. → *intermediate*

Internet *(int)* The entire collection of connected worldwide networks, including those used solely for the Web. The Internet was originally funded by the United States Department of Defense. → *browser (1); World Wide Web (WWW)*

Text **interlock** is mostly used for display

browser produced by Microsoft.

Internet Protocol *(int)* The networking rules that tie computers together across the Internet.

Internet Protocol address *(int)* The unique numeric address of a particular computer or server on the Internet (or any TCP/IP network). Each one is unique and consists of a dotted decimal notation – for example, 194.152.64.68.

Internet Relay Chat *(int)* An Internet facility provided by some ISPs, which allows multiple users to type messages to each other in real-time on different 'channels', sometimes referred to as 'rooms'.

Internet Service Provider (ISP) *(int)* Any organization that provides access to the Internet. At its most basic, this may merely be a telephone number for connection, but most ISPs also provide other services such as e-mail addresses and capacity for your own webpages. Also called 'access provider'.

interpolate/interpolation *(com)* A computer calculation used to estimate unknown values that fall between known values. This process is used, for example, to redefine pixels in bitmapped images after they have been modified in some way, such as when an image is resized (called 'resampling') or rotated or if colour corrections have been made. In such cases, the program makes estimates from the known values of other pixels lying in the same or similar ranges. Interpolation is also used by some scanning and image-manipulation software to enhance the resolution of images that have been scanned at low resolution. Inserting animation values between two keyframes of a film sequence are also interpolations. Some applications allow you to choose an interpolation method – Photoshop, for example, offers *Nearest Neighbor* for fast but imprecise results that may produce

jagged effects. ➜ *descreen(ing); dither(ing) (1); resampling*

interpreter *(com)* Software that converts program code into machine language piece by piece as it is required, as distinct from a 'compiler', which converts a program in its entirety. ➜ *code; compiler*

interrupt button *(com)* On Macintosh computers, a hardware button that allows programmers to debug software.

intersect(ion) *(com)* In some drawing and page-layout applications, a feature that allows you to create a shape from two or more others that overlap, or 'intersect' each other.

intranet *(int)* A network of computers similar to the Internet but to which the general public do not have access. A sort of 'in-house' Internet service, intranets are used mainly by large corporations, governments and educational institutions to provide information and support to staff. ➜ *Internet*

intrinsic mapping *(com)* A 3-D method of mapping a texture to a surface by using the object's own geometry as a guide to placement, rather than the geometry of another shape such as a cylinder or sphere.

introduction *(gen)* The opening part of a publication, following the prelims, commenting on the purpose, content and logic of the work, usually (although not necessarily) written by its author. ➜ *prelims/preliminary pages*

inverse kinematics *(com)* Or IK for short. When animating hierarchical models, IK can be applied so that moving the lowest object in the hierarchy has an effect on all the objects further up. This is the inverse of how forward kinematics works. ➜ *forward kinematics*

invert (1) *(com)* A feature of many applications, in which an image bitmap is reversed so

I

invert (1) *(com)* A feature of many applications, in which an image bitmap is reversed so that the black pixels appear white and vice versa, making a negative image. Inverting also affects colours, turning blue to yellow, green to magenta and red to cyan. 'Invert' is sometimes used synonymously (and confusingly) with 'inverse', although the latter is more often used to mean reversing a selected area so that it becomes deselected.

invert (2) *(com)* In some page layout applications, the facility to flow text within a runaround path or picture shape rather than around it. → *runaround/run round*

inverted commas *(typ)* A pair of commas used to open or close a quotation. In the English language, they are used "thus", whereas in German they are sometimes used „thus". Some other European languages alternatively use 'duck foot quotes': «thus» or »thus«. → *duck foot quotes; quotation/quote marks/quotes*

invisible character/invisibles *(com)* Any character that may be displayed on screen but which does not print, such as spaces (·), paragraphs (¶), etc. Also called 'non-printing characters'.

invisible file *(com)* Any file that is not visible but nonetheless exists, such as directory files and icon files. Files can, for security reasons, be made invisible using a suitable utility program, although such files may still appear in directory dialog boxes. It is common practice to make the support files of multimedia applications invisible.

I/O *(com) abb.:* input/output. The hardware interactions between a computer and other devices, such as the keyboard and disk drives. → *BIOS*

IP *(int) abb.:* Internet Protocol. → *Internet; Internet Protocol; Internet Protocol address; IPnG*

IPA *(gen) abb.:* International Phonetic Alphabet. → *phonogram*

IP address *(int) abb.:* Internet Protocol address. → *Internet Protocol; Internet Protocol address; TCP (TCP/IP)*

iph *(pri) abb.:* impressions per hour. The speed at which a printing press prints each sheet.

IPnG *(int) abb.:* IP next generation. A new generation of Internet Protocols, which will expand the number of available Internet addresses. → *Internet Protocol*

IRC *(int) abb.:* Internet Relay Chat. → *Internet Service Provider (ISP)*

iris diaphragm *(pho)* → *diaphragm*

ISBN *(gen) abb.:* International Standard Book Number. → *International Standard Book Number*

ISDN *(int) abb.:* Integrated Services Digital Network. A telecommunication technology that transmits data on special digital lines rather than on old-fashioned analog lines, and is thus much faster. DSL (Digital Subscriber Line) links are even faster than ISDN. → *ADSL*

ISO (1) *(gen) abb.:* International Standards Organization. A Swiss-based body responsible for defining many elements common to design, photography and publishing, such as paper size film speed rating, and network protocol ('ISO/OSI' protocol).

Invert can refer to text within a path

The negative (right) is known as **invert**

ISO (2) *(pho)* An international standard rating for film speed, with the film getting faster as the rating increases. ISO 400 film is twice as fast as ISO 200, and will produce a correct exposure with less light and/or a shorter exposure. However, higher speed film tends to produce more grain in the exposure, too.

ISO/Adobe character set *(com)* The industry standard character set for PostScript text faces. Access to certain characters depends upon which operating system and application is being used. ➜ *character set*

ISO A-series paper sizes *(pap)* The 'A' series system of defining paper sizes was first adopted in Germany in 1922, where it is still referred to as 'DIN-A'. The sizes were calculated in such a way that each is a division into two equal parts of the size immediately above, and, because each uses the same diagonal, the proportions are geometrically identical. The basic size (A0) is one square metre in area, 841 x 1189mm (33.11 x 46.81in). 'A' series sizes refer to the trimmed sheets, whereas untrimmed sizes are known as 'RA' or, for printing work with bleeds, 'SRA'. 'B' sizes are used when intermediate sizes are required between any two adjacent A sizes, while 'C' sizes refer to envelopes. More than 26 countries have now officially adopted the ISO system, and it is likely that this system will gradually replace the wide range of paper sizes still used in the US and some other countries. Unlike the metric ISO series of paper sizes, the American and British systems of sizing paper refer to the untrimmed sheet size.

ISOC *(int)* Acronym for The Internet Society. A governing body to which the Internet Architecture Board (IAB) reports. ➜ *IAB*

isotype *(gen)* A method for graphically presenting statistical information, using pictograms or ideograms, pioneered by Otto and Marie Neurath's 'Isotype Institute'.

ISP *(int) abb.:* Internet Service Provider. ➜ *Internet Service Provider (ISP)*

ISSN *(gen) abb.:* International Standard Serial Number. A unique eight-figure number allocated to and appearing on periodicals, which identifies the country of publication as well as the title. ➜ *International Standard Book Number*

issue (1) *(gen)* The term describing part of an edition that, although comprised mostly of pages printed with the first printing, may have new front and/or end matter.

issue (2) *(gen)* One complete printing of all the copies of a periodical published at one time, as in 'July issue'.

IT *(com) abb.:* information technology. Anything to do with computers or telecoms, particularly networking and databases.

italic *(typ)* The sloping version of a roman type design, derived from cursive handwriting and calligraphic scripts, and intended for textual emphasis. The first italic type was cut by Aldus Manutius in about 1499. A version of italic, often called oblique or sloped roman, can be generated digitally by most applications, but this merely slants the roman style to the right and so is a poor substitute for the real thing. ➜ *contra italic*

IT-8 *(gen)* A series of test colour targets and tools for measuring colour behaviour of materials and devices, defined by the ANSI committee for digital data exchange standards. Different IT-8 targets are used to evaluate different devices. In colour management, an IT-8 target is used for building scanner or digital camera profiles.

item *(com)* A general term used to describe virtually any individual object created in a computer application, such as text boxes, picture boxes and rules.

Item tool *(com)* In some applications, a tool for selecting, modifying or moving items.

ivory board *(pap)* High-grade board made of one or more laminations of identical-quality sheets and having characteristic features of translucency and rigidity. ➜ *board (1)*

jacket flaps *(gen)* The extremities of a dust jacket, which fold inside the front ('front flap') or back ('back flap') of a book. Usually applies to hardback.

jacketing machine *(fin)* A machine that automatically wraps dust jackets around bound books – a practice that, although such machines were introduced in the 1950s, is still carried out by hand in many parts of the world where labour is cheap.
→ *dust jacket/wrapper*

jaconet *(fin)* A glazed cotton fabric used for lining the spines of books. → *mull*

Japanese vellum *(pap)* A thick paper, hand-made in Japan, with an ivory colour and smooth surface that becomes furry with excessive handling.

Java *(int)* A programming language devised by Sun Microsystems for creating small applications ('applets') that can be downloaded from a Web server and used, typically in conjunction with a Web browser, to add dynamic effects such as animations.
→ *applet; Web browser*

Java-based Extendable Typography (JET) *(int)* → *JET*

Java class library *(int)* Groups of frequently used Java routines that programmers use to add common functionality to Java applets. → *applet; Java*

JavaScript *(int)* Netscape's 'scripting' language, which provides a simplified method of applying dynamic effects to webpages, not to be confused with Sun Microsystem's Java. Microsoft's version of JavaScript for use in some versions of Internet Explorer is called 'JScript'.

Java virtual machine *(int)* A process that converts programming code into machine language.

jaw folder *(fin)* A folding unit fitted to a web press, which cuts and folds signatures.

JET *(int) abb.:* Java-based Extendable Typography, a font enhancement for Java.
→ *font embedding*

jim-dash *(gen)* A short rule that divides items in a newspaper, also called a 'dinky dash'.

Jacket flaps will often feature information about the book and its author

```
var x = 121;
var y = 1;
function Reload() {
x = x - y;
document.form1.clock.value = "reload in " + x + " seconds";
timerID = setTimeout("Reload()", 1000);
}
var timerID = null;
var timerRunning = false;
function stopclock() {
if(timerRunning) clearTimeout(timerID);
```
Untitled.txt

Some **JavaScript** as it appears in a text editor

JACKET FLAPS

These images show the effect of **JPEG** compression. As the quality setting (and file size) is reduced, blockiness increases

Original Image   100% Quality, 36Kb   50% Quality, 8Kb   0% Quality, 2.5Kb

jobbing *(pri)* Description of general, non-specialist printing, usually comprising short runs. The term originally described any printed job that could be achieved from a single sheet of paper, such as letterheads, business cards, menus, invitations, and so on. Also known as 'quick printing'.

job inks *(pri)* The term used to describe printing inks used for general printing, comprised of 75 per cent medium and 25 per cent pigment.

job jacket, job bag *(gen)* A folder or large envelope, which contains all matter relating to a particular project in progress, including all copy, transparencies, art, specifications and so on.

jog(ging) *(fin)* The process of shaking a pile of paper, either by hand or by machine, so that the edges of each sheet align before trimming. A 'jogger' may be attached to a press or form a separate unit. Also called 'knocking up'.

joint *(fin)* The point at which the spine and the boards of a casebound book are hinged. → *crash (3); nip (1)*

Joint Photographic Experts Group (JPEG) *(com)* → *JPEG*

joule *(pho)* Unit of electronic flash output, equal to one watt-second.

JPEG *(com)* (pron.: 'jay-peg') Acronym for Joint Photographic Experts Group. An ISO group that defines compression standards for bitmapped colour images. The abbreviated form gives its name to a 'lossy' (meaning some data may be lost) compressed file format, in which the degree of compression from high compression (low-quality) to low compression (high-quality) can be defined by the user. This makes the format doubly suitable for images that are to be used either for print reproduction or for transmitting across networks such as the Internet.

jump *(gen)* To continue a text or story on a succeeding page of a publication. → *jump line*

jump line *(gen)* A reference indicating that the text or story is continued elsewhere in the publication – for example, 'continued on page X'. → *jump; slug (2)*

justification *(typ)* The distribution of space between words and letters in lines of text so that all lines in the column have uniform ('flush') left and right edges. Text set like this may, in some applications, be called 'horizontal' justification, especially when that application offers an option for 'vertical' justification, in which spaces are inserted between lines of text so that it fills the column from top to bottom. → *hyphenation and justification (H&Js, H/Js); unjustified*

jute board *(pap)* A strong, light and durable board used particularly in binding.

*!?

J

K (1)/k *(gen) abb.:* key (plate). The black printing plate in four-colour process printing, but now the name is more commonly used as shorthand for the process colour black itself. Using the letter 'K' rather than the initial 'B' avoids confusion with blue, even though the abbreviation for process blue is 'C' (cyan).

K (2) KB/Kbyte *(com) abb.:* kilobyte. An uppercase KB stands for kilobyte while the upper and lower form, Kb, means kilobit. The letter K on its own isn't strictly enough to indicate either form clearly. Modem speed, for example, is often described as, say, 65K, when what is actually meant is 65 kilobits – which could also be expressed as 56kbps. ➔ *kilobyte (KB/Kbyte)*

K (3) *(gen)* ➔ *Kelvin temperature scale (K)*

kaolin *(pap)* ➔ *china clay*

Kbps *(com) abb.:* kilobits per second.
➔ *kilobyte (KB/Kbyte)*

keep down/up *(typ)* An instruction to set all text in lower case (keep down) or upper case (keep up) type. As distinct from 'put up' and 'put down' – changing characters already set. ➔ *put down/up*

keep in/out *(typ)* An instruction to make word spaces narrow (keep in) or wide (keep out).

keep standing *(pri)* An instruction to keep printing plates in readiness for a possible reprint.

Kelvin temperature scale (K) *(gen)* A unit of measurement that describes the colour of a light source, based on absolute darkness rising to incandescence. ➔ *colour temperature*

kenaf *(pap)* An Indian plant fibre used for making paper.

kermit *(int)* An older (thus slower) communications protocol.

kern *(typ)* The part of a metal type character that overhangs the next. ➔ *kerning*

kerning *(typ)* The adjustment of the space between adjacent type characters to optimize their appearance. Traditionally, kerned letters were those that physically overhung the metal body of the next character – particularly important in italic typefaces. The roman versions of most metal fonts were designed so that they did not require kerning. Kerning should not be confused with 'tracking', which is the adjustment of space over a number of adjacent characters. Also known as 'mortising'. ➔ *kerning pair; kerning table; kerning value; mortise (2); tracking (1)*

kerning pair *(typ)* Any two adjacent characters to which a specific kerning value has been applied. ➔ *kerning*

kerning table *(typ)* In some applications, a list of information describing the automatic kerning values of a font, which can sometimes be modified. ➔ *kerning*

A **kerning pair**, with no changes to the left, and altered on the right

kerning value *(typ)* The space between two adjacent characters, usually measured in units of an em. ➔ *em; kerning*

key (1) *(pri)* A printing plate – traditionally called the 'key plate' – or piece of artwork that acts as a guide for positioning and registering other colours. ➔ *K (1)/k*

key (2) *(com)* To enter matter ('input') into a computer via a keyboard.

key (3) *(aud)* The process of electronically substituting an alternative image or sequence into an area within a video picture. Used, for example, in TV weather broadcasts where a presenter appears to be standing in front of a computer-generated weather map. The overlaid image is keyed to a specified colour (chroma) or brightness level (luma).

keyboard *(com)* A device for entering data into a computer.

keyboard character *(com)* Any character generated by typing a key on the keyboard ➔ *keyboard; keyboard equivalent/shortcut*

key(board) combination *(com)* A combination of keys that, when pressed together, execute a specific computer function.

keyboard equivalent/shortcut *(com)* A command given to your computer made via the keyboard rather than by selecting the equivalent menu command. Typical keyboard equivalents usually require the use of a 'modifier' key such as 'Option' or 'Command' (Mac) or 'Alt' (Win). ➔ *Fkey; macro (1)*

keyboard event *(com)* The computer process generated when you press a keyboard key, occurring either at the moment you press down on the key ('key down') or when you release it ('key up'). If you hold down a key so that a process is repeated, it is called an 'auto-key event'. ➔ *event*

keyboard map *(com)* Characters as displayed on a monitor, which correspond with the arrangement on a keyboard.

keyboard special character *(com)* ➔ *keyboard equivalent/shortcut*

keyboarding *(com)* A term used, traditionally, to describe the typesetting procedure of inputting copy, but now referring to the action of computer input via a keyboard. ➔ *key (2)*

keyframe *(aud)* Used to control motion effects or animation, a keyframe is a point on the timeline where specified changes to an effect or object will take place. The editing application then interpolates how this will affect the frames between keyframes to create a smooth result.

key frame *(com)* In a QuickTime sequence, a single animation frame where information is stored as a reference. Subsequent frames store only changes in the frame, rather than storing the whole frame each time, thus making the file smaller. The frames based on changes are called 'delta frames' or 'difference frames'.

key letters/numbers *(gen)* Letters or numbers added to an illustration in order that specific elements can be linked to a description in a caption.

key light *(pho)* The main light source in a photographic setup.

key mapping *(aud)* The mapping of any digital function, sound, sample or instrument, to a specific key on a keyboard, usually a real or virtual music keyboard. An example would be mapping individual drum samples to specific keys, so that playing each key in turn creates an entire drum kit.

key plate *(pri)* ➔ *key (1)*

key reading *(pho)* In a photographic setup, an exposure reading of the key tone only. ➔ *key tone*

key repeat rate *(com)* ➔ *auto-key rate*

key tone *(pho)* The most important tone in a photographic scene, which must be recorded accurately.

keying *(com)* ➔ *key (2)*

K

keyline (1) *(pre)* In the conventional preparation of artwork (i.e. not involving a computer), an outline drawing that indicates areas to be filled with mechanical tints. → *mechanical tint*

keyline (2) *(gen)* A line drawing indicating the size and position of an illustration in a layout.

keyline (3) *(pre)* The outline on artwork that, when printed, will act as a guide for registering other colours.

keyline view *(com)* In some applications, a facility that provides an outline view of an object or illustration without showing attributes such as colours and line thicknesses.

keystroke *(com)* A single press of any key on a keyboard, whether or not it generates a character (a space, for example). The traditional means of assessing the cost of typesetting.

kicker *(gen)* A newspaper and magazine term for a line of text that appears above or below the title of a feature.

kill *(typ)* A largely obsolete term used to instruct a typesetter to dismantle a job, emanating from the tradition of 'dissing' (distributing) metal type into their respective cases upon completion of a job.

kilo *(gen)* A unit of metric measurement representing 1000 (from the Greek *'khilioi'*, meaning 'thousand'). However, although the term is widely used as a measure of computer data ('kilobyte', for example), computers use a binary system (pairs of numbers) in which each number is doubled: 2; 4; 8; 16; 32; 64; 128; 256; 512; 1024; etc. Thus 'kilo' in a data context does not mean 1000, but 1024. → *mega; mille*

kilobit (kb/kbit) *(com)* One kilobit is equal to 1024 bits. → *bit; kilobyte (KB/Kbyte)*

kilobits per second *(com)* A measurement of the speed at which data is transferred across a network, a kilobit being 1024 bits or characters.

kilobyte (KB/Kbyte) *(com)* One kilobyte is equal to 1024 bytes.

kinematics *(com)* Animated motion.

kipskin *(fin)* An animal skin sometimes used for bookbinding.

Kirlian photography *(pho)* A photographic technique in which the subject is placed against film and its image appears as an outline of electrical discharge.

kiss impression *(pri)* In printing, the term describing the lightest possible pressure required to make a perfect impression, particularly important when printing on coated papers. → *dwell*

Klischograph *(pri)* An electronic photoengraving machine, developed in Germany, which produces plastic or metal plates.

knife folder *(fin)* A folding machine in which a blunt knife forces the sheet of paper between two rollers, folding it in the process. → *buckle folder; combination folder*

knocked-out type *(typ)* → *dropped-out type*

knocking up *(fin)* → *jog(ging)*

knockout *(pre)* An area of background colour that has been masked ('knocked out') by a foreground object, and thus does not print. The opposite of 'overprint'. → *overprint (2)*

knowledge fade *(gen)* An expression that describes the condition arising from lack of continual familiarity with a process or, more commonly these days, with computer software. In other words, unless you use a particular application frequently, your knowledge of it will rapidly diminish.

Kodalith MP System *(pre)* A proprietary orthochromatic film system. → *orthochromatic*

kraft (paper) *(pap)* Strong brown paper made from sulphate wood pulp, used in packaging.

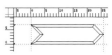

The lower illustration is a **keyline** of the top one

KEYING

Lab color *(com)* Lab color (as opposed to the CIE L*a*b* color model) is the internal colour model used by Photoshop when converting from one colour mode to another. 'Lab mode' is useful for working with PhotoCD images.

laced on *(fin)* A description of bindings in which the boards are affixed to the book by means of cords onto which the sections have been sewn.

lacing in *(fin)* The stage of binding in which the boards are attached to a hand-sewn book before a leather cover is fitted.

lacquer *(fin)* A solution that provides a glossy finish and a protective coating.

lacuna *(typ)* A traditional term for a blank space in a piece of text, caused by damaged or missing copy. From the Latin *'lacus'*, meaning 'lake'.

laid paper *(pap)* Paper made with subtle parallel lines in its surface instead of the smooth surface of wove paper. The laid finish is impressed by a dandy roll on a fourdrinier machine. → *chain lines/marks; dandy roll; fourdrinier*

lamination/laminate *(fin)* An item composed of two or more layers of material. In print finishing, this usually means applying transparent or coloured plastic films, with any degree of shininess, to printed matter to protect or enhance it.

lampblack *(pri)* A pigment made from carbon, which is used to make black printing ink.

LAN *(com)* *abb.:* local area network. → *network*

lands (1) *(pri)* The unetched grid on a gravure plate that forms the edges of the ink-bearing recessed cells. → *gravure*

lands (2) *(com)* → *CD-ROM*

landscape format *(gen)* An image or page format in which the width is greater than the height. Also called 'horizontal' format. → *portrait, upright format*

lap *(pre)* Abbreviation for overlap, describing colours that overlap to avoid registration problems ('trapping'). → *trapping*

lapis lazuli *(gen)* A mineral used to make ultramarine colour pigment.

lap lines *(pri)* A printing aberration of fine lines between images, caused by two adjacent pieces of film touching each other when assembled prior to platemaking. Also called 'butt lines'.

laptop (computer) *(com)* A small, portable computer, as distinct from the larger 'desktop' variety.

large-screen emulation *(com)* A feature of certain utilities to provide a larger screen size than you may already have. When the pointer reaches the edge of the screen, the screen automatically scrolls. → *emulation*

laser *(com)* Acronym for light amplification by stimulated emission of radiation. The process of generating an intense, fine beam of light, sometimes with considerable energy (the term also describes the device used to generate the light). It is used extensively in computer hardware such as optical discs, printers and scanners, and for various commercial printing activities such as platemaking and engraving.

laser font *(com)* → *outline font*

laser printer *(com)* A printer that uses a laser as part of the mechanical process of printing onto paper. → *demand printing; laser*

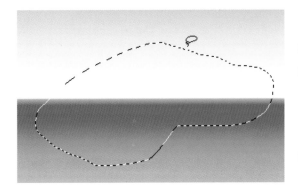

Lasso tool *(com)* The freehand selection tool indicated by a lasso icon in the Photoshop Toolbar. There are many other variations on the basic lasso, such as the *Magnetic Lasso* (which can identify the edges nearest to the selection path, aiding accurate selection of discrete objects) and the *Polygon Lasso* (which allows straight-edged selections to be made). In the case of the latter, to draw a straight line, place the cursor point at the end of the first line and click; place the cursor at the end of the next line and click again to select the second segment.

latency *(aud)* In the analog audio world, sound travels at 344 metres/376 yards per second. In the switched-on, switched-off world of computers, however, digital audio is data that has to be buffered, just like any other data. It also has to be converted between analog and digital at the recording stage, then back again on playback and monitoring. This can mean that you hear (and see) perceptibly slow response times when you are dealing with audio in real time, especially when you are monitoring via ASIO to external monitors, using a number of VST plug-ins, or watching the signal peaks in your virtual mixer. This is known as the 'latency' of the system, and it is measured in milliseconds.

latency time *(com)* → *access time*

latent image *(pho)* An image that lies dormant until something happens to it to make it appear. In photography, this is used to describe a recorded image that only becomes apparent after it is processed.

lateral reverse *(gen)* The transposing of an image from left to right, as in a mirror reflection. → *reflection tool*

lathe/lathing *(com)* In 3D applications, a technique of creating a 3D object by rotating a two-dimensional profile around an axis – just like carving a piece of wood on a real lathe.

Latin (1) *(typ)* The standard alphabet used in most European languages, consisting of the upper- and lower-case characters from A to Z. The exceptions are Greek and Cyrillic. Oriental languages, including Arabic and Hebrew, are classified as 'exotics'. → *exotic*

latin (2) *(typ)* A term sometimes given to typefaces derived from letterforms common to Western European countries, especially those with heavy, wedge-shaped serifs.

Latin text *(typ)* → *dummy text*

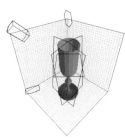

A cup created in 3D by **lathing** a 2D shape

The **Lasso tool** is perfectly suited to selecting random shapes

LASER

latitude *(pho)* The range of exposures that produce an acceptable image on a given type of film.

launch *(com)* To open, or start, a software application. You can do this by (a) double-clicking on the application's icon, (b) highlighting the icon and choosing 'Open' from the File menu or 'Start', or (c) using either of these techniques to open a document created in that application. Some applications will permit you only to open a document from within the application – i.e. you have to launch the application itself and then use the 'Open' command to access the document.

lay edges *(pri)* The two edges of a sheet that are placed flush with the side and front marks on a printing machine, to make sure the sheet will be removed properly by the grippers and have uniform margins when printed.

layer *(com)* In some applications and webpages, this is a level to which you can consign an element of the design on which you are working. Selected layers may be active (meaning you can work on them) or inactive. Some applications may not provide

Using a **layer mask** to hide areas from editing

This image was created using two separate **layers**, the background and the woman can be moved and edited independently

a layering feature but nonetheless may lay items one on top of another in the order that you created them, and in some cases will allow you to send items to the back or to bring them to the front of the stack.

layer effects/layer styles *(com)* Series of effects, such as *Drop Shadow*, *Inner Glow*, *Emboss* and *Bevel*, enacted on the contents of a layer.

layer mask *(com)* A mask that can be applied to the elements of an image in a particular layer. The layer mask can be modified to create different effects, but such changes do not alter the pixels of that layer. As with adjustment layers (of which this is a close relation), a layer mask can be applied to the 'host' layer (to make the changes permanent) or removed, along with any changes. → *adjustment layer*

layer menu *(com)* Menu dedicated to layer manipulations. Options allow you to create, delete or duplicate layers; link, group and arrange layers; and flatten an image.

laying on *(fin)* The term describing the process of applying gold leaf to a surface.

layout *(gen)* A drawing that gives the general appearance of a design, indicating, for example, the position of text and illustrations. The term is also more used in the context of preparing a design for reproduction, where it is called a 'tissue' or 'overlay', the terms deriving from the transparent paper often used for drawing layouts. → *tissue*

layout element *(int)* The description of any component in the layout of an HTML document – a webpage, for example – such as a graphic, list, rule or paragraph. → *HTML*

layout paper *(pap)* → *detail/layout paper*

lay sheet (1) *(pre)* A sheet of glass on which flats are assembled prior to printing down to a photo-offset plate. → *flat (1)*

lay sheet (2) *(pri)* The term describing the first of many sheets passed through a press to check such things as register.

lc, l/c *(typ) abb.:* lower case. → *lower case*

LCD (1) *(com) abb.:* liquid crystal display. → *liquid crystal display; monitor*

lcd (2) *(gen) abb.:* lowest common denominator. The most basic level that can be understood by everyone concerned.

leaded *(typ)* Type set with space, or 'leads', between the lines. → *leading*

leader line/leader rule *(gen)* A line keying elements of an image to annotation or a caption. → *dogleg; leader(s)*

leader(s) *(gen)* A row of dots, dashes or other characters, used to guide the eye across a space to other relevant matter. In some applications, leaders can be specified as a 'fill' between tab stops in text. → *leader line/leader rule*

leading *(typ)* Space between lines of type, originating from the days of metal typesetting when strips of lead ('leads') were placed between lines of type to increase the space. In digital applications, leading can be specified as a) absolute: a specific value given to spaces between lines of text, b) auto: the value given to automatic line spacing by means of a user-definable preference, or c) incremental: a value given to line spacing, which totals the largest character on the line plus or minus a user-defined value. → *leads*

leads *(typ)* In conventional metal typesetting, the thin strips of lead used to separate lines of text, giving rise to the term 'leading'. → *leading*

leaf (1) *(gen)* Each of the folios of a sheet after it is folded, resulting in a page on each side.

leaf (2) *(pap)* A newly made sheet of paper before it is dried and finished.

leaf edge *(pri)* The edge of a paper sheet opposite the gripper edge. → *gripper edge*

leak(s) *(pri)* The term describing the tiny gaps that may occur when adjoining colours misregister during printing.

lean matter *(typ)* → *fat matter*

leatherette *(pap)* A simulation of real leather made from a strong, embossed 'machine glazed' (MG) paper.

LED *(com) abb.:* light emitting diode. An electronic component providing miniature light sources, which are used to display alphanumeric characters on some hardware devices.

left-aligned *(typ)* → *unjustified*

legal *(pap)* A US size of paper measuring 8½ x 14in (215.9 x 355.6mm).

legal colours *(gen)* Colours that fit within the standards of the governing broadcast bodies in a given territory. Computer monitors can display some colours that fall outside of the capabilities of the TV screen, and particular colours with high luminance values (particularly reds) are forbidden by the major broadcast authorities.

legend *(gen)* The text printed below an illustration or map, describing the subject or the symbols used. More commonly called a caption, albeit inaccurately. → *caption*

length *(int)* A CSS webpage measurement expressed in units such as pixels or points. → *cascading style sheet (CSS)*

A computer-generated effect using the **Lens Flare filter**

lens *(pho)* The name describing a cylindrical tube that contains one or more glass elements, which collect and focus light rays to create an image.

lens flare *(pho)* → *flare*

Lens Flare filter *(pho)* A render filter that introduces (controllable) lens flare into images that previously had none. Lens flare can often be simulated for a variety of lenses – for example, using multiple artefacts for multi-element zooms.

lens speed *(pho)* → *f-number/f-stop*

letter *(pap)* A standard size of US paper measuring 8½ x 11in (215.9 x 279.4mm).

The Photoshop **Levels** dialog

letter fold *(fin)* A sheet of paper folded two or more times with the crease running in the same direction.

letterform *(typ)* The description of any drawn or designed alphanumeric character, whether used as a typeface or as a hand-drawn script.

letterhead(ing) *(gen)* Strictly speaking, the heading – name, address and telephone number of a business or individual – on any item of stationery, but sometimes used to describe the item of stationery specifically used for writing letters.

letterpress *(pri)* The original relief printing process, in which the surface of a raised, or relief, image or piece of type is inked and then pressed onto paper or some other surface.

letterpress binding *(fin)* A term that distinguishes the bindings of books that are to be read from those that are to be written in ('stationery binding').

letterset *(pri)* A contraction of letterpress and offset. A method of offset printing from a relief plate. Also called 'letterset', 'indirect letterpress' and 'relief offset'.

letterspacing/letterfit *(typ)* The adjustment of space between type characters (from that allocated by the font designer) by kerning or by increasing or decreasing the tracking.
→ *differential letterspacing; kerning; tracking (1)*

levelling *(fin)* A stage in perfect binding in which a small amount is shaved off the spine, therefore making it flat and square.

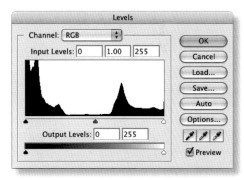

Levels *(com)* An image-editing tool that maps tones in an image, from the darkest shadows to the brightest highlights, as a histogram. By adjusting sliders on the histogram, you can remap tones across the image to improve the use of tonal range.

lexicon *(gen)* The term describing, originally, a dictionary of languages such as Greek and Hebrew, but now used more for dictionaries on specific subjects, like *The Designer's Lexicon*.

LEXICON

lhp *(gen) abb.:* left-hand page, or 'verso'.
→ *recto; verso*

library *(com)* A feature of some applications. It provides a facility for storing those frequently used items or attributes (such as colours) that have been created so that they can be accessed immediately from within any document.

library edition/binding *(fin)* Part of a standard edition that is specially bound with strengthened stitching, endpapers, joints, covers and so on, to endure continual handling. In the US, specifications for library bindings are determined by the American Library Association (ALA).

Library of Congress number (LOC) *(gen)* In the context of publishing, a reference number applied to books published in the USA and recorded at the Library of Congress.

library picture/pic *(gen)* → *image library*

library shot *(gen)* → *image library*

license/licensing *(gen)* The right granted to someone so that they can use something that belongs to someone else. The term describes two opposing views of the same meaning: either the licensor licenses the right to use, say, an intellectual asset to a licensee (to collect a fee), or the licensee licenses it from a licensor (by paying a fee).
→ *copyright*

lift *(pri)* An unquantifiable measure of the total amount of ink applied to the surface of paper in multicolour printing.

lifted matter *(gen)* Text, already typeset, that is taken from one job and used in another.

ligature *(typ)* Two or three type characters tied, or joined together, to make a single type character. Also called 'tied letters' or 'tied characters'.

light emitting diode (LED) *(com)* → *LED*

lightfast *(gen)* A description of ink or other material whose colour is not affected by exposure to artificial or natural light, atmosphere or chemicals. Also called 'colourfast'.

light/light face *(typ)* Type with an inconspicuous light appearance, based on the same design as medium, or roman, weight type in the same type family. The opposite of bold face. → *weight (1)*

light metre *(pho)* → *exposure metre*

lightness *(gen)* The tonal measure of a colour, relative to a scale running from black to white. Also called 'brightness' or 'value'.

light sensitive *(gen)* Any material or device that responds either chemically or digitally to light striking it, such as a photographic emulsion or a photosite (the light sensor of a CCD). → *CCD; emulsion*

light table/box *(pho)* A table or box with a translucent glass top lit from below, giving a colour-balanced light suitable for viewing colour transparencies and for colour-matching them to proofs.

light tent *(pho)* Translucent material placed around a subject, lighting being directed through the material to give a diffused effect, thus simplifying reflections.

lightweight paper *(pap)* An imprecise grouping of thin, tough papers of a substance ranging from about 20 to 50gsm (or less than 80gsm for coated papers), or 17 to 40lb per 25 x 38in ream.

limitcheck error *(com)* An error sometimes encountered when printing a complex document, caused either by too little RAM in the printer or by an illustration containing too many line segments for PostScript to handle. → *RAM*

limited edition *(gen)* An edition of a publication that is confined to a specified number of copies is usually numbered, and in some cases signed, by its author.

Examples of roman and italic **ligatures**

L

limiting *(aud)* Inhibiting certain audio frequencies or setting amplitude parameters during recording, mastering or playback. A hard limiter effect will allow a signal level to increase, but will attenuate any portions of a sample that are going past the defined limit (often 0 dB in digital audio) so that clipping does not occur. This is related to compression.

limpback *(fin)* → *paperback*

limp binding *(fin)* A form of binding using a flexible material such as paper, cloth or leather, with no stiffening, as distinct from case binding. Bibles are often bound in this way, with overhanging, or 'yapp', edges.
→ *circuit edges; Yapp binding*

limp flush *(fin)* → *flush cover/boards*

lineal type *(typ)* → *sans serif*

line and halftone *(pre)* Halftone and line work combined onto one set of films, plates, or artwork, as distinct from the tone-line process. → *tone-line process*

line and halftone fit up *(pre)* → *combination line and halftone*

linear gradient *(com)* Option of most gradient tools. Shades uniformly along a line drawn across the selection. The start point is coloured in the first colour (or foreground colour, in a foreground to background gradient) and the end point in the last colour (or background). A gentle gradient is achieved by drawing a long line over the selection (which can extend beyond the selection at

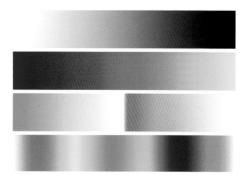

either extreme); a harsher gradient will result from drawing a short line within the selection.

linear motion style *(com)* A 3D calculation of the unknown values between two known key frame values of an animation, done by calculating the shortest distance between the two.

linear screen *(pre)* A halftone screen that uses lines rather than dots to prepare an image for reproduction. Used for effect rather than for any particular benefit. → *dot shape*

line art(work) *(pre)* Artwork or camera-ready copy consisting only of black on white, with no intermediate tones and thus not requiring halftone reproduction. Also called 'line copy', 'line work' or 'line original'.
→ *mechanical tint*

line block *(pri)* A relief printing plate used to reproduce images consisting of lines or solid areas with no tonal graduation.

line board *(gen)* A general term for smoothly finished boards with low absorbency, suitable for drawing line artwork with Indian ink.

line conversion (technique) *(pre)* The photographic or electronic method of eliminating the middle tones from a continuous tone original so that it can be treated as line artwork. Also called 'drop tone'.

A **line conversion** removes all shading

A selection of **linear gradients**, ranging from the traditional two-tone to various combinations at different speeds

lined characters *(typ)* ➔ *strike through (2)/ strike thru*

line engraving *(pri)* An intaglio printing process in which the design is cut into the surface of a copper plate – no acid is used. Tonal variations are achieved by hatched lines.

line feed *(typ)* ➔ *line interval/line feed*

line film *(pre)* Negative or positive photographic film in which the image consists of solid elements, such as lines or text matter, with no continuous tones or halftones (actually, halftones are usually printed to line film because they consist entirely of solid dots). ➔ *orthochromatic*

line gauge *(typ)* A rule marked with a scale of measurements in varying increments of point size.

line increment *(typ)* The smallest allowable increase in the basic measure between typeset lines (leading). ➔ *leading*

line interval/line feed *(typ)* The phototypesetting equivalent of 'leading', measured from baseline to baseline in millimetres, inches or points. ➔ *leading*

linen faced *(pap)* Originally, paper lined on one or both sides with linen but now known as 'cloth faced' or 'cloth lined'. ➔ *linen finish; linen paper*

linen finish *(pap)* Paper embossed to resemble coarsely woven cloth. ➔ *linen paper*

linen paper *(pap)* Originally, paper made with linen rags, but the term now describes paper embossed to resemble linen ('linen finish'). ➔ *linen finish*

linen tester *(gen)* ➔ *magnifier/magnifying glass*

line pattern *(typ)* The sequence of dots, dashes and spaces in a rule.

liners *(fin)* The term describing thin, strong paper used to line the boards of a cased book, particularly those bound in leather.

line spacing *(typ)* ➔ *leading*

lines per inch (lpi) *(pre)* The measurement of the resolution, or coarseness, of a halftone, being the number of rows of dots to each inch. It is not to be confused with screen resolution, which is measured in pixels per inch. ➔ *pixels per inch (ppi); resolution (1); screen resolution*

Line tool *(com)* In graphics applications, the tool used to draw lines and rules. If the tool can only draw horizontal and vertical rules, it is usually called an 'orthogonal' line tool. ➔ *tool*

line up *(gen)* ➔ *alignment*

line weight *(gen)* The thickness of a line or rule.

Lingo *(com)* A computer programming language used by Macromedia's multimedia software, Director. ➔ *script (1); scripting language*

lining figures/numerals *(typ)* A set of numerals aligned at top and bottom. Sometimes called 'modern' numerals.

lining/lining up *(fin)* A bookbinding term for strengthening the back of a book with mull. ➔ *mull*

lining papers *(fin)* ➔ *endpapers*

link (1) *(int)* A pointer, such as a highlighted piece of text, in an HTML document (a webpage, for example) or multimedia presentation, which takes the user to another location, page or screen just by clicking on it. ➔ *hyperlink*

link (2)/linking *(com)* In some frame-based page-layout applications, the facility to connect two or more text boxes so that text flows from one box to another.

linocut *(pri)* A crude relief printing block with a linoleum surface, into which the design is cut.

Drawing a curved line with a **Line tool**

*!?

The blue highlighted text areas are all **links**

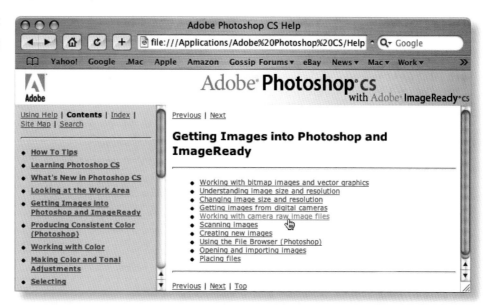

Linotype *(typ)* A type foundry and manufacturer of typesetting equipment and digital fonts. The original Linotype machine was the first keyboard-operated composing machine to employ the principle of a 'matrix', which cast hot metal type in solid lines, or 'slugs'. It was invented by the German-born American engineer Ottmar Mergenthaler and patented in 1884. The Monotype machine was invented almost simultaneously, in 1885. → *casting; Monotype*

linting/lint *(pap)* → *fluff(ing)*

lip *(fin)* The term describing the extended edge of a signature, which is gripped during saddle-stitch binding. → *saddle-stitched; signature (1)*

liquid crystal display *(com)* A digital display technology commonly seen on calculators, clocks and computer displays, particularly on portables and laptops.

list element *(int)* Text in a webpage that is displayed as a list and which is defined by the HTML tag <LI> (list item). This tag is also called the 'list tag'.

listserv *(int)* An automated mailing list distribution system, typically based on UNIX servers.

literal *(gen)* An error that may occur at any stage of copy preparation, from author's manuscript to typeset galleys, such as a spelling mistake. As distinct from a 'typo', which is an error occurring during typesetting, such as the wrong font. → *typo*

lith (film) *(pre)* → *orthochromatic*

lithography *(pri)* A 'planographic' printing process invented in 1798 by a German, Aloys Senefelder, in which an image is produced from a dampened, flat surface, using greasy ink. Based on the principle of the mutual repulsion of oil and water.

live matter *(pri)* Any matter, such as type or plates, that is waiting to be printed.

loading *(pap)* The action of adding a substance such as china clay during papermaking to improve or alter the characteristics of the finished product.

LOC *(gen)* abb.: Library of Congress → *ISBN; Library of Congress number (LOC)*

loc. cit. *(gen)* abb.: *loco citato*. A Latin term meaning 'in the place named', and used as a reference in footnotes.

lock (1) *(com)* A facility in some applications for securing, or anchoring, an item, either so that it cannot be moved or so that it cannot be modified.

lock (2) *(com)* → *locked file*

locked disk *(com)* A removable or floppy disk that is write-protected and thus can only be read.

locked file *(com)* A data file that cannot be modified or deleted.

lock on *(pri)* → *trapping*

logical volume *(com)* A volume (such as a partition) created by software, as distinct from a physical volume such as a disk. → *partition(ing)*

logic board *(com)* → *circuit board*

logo/logotype *(gen)* Traditionally, a 'logotype' is any group of type characters, such as company names or emblems, which are cast together on one metal body. However, the term is now used to describe any design or symbol, such as a pictogram, which forms the centrepiece of a corporation's or organization's corporate identity. → *pictogram/pictograph*

logography *(gen)* → *logo/logotype*

log on *(com)* To connect to a network.

long-bodied type *(typ)* The term describing metal type characters cast on larger bodies than usual, thus increasing the space between lines without the need for leading.

long descenders *(typ)* The descenders, such as g, j, p, q, and y, that are particularly long on certain typefaces and which are offered as an alternative to the standard characters of the typeface.

long-focus lens *(pho)* A camera lens with a focal length longer than the diagonal measurement of the film format. Thus, for 35mm film, a lens longer than about 50mm is long-focus. → *short-focus lens; telephoto lens*

long grain *(pap)* → *machine direction*

long ink *(pri)* Printing ink mixed to a consistency so that it does not break when drawn out in a thread. The opposite of 'short ink'. → *short ink*

long page *(gen)* A page on which the type area has been extended by one or two lines to avoid an inconvenient break.

long primer *(typ)* A former size of type, about 10 point.

long s *(typ)* A lower-case 's' used in old forms of printed English, resembling an 'f'. On some character sets, a 'long s' is called a 'florin'.

look-through *(pap)* A term used when describing the opacity of a paper, whereby text or images printed on one side of a sheet are visible from the other side. This may be caused by the use of incompatible inks and papers, but more often it is because the paper is too thin. Also called 'show-through' or 'see-through'.

lookup field *(com)* A field in a database file, which provides the same information as a specified field in another file. → *database*

lookup table *(com)* → *CLUT*

loop *(aud)* In electronic music, a loop is a piece of rhythm or percussion that loops seamlessly to a specific tempo.

loop stitching *(fin)* A technique of saddle-stitching in which the wire forms a loop that extends beyond the spine, thus providing an alternative to drilled holes as a means of attaching the publication to a post or ring binder.

loose insert *(fin)* → *insert (2)*

loose-leaf binding *(fin)* A binding method that allows easy insertion or removal of individual leaves of paper, as in 2-, 3-, or 4-ring binders.

When saving files, many applications offer an **LZW** compression option

loose line, loose setting *(typ)* Lines of justified type that have been set with excessive word spacing, causing 'rivers' of white space to flow down the column of text. → *river*

lossless/lossy *(com)* Refers to the data-losing qualities of different compression methods. 'Lossless' means that no information is lost; 'lossy', which specifically refers to still and moving image compression, means that some (or much) of the image data is lost in the compression process (but the data will download quicker).

loudspeaker *(aud)* A device that converts electrical impulses to acoustic energy, turning signals to sounds.

loupe *(gen)* → *magnifier/magnifying glass*

low-bulk paper *(pap)* Thin, smoothly finished paper.

This is a **low-key** image

low contrast *(gen)* → *contrast*

lower case *(typ)* The small letters in a font, as distinct from capitals ('upper case'). Also called 'miniscules'. → *case (2); upper case*

lower-third *(typ)* A common form of caption, which usually appears in the lower-third of the screen.

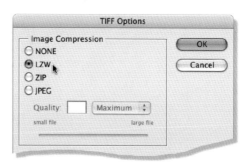

low key *(pho)* A photographic image that is given overall dark tones either by lighting or by processing. → *contrast*

low-profile *(gen)* Any item that is at the same level as surrounding items, or which blends in with its surroundings. The opposite of high-profile. → *high-profile*

lpi *(pre) abb.:* lines per inch. → *lines per inch (lpi)*

luma *(aud)* Shortened form of 'luminance'. The technical name for the brightness component of a video signal.

luminaire *(pho)* A large photographic tungsten lamp, which is focused by means of a fresnel lens. → *fresnel lens*

luminance *(gen)* The brightness of a colour, from solid black to the brightest possible value.

lupe *(gen)* → *magnifier/magnifying glass*

Lynx *(int)* A UNIX-based Web browser that runs in character, or text, mode.

LZW *(com) abb.:* Lempel-Ziv-Welch. A widely supported 'lossless' compression method for bitmapped images, giving a compression ratio of 2:1 or more, depending on the range of colours in an image. Thus an image with large areas of flat colour will yield higher compression ratios. → *compression (1)*

L

Mm

m (1) *(gen) abb.:* magenta. ➔ *magenta (m)*

m (2) *(gen) abb.:* mille. The Latin term meaning 'one thousand'.

MacBinary *(com)* A file format that allows Apple Macintosh files to be transferred via modem or shared with non-Mac computers by ensuring that all component parts such as the 'resource' and 'data' forks remain together.

machine-binding process *(fin)* The entire automated process of bookbinding, usually in separate units that may or may not be linked together. This comprises bundling, affixing endpapers, gathering, sewing, nipping, trimming, glueing, rounding and backing, lining, casing-in and pressing.

machine clothing *(pap)* The wire, press felts and drier felts on a papermaking machine.

machine-coated paper *(pap)* ➔ *imitation art (paper)*

machine code *(com)* The lowest level of programming code – i.e. the one least understandable to the user but most easily understood by a computer. ➔ *code*

machine direction *(pap)* The path of paper through a papermaking machine that determines the grain. 'Long grain' indicates the direction of the paper path, whereas 'short grain' is at right angles to it. ➔ *grain direction*

machine dot *(com)* The tiny dots made by an imagesetter, which form everything in the output image, including halftone dots. They are invisible at high resolutions, even when magnified. The shape of a machine dot is consistently square and cannot be modified as a halftone dot's shape can. Changing the resolution of machine dot ('printer resolution') does not affect the resolution of halftone screen ruling, although the relationship between screen ruling and printer resolution determines the tonal range that can be printed. As the screen ruling increases, the size of the halftone 'cell' (the largest size of halftone dot) decreases, thus fewer machine dots are used to create the halftone dot, so fewer shades will be rendered. Machine dots are also called 'printer dots' or 'recorder elements'. ➔ *halftone dot; scan dot*

machine engraving *(pri)* The process of cutting an image into a gravure printing cylinder with mechanized engraving tools.

machine finish (MF) *(pap)* Paper with a smooth, though not glossy, surface, made by passing it through heavy polished rollers ('calenders'). MF paper is suitable for printing text and line illustrations but does not reproduce fine halftones well. Also called 'mill-finished'. ➔ *machine glazed (MG)*

machine glazed (MG) *(pap)* Paper with a highly polished surface on one side and a rough surface on the other. ➔ *machine finish (MF)*

machine-made paper *(pap)* Paper made as a continuous web on cylinder or fourdrinier machines. ➔ *fourdrinier*

A typical screen using Apple's **Mac OS**

$\bar{a}$

A **macron** denotes a long vowel

machine proof *(pri)* A final ink proof made on a press similar to the one on which it will be printed. Also called a 'press proof'.

machine readable *(com)* Text or data that can be read by a machine and converted to a digital format, such as in magnetic ink character recognition (MICR) or optical character recognition (OCR). → *MICR; OCR*

machine revise *(pri)* → *press revise*

machine ruling *(pri)* → *ruling machine*

machine-sewing *(fin)* A mechanical bookbinding process in which the individual leaves of a folded section are sewn together at the same time as the sections are sewn together.

machine sheet *(pri)* Any printed sheet coming off a press.

Macintosh *(com)* The brand name of the Apple Computer's range of personal computers. The Macintosh was the first commercially available computer to successfully utilize the 'graphical user interface' (GUI), pioneered by Xerox Corporation's Palo Alto Research Center (PARC), although the concept was first seen in Apple's unsuccessful 'Lisa' computer. The Macintosh heralded the concept of 'plug and play' computing, while the use of a GUI provided the platform for the software applications that gave rise to

the phenomenon of 'desktop publishing' (DTP). This revolutionized not only the graphic design profession but the entire graphic arts industry – all in the space of 10 years. → *desktop publishing (DTP); GUI; Mac OS*

mackle *(pri)* A printing fault resulting in blurring or a double impression, caused by movement of the paper while printing. → *slur*

Mac OS *(com)* The operating system used on Apple Computer's 'Macintosh' series of computers, which provides the underlying 'graphical user interface' (GUI) on which all applications and files depend. Unlike other operating systems, such as Microsoft's 'DOS' and 'Windows', which are entirely software-based, the Mac OS is part software and part 'firmware' (software built into a hardware 'ROM' chip on the Mac's motherboard). This provides a consistent interface with standard control mechanisms, such as dialog boxes and windows, and this allows all software written for the Macintosh to have the same look and feel. → *graphical user interface (GUI); MS-DOS; ROM; Windows*

macro (1) *(com)* A term deriving from the Greek *makros*, meaning long or large. 'Macroscopic', for example, means large units, whereas 'microscopic' describes small things. In computer parlance, a macro is a single command containing several other commands – one large unit comprised of smaller units. Thus the term describes a sequence of actions or commands that have been recorded so that they can be repeated at any time using a single command (usually a keystroke). → *function keys*

macro (2) *(pho)* A mode offered by some lenses and cameras to enable the lens or camera to focus in extreme close-up.

macron *(typ)* A pronunciation symbol representing a long vowel, indicated by a line above a letter.

macrophotography *(pho)* The photography of large-scale objects, often used erroneously to describe 'photomacrography', which is close-up photography
→ *photomacrography; photomicrography*

MacTCP *(int)* Acronym for Macintosh transmission control protocol, the Mac OS version of TCP. → *(TCP/IP)*

made-up proofs *(gen)* → *page proofs*

magenta (m) *(gen)* With cyan and yellow, one of the three subtractive primaries, and one of the three process colours used in four-colour printing. Sometimes called 'process red'. → *CMY; CMYK*

magenta printer *(pre)* In four-colour process printing, the plate or film used to print magenta ink.

magnetic disk *(com)* → *disk*

magnetic induction *(aud)* A process by which electrical impulses cause the magnets in a loudspeaker to vibrate, thus transmitting sound.

magnetic ink character recognition (MICR) *(com)* A process in which specially designed characters are printed with a magnetic ink so that they can be 'read' by a machine. Used widely for security printing – for example, bank cheques. → *OCR*

magnetic ink characters *(typ)* Characters that are readable by an MICR machine.
→ *magnetic ink character recognition (MICR)*

magnetic media/storage *(com)* Any computer data storage system that uses a magnetic medium, such as disk, tape or card, to store information. → *disk*

magneto-optical disc (MO/MOD) *(com)* A rewritable storage medium that combines the technologies of a laser and an electromagnet for writing and reading data, the result being that data cannot be corrupted by stray magnetic fields.
→ *disc; disk; floptical*

magnifier/magnifying glass *(gen)* A lens used to inspect the quality of printing proofs, film, photographic transparencies, etc. Some magnifiers incorporate additional features such as adjustable focus, built-in measuring scales and a light source. Also called 'loupe', 'lupe' or 'linen tester' (after the folding device used in the textile industries for counting threads in linen).

Magnify tool *(com)* A tool in most computer applications, which will enlarge or reduce an area of the screen or part of a document. Also called a 'reduction tool' or 'reduction glass'.

A typical **Magnify tool** icon

mailto: *(int)* A hyperlink code used in webpages or e-mail applications that, when prefixed to an e-mail address and double-clicked, creates a new e-mail message for sending direct to the addressee. → *e-mail*

main board *(com)* → *motherboard*

main exposure *(pre)* The first exposure in the conventional processing of a halftone image.
→ *flash exposure*

mainframe (computer) *(com)* A large computer system used mainly to manage vast databases where simultaneous processing of transactions is required, such as in banks or insurance companies.

main memory *(com)* A term used to describe installed memory (RAM) to distinguish it from 'virtual memory'. → *RAM; virtual memory*

majordomo *(int)* A system of automated multiple electronic mailing lists, which users can subscribe to or unsubscribe from at will.

majuscule *(typ)* Another term for capital letters.

make even *(typ)* An instruction to extend a line of type to the full measure by adding spaces. → *end even; full out*

makeover (1) *(pre)* To produce screened separations in a variety of sizes from one set of continuous-tone separations.

makeover (2) *(pre)* To remake a defective printing film or plate.

make-ready *(pri)* The process of preparing a printing press before a new run, to establish register, ink density, consistent impression, etc. → *packing*

make–up (1) *(pre)* The final preprint assembly, whether it be on paper, film or computer, of all the various elements to be printed.

make–up (2) *(fin)* A mock-up assembly of all the printed sections of a publication for use as a guide by the bindery.

making *(pap)* One entire batch of machine-made paper ('a making').

manila *(pap)* A very strong paper usually made from vegetable fibre such as hemp or jute, the term deriving from fibres used to make the paper which were grown in the Philippines.

manuscript (MS/MSS) *(gen)* An original text submitted for publication.

map file *(int)* → *image map*

mapping (1) *(com)* Converting data between formats, particularly databases.

mapping (2) *(com)* Assigning attributes, such as colours, to a computer image.

mapping (3) *(com)* The process of applying textures to an object by defining a suitable projection method.

mapping resource *(gen)* A ready-made 'kit' of files with which you can generate cartographic maps – for example, 'Mountain High Maps'. → *DEM; relief map*

maquette binding *(fin)* A sample case submitted by the bookbinder for client approval.

marbled calf *(fin)* A traditional method of making a decorative binding material by using dilute acid to stain calfskin, producing a marbled pattern. → *marbling*

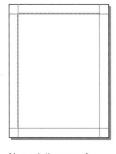

Non-printing **margin guides** are a feature of most word-processing and page-layout applications

marbling *(pap)* A traditional method of decorating paper by floating colours on the surface of a gum solution. The colour adheres to the sheet producing interesting random patterns. Marbled papers were used traditionally for book endpapers.

marching ants *(com)* → *marquee*

marginal notes *(gen)* Text printed in the margin of a main text column, adjacent to the passage to which it refers. → *cut-in side notes*

margin guides *(com)* A feature in some applications in which non-printing guides define areas of text or images.

margin(s) *(gen)* The blank area of a page that surrounds the text or image area.

maril *(fin)* A bookbinding of marbled inlaid leather.

marked proof *(gen)* A typeset or printed proof marked for corrections prior to being given to its author.

markup (1) *(gen)* A set of instructions and specifications for any material prepared for typesetting, reproduction or printing. → *spec(ification)*

markup (2) *(int)* The technique of embedding 'tags' (HTML instructions) within special characters ('metacharacters'), which tell a program such as a Web browser how to display a page. → *HTML; markup language; metacharacter*

markup language *(com)* A defined set of rules describing the way files are displayed by any particular method. HTML is one such language, used for creating webpages. → *HTML; markup (2)*

marquee *(com)* A moving broken line drawn (in many software applications) around an object or area in order to 'select' it or, in some cases, an area defined by an

application to show that the space within is active or selected. The moving lines are colloquially known as 'marching ants'. → **select(ing)**

mask (1) *(gen)* Any material used to protect all or part of an image or page in photomechanical reproduction, photography, illustration or layout. Many computer applications provide a masking feature that enables you to apply a mask to all or selected parts of an image. Such masks are stored in an 'alpha channel' and simulate the physical material used in platemaking to shield parts of a plate from light. → **alpha channel**

mask (2) *(pho)* A photographic image modified in tone or colour.

masking (1) *(pre)* To block out an area of an image with opaque material to prevent reproduction or to allow for modifications such as adjusting the values of colour and tone. → **mask (1)**

masking (2) *(gen)* A protective layer of film or paper ('frisket') applied to an illustration to protect an area while other parts are painted or airbrushed. → **frisket**

masking film (1) *(pre)* → **Rubylith**

masking film (2) *(gen)* → **frisket**

master *(gen)* An original item from which all copies are made, or upon which any changes are marked or made.

master cylinder *(pri)* The cylinder of a printing press, which transfers ink from reservoir to plate. → **blanket cylinder**

master directory block *(com)* The area of a computer disk that contains the disk directory (the catalog of files), and which is put into RAM when you start or insert the disk. → **directory (2)**

master page *(com)* In some applications, a template that contains attributes that will be common to any specified page or pages, such as the number of text columns, page numbers or type style. → **template (2)**

master plate *(pri)* The plate containing the image in offset litho printing.

master proof *(gen)* The final proof, which combines the author's and editor's comments or corrections. → **master**

Master/Slave *(com)* The use of any hardware or software device to control another. In analog audio, this might be two tape machines, for example; and in digital audio, one software program setting parameters for another, via a protocol such as ReWire.

Rectangular and elliptical **Marquee** tools

In this series of images, a **mask** is applied to the dark original, which appears red (middle). This allows a brightening effect to be applied to the unmasked area which lightens the background without affecting the foreground

masthead (1) *(gen)* The title of a newspaper or journal as it appears on the front page, also called a 'nameplate'.

masthead (2) *(gen)* Details about a publication and its publisher, such as ownership and subscription rates, usually printed on its contents page. Also called a 'flag'.
→ *masthead (1)*

MatchPrint *(pre)* A proprietary dryproofing system from 3M, which uses toners on light-sensitive paper and which is used for checking colour reproduction of film prior to printing. An alternative to a 'wet proof' (one that uses printing ink). Also called an 'off-press proof' or 'prepress proof'.
→ *Cromalin*

material *(com)* In 3D applications, the aggregate of all surface attributes for an object.

math coprocessor *(com)* → *coprocessor*

mathematical setting *(typ)* The typesetting of mathematical characters and formulae.
→ *mathematical signs/symbols*

mathematical signs/symbols *(typ)* Characters used as a shorthand for mathematical concepts and processes, such as '+' (add), '÷' (divide), '√' (radical, or square root).

mat(rix) *(typ)* In traditional typesetting, the copper mould used for casting hot metal type. The term later was adapted to mean the negative on phototypesetting machines from which characters are generated.

matrix *(pri)* The mould used for making the rubber plate in flexographic printing, and also the papier-mâché mould taken from a page of type to be used for stereotyping.
→ *flexography/flexo; stereo(type)*

matt art *(pap)* A coated paper with a dull finish. The US equivalent is 'cameo coated paper'.
→ *cameo (2)*

Matte *(aud)* An area of the screen designed to mask or reveal the video running on another layer in order to create composite images.

matt(e) finish *(pap)* A paper with a flat, slightly dull surface.

matter *(gen)* The traditional term for anything that is to be printed, at whatever stage. The term particularly applies to material (a manuscript, for example) that is to be typeset.

Mb *(com)* *abb.:* megabit. → *megabit (Mb/Mbit)*

MB *(com)* *abb.:* megabyte. → *megabyte (MB/Mbyte/meg)*

Mbps *(com)* *abb.:* megabits per second.
→ *megabit (Mb/Mbit)*

mean line *(typ)* → *x-height*

mean noon sunlight *(pho)* An arbitrary colour temperature to which most daylight colour films are balanced, based on the average colour temperature of direct sunlight at midday in Washington DC (5400K Kelvin).

measure *(typ)* The width of a justified typeset line or column of text, traditionally measured in picas, points, didots or ciceros but now commonly in inches and millimetres as well. Also called 'line length'.

mechanical *(gen)* → *camera-ready copy/art (CRC)*

mechanical binding *(fin)* A binding method in which individual sheets are held together with a plastic comb, wire or metal rings.
→ *plastic comb/coil; binding; spiral binding*

mechanical ghosting *(pri)* An aberration in printing when the density of ink film varies dramatically, caused by large areas of colour consuming too much ink. Also called 'ink starvation ghosting'.

mechanical tint *(pre)* Line or dot tints in various percentages preprinted onto thin adhesive film. These were used in traditional artwork to fill a given area with a tint, but have all but been replaced by digital processes. → *benday/Ben Day tints; Zip-a-tone/Zipatone*

mechanical (wood) pulp *(pap)* Untreated paper pulp used for low-quality papers such as newsprint. Also called 'groundwood'.
→ *chemical pulp; woodfree paper*

medallion *(fin)* An illustration printed on paper and pasted onto the case of a book.

media (1) *(gen)* A plural term now accepted as a singular to cover any information or communications medium, such as 'broadcast media' (television, radio, etc.) and 'print media' (newspapers, magazines, and such like).

media (2) *(com)* A plural term now accepted as a singular to describe the actual item on which digital data is stored, such as a floppy, hard, CD-ROM, etc., as distinct from the devices in which they are used. → *disk*

MediaManager *(com)* Avid Unity MediaManager is an 'asset management suite' that allows production assistants to access and manage bits of digital media from any networked or Internet-ready computer, thanks to a browser-based interface. The Select version of the software manages video clips on a LAN (Local Area Network); both versions are available for Mac or Windows systems.

median (filter) *(com)* A filter in some image-editing applications that removes small details by replacing a pixel with an averaged value of its surrounding pixels, ignoring extreme values.

medical and pharmaceutical symbols *(typ)* Typographical symbols representing: dram, drop, gallon, grain, minim, of each, ounce, pint, recipe, semi, signa, etc.

medical lens *(pho)* A type of camera lens designed specifically for medical use, with close-focusing capability and a built-in ringflash (a flash unit that fits around the camera lens).

medium (1) *(gen)* A substance, such as linseed oil or gum arabic, into which pigment is mixed to create printing ink or artist's paint. Also called a 'vehicle'. → *ink*

medium (2) *(pap)* Formerly the size of a standard printing sheet: 18 x 23 inches.

An image before and after a **median filter** was applied.

medium (3) *(typ)* The weight of a type design halfway between light and bold, sometimes described as 'roman'.

medium (4) *(pre)* An alternative name for a benday tint. → *benday/Ben Day tints*

meeting guards *(fin)* V-shaped guards of paper sewn to folds of sections to enable the flatter opening of a book, particularly one with narrow page margins.

meg *(com)* → *megabyte (MB/Mbyte/meg)*

mega *(com)* A unit of metric measurement representing 1,000,000. Although the term is used widely as a measure of computer data ('megabyte', for example), computers use a binary system (pairs of numbers) in which each number is doubled. Thus 'mega' in a data context does not mean 1,000,000 but 1,048,576. → *kilo*

megabit (Mb/Mbit) *(com)* 1,024 kilobits or 1,048,576 bits of data.

megabyte (MB/Mbyte/meg) *(com)* 1024 kilobytes or 1,048,576 bytes of data → *gigabyte (GB/G/gig); kilobyte (KB/Kbyte); terabyte*

megahertz (MHz) *(com)* One million hertz (or cycles, occurrences or instructions per second), often used as an indication (not necessarily accurate) of the speed of a computer's central processing unit (CPU), and thus sometimes referred to as 'clock speed'.

megapixel *(pho)* A rating of resolution for a digital camera, directly related to the number of pixels forming or output by the CMOS or CCD sensor. The higher the megapixel rating, the higher the resolution of images created by the camera.

membrane *(fin)* A skin parchment.

memory *(com)* The recall of digital data on a computer. This is typically 'dynamic RAM', the volatile 'random access' memory that is emptied when a computer is switched off (data should be stored on media such as a hard disk for future retrieval), or ROM, the stable 'read only' memory that contains unchanging data. As an analogy, think of your own memory – when you die, everything in your head is lost unless you write it down, thus 'saving' it for posterity. 'Memory' is often erroneously used to describe 'storage', probably because both are measured in megabytes. → *RAM; ROM*

memory allocation *(com)* The allocation of memory to specific tasks, thus enabling system software, application software, utilities and hardware to operate side by side. → *application memory (heap); heap; system heap*

memory card *(pho)* The media employed by a digital camera to save photos. This can be Compact Flash, Memory Stick, SD Cards or Smart Media – all store images which can then be transferred to the computer.

menu *(com)* The display on a computer screen showing the list of choices available to a user.

menu bar *(com)* The horizontal panel across the top of a computer screen containing the titles of available menus. → *menu*

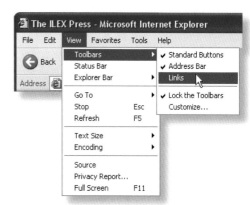

A pull-down menu showing **menu indicators**

menu command *(com)* A command given to your computer from a list of choices available within a menu, as distinct from a command made via the keyboard ('keyboard command').

menu-driven *(com)* A computer or application interface in which commands are given through a list of choices available from a hierarchy of menus. Synonymous with a 'command-line interface'. → *command-line interface; GUI*

menu indicator *(com)* Symbols within a menu that expand the range of options. An ellipsis (...) following an item means that selecting it will display a dialog box before the command can be executed; a check-mark indicates a command is already active; a right-pointing triangle points to a submenu; and a down-pointing triangle indicates that there's more on the menu. → *menu*

A Mac OS **menu bar**

MENU INDICATOR

menu title *(com)* The title of a menu as displayed in the menu bar. → *menu bar*

mercator (map) projection *(gen)*
→ *cylindrical (map) projection*

merge *(com)* The facility of some applications to combine data from two or more sources or to combine two or more graphic items.

MESECAM *(com)* → *SECAM*

mesh (1) *(pri)* The interlaced structure of the threads in screen printing fabric.

mesh (2) *(com)* Vertices that are linked together to form Polygon or NURBS (or other) surfaces.

mesh marks *(pri)* In screen printing, a cross-hatch pattern on the printed surface, left by the mesh of the screen fabric and caused by incorrect ink consistency. Also called 'screen marks'. → *mesh (1)*

mesh warp *(com)* In some applications, the facility to distort an image by means of dragging 'handles' at the intersections of the lines of a grid ('mesh') placed over the image. Also called 'rubber sheeting'.

message box *(com)* → *alert box*

metacharacter *(int)* Characters within text that indicate formatting, such as the 'tags' in an HTML file. Angle brackets () and ampersands (&) are typical metacharacters. → *HTML; markup (2); markup language*

metadata *(gen)* Data about data, such as XMF and XML, which is embedded into differing technologies. The use of metadata allows different data sets, computing platforms, databases and mobile technologies to share information and communicate, regardless of their provenance. In an audio environment, it means packets of different data types can be sent to any compatible device.

meta-information *(int)* Optional information provided in an HTML document to help search engine databases place websites in the correct category. This facility is often abused by less scrupulous websites, and is falling out of favour with search engine providers whose 'spider' programs trawl the Web to add sites to their databases. → *spider*

metallic ink *(pri)* An ink to which a metallic powder such as bronze or aluminium has been added to give the effect of gold, silver or other precious metals.

metallography *(pri)* A contraction of 'metal-lithography', a traditional lithographic printing process in which metal plates are used instead of stone. → *lithography*

metameric *(gen)* A colour that changes hue under different lighting conditions.

metamerism *(pri)* An undesirable property of printed material, by which the grey balance appears to change in response to the lighting conditions, depending on the spectral content of the lighting. This is the effect responsible for items whose colours match under one lighting type (fluorescent, for example) but no longer match under another (daylight or incandescent).

meteorological symbols *(gen)* A collection of internationally agreed symbols for recording weather. Since that agreement took place in 1935, however, the rapid expansion of graphic design as a profession has meant

Photoshop's *Liquify* filter is a **mesh warp**

The grainy effect of a **mezzograph**

that such symbols have largely been replaced by altogether more appropriate and pleasing graphics, particularly in weather forecasting.

metrication *(gen)* The introduction of a decimal system of measurement by certain countries. However, even in some countries that have adopted metrication there are inconsistencies – the UK still uses the Anglo-American point system for measuring type.

metrics *(com)* Font information such as character width, kerning, ascent and descent.

mezzograph/metzograph *(pre)* A halftone screen that, emulating a 'mezzotint', uses a grain formation rather than a regular ruling. Similar to a 'stochastic' screen, although a lot coarser. → *mezzotint; stochastic screening*

mezzotint *(pri)* A traditional intaglio engraving process for reproducing tones rather than lines. → *intaglio; mezzograph/metzograph*

MF *(pap) abb.:* machine finish. → *machine finish (MF)*

mf/mtf *(gen) abb.:* more follows/more to follow. Used when preparing a manuscript for typesetting.

MG *(pap) abb.:* machine glazed. → *machine glazed (MG)*

MICR *(com) abb.:* magnetic ink character recognition. → *magnetic ink character recognition (MICR)*

microchip *(com)* → *chip/microchip*

microfiche *(gen)* → *microform publishing*

microform publishing *(gen)* The storage of data on microfilm, requiring a viewer or projector to enlarge the data to a readable size. Also called 'microfiche'.

micrometer *(gen)* An instrument for measuring thickness, usually of paper.

microphone *(aud)* A device that picks up sounds and converts them to electrical impulses, which can be recorded, or converted to digital information. A mic may be directional, which means it picks up sound primarily from one direction, or omnidirectional, when it picks up sounds equally from all directions.

microprocessor *(com)* → *processor (chip)*

microwave drying *(pri)* A method used to dry inks in the drying units of high-speed web presses.

MID *(aud)* MIDI file format. → *MIDI*

middle A *(aud)* 440 Hz, otherwise known as the 'concert pitch' to which orchestra musicians tune their instruments.

mid(dle) space *(typ)* In traditional metal typesetting, a standard word space measuring one quarter of an em. → *space*

MIDI *(com) abb.:* musical instrument digital interface. The lingua franca of digital music. A 1980s-developed asynchronous serial protocol that allows compatible devices – including most hardware keyboards, synths, samplers and signal processors, and many multitrack recorders and portable studios – to exchange musical and non-musical instructions. Audio and MIDI sequencing

M

applications and virtual studio packages accept and manage MIDI data, and allow you to control soft synths and other virtual instruments via an external keyboard.

midtone dot *(pre)* Halftone dots of the middle tone areas of a halftone image, shown on close examination as the square dots of a chequerboard. ➔ *halftone dot; midtone/middletone*

midtone/middletone *(gen)* The parts of an image that are approximately average in tone, falling midway between the highlights and shadows.

milking machine *(typ)* ➔ *text retrieval terminal*

millboards *(fin)* Strong boards used for the covers of books. Also called 'pressboards'.

mill brand *(pap)* The brand name and/or trademark of a paper or manufacturer.

mille *(gen)* Latin for 'one thousand'. Used in the paper industry to describe the unit of quantity in which sheets of paper are sold. In a modern context, the unit can be confusing since, in its abbreviated form ('m'), it can easily be mistaken for 'mega', which means 1,000,000, or 'kilo', which is also 1,000. ➔ *kilo; mega*

mill-finished *(pap)* ➔ *machine finishe (MF)*

millisecond (ms) *(gen)* One thousandth of a second. ➔ *seek time*

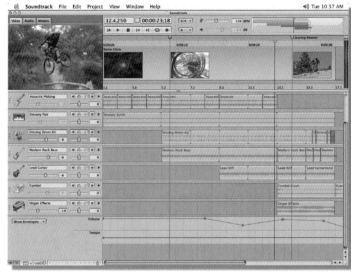

Apple's Soundtrack uses **MIDI** sources

mill ream *(pap)* A bulk quantity of 472 sheets of handmade or mouldmade paper, made up of 18 x 24 sheets ('inside quires') and 2 x 20 sheets ('outside quires'). ➔ *printer's ream; publisher's ream; ream; short ream*

MIME *(int) abb.:* multipurpose Internet mail extension. ➔ *content-type; multipurpose Internet mail extension (MIME)*

minidisc (MD) *(aud)* A small disc used for recording and playback of audio. It uses ATRAC 1:5 audio compression, has a sampling rate of 44.1kHz, a frequency range of 20Hz to 20kHz and a dynamic range of 92dB+.

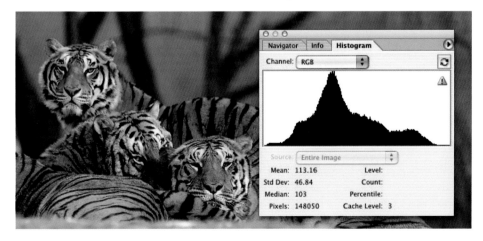

In this image, there is a high concentration of **midtones** and few very dark or very light areas, as indicated by the histogram spike in the middle rather than the ends

minion *(typ)* A former size of type, now standardized as 7 point.

miniscule *(typ)* An alternative name for a lower-case or small letter. → *lower case*

mint *(gen)* As new – anything in excellent condition, usually applied to secondhand goods.

minus leading/linespacing *(typ)* → *negative leading/line spacing*

mips *(com) abb.:* million instructions per second. Usually used in the context of processor speeds. → *hertz (Hz); processor (chip)*

mirror lens *(pho)* A camera lens that forms an image by reflecting it from curved mirrors rather than by refraction through a series of lenses. A mirror lens is more compact than a traditional lens of the same focal length (a telephoto lens, for example). Also called a 'catadioptic lens'. → *telephoto lens*

missal caps *(typ)* Decorative black letter capitals. → *black letter*

misting *(pri)* Mist in a press room formed from ink droplets suspended in the air. → *flying*

mitred/mitre (1) *(fin)* Said of the corners of a book cover material that have been folded inside to meet at an angle of 45 degrees.

mitred/mitre (2) *(com)* The bevelled ends of right-angled frame rules used in traditional typesetting. Also used in software applications as a method of defining the 'end caps' in rules or lines. → *end cap*

mix *(aud)* This refers to adjusting the levels and EQ of various recorded and/or live tracks to achieve a desired overall sound.

mixed composition *(typ)* The traditional description of a paragraph of text matter set in a variety of fonts.

mixed lighting *(gen)* Lighting comprising several different sources, such as tungsten and fluorescent or other artificial sources, mixed with daylight. Such mixes are difficult to compensate for but can be used to creative effect.

The Windows XP Shut Down dialog is a **modal dialog box**. It has to be clicked before another screen shows

MME *(aud)* (PC) Microsoft standard wave driver for soundcards. Like DirectSound, it may cause problems with sophisticated virtual instruments.

mnemonic *(com)* Anything that aids memory, frequently an abbreviation, such as a keyboard equivalent command that uses the initial letter of the command (O = Open, C = Copy).

mock-up *(gen)* → *comprehensive*

modal dialog box *(com)* A dialog box that, until it is closed, will not allow any activity to take place on screen other than that within its box.

model *(gen)* Any control specification used to compare the behaviour of complex systems – a colour model, for example. → *colour model*

modelling lamp *(pho)* A lamp used to demonstrate what the lighting effect will be on a subject but which does not interfere with the actual exposure.

modem *(int)* Abbreviation for modulator-demulator. A device that converts digital data to analogue for transfer from one computer to another via standard telephone lines. The receiving modem converts it back again.

MO/MOD disc *(com)* → *magneto-optical disc (MO/MOD)*

modern face *(typ)* A typeface characterized by vertical stress, strong stroke contrast and thin, unbracketed serifs – Bodoni and Walbaum, for example.

modern numerals *(typ)* → *lining figures/numerals*

modifier key *(com)* A non-printing key (on a keyboard) that, when used in conjuction with a character key, enables the selection of a character not normally visible on the keyboard, such as accented letters or other symbols (©, ®, Ω, etc). The most commonly used modifier keys are Shift, Command, Option/Alt and Control, or a combination of these. Modifier keys can also be used as keyboard shortcuts. → *character key; keyboard equivalent/shortcut*

modular system *(gen)* Any system, such as a computer system, made up from self-contained but separate parts ('modules'), rather than a single item that contains all of the parts. For example, a computer that does not incorporate the monitor in its case.

modulate *(aud)* To alter a sound in some way, as with a musical instrument or a human voice.

module *(com)* In software, a self-contained but separate element of a program that connects with other elements, such as a 'plug-in'. → *plug-in*

moiré *(pre)* An unintended pattern that occurs in halftone reproduction when two or more colours are printed and the dot screens are positioned at the wrong angles. The correct angles at which screens should be positioned usually depends upon the number of colours being printed, but the normal angles for four-colour process printing, and thus the default setting in many computer applications, are: cyan 105; magenta 75; yellow 90; black 45. A moiré pattern can also be caused by scanning or

The image (left) shows a normal halftone, while that to the right has had a second halftone applied, leaving a subtle **moiré** effect

rescreening an image to which a halftone screen has already been applied.
→ *circular screen; colour rotation/ sequence; descreen(ing); dot pattern*

mold *(gen)* → *mould/mold*

mold-made paper *(pap)* → *mould-made paper*

monetary symbol/currency symbol *(typ)* A symbol denoting a unit of currency, such as $ (dollar); ¢ (cent); £ (sterling); € (Euro); ¥ (yen). The Euro currency symbol has replaced the general currency symbol (¤) of the 'ISO/Adobe' character set in recently issued fonts. → *ISO/Adobe character set*

monitor *(com)* The unit comprising your computer screen. Monitors display images in colour, greyscale or monochrome, and are available in a variety of sizes from 9in (229mm) (measured diagonally) to 21in (534mm) or more. Although most monitors use cathode ray tubes, some contain liquid crystal displays ('LCDs'), particularly portables and laptops and, more recently, 'gas plasma' (large matrices of tiny, gas-filled glass cells). Monitors are variously called 'screens', 'displays', 'VDUs' and 'VDTs'. → *cathode ray tube (CRT); convergence (1); gas plasma monitor; LCD*

monk *(pri)* The traditional term for an ink blot or splash on a printed sheet.

Nn

An example of a **modern face**

MODERN FACE

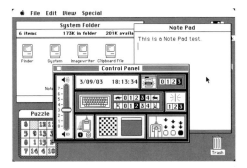

Mac OS 1.1 worked in **monochrome**

A typical **monogram**

A simple **montage**

monobloc *(pho)* An all-in-one flash unit with the controls and power supply built-in. Monoblocs can be synchronized together to create more elaborate lighting setups.

mono(chrome)/monochromatic (1) *(gen)* An image of varying tones reproduced in a single colour. → *monotone*

mono(chrome)/monochromatic (2) *(com)* A computer monitor that displays pixels as either black or white, rather than in shades of grey as per 'greyscale' monitors. → *monitor*

monogram *(typ)* A design comprised of interwoven characters, usually two or more.

monograph *(gen)* A treatise on a single subject.

monophonic (mono) *(aud)* Describing sound that is stored and played back using only one channel – as opposed to stereo sound, which uses a left and right channel, or surround sound, which uses multiple channels.

monorail *(pho)* A type of studio support for standard view cameras, and also the name given to such cameras.

monospaced (font) *(typ)* A font in which the type characters all occupy the same width space (as on a typewriter), as distinct from proportionally spaced fonts, which are more common. 'Courier' is a monospaced font. Also called 'fixed-width fonts'.

monotone *(gen)* Reproduction in a single colour, without tonal variation. → *mono(chrome)*

Monotype *(typ)* The name of a type foundry, Monotype Corporation, which designs and supplies digital fonts. Originally, Monotype was the manufacturer of a typesetting process invented in 1885 by Tolbert Lanston of Ohio (one year after the invention of the Linotype machine), which employed a keyboard-operated composing machine to cast type as individual letters. → *Linotype; casting*

montage *(gen)* An assembly of several images, forming a single original. A montage of photographs is called a 'photomontage'.

mordant (1) *(fin)* An adhesive for affixing gold leaf.

mordant (2) *(pri)* Any fluid used to etch a printing plate. → *etch*

morocco *(fin)* Glazed and polished goatskin, used for bookbinding. → *cross-grained morocco*

mortise (1) *(pre)* Traditionally, a space cut out of a printing plate in order to insert type or another plate. In modern usage, fitting a correct piece of text film into a hole left in the film when incorrect text was removed. → *pierced*

mortise (2) *(typ)* Cutting away the sides of type to allow closer setting – also known as 'kerning'. → *kerning*

mosaic binding *(fin)* Book covers decorated with contrasting leather inlays. → *inlaying*

*!?

mosaic gold *(fin)* Imitation gold made from bisulphide of tin and mercury, a cheaper substitute for powdered gold. Also called 'aurium musicum'. ➔ *oriental leaf*

MOTD *(int)* abb.: message of the day. A message posted by an ISP (Internet Service Provider) on its server to inform its users of any known problems that may be affecting the network that day. An MOTD is read either by using special software that 'fingers' the server, or by using a World Wide Web browser. ➔ *finger(ed)/fingering; ISP; World Wide Web (WWW)*

motherboard *(com)* ➔ *circuit board*

mother set *(pri)* The master set of printing plates kept for electrotyping further sets. ➔ *electro(type)*

motif *(gen)* A decorative design or pattern.

Motion blur filter *(com)* One of the Adobe blur filters, *Motion Blur* creates a linear blur (implying movement) at any angle. The degree of blur can be altered between arbitrary levels that introduce mild through to excessive blurs. It works most effectively when applied to an inverted selection: an object is selected, the selection is inverted and the filter applied to the inverse selection.

motion channel *(com)* An animation parameter that controls how an object moves (for example, rotation x, y, z and translation x, y, z are all motion channels).

Motion Picture Experts Group (MPEG) *(com)* ➔ *MPEG*

motor-drive *(pho)* A device that drives the film advance in a camera, enabling a rapid sequence of photographs to be taken.

mottled calf *(fin)* Calfskin that has been given an irregular pattern with coloured dyes, used for book covers.

mottle/mottling *(pri)* A printing fault appearing as a random, uneven, blotchy effect, caused by too much pressure or unsuitable paper or ink.

mould-made paper *(pap)* A manufactured paper that simulates handmade paper. ➔ *mould*

mould/mold *(pap)* The wire cloth and frame on which pulp is formed into sheets of paper.

mounting and flapping *(gen)* A method of presenting artwork in which the work is mounted on board and protected by a hinged sheet of cellulose acetate or paper.

mounting board *(pap)* A heavy board used for mounting artwork or photographs.

mouse *(com)* The small, handheld device that is manipulated to position the pointer on a computer monitor.

mouse-down *(com)* ➔ *mouse event*

mouse event *(com)* The action ('event') initiated by pressing the button on your mouse. This can happen at the moment you press the button down ('mouse-down'), or when you release it ('mouse-up'). ➔ *mouse*

mouse mat/pad *(com)* A small pad designed to enable the smooth motion of a mouse.

mouseover *(com)* The mouse event that occurs when the mouse pointer rolls over a navigation button.

mouse-up *(com)* ➔ *mouse event*

- Working with bitmap images and ve
- Understanding image size and resolu
- Changing image size and resolution
- Getting images from digital cameras
- Working with camera raw image file
- Scanning images
- Creating new images
- Using the File Browser (Photoshop)
- Opening and importing images
- Placing files

Using a scripting language, a **mouseover** event is defined that turns the link red as the pointer moves over it

Motion blur creates an impression of movement

MOV *(aud)* The filename suffix for standard QuickTime films: 'moviename.mov'. Not required for use on Macintosh computers, but needed for servers and Windows-based computers. → *QuickTime*

movable type *(typ)* The principle of the original method of typesetting, in which type was cast as single letters and assembled by hand in a composing stick rather than by a hot metal machine. → *hot metal (type)*

moving banner *(int)* An animated advertisement used within webpages. → *banner (2)*

MPEG *(com)* (pron.: 'em-peg') Acronym for Motion Picture Experts Group. The acronym has come to stand for compression formats for digital audio and video. Full-screen, VHS-quality digital video files and animations can be compressed by ratios of up to 200:1.

MPPP *(int)* abb.: Multilink Point-to-Point Protocol. → *Multilink Point–to–Point Protocol*

MP3 (file format) *(aud)* abb.: Motion Picture Experts Groups level three. The most common format for sound files on the Internet. MP3 offers good levels of compression, generally around 10:1, although this depends on the quality settings used to create it. It is widely used in portable audio players, such as Apple's iPod. Due to its lossy compression, MP3 is generally best for personal archiving and playback rather than mastering work.

ms *(gen)* abb.: millisecond. → *millisecond (ms)*

MS-DOS *(com)* abb.: Microsoft Disk Operating System, the operating system used on Intel-based personal computers (PCs). MS-DOS (or just plain 'DOS') also provides the skeleton on which Microsoft's 'Windows' operating system hangs. → *command-line interface; operating system*

ms(s) *(gen)* abb.: manuscript.

mull *(fin)* A coarse muslin that forms the first lining of a casebound book. Also called 'scrim' or 'super' (US).

mullen tester *(pap)* A machine for measuring the bursting strength of paper.

Multilink Point-to-Point Protocol *(int)* An Internet protocol that provides simultaneous multiple connections between computers.

multimedia *(com)* A generic term for any combination of various digital media, such as sound, video, animation, graphics and text, incorporated into a software product or presentation.

MultiMedia Cards (MMC), Secure Digital (SD) cards and others *(aud)* Portable card devices offering fast transfer speeds. Many audio players accept MMC and newer SD cards; they are used to store MP3 files for playback. Some other Flash RAM cards, including SmartMedia, Memory Sticks and CompactFlash, are compatible with certain audio devices as well.

multi-pass rendering *(com)* The process whereby a single scene is rendered in multiple passes, each pass producing an image (or film or image sequence) containing a specific portion of the scene but not all of it (for example, one part of a multi-pass render may contain just the reflections in the scene, or just the specular highlights. It may also contain single objects or effects).

multi-pattern metering *(pho)* An exposure metering system, in which areas of the image are measured separately and assessed according to a predetermined programme.

multiple exposure *(pho)* Two or more photographic images, which may be the same or different, superimposed during exposure or processing to form a single image.

M

multiple flash *(pho)* Repeated firing of a flash unit to increase the exposure of a (static) subject. Also called 'serial flash'.

multiple flats *(pre)* Flats used to print successive pages in which some elements of the design are repeated from page to page. → *flat (1)*

multiple screens/multi screen *(com)* Two or more monitors attached to a single computer, used for presentations or to increase the workspace.

multiple-selected items *(com)* The selection of two or more items so that they can be modified or moved as one – for example, move, group or resize.

multiplex(ing) *(int)* The term for 'many'. In communications, the simultaneous transmission of many messages along a single channel.

multipurpose Internet mail extensions (MIME) *(int)* A format for conveying Web documents and related files across the Internet, typically via e-mail.

multiring binder *(fin)* A mechanical binding method, in which the leaves are secured by closely spaced rings. → *mechanical binding*

multitasking *(com)* The ability of a computer to do many things at once, such as run several applications simultaneously. Most computers aren't true multitasking machines, although they can usually work on several tasks or applications simultaneously by switching very rapidly from one to another (sometimes called 'time-slicing'). → *time-slicing*

multithreaded *(com)* A concept of operating systems in which they, or the applications that run on them, divide into smaller 'subtasks', each of which runs independently but which combine to perform a primary task. → *multitasking; time-slicing*

multitracking *(aud)* Using more than one channel – or track – to record separate sounds, which can later be mixed.

multi-user *(com)* A qualification of a license agreement that allows more than one person to use a single piece of software.

mump *(typ)* A typesetting term, meaning to move or copy fonts from one establishment to another (usually unauthorized). The term originally referred to moving hot metal matrices, and is still used today with reference to digitized fonts. Mump probably derives from the old Dutch word *'mompen'*, meaning 'to cheat'.

murex *(gen)* A purple dye, variously known as Tyrian, Royal and Phoenician purple, obtained from the shellfish murex.

musical instrument digital interface (MIDI) *(com)* A hardware and software standard for digitally synthesized musical sound.

music printing *(pri)* The printing of musical notation, now done digitally, but traditionally done by engraving directly onto metal plates or by using movable type on previously printed staves.

music program *(com)* Any application in which music can be composed, recorded, manipulated, edited, played and output, either with or without a musical keyboard or other audio equipment. → *MIDI*

mutton/mutt *(typ)* → *em quad*

M weight *(pap)* The weight of 1,000 sheets of a given paper size, 'm' being an abbreviation of the Latin *'mille'*, meaning 'one thousand'.

MULTIPLE FLASH

Nn

nailhead *(fin)* A paperback book, so-called because its cross-section resembles a nail, thicker at the spine and tapering to the fore-edge.

nameplate *(gen)* → *masthead (1)*

nanosecond (ns) *(com)* One billionth of a second, usually used in the context of measuring the speed of memory chips. The fewer the number of ns, the faster.

nap roller *(pri)* A superior type of lithographic roller with a cover of French calf. The nap or skin side is outermost and is treated with oil to make it waterproof and supple before being varnished to make it smooth.
→ *French calf*

narrowcasting *(int)* The targeting of content to a specific type of audience via the Internet.

narrow copy *(fin)* An elongated, tall book.
→ *tall copy*

National Center for Supercomputing Applications (NCSA) *(int)* A group of programmers at the University of Illinois, who developed the first Web browser and who produce software such as NCSA Telnet for the scientific community.

National Television Standards Committee (NTSC) *(com)* A television and video standard used mainly in the United States and Japan, which uses 525 lines and displays images at 30 frames per second.

native file format *(com)* A file format for exclusive use by the application in which the files were created, although some applications may be able to read files created in another's native format.

natural letter spacing *(typ)* Type characters designed so that letters and numbers occupy an appropriate amount of space for their shape. For example, this would be used to accommodate the difference in width between 'm' and 'i'. Also called 'proportional letter spacing'.
→ *centrefold/spread; differential letterspacing; letterspacing/letterfit monospaced (font)*

natural tint *(pap)* Paper that is pale cream in colour.

navigate *(com)* The process of finding your way around a multimedia presentation or website by clicking on words or buttons.

navigation bar *(com)* A special bar in a Web browser, webpage or multimedia presentation, which helps you to 'navigate' through pages by clicking on buttons or text. → *navigate*

Safari has a **navigation bar** with various links

navigation button *(com)* A button in a Web browser, webpage or multimedia presentation, which links you to a particular location or page.
→ *navigate; navigation bar*

Navigator *(int)* A cross-platform Web browser produced by Netscape. → *browser (1)/ Web browser; Explorer*

NC *(com) abb.:* network computer. → *network computer (NC)*

NCR paper *(pap)* → *carbonless paper*

NCSA *(int) abb.:* National Center for Supercomputing Applications. → *National Center for Supercomputing Applications (NCSA)*

near-print *(pri)* Prior to the desktop publishing era, a general term used to describe substitute printing processes such as typewriter composition and 'offset duplicating' (using small offset litho presses). Also called 'near letter quality' (NLQ).

neck *(typ)* The part of a metal type character between the shoulder and face, also known as the bevel.

neck line *(typ)* The amount of white space or leading underneath a running head.

negative/neg (1) *(pho)* Photographic film or paper in which all the dark areas appear light and vice versa. Negative film is used extensively in the reproduction process and is either made direct from originals or produced by an imagesetter.

negative (2) *(com)* → *invert (1)*

negative element *(pho)* → *diverging/ divergent lens*

negative leading/line spacing *(typ)* In text, vertical line spacing that is less than the type size. Also called 'minus leading' or 'minus line spacing'. → *leading*

A series of
nested folders

negative light *(com)* In a 3D environment, lighting with an intensity value below zero.

negative-working plate *(pre)* A printing plate that has been exposed through negative film, as distinct from one exposed through positive film ('positive-working plate').
→ *positive-working plate*

nested folder *(com)* In GUIs, a folder that is placed inside another folder. → *GUI*

nesting *(com)* Items placed inside other items such as tables within tables on a webpage.

netiquette *(int)* A play on the word 'etiquette', describing the notional rules – written or unwritten – for polite behaviour for users of the Internet.

Some classic
navigation buttons

Netscape *(int)* Company responsible for pioneering the Web browser with its Navigator and Communicator products.

NetShow *(int)* Microsoft's technology for delivery and playback of multimedia on the Internet, supporting both live and on-demand video.

netTV *(int)* A system for accessing the World Wide Web via a television set. → *set-top; television service provider (TVSP)*

netTV viewers *(int)* Users who gain access to the Internet via netTV. → *netTV*

network *(com)* The connection of two or more computers or peripheral devices to each other, and the hardware and software used to connect them. → *bridge*

network computer (NC) *(com)* A cut-down computer with no other means of operating than on a network where it relies on the software and storage facilities of a server computer. → *server*

NAVIGATION BUTTON

network link *(com)* The part of the network that forms the link between your computer and the network itself, such as a telephone line or Ethernet cable.

Network News Transfer Protocol *(int)* A standard for the retrieval and posting of news articles.

neutral density filter *(pho)* A filter that uniformly reduces all colours of light during an exposure.

new edition *(gen)* → *revised edition*

new line character *(com)* In some applications, a character that can be inserted to start a new line without starting a new paragraph.

newsgroup *(int)* A group of like-minded individuals who 'post' and collect articles of common interest on the Internet. → *UseNet*

newsprint *(pap)* An unsized – and thus absorbent – paper made from mechanical pulp and used for printing newspapers. → *mechanical (wood) pulp*

news server *(int)* → *Network News Transfer Protocol*

Newton's rings *(pho)* Patterns of banded colour with the appearance of watered silk or contour lines. These occur as a result of interference in the path of light, when two lenses or pieces of film or glass are placed in contact with each other.

next reading/text matter *(gen)* An instruction to place advertisement copy next to editorial copy in a publication.

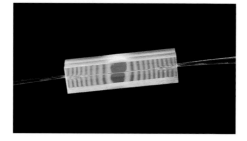

Two lenses revealing
Newton's rings

NFNT *(com) abb.:* new font numbering table. → *font ID conflict*

nib/nibbed *(fin)* A tongue of paper on a folded insert in a book (a map, for example), enabling the insert to open more easily.

nibble/nybble *(com)* Half a byte, or four bits. → *bit; byte*

nick *(typ)* A small groove on a piece of metal type, which identifies its orientation.

nickname *(int)* An abbreviated e-mail address.

night lens *(pho)* A camera lens designed for optimum use at a wide maximum aperture.

nip (1) *(fin)* The crease at the joint of a casebound book. → *joint*

nip (2) *(pri)* The point of contact between cylinders on a press.

nippers *(fin)* Heated clamps that are used to secure the book and case together on a bookbinding line.

nipping *(fin)* The process of clamping book blocks to reduce the swelling caused by sewing when bookbinding. Sometimes called 'smashing', although this term is more correctly applied to books printed on soft paper. → *smash(ing)*

nipping up *(fin)* A stage in the process of handbinding, which gives shape to the bands. → *head/tail band*

NLQ *(pri) abb.:* near letter quality. → *near-print*

NNTP *(int) abb.:* Network News Transfer Protocol. → *Network News Transfer Protocol; newsgroup; UseNet*

no-carbon-required paper (NCR) *(pap)* → *carbonless paper*

node (1) *(int)* A basic object, such as a graphic within a scene, used in the VRML environment. → *VRML*

node (2) *(com)* Any device connected to a network, such as a computer, printer or server.

*!?

nodename *(int)* A name that identifies an individual computer on a network or the Internet.

noise (1) *(int)* Undesirable fluctuations or interference in a transmitted signal, such as across telephone lines.

noise (2) *(gen)* Random pattern of small spots on a digital image, which are generally unwanted and are caused by non-image-forming electrical signals.

noise function *(com)* A random pattern generator that, in 3D scenes, improves photorealism.

noise reduction *(aud)* Procedure that is meant to reduce the amount of noise produced by audio components and systems; this can be done digitally using a variety of software methods.

nom-de-plume *(gen)* A pen name, adopted to hide the real name of an author.

non-actinic (light) *(pho)* A light source that is normally non-reactive to a sensitized photographic surface, and is thus used in photographic darkrooms. Sometimes called 'safelight'.

non-breaking space *(com)* A character placed between two words to prevent them from being separated at the end of a line. Also called a 'hard space'.

non-contact printing *(pri)* → *non-impact printing*

non-contiguous *(com)* The opposite of contiguous. → *contiguous*

non-contiguous selection *(com)* A feature of some applications, which allows you to select disconnected pieces of text.

non-contiguous space *(com)* Free space on a computer disk, which is broken up into small chunks, as distinct from being arranged continuously. → *contiguous*

non-discrete value *(gen)* → *discrete value*

None *(com)* A QuickTime compression codec meaning no compression. → *codec (1)*

non-gear streaks *(pri)* Marks that appear on a printed sheet, parallel with the printing cylinder.

non-image area *(pri)* The non-printing area of a litho plate that has been treated to accept water, thus repelling ink.

non-impact printing *(pri)* Printing processes in which the printing surface does not strike the surface of the substrate. Used by plotters, land laser and inkjet printers.

non-lining figures/numerals *(typ)* Numerals designed with descenders and ascenders rather than those of a standard height and alignment, which are known as 'lining figures'. Also known as 'hanging figures'. → *lining figures/numerals*

nonpareil *(typ)* An old type size, now standardized as 6 point. The name is still sometimes used (although increasingly rarely) as an alternative term to indicate 6-point leading.

non-printing characters *(typ)* → *invisible character/invisibles*

non-read colour *(pre)* → *dropout blue*

A digitally created **noise** effect

1234567890

An example of **non-lining figures**

non-read ink *(pre)* → *dropout ink*

non-reflective ink *(pri)* A special ink used to print information so that it can be easily read by OCR devices. → *OCR*

non-repro blue *(pre)* → *dropout blue*

normal(s) *(com)* In 3D objects, the direction that is perpendicular to the surface of the polygon to which it relates. → *front-facing polygons*

normalization *(aud)* The process of increasing the amplitude of a sound wave's peak to a reference level in an editing package – for example, importing a WAV into BIAS Peak software, then asking the application to locate the loudest point and increase the volume of the whole track until the peak hits 0 dB.

northlight *(pho)* A lighting set-up with diffuse but directional qualities, which emulates that from a north-facing window.

not *(pap)* A term meaning 'not glazed', used to describe unglazed 'rag' papers that are midway between a hot pressed and a rough finish. → *rag paper/pulp*

notch binding *(fin)* A method of perfect binding in which small glue–retaining slits are applied to the spine of a book. → *perfect binding*

np *(gen)* abb.: new paragraph. A mark used in editing and proof correction to indicate the creation of a new paragraph.

ns *(com)* abb.: nanosecond. → *nanosecond (ns)*

NTSC *(aud)* National Television Standards Committee. This is the TV standard employed in the US, Canada, Japan and other countries in South America and many nations in the Pacific. NTSC uses 525 lines made up of two interlaced fields scanning at 29.97 frames per second or 59.94 fields per second. SECAM recordings will often play in monochrome on PAL TV receivers.

NuBus *(com)* The 'bus architecture' found in very old Macintosh computers, which provides 'slots' for adding circuit boards such as video cards and accelerator cards. → *bus (1); circuit board*

nudge *(com)* A feature of some applications, which enables you to move items in increments of, say, one pixel or one point (or even a fraction of a point), using a keyboard command.

null modem cable *(com)* A communications link between two computers, usually over a short distance, without using a modem (null = non-existent).

numbered copy *(gen)* An individual book taken from a limited-edition print run in which each copy has received an identifying number, such as 3/200 (the third copy from a run of 200 copies).

numbered list *(int)* An HTML style that numbers paragraphs for use in list form. → *HTML*

numbering format *(typ)* The style of numbering used for page numbers: 1, 2, 3; I, II, III, etc.

numerals *(typ)* Alternative term for numbers.

numerator *(typ)* The number above the line in a fraction. → *decimal point; denominator; fraction; separator*

numeric coprocessor *(com)* → *coprocessor*

numeric keypad *(com)* A cluster of number keys (normally) situated to the right on most keyboards.

NURBS *(com)* Non-Uniform Rational B-Spline. A special curve (and when linked together, a surface) in 3D programs, which is defined by a mathematical equation. Requires fewer points than polygons to achieve smooth flowing lines and surfaces.

Nyquist Theorem *(aud)* In digital audio, the sampling rate must be twice as high as the highest frequency in the sound to be represented digitally.

oasis goat *(fin)* Bookbinding leather obtained from a South African goat. Also used as a trade name for West African tanned morocco skin. → *morocco*

o.b.a. *(pap)* abb.: optical bleaching agents. → *optical bleaching agents (o.b.a.)*

obelisk *(typ)* → *dagger*

obelus *(typ)* → *dagger*

object *(com)* Any multimedia or webpage element, such as an image or block of text, or any single element in a 3D space. → *child object; parent object*

object linking and embedding (OLE) *(com)* Microsoft technology in which a linked object – an image created in a graphics application, for example – has been placed ('embedded') into another application. It will be updated each time it is altered in the source application. An embedded object will, when 'double-clicked', fire up the source application in anticipation of additional editing.

object-oriented *(com)* A software technology that uses mathematical points, based on 'vectors' (information giving both magnitude and direction), to define lines and shapes, these points being the 'objects' referred to. (This is distinct from a graphic shape as an object; an 'object' in computer programming is a database of mathematical formulae.) The data for each shape is stored in these points, which in turn pass information from one to another on how the paths between them should be described – as straight lines, arcs or Bézier curves. The quality of the line between each point is determined entirely by the resolution of the output device. A line produced by an imagesetter at 2400dpi will be much smoother than the same line output on a LaserWriter at 300dpi or when viewed on a monitor. The alternative technology for rendering computer images is that of 'bitmapped' graphics, which are edited by modifying individual pixels or by turning them on or off. → *point (2)*

oblique *(com)* An alternative term for 'italic', although in digital typography it is more commonly used to refer to a roman character that has been distorted to simulate italic. → *italic*

Oblique Strategies *(aud)* Brian Eno's series of 'over 100 worthwhile dilemmas' is actually a list of phrases intended to help creative people think of new ways of solving problems or approaching situations in their work. These are published on cards, but many different versions are also available online.

oblique stroke *(typ)* → *slash*

oblong *(gen)* A book of 'landscape' format, i.e. wider than it is tall.

OBR *(gen)* abb.: optical bar recognition. → *bar code*

obsolete (element) *(int)* HTML code that is out of date and thus no longer supported by current generations of browsers. → *HTML*

OCR *(com)* *abb.:* optical character recognition. → *ICR; non-reflective ink; optical character recognition (OCR)*

OCR-A *(typ)* → *optical (type) font*

OCR-B *(typ)* → *optical (type) font*

octavo *(pap)* A sheet of paper folded in half three times, to make eight or sixteen pages. It also refers to a standard 'broadside' divided into eight parts. → *broadside/ broadsheet*

octodecimo *(gen)* → *eighteenmo/18mo*

odd *(pap)* A papermaker's term for paper that does not conform to regular or standard sizes, finishes, etc.

OEM *(com)* *abb.:* original equipment manufacturer. → *original equipment manufacturer (OEM)*

off-cut *(fin)* Trimmed parts of paper, board, etc., which may be used for other jobs.

offline converting/finishing *(fin)* Any post-print process, such as trimming or folding, that is not performed on the same press used for printing the job. → *converting; in-line converting/finishing*

off-line/offline *(com)* Work done on a computer with access to a network or the Internet, but not actually while connected to the network. The opposite of online. → *online/on-line*

off-press proofing *(pre)* A method of proofing by exposing each separation positive onto laminated light-sensitive paper to create an accurate simulation of a 'wet proof' (one made with printing inks). Also known as 'prepress proofing' or 'dry proofing'. → *Cromalin; dry proof; MatchPrint*

off-print *(pri)* An article or other part of a publication printed with the main run but produced as a separate item. Also called a 'separate'. → *separate*

In **offset litho** printing, ink is transferred via a blanket cylinder to the paper

offset (1) *(pri)* A printing technique in which the ink is transferred from the printing plate to a 'blanket' cylinder and then to the paper or material on which it is to be printed. → *letterset; offset litho(graphy); offset gravure*

offset (2) *(pri)* To reproduce a book by photographing a previously printed edition.

offset blanket *(pri)* The rubber-coated blanket used in offset litho printing to transfer the inked image from plate to paper.

offset cartridge *(pap)* A good-quality smooth paper suited to offset litho printing.

offset gravure *(pri)* A method of gravure printing that uses a rubber-coated blanket to transfer the inked image from plate to paper. → *gravure*

offset ink *(pri)* An ink developed for use on offset litho presses. It must not react to the rubber in the blanket; it must have a high concentration of pigment, since not all the ink is transferred from blanket to paper; and it must be free from water–soluble particles.

offset letterpress *(pri)* → *letterset*

offset litho(graphy) *(pri)* A lithographic printing technique, developed in the US in the early 1900s, in which the image is printed indirectly by 'offsetting' it onto a rubber-covered cylinder, called a 'blanket' cylinder, from which the image is printed.

213

It is one of the most widely used commercial printing processes. This book was printed by the offset lithography process. → *direct litho(graphy); offset gravure*

offside *(fin)* The part of the case that is at the end of a book.

OK press/sheet *(pri)* Authorization that a job has had all corrections made and is ready for press. Also known as 'pass for press'.

old English *(typ)* → *black letter*

old face *(typ)* A type design characterized by its diagonal stress and sloped, bracketed serifs – for example, Garamond.

old style *(typ)* → *old face*

old-tech *(gen)* A colloquial expression referring to prepress technology that has largely been replaced by new, mostly computer-based, technology.

OLE *(com) abb.:* object–linking and embedding. → *object linking and embedding (OLE)*

olivined edges *(fin)* Green staining applied to the edges of a book.

OMF Open Media Framework *(aud)* Facility that permits the import and export of sound sessions from programs such as Digital Performer, Pro Tools and Cubase/Nuendo, and also from and to video suites such as Final Cut Pro.

omnibus book *(gen)* A single edition comprising a number of books previously published separately.

omni light *(com)* In a 3D environment, a light that shines in every direction (360°) from the Latin *'omnis'*, meaning 'all').

OMR *(gen) abb.:* optical mark recognition. → *bar code*

on-demand *(gen)* A description of anything that is supplied only when it is asked for, rather than 'live' (as it happens) or automatically.

on-demand printing *(pri)* → *demand printing*

one-and-a-half-up *(gen)* → *half-up*

one on and two off *(fin)* A method of binding in which a single width of paper is glued to the back of the book, then double-folded, and the resulting two layers glued together to add support to the spine. When a double layer of paper is glued to the back, it is known as 'two on and two off'.

one-piece film *(pre)* → *flat (1)*

one-up *(pri)* A single printing of a single signature or image on a press sheet. → *two-up*

one-way halftone *(pre)* → *single-line halftone*

onionskin *(pap)* A very lightweight, semi-translucent paper with a cockle finish.

onlaying *(fin)* The traditional method of decorating a calf- or morocco-bound book cover, using additional pieces of very thin leather of contrasting colours glued to the surface. → *inlaying*

online help *(com)* In most applications, a file that gives help and advice, always available while that application is being used.

online/on-line *(com)* Any activity taking place on a computer or device while it is connected to a network such as the Internet. The opposite of offline. → *in-line; network; off-line/offline*

online service provider *(int)* → *service provider*

ooze leather *(fin)* Bookbindings made of sheepskin or calfskin with the flesh ('nap') side outermost, giving a suede finish.

o.p. *(gen) abb.:* out of print. → *out of print (o.p.)*

opacity *(com)* The degree of transparency that each layer of an image has in relation to the layer beneath. Layer opacities can be adjusted using an opacity control in the *Layers* palette. Available in many image editing applications, most notably in Adobe Photoshop.

This car has 100% **opacity** on the left fading to zero

opaline *(pap)* Semi-opaque paper with a glazed finish.

opaque *(gen)* The opposite of transparent. Any material that does not allow light to shine through. → *photo-opaque*

opaquing *(pre)* To paint out unwanted marks or areas on a negative or positive film with opaque solution prior to platemaking. → *photo-opaque*

op. cit. *(gen)* abb.: *opere citato*. Latin for 'in the work already quoted', used as a footnote reference.

open (1) *(com)* A standard operating system command, which reveals the contents of a selected file or folder or launches an application. → *launch*

open (2) *(gen)* The appearance of a design in which the text and pictorial elements are not crammed together.

open architecture *(com)* The facility, in the design of a computer system, for unrestricted modification and improvement of the computer and its system. Macintosh computers are not open, in as much as the ROM chip used as the basis of the operating system can not be used by other computer manufacturers to make cloned Macs.

open back *(fin)* → *hollow back*

open curve *(com)* A curve that does not form a closed loop.

OpenDoc *(com)* Obsolete Mac OS technology that allowed users to work on different types of data within a single document by using several applications to do so.

open flash *(pho)* The technique of illuminating a subject by leaving the camera shutter open and firing the flash manually.

opening *(gen)* Any pair of facing pages, which may or may not form a double-page spread.

open letters *(typ)* → *outline letter/outline font*

open matter *(typ)* Type that has been set with extra leading to give an 'open' appearance.

open prepress interface (OPI) *(pre)* A prepress protocol that enables low-resolution (positional) scanned image files to be automatically substituted for high-resolution versions when the file is output to an imagesetter or other high-resolution device.

open/standing time *(gen)* Spare production time due to a break in the schedule. You should be so lucky. → *down time*

OpenType *(com)* A development of Microsoft's 'TrueType Open' font format, which adds support for Type 1 font data. An OpenType font can contain Type 1 data only, TrueType data only, or both. The Type 1 data can be rendered ('rasterized') by a utility such as Adobe Type Manager, or converted to TrueType data for rasterization by the TrueType rasterizer. This font format is a superset of the existing TrueType and Type 1 formats, and is designed to provide support for type in print and on-screen and, with its compression technology, is also relevant to the Internet and the World Wide Web, since it allows for fast download of type. → *font embedding; TrueType; Type 1 font; WEFT (2);*

open up *(pre)* A method of obtaining a lighter printed result by slightly overexposing a halftone negative so that the dots appear smaller.

operating system *(com)* The software (and in some cases 'firmware') that provides the environment within which all other software and its user operates. The major operating systems are Microsoft's 'Windows', Apple's 'Mac OS' and AT&T's 'UNIX'. → *firmware*

OPI *(pre) abb.:* open prepress interface.
→ *CEPS; DCS; open prepress interface (OPI)*

optical alignment *(gen)* Curved or pointed characters or shapes that project beyond the margin when aligned, giving the overall appearance of being in a straight line.

optical bleaching agents (o.b.a.) *(pap)* An additive to pulp, which makes paper look whiter under particular lighting conditions. Despite the name, bleaching agents are not used. The paper reflects more light by absorbing invisible ultraviolet light, which is then re-emitted as visible light.

optical centre *(gen)* A point within a scene, usually slightly higher than the actual geometric centre, at which the main subject appears to be centrally placed.

optical character recognition (OCR) *(com)* A means of inputting copy without 'keying' it in. This is achieved with software that, when used with a scanner or 'page reader', converts typescript into editable digital text.

optical disc/media *(com)* A medium for storing digitized data by means of minute pits embedded into the surface of the disc. The binary digits of 1 and 0 are determined by the size and presence of the pits, and these are 'read' by an optical pick-up using

a laser, which is reflected off a shiny metallic layer on the disc's surface. Optical discs are widely used for audio and video recording and for computer data storage, and are capable of holding huge amounts of data. Commonly called CDs (compact discs) or DVDs (digital versatile discs), optical discs are more resilient than magnetic media and thus provide more secure data storage.

The subject of this image has been placed in the **optical centre**

optical(ly) even spacing *(typ)* The adjustment of the spaces between characters to create an even appearance in a line of type.

optical (type) font *(typ)* Fonts used in some methods of optical character recognition, having character shapes that are both distinguishable by computers and readable by people. The most common OCR fonts are 'OCR-A' and 'OCR-B', the latter designed by Adrian Frutiger. → *OCR*

optimize/optimizing *(com)* The technique of speeding up disk operations by using special 'utility' software to shuffle files around and merge those that, due to a shortage of contiguous storage space on the disk, have become 'fragmented' (split into smaller pieces). This also creates

*!?

contiguous areas of unused storage space on your drive, thus allowing files to be written to disk faster when you save them. → *contiguous; defragment(ing)*

Option key *(com)* Any keyboard key, button, checkbox, menu or command that allows you an alternative choice. On keyboards, this is provided by the 'Option' (Macintosh) and 'Alt' (Windows) keys, and when used in conjunction with another key, these provide a special character or a shortcut to menu commands. → *modifier key*

Orange Book *(com)* The document that specifies all parameters for recordable CD (CD-R) technology, developed by Sony and Philips. → *CD-R/CD-RW*

orange peel *(fin)* An undesirable effect on laminated surfaces, usually caused by too much set-off spray being used after printing. → *set-off*

ordinal numbers *(gen)* Numbers that indicate placement – first, second, third, etc. – as opposed to cardinal numbers used for sequential counting – 1, 2, 3, etc. → *cardinal numbers*

oriental leaf *(fin)* An alternative to gold foil made from a mixture of brass and bronze. → *mosaic gold*

oriental type *(typ)* → *exotic*

orientation *(gen)* The print direction of a page, or the format of an image (portrait or landscape).

origin *(com)* The fixed, or zero, point of horizontal and vertical axes, or of the rulers featured in most applications from which measurements can be made.

original equipment manufacturer (OEM) *(com)* The manufacturer of an item that may be marketed under a different name – common practice with disk drives. Sometimes called a 'third-party' supplier.

origination *(pre)* → *prepress*

o-ring *(com)* The rubber ring designed to prevent leaks in a waterproof housing.

ornament *(typ)* → *flower*

orphan *(typ)* A short line, usually the first or last line of a paragraph, that falls at the top or bottom of a column of text. Also known as 'club line'.

orphan file *(int)* A file on a website that is not referred to by any link or button and thus cannot be reached by any means other than through its absolute URL. To find it, you must know its exact pathname. → *absolute URL; URL*

orthochromatic *(pre)* A photographic emulsion that is sensitive to all colours except red, and used extensively in conventional reproduction. Also called 'lith film'. → *orthographic (1)*

ortho film *(pre)* → *orthochromatic*

orthogonal line tool *(com)* → *Line tool*

orthographic (1) *(pho)* Photographic emulsion that is sensitive only to green, blue and ultraviolet light. → *orthochromatic*

orthographic (projection) (2) *(gen)* An illustration technique in which there is no perspective (or the perspective is infinite), thus giving parallel projection lines.

OS *(com)* → *operating system*

oscillator *(aud)* Often associated with synthesizers, this is a device that can be made to generate a tone at any frequency.

OTF metering *(pho)* abb.: off-the-film metering. A 'through-the-lens' (TTL) system in which the exposure is determined from the image that is projected onto the film plane inside the camera.

out *(typ)* Text that has been unintentionally omitted from composition.

outer margin *(gen)* → *fore-edge*

outline font *(com)* A vector-based digital font drawn from an outline that can be scaled or rotated to any size or resolution, as distinct from 'bitmapped fonts', comprised of pixels and used primarily for screen display in the case of PostScript fonts. Also called 'printer fonts' or 'laser fonts' (because they are essential for rendering fonts accurately when output on laser printers and imagesetters), or 'scalable fonts'. ➜ *bitmapped font; Type 1 font*

outline halftone *(gen)* ➜ *cutout (1)*

outline letter/outline font *(typ)* A type design in which the character is formed of outlines rather than a solid shape or, alternatively, a font 'style' option in many applications, which renders just the outline of a font without filling it in, usually with appalling results.

outliner *(com)* The part of a word-processing application that shows the structure of a document, such as headings and text.

out-of-memory message *(com)* A message that tells you that there is not enough memory (RAM) available to perform the task that you require. Typical out-of-memory messages relate to having too many applications open at once. Less obvious reasons can include the system heap being too small, having too many system files open (such as fonts), or a particularly memory-intensive task (such as those involving bitmapped images) exceeding available RAM. ➜ *application memory (heap); system heap*

out of print (o.p.) *(gen)* A book that is not in a publisher's current list and is unlikely to be reprinted. ➜ *in print*

out of register *(pri)* ➜ *register/registration*

out of series *(pri)* ➜ *retree copy*

output *(com)* Any data or matter extracted from a computer, by whatever means, but typically via a monitor, printer or storage device.

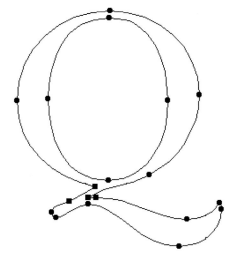

Outline fonts are drawn from vectors

output device *(com)* Any hardware device capable of producing or displaying computer data in a visible form, such as a monitor, printer, plotter, imagesetter, etc.

output resolution *(pre)* The resolution of a printer, monitor, imagesetter or similar device, usually measured in dpi (dots per inch), though more correctly ppi (pixels per inch) for displays. The relationship between output resolution and halftone screen ruling determines the tonal range that can be printed. The following formula should be used to calculate the optimum number of greys that can be achieved (remembering that 256 is the PostScript maximum): $(\text{output resolution} \div \text{screen ruling})^2 + 1 =$ shades of grey. Therefore an image output at 1200dpi and printed with a screen ruling of 90lpi will produce 178 shades of grey. Increasing the screen ruling creates smaller halftone dots and adds detail to an image, but it also reduces the number of greys, so the same image output at 1200dpi and

Out-of-memory messages are often reduced by using Hard Disk space as Virtual RAM. This means you can run out of this kind of storage too

OUTLINE FONT

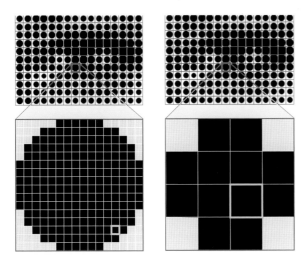

Output resolution
showing a high-resolution halftone dot on a 16x16 matrix of machine dots (left) and a low-resolution dot on a 4x4 matrix (right)

An example of an **overexposed** picture

printed with a screen ruling of 175lpi will produce only 48 shades of grey. A typical resolution for a monitor is 72–90dpi, for a laser printer 600dpi, and for an imagesetter anything upward of 1000dpi. → *halftone screen; machine dot; screen ruling*

outrig frame *(pho)* A metal frame fitted in front of a lamp and used to carry filters, gels, diffusing filter, etc.

outsert/outset *(fin)* → *insert (1)*

outside margin *(gen)* → *fore-edge margin*

outsides *(pap)* Damaged sheets in a batch of handmade paper, having torn edges, creases or a damaged surface. These are marked 'XXX'.

Oval tool *(com)* → *Ellipse/Oval tool*

overcasting *(fin)* → *oversewing*

overdevelop *(pho)* To allow an exposed photographic image to remain in the developing solution longer than necessary for a correct exposure.

overdub *(aud)* Sound added to an existing recording to enhance or correct it. This can refer to plain sounds or music.

overexpose/overexposure (1) *(pho)* A photographic image that has a bleached-out, pale appearance, with subsequent loss of detail, caused by too much light reaching the film during exposure.

overexpose/overexposure (2) *(pri)* A fault in platemaking caused when the light source is too close or too bright.

overflow *(typ)* → *overmatter*

overhang cover *(fin)* A book cover that projects past the trimmed edges of the leaves, common with casebound books.

overhead *(com)* The unseen formatting data contained within a document file, which is saved along with the visible data.

overhead cost *(gen)* The residual costs that are inherent in any project, such as office rental, stationery, staff, entertainment, vehicles, etc., as compared with the costs specifically attributed to the project itself, which would not occur if the project did not proceed (printing the job, for example). → *direct cost*

overhead projector *(gen)* A device for making presentations in which images that have been created or output on transparent cellulose acetate are projected onto a flat surface or screen.

overlay *(gen)* → *tissue*

overlaying *(pri)* A method of varying the pressure of a printing plate on a press by adding pieces of paper to the tympan, thereby darkening or lightening the impression. → *make-ready*

overmatter *(typ)* Typeset matter that will not fit within the space designed for it (if set by a typesetter, a charge is incurred for overmatter). Also called 'overset' or 'overflow'. → *overflow*

overprint (1) *(pri)* To make a second printing or 'pass' on a previously printed sheet. Also called 'surprinting'.

overprint (2) *(pri)* To print two or more colours so that they overlap, either to produce more colours or to avoid registration problems. The opposite of 'knockout'. → *lap*

overprint (3) *(pri)* → *off-print*

overprint colour *(pri)* → *secondary colour*

overrun *(typ)* Words that move from one line to the next, possibly for several successive lines, as a result of newly inserted text or a correction. The opposite of 'run back'.
→ *run back*

overs *(pri)* A number of copies of a publication printed beyond the number ordered. This is usually deliberate, to allow for copies that may be spoiled during finishing or lost or damaged during shipping. → *printer's ream; run on (1)*

overset (1) *(typ)* Typeset characters that accidentally extend beyond the specified measure.

overset (2) *(typ)* → *overmatter*

oversewing *(fin)* A method of sewing books comprised of separate leaves, using a stitch similar to that found on the edge of blankets. Also called 'overcasting' or 'whipstitching'. → *whipstitching*

oversize (1) *(gen)* Artwork drawn to a larger size than that intended for reproduction.

oversize (2) *(com)* In some applications, a description of a page size that is larger than the size of paper it is to be printed on.

oversize (3) *(pap)* A size of paper cut larger than the basic size.

oversize (4) *(fin)* A size of book or publication that is physically too large for the printing and binding process and which may therefore involve some handwork.

own ends *(fin)* → *self ends*

Oxford corners *(gen)* A box rule where the lines project beyond the frame corners.

Oxford rule *(gen)* The combination of a thick and a thin rule.

Ozalid *(pre)* The proprietary name for a diazo process paper, often used to make prepress proofs of an imposed publication. Such proofs are therefore frequently called 'Ozalids'. → *blueline (1); diazo(type)/ diazo process*

Pp

p/pp *(gen)* abb.: page/pages.

packet *(int)* A bundle of data – the basic unit transmitted across networks. When data is sent over a network such as the Internet, it is broken up into small chunks called 'packets', which are sent independently of one another.

packing *(pri)* A method involving the placing of material (usually paper or rubber) between the cylinder and the plate/blanket on a printing press. The increased pressure results in a heavier impression being transferred from the plate to the blanket or from the blanket to the paper. → *make-ready*

page (1) *(int)* An HTML document (text structured with HTML tags) viewed with a Web browser. → *HTML; Web browser*

page (2) *(gen)* One side of a leaf. → *leaf (1)*

Adobe InDesign is a popular **page-layout** application

page (3) *(com)* A contiguous segment of memory. → *memory*

page break *(gen)* In continuous text, the place at which text is broken to be taken on to the following page.

page description language (PDL) *(com)* A programming language via which a computer communicates with a printer, describing to it image and font data so that it can construct and print the data to your specifications. PostScript is the most widely used PDL.

paged memory–management unit (PMMU) *(com)* A microchip on older Macintosh computers that enhances memory capabilities, such as enabling the use of virtual memory. The PMMU is integrated into the CPU of more modern computers. → *CPU*

page flex *(fin)* The amount of stress that a bound book can endure before the pages become loosened.

page flipping *(int)* An HTML structure for webpages, which allows users to see successive screens without needing to scroll. → *HTML*

page guides *(com)* In some applications, non-printing guides that show the width of margins, position of columns, etc. → *guides*

page head *(gen)* → *headline (1)*

page-layout/make-up application *(com)* Any application that enables you to carry out all of the functions normally associated with page design, layout and make-up.

page preview *(com)* A feature in some applications, such as word processing applications and databases, that allows you to view a page as it will look when printed.

page proofs *(gen)* A proof of pages that have been paginated (put into the correct page sequence). Traditionally, this is the secondary stage in proofing (after galley proofs and before machine proofs) although there may be other stages either before or after, such as the 'blues' used to check imposition. Also called 'made-up proofs'. ➔ *proof*

page reader *(com)* ➔ *OCR*

Page Setup *(com)* A dialog box that enables you to select various options for printing, such as paper size, enlargement or reduction, paper orientation, inversion, etc. The available options depend on the printer you are using.

pages to view *(pri)* A reference to the number of pages that will be visible on one side of a sheet that will be printed on both sides.

pagination *(gen)* Strictly speaking, the numbering of book pages, but also commonly used to describe the make-up of material into pages.

Paintbucket *(com)* A tool used to fill an outlined area with texture and colour.

painted edges *(fin)* ➔ *fore-edge painting*

paint(ing) application *(com)* Applications using bitmaps of pixels to create images rather than the vectors that describe lines in drawing applications. Increasingly, graphics applications combine both. ➔ *image-editing application/image editor; vector*

paint program *(com)* ➔ *image-editing application/image editor*

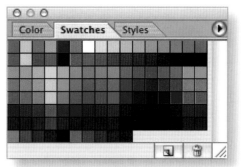

Palettes act as little windows that can be arranged to suit the user, but remain to hand like an artist's palette

PAL *(aud)* Acronym for phase alternation line. The standard TV display format for the UK, most other European countries (with the exception of France), Australia, New Zealand and several African nations, including South Africa. PAL is made up of 625 lines, using 25 frames made up of two interlaced fields, thus producing 50 fields per second.

palette *(com)* A window, often 'floating' (movable), that contains features such as tools, measurements or other functions.

pallet (1) *(fin)* A brass finishing tool used for impressing straight lines onto the spines of books.

pallet (2) *(fin)* A small hand tool in which type characters are placed prior to being heated, after which it is used to stamp the cover of a book.

Corel Painter is a **painting application** with features designed to simulate traditional artistic materials

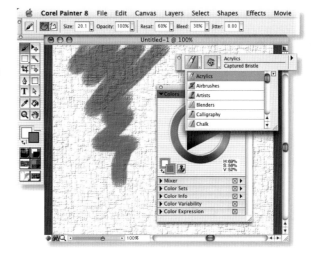

pamphlet *(gen)* A short publication, usually on a subject of current interest, presented unbound and in a soft cover. ➔ *booklet*

pan (1) *(aud)* To create an apparent location for a signal within the stereo spectrum. In a musical recording for example, some sounds are panned a little bit to the right or left, to represent the actual physical area at which that instrument might appear. It is also commonly used for special effects.

pan (2) *(aud)* In video, a smooth camera movement where the horizontal angle of the camera changes, either to show more of the scene or to follow characters as they move through it.

panchromatic *(pho)* Photographic emulsion that is sensitive to all colours in the visible spectrum. ➔ *orthographic (1)*

panel *(pri)* The part of a printed page or sheet defined by folds.

panel back *(fin)* A handbound book with a decorative panel on its spine.

panel printing *(pri)* A preprinted area of flat colour used as a base for further printing.

panel stamp *(fin)* An engraved block used to create an embossed image on a book cover.

pan film *(pho)* – ➔ *panchromatic*

pan(ning) *(pho)* The rotation of a camera from side to side along its vertical axis, an animation feature of most 3D applications. ➔ *camera moves; dolly (shot); tracking (2)*

panorama *(pho)* A wide-framed image, generally at least twice as wide as high.

pantograph *(pho)* A device that allows the easy extension and retraction of photographic lamps.

PANTONE® *(gen)* The proprietary trademark for Pantone Inc's system of ink colour standards, control and quality requirements, in which each colour bears a description of its formulation (in percentages) for subsequent printing. The PANTONE MATCHING SYSTEM® is used throughout the world so that colours specified by any designer can be matched exactly by any printer.

paper absorbency *(pap)* The ability of paper to retain or absorb fluids, particularly ink.

paperback *(fin)* A book with a soft outer cover, usually made of thick paper, as distinct from 'limp binding', which may be made from other materials. Also known as a 'softback' binding. ➔ *paper covers; softback edition*

paper basis weight *(pap)* The weight of a ream of paper (500 sheets) cut to a given standard size. ➔ *paper weight*

paperboard *(pap)* The heaviest weights of paper. Also called 'cardboard'. ➔ *board (1)*

paper boards *(fin)* A cased binding of paper rather than cloth.

paper covers *(fin)* A style of binding (without boards) for ordinary books sewn in sections, as distinct from mass-produced paperbacks, which are generally 'perfect bound'. ➔ *paperback; perfect binding*

paper grade *(pho)* ➔ *grade*

paper permanence *(pap)* The longevity of paper – for example, its resistance to discolouration. Rag-based papers withstand discolouration and brittleness better than most. ➔ *rag paper/pulp*

paper sizes *(pap)* ➔ *ISO A-series paper sizes*

paper substance *(pap)* The measure of paper by weight alone ('substance') rather than by weight related to a given size or number of sheets. Thus in many parts of the world paper substance is expressed in grammes per square metre (gsm) – a basis that does not change whatever the size or number of sheets – rather than, say, pounds per ream of 500 sheets of a certain size, which makes it difficult to assess actual substance. ➔ *equivalent weight; weight (2)*

*!?

paper to paper *(fin)* → *fold to paper*

paper weight *(pap)* The actual weight of a paper measured either in pounds per ream of 500 sheets or in grammes per square metre (gsm, g/m^2). However, paper weight is not necessarily an indication of substance. Alternatively, the thickness of the paper or board is measured in microns (one micron = one millionth of a metre). → *paper basis weight; paper substance*

paper wrappered *(fin)* A paper–covered book. → *paper covers*

papeterie *(pap)* A type of heavy, uncoated paper with a range of smooth or embossed finishes.

papier mâché *(pri)* A paper pulp used to create moulds for casting stereotypes. → *flong; stereo(type)*

papyrus *(pap)* A form of writing material used by early Egyptians and made from the giant papyrus rush found around the River Nile. Papyrus was the origin of the word 'paper' (via the Anglo-French *'papir'*).

paragon *(typ)* The name (now defunct) of a size of type that is approximately 20 points, originating in 16th-century Holland. It was also described as a 'two-line primer'.

paragraph *(int)* In an HTML document, a markup tag used to define a new paragraph in text.

paragraph format *(com)* → *format (3)*

paragraph mark *(typ)* → *blind P*

parallax *(gen)* The apparent movement of two objects relative to each other when viewed from different positions.

parallel fold *(fin)* A series of folds aligned in the same direction in a sheet of paper, and usually of equal size.

parallel interface *(com)* A computer connection in which data is transmitted simultaneously in the same direction along a single cable. As distinct from serial interface in which data is transmitted sequentially, one at a time. → *serial interface*

parallel mark *(typ)* A type character ('ll') used to denote a reference mark.

parallel rule *(gen)* The term used to distinguish a rule comprising two lines of the same thickness (made from brass in traditional typesetting) from one comprising two lines of different thickness (called a 'double rule'). → *double rule*

parameter *(com)* A limit, boundary or, in programming, a qualifier that defines the precise characteristics of a piece of software.

parameter RAM *(com)* An area of memory – stored in a chip – in Macintosh computers that maintains basic settings such as time and date, even when it is switched off (unlike the memory provided by RAM, which is lost when the computer is switched off). The PRAM chip is provided with a continuous power supply from its own lithium battery.

parchment *(pap)* An early form of fine, translucent writing material made from the skin of a goat or sheep. It is prepared by first scraping and then dressing with pumice or lime. Nowadays, parchment generally comes as a paper simulation called 'artificial parchment'.

parenthesis *(typ)* A pair of rounded brackets ( ), although, accurately, the term means a non-essential word, clause or sentence inserted into a text, which can be marked off by dashes or commas as well as brackets.

parent object *(com)* In a series of linked 3D objects, the one that is at the top of the hierarchy. ➔ *child object; down tree*

parent relative *(com)* The position and orientation of a 3D object in relation to its parent.

Pareto diagram *(gen)* A diagram that illustrates the theory (the 'Pareto principle') that 80 per cent of the effects of a situation come from only 20 per cent of possible causes.

paring *(fin)* In traditional bookbinding, the process of thinning the edge of a leather sheet to enable a neater finish when it is folded around the edge of a cover board.

parity bit *(com)* An extra bit of data used to verify that the bits received by one communications device match those transmitted by another. ➔ *bit*

parked *(com)* The state of a disk drive's read/write heads when they are at rest, important if the drive or cartridge is to be moved without damage to the disk.

partition(ing) *(com)* The division of a hard disk into smaller volumes, each of which behaves as if it were a separate disk. There are two kinds of partitions: 'real partitions' (sometimes called 'SCSI partitions') in which you divide the disk up during formatting, and 'file partitions' (also called 'disk images'), which are large files created on an existing disk drive. ➔ *disk image*

partwork *(gen)* A complete work, such as an encyclopedia, published as smaller individual issues, usually in weekly instalments. ➔ *fascicule*

Pascal *(com)* A programming language. ➔ *programming language*

pass *(pri)* One cycle of a printing surface through a printing press, whether it be a single- or four-colour press. Subsequent passes may be required to achieve the desired result – for example, to add more colour than was possible on the first pass.

pass for press *(pri)* A printing job that has had all corrections approved and is thus ready for press.

passive matrix display *(com)* An LCD (liquid crystal display) monitor technology, usually found on cheaper laptop computers, which uses fewer transistors to generate the display, thus giving an inferior image quality to 'active' matrix displays. ➔ *active matrix display; liquid crystal display*

pass sheet *(pri)* A printed sheet of optimum print quality, which is removed from the run so that subsequent sheets can be compared with it.

paste *(com)* A command that places a copied item into a document. ➔ *clipboard; copy (2); cut (7); cut and paste*

pasteboard (1) *(com)* In some applications, the non-printing area around the page, on which items can be kept for later use.

pasteboard (2) *(pap)* Two or more laminations of paper, typically used for business cards. ➔ *cardboard/card*

pasted down to ends *(fin)* ➔ *glued down to ends*

Using applications like Apple's *Disk Utility,* you can format and **partition** your computer's hard disk

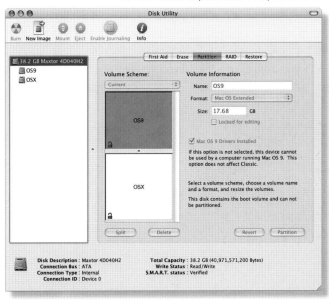

PASTED DOWN TO ENDS

paste-downs *(fin)* The half of an endpaper that is glued to the cover boards, leaving the other half free ('fly leaf'). ➜ *endpapers; fly leaf*

paste-grain *(fin)* A binding material with a polished surface, made from hardened sheepskin coated with paste.

paste in *(fin)* ➜ *tip in/on, tipped in/on*

pastel shades *(gen)* Lighter shades of colour.

paste on *(fin)* A method of glueing a printed image into a book by applying paste all over ➜ *tip in/on, tipped in/on*

paster (1) *(fin)* The component of a binding line that applies adhesive rather than stitching in the manufacture of booklets. The term also describes the product of the process.

paster (2) *(pri)* An automatic splicer on a web press.

paste-replace *(com)* The action of replacing one 3D object by pasting in another to the same position and orientation.

paste-up/pasteup *(gen)* The layout of a design, including all elements such as text and illustrations. A paste-up will either be 'rough' for layout and mark-up purposes or 'camera-ready' (also known as 'mechanical'), which will be used to make film for reproduction. ➜ *camera-ready copy/art (CRC)*

pasting *(fin)* In bookbinding, the application of adhesive by hand or machine. ➜ *gluing-up*

pasting down *(fin)* In bookbinding, the affixing of endpapers to the inside boards of a case.

patch *(com)* A small piece of program code supplied for fixing bugs in software. ➜ *bug*

patent *(gen)* The authority granted by a government agency to protect an invention from being copied.

path (1) *(com)* The hierarchical trail through disk and folders to a particular file. ➜ *pathname*

path (2) *(com)* A line drawn in an object-oriented application. ➜ *object-oriented*

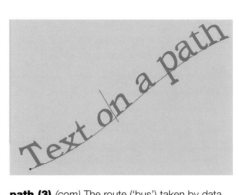

Many applications allow you to run text along a **path**

path (3) *(com)* The route ('bus') taken by data as it travels along circuits from chip to chip or device to device.

path (4) *(gen)* A line, often invisible, which is used to control or constrain the flow of text. A path can be straight, curved or irregular, and the text often flows along the top of it.

pathname *(com)* A string of words identifying the entire path from disk to file, such as 'mydisk:myfolder:myfile', indicating that the file named 'myfile' is inside the folder named 'myfolder', which is on the disk called 'mydisk'. Colons (:) or forward slashes ('/') are generally used to separate each name in the path, which is why colons or slashes should not be used in file names.

PC *(com) abb.:* personal computer. The name originally used to describe IBM PCs but now used to describe any personal computer that is IBM-compatible or that runs the Windows operating system. As distinct from computers running the Mac OS although, strictly speaking, they are also personal computers.

Examples of **pastel shades**

PC board *(com) abb.:* printed circuit board. ➜ *circuit board*

PCI *(com) abb.:* peripheral component interconnect. ➜ *bus (1); peripheral component interconnect (PCI)*

PC lens *(pho) abb.:* perspective correction lens. ➜ *perspective correction (PC) lens*

PASTE-DOWNS

PCM *(aud)* Pulse code modulation, the uncompressed data format used in most standard digital audio file types. Standards body the Audio Engineering Society (www.aes.org) recommends a sampling frequency of 48 kHz for the origination, processing and interchange of audio programs employing PCM, but recognizes 44.1-kHz sampling rates.

PCMCIA *(com) abb.:* Personal Computer Memory Card International Association. → *Personal Computer Memory Card International Association (PCMCIA)*

PCS *(com) abb.:* profile connection space. A component of a colour management system used to transform colour information between device-specific colour profiles. In commercial products, the PCS is a device-independent colour model, such as CIE LAB or CIE XYZ.

PD *(gen) abb.:* public domain.

PDF *(com) abb.:* portable document format. The cross-platform, cross-application page description format created by Adobe that allows complex, multi-featured documents to be created, retaining all text and picture formatting, and then viewed and printed on any computer that has an appropriate 'reader' installed, such as Adobe Acrobat Reader.

PDL *(com) abb.:* page description language. → *page description language (PDL)*

PDS *(com) abb.:* processor direct slot. → *processor direct slot (PDS)*

PE *(typ) abb.:* printer's error. A mark on a set of proofs indicating an error that has been caused by the typesetter and not the author or editor.

peaking *(com)* A method of digitally sharpening images by using a filter that increases the difference in density where two tonal areas meet. Also called 'sharpen edges'. → *unsharp masking (USM)*

pearl *(typ)* The name (now defunct) of a size of type of approximately 5 points.

peasant binding *(fin)* A binding of inferior quality used in 17th-century Europe for Bibles made for rural home use.

pebbling *(fin)* A technique of embossing paper after it has been printed to create an undulating effect.

peculiars *(typ)* → *special sorts*

peer-to-peer *(com)* A network system in which files are spread around different computers, the users of which access them from each other rather than from a central 'server'.

PEL *(com) abb.:* picture element. The smallest unit of a computer display that can be assigned an individual colour and intensity. It is more commonly called a pixel.→ *pixel*

percussion *(aud)* Sound made by the impact of an object when striking a resonant surface; drums are percussion instruments.

perfect *(pri)* The point at which some or all printed sheets of an edition are ready for binding. → *perfect copy*

perfect binding *(fin)* → *threadless binding*

perfect copy *(fin)* A complete set of printed and folded sheets, ready for binding. → *perfect*

perfecting *(pri)* → *back up/backing up (2)*

perfecting press/perfector *(pri)* → *blanket-to-blanket press*

perforate/perf *(pap)* A line of punched holes, which allows a sheet of paper to be torn or folded accurately.

perf strip *(fin)* A narrow strip of paper bound in to a saddle-stitched publication, which allows single leaves to be tipped in.

period *(typ)* A full stop, or full point.

peripheral cable *(com)* A cable that connects a peripheral device to a computer.

peripheral component interconnect (PCI) *(com)* A high-performance, 32-bit or 64-bit 'bus' for connecting external devices to a computer. → *bus (1)*

peripheral device *(com)* → *device (1)*

Perl *(int)* A programming language much favoured for creating CGI programs. → *CGI (2)*

permanence *(pap)* → *paper permanence*

permanent font *(com)* A misnomer sometimes used to describe fonts that are manually downloaded to a printer, even though they are permanent only until the printer is switched off, in which case they must be downloaded again when it is switched on. As distinct from an automatically downloaded ('transient') font, which lasts in memory only while a document is being printed. Not to be confused with a 'resident font', which resides on the printer's hard disk or ROM.

Personal Computer Memory Card International Association (PCMCIA) *(com)* A standard format for a type of expansion card that is used mainly in portable computers for adding features such as external devices, modems and memory. Also known as 'PC Card'.

personal Java *(int)* A variation of Java designed for specific Internet devices such as netTVs. → *Java*

perspective *(gen)* A technique of rendering 3D objects on a 2D plane, duplicating the 'real world' view by giving the same impression of the object's relative position and size when viewed from a particular point – the shorter the distance, the wider the perspective; the greater the distance, the narrower the perspective.

perspective correction (PC) lens *(pho)* A camera lens used mainly to correct converging verticals in architectural photography. Also called a 'shift lens'.

PFR *(int)* abb.: portable font resource. → *font embedding*

phase *(aud)* When two audio waveforms match each other and are playing simultaneously, they are in phase, and as such they reinforce each other. If one of these waveforms is playing back at a slightly different speed, they are out of phase, and this causes them to weaken each other. If one waveform is exactly 180° out of phase (say, if the polarity is reversed on one stereo speaker), the waveforms will cancel each other out. A phasing effect involves playing a copy of a sound simultaneously while varying the delay by anywhere from about 1 to 10 milliseconds.

phase alternation by line (PAL) *(com)* → *PAL*

Phong shading *(com)* A superior but time-consuming method of rendering 3D images, which computes the shading of every pixel. Usually used for final 32-bit renders.

phonogram *(gen)* A symbol, which may or may not correspond to the International Phonetic Alphabet (IPA), devised as the written equivalent of a spoken sound.

phosphor *(com)* The light-sensitive coating in a CRT screen, which glows when hit by a beam from the electron gun. Phosphors are arranged in patterns of red, green and blue in order to create the appearance of a full-colour display through additive colour mixing. → *cathode ray tube (CRT)*

Photo CD *(com)* A proprietary, cross-platform technology developed by Kodak for scanning and storing photographs on CD-ROM. Photo CD files can be opened and edited with most image-editing applications.

photocell *(com)* → *photoelectric cell*

photocomposition *(typ)* → *filmsetting*

photodirect *(pre)* A method of producing litho plates direct from artwork without an intermediate negative being made first.

photoelectric cell *(com)* A device that produces an electric signal in response to the amount of light striking it. Also called a 'photocell' or 'photosite'. → *CCD*

photoengraving *(pri)* The method of engraving or etching printing plates using a photomechanical transfer of the image.

A cube drawn in **perspective**

photoflood *(pho)* A high-rated tungsten lamp used in photography, with a colour temperature of 3400K.

photogelatin printing *(pri)* → *collotype*

photogram *(pho)* A photographic image made by placing an object on a sheet of emulsion and briefly exposing it to light, resulting in a kind of shadow picture.

photographic film *(pho)* → *film (2)*

photography *(pho)* The method of recording an image by the action of light on materials affected by it, such as a sensitized film emulsion or increasingly since the advent of digital cameras, a tiny light-sensitive sensor. → *camera; digital camera*

photogravure *(pri)* The photomechanical preparation of plates for use in intaglio printing processes. → *gravure; intaglio*

Photo JPEG *(com)* A QuickTime compression setting ('codec') generally used for still photographic image. Useful for films with a slow frame rate, such as slide shows or Web films. → *QuickTime*

photolithography *(pri)* → *offset litho(graphy)*

photomacrography *(pho)* Close-up photography with magnifications in the range of about one to ten times that of the original (and thus not 'photomicrography'). → *photomicrography*

photomechanical (1) *(pri)* The preparation of printing plates involving photographic techniques.

photomechanical (2) *(pre)* The full version of the term 'mechanical'. → *camera-ready copy/art (CRC)*

photomechanical reproduction *(pri)* → *photoengraving*

photomechanical transfer (PMT) *(pre)* A method of transferring images onto paper, film or metal litho plates by means of photography. An image produced by this method is also known as a PMT. Also called 'diffusion transfer', 'chemical transfer' or 'velox'.

photomicrography *(pho)* Photography at great magnifications using a microscope. → *darkfield lighting; photomacrography*

photomontage *(gen)* → *montage*

photo-opaque *(pre)* A liquid used to paint out 'pinholes' and other areas on negative or positive printing film. → *opaquing*

photopolymer (printing) plates *(pri)* Relief printing plates made with a light-sensitive polymer (plastic) coating, used mainly for flexographic printing.

photoresist *(pri)* A coating selectively applied to a printing plate to protect it from etching chemicals.

photo-sensitive *(pho)* Any material that has been chemically treated to make it sensitive to light, typically photographic emulsion.

photosite *(com)* → *CCD*

phototypesetting *(typ)* → *filmsetting*

physical dot gain *(pri)* The increase in the size of a halftone dot caused by the spread of ink during printing. → *dot gain; ink spread*

pica *(typ)* A typographer's and printer's unit of linear measurement, equivalent to 12 points. One inch comprises 6.0225 picas, or 72.27 points. Computer applications, however, use the PostScript value of exactly six picas, or 72 points, to the inch. → *point (1)*

pi character *(typ)* → *special sorts*

picking *(pri)* The lifting of fibres on the surface of paper during printing, caused either by sticky ink, poor quality paper or suction from the blanket cylinder. Also called 'plucking' or 'pulling'. → *blanket piling; bonding strength (1); fluff(ing)*

P

pick resistance *(pap)* The ability of a paper surface to withstand wear.

pick-up *(pri)* A traditional printing term for the reuse of materials from a previously completed print job.

PICS animation *(com)* A Macintosh animation format that uses PICT images to create a sequence, no longer used by authoring or animation tools.

PICT *(com)* Abbreviation for picture. A standard file format for storing bitmapped and object-oriented images on Macintosh computers. Originally the format supported only eight colours, but the newer PICT-2 supports 32-bit colour.

pictogram/pictograph *(gen)* A simplified, pictorial symbol distilled to its salient features to represent an object or concept. → *glyph (1); isotype; symbol*

picture box *(com)* A box that holds a picture, as distinct from a text box.

picture library *(gen)* → *image library*

picture skew *(com)* The distortion of an image by slanting the two opposite sides of a rectangle away from the horizontal or vertical.

piece fraction *(typ)* → *split fraction*

pie diagram *(gen)* → *cake/pie diagram/chart*

pierced *(pri)* A block that has been cut away to allow for type to be inserted. → *mortise (1)*

pie (type) *(typ)* Traditionally, composed type that has been inadvertently mixed up.

pi font *(typ)* A font of various characters such as shapes, logos, accents, dingbats, etc., which do not form part of a standard character set. → *dingbat; standard character set*

PIG chart *(pri)* abb.: process ink gamut chart. → *process ink gamut chart (PIG)*

pigment *(gen)* Ground particles of colour dissolved in a suitable medium to form ink or paint.

piling *(pri)* The accumulation of debris on an offset blanket or press rollers, affecting print quality.

pincushion *(com)* The tendency of a monitor image either to bulge out or curve in along its vertical sides. → *ballooning*

Adjusting a monitor's **pincushion** setting affects the sides

pinholes *(pho)* Tiny transparent specks on processed photographic emulsion, usually caused by dust on the lens or film. Also called 'point holes'. → *opaquing*

pin register *(pre)* A method of securing overlays and flats to keep them in register. Also known as a 'punch register'.

pin seal *(fin)* Young sealskin, once used for exotic bindings.

pin seal morocco *(fin)* Goatskin that has been treated to resemble pin seal. → *pin seal*

pinxit *(gen)* Latin for 'he painted it', often following an artist's name – on coloured engravings, for example. Sometimes abbreviated to 'pinx'.

pipe *(int)* The bandwidth of the actual connection between your computer and a server on the Internet. → *bandwidth*

pit *(com)* A tiny cavity burned by a laser in the surface of an optical disk. It equates to one bit of digital information. → *lands (2)*

pitch (1) *(typ)* A unit measure of type width equivalent to the number of characters per linear inch – 8-pitch, for example, equals 8 characters per inch.

pitch (2) *(com)* In 3D construction, the rotation around the x-axis.

pitch (3) *(com)* An expression of the resolution of imaging devices. For example, 'dot pitch' refers to the frequency of dots in, say, a monitor or imagesetter.

pixel *(com)* Abbreviation for picture element. The smallest component of a digitally generated image, such as a single dot of light on a computer monitor. In its simplest form, one pixel corresponds to a single bit: 0 = off, or white, and 1 = on, or black. In colour or greyscale images or monitors, one pixel may correspond to several bits: an 8-bit pixel, for example, can be displayed in any of 256 colours (the total number of different configurations that can be achieved by eight 0s and 1s). ➔ *pixels per inch (ppi); resolution (2)*

pixelation/pixelization *(com)* An image that has been broken up into square blocks resembling pixels, giving it a 'digitized' look. ➔ *aliasing*

pixel depth *(com)* The number of shades that a single pixel can display, determined by the number of bits used to display the pixel. One bit equals a single colour (black), four bits produces 16 shades, while 24 bits allows for 16.8 million colours.

pixels per inch (ppi) *(gen)* A unit of measurement that defines the number of pixels a bitmap image contains in every inch. The higher the number the greater the image's resolution. The term strictly refers to screen resolution, but is often confused with printer resolution, which is measured in lines per inch (lpi). ➔ *lines per inch (lpi); resolution (1)*

place *(com)* In many applications, the command used to import an image and position it in a document.

plagiarism *(gen)* The abuse of another's original work by copying it and passing it off as one's own.

planographic (printing) *(pri)* Printing from a flat surface (plane) – for example, lithography. ➔ *lithography*

plastic comb/coil binding *(fin)* A method of binding using rings attached to a plastic spine to secure the pages. ➔ *spiral binding*

plastic plates *(pri)* Plastic printing plates that are hard-wearing and light.

plate (1) *(pri)* A metal, plastic or paper sheet from which an image is printed. ➔ *curved plate*

plate (2) *(pri)* A book illustration printed separately from the main body and then tipped or bound into the book, although the term is now widely used (erroneously) to describe an illustration printed in a book. ➔ *figure (2)*

plate (3) *(pho)* A size of photographic film, a whole plate measuring 6½ x 8½in, and a half-plate measuring 4 x 6½in. ➔ *figure (2)*

plate-boring machine *(pri)* A machine used to bore out a stereotype plate to reduce it to the required thickness. ➔ *stereo(type)*

plate cylinder *(pri)* The cylinder on a printing press onto which the plate is fixed.

plated paper *(pap)* A paper containing a mixture of rags and clay, giving an excellent surface on which to print copper engravings and etchings.

plate finish/glazed *(pap)* The smooth surface on paper obtained by 'supercalendering' (passing it through heated, polished rollers).

plate folder *(fin)* ➔ *buckle folder*

platemaking *(pri)* The process of making an image on a printing plate by whatever means, but usually photomechanically transferring it from film.

plate mark *(pri)* ➔ *facet edge*

platen press *(pri)* A traditional flat bed press that uses a heavy plate ('platen') to press paper to the inked surface to create an impression.

plating *(pri)* The making of a stereotype or electrotype from setup type.

platter *(com)* A single, circular, magnetically coated metal disk that, usually with others, forms the storage medium of a hard disk drive.

playback *(com)* The rerun of an audio, video or animation sequence.

plotter *(com)* An output device that uses inked pens, to produce large format prints, particularly in the CAD and CAD/CAM industries.

plug and play *(com)* The marketing description of computer or hardware devices that do not require complicated 'setting up' – in other words, you just plug them in and start playing with them. ➔ *Macintosh*

plugging *(pri)* An aberration in platemaking by which dot areas become filled in, caused by damage to the plate.

plug-in *(com)* Software, usually developed by a third party, which extends the capabilities of a particular program. Plug-ins are common in image-editing and page-layout applications for such things as special effect filters. Plug-ins are also common in Web browsers for such things as playing films and audio, although these often come as complete applications ('helper applications') that can be used with a number of browsers rather than any specific one.
➔ *extension (1); helper application*

ply *(pap)* The measure of the thickness of board stock.

ply thickness *(pap)* The number of layers that comprise a sheet of paperboard.

PMMU *(com)* abb.: paged memory management unit. ➔ *paged memory management unit (PMMU)*

PMS *(gen)* abb.: PANTONE MATCHING SYSTEM®. ➔ *PANTONE®*

PMT (1) *(pre)* abb.: photomechanical transfer. ➔ *photomechanical transfer (PMT)*

PMT (2) *(pre)* abb.: photomultiplier tube. The light-sensing element in a drum scanner. PMTs are more expensive to make than CCDs. Since they amplify incoming light signals, they are capable of better discrimination of tonal levels and hence better dynamic range. In reprographics, PMT can also stand for Photo-Mechanical Transfer, a process that creates high-quality, black and white prints on photographic paper. This is not part of a digital workflow and for most practical purposes is now virtually obsolete.

PNG *(int)* abb.: portable network graphics. ➔ *alpha channel; Portable Network Graphics*

pocket edition *(gen)* A small book, usually no larger than approximately 6¾ x 4¼ in.

pocket envelope *(pap)* A rectangular envelope with the opening on the shorter side.

point (1) *(typ)* The basic unit of Anglo-American type measurement. In the past, no two printers could agree on a standard system of type measurement, so type cast in one foundry could not be mixed with that cast in another. However, in the mid-18th century, the French typographer Pierre Simon Fournier introduced a standard unit, which he called a 'point'. This was further developed by François Didot into a European standard ('Didot point'), although this was not adopted by either Britain or the US. The Anglo-American system divides one inch into 72 parts, each one a 'point'. There is no relationship between the Anglo-American point and the Didot point, and neither of them relate to metric measurement. The introduction of the computer as a design tool has established a new international standard of measurement based on the Anglo-American system. However, one point measures 0.013889in on the computer, and 72 points equal exactly one inch – no coincidence, then, that Macintosh computer monitors have a standard resolution of 72dpi. ➔ *cicero; Didot point; pica*

point (2) *(com)* In object-oriented drawing applications, the connections ('Bézier points') that mathematically define the characteristics of line segments, such as where they start and end, how thick they are, and so on (each point is a 'vector' or

Photomerge is a **plug-in** for Adobe Photoshop

P

Examples of different
pointer styles

tiny database of information). Lines are manipulated by dragging 'control handles' (sometimes called 'guidepoints') from the point, which act on the line like magnets.
→ *Bézier; object-oriented; vector*

pointer *(com)* A general term refering to any of the many shapes on a monitor that indicate the location and operating mode of the mouse. Typical pointer shapes are the arrow pointer, vertical bar, I-beam, crossbar or crosshair, and wristwatch. Sometimes confused with the 'cursor' (the typing location within a field or piece of text).
→ *crosshair/crossbar pointer; cursor*

point holes *(pho)* → *pinholes*

pointing interface *(com)* → *GUI*

point of sale *(gen)* Advertising material or goods displayed near the cash register.

Point-to-Point Protocol (PPP) *(int)* The most common means of establishing dial-up connections to the Internet. It provides a method for transmitting packets over serial point-to-point links. It also allows you to use other standard protocols (such as IPX and TCP/IP) over a standard telephone connection and can be used for local area networks (LAN) connections.

poise *(pri)* → *viscosity*

A 3D shape made
up of **polygons**

Polar Coordinates filter *(com)* Distort filter that converts an image's coordinates from conventional rectangular x–y axis to polar, and vice versa. The rectangular-to-polar conversion produces cylindrical anamorphoses that make no obvious logical sense until a mirrored cylinder is placed over the centre, when the image is displayed in conventional form again.

polarize/polarization *(pho)* To restrict light vibrations to one direction. Polarizing lens filters reduce the reflective qualities of light and are thus used to minimize reflections and glare, and to enhance colour balance.

A **polarizing filter**
reduces reflection

polarizing filter *(pho)* → *polarize/polarization*

Polaroid *(pho)* A proprietory 'in-camera' method of self-processing photographic materials and equipment, used extensively by professional photographers as a means of instantly assessing composition and lighting prior to the actual exposure of a shot. → *in-camera (1)*

polished calf *(fin)* High-quality bookbinding material made from calfskin.

polygon *(com)* The smallest unit of geometry in 3D applications, the edges of which define a portion of a surface. → *polygon resolution*

polygon resolution *(com)* The detail in a 3D scene, defined by the number of polygons in a surface, which, in turn, determines the detail of the final render – the more polygons, the finer the detail. → *polygon*

polygon tool *(com)* A tool in some applications with which you can create irregular-shaped boxes, in which text, pictures or fills can be placed.

polyline *(com)* In 3D applications, a line with more than two points that defines a sequence of straight lines.

polymesh *(com)* A 3D object comprising shared vertices in a rectangular shape.

polyphony *(aud)* This refers to music or a synthesized sound that is made up of a combination of more than one melodic sequence simultaneously to produce intertwining harmonies.

POP (1) *(int) abb.:* Point of Presence. Usually referring to a city or location to which a network can be connected, such as the actual location of the server of your ISP (Internet Service Provider).

POP (2) *(int) abb.:* Post Office Protocol. → *Post Office Protocol*

POP account *(int) abb.:* Post Office Protocol account. → *Post Office Protocol (POP)*

pop-down menu *(com)* → *drop-down menu*

pope roll *(pap)* In the papermaking process, a roller on which the dry paper is reeled.

pop-up menu *(com)* A menu in a dialog box or palette, which 'pops up' when you click on it. Pop-up menus usually appear as a rectangle with a drop shadow and a downward or side-pointing arrow.

pop-ups *(fin)* A folded paper sheet that is die-cut and creased to lie flat when closed, but expands into a 3D model when opened.

porosity *(pap)* The degree to which paper can absorb ink and air.

port *(com)* A socket in a computer or device into which other devices are plugged.

portable document format (PDF) *(com)* → *PDF*

Portable Font Resource (PFR) *(int)* → *font embedding*

Portable Network Graphics *(int)* A file format for images used on the Web, which provides 10–30% 'lossless' compression, or a 'lossy' option. It was created as an alternative to the GIF and JPEG file formats, but has not yet displaced either.

port address *(com)* The precise address (of the program on the receiving end) to which data is delivered by a remote computer on a network.

portrait monitor *(com)* A monitor in which the screen is in an upright format, as distinct from the more usual landscape format. → *monitor*

portrait, upright format *(gen)* An image or page in a vertical format. → *landscape format*

position marks *(pre)* → *register marks/ registration marks*

position proof *(pre)* A colour proof (for checking prior to printing) on which all elements of the final page are present. Traditionally, a variety of colour sets were first scatter proofed without text in position. → *Ozalid*

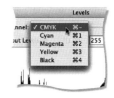

An example of a
pop-up menu

positive *(pho)* An image emulating an original scene, made photographically on paper or film, usually from a negative. → *negative (1)*

positive reversal process *(pre)* → *deep-etch(ing)*

positive-working plate *(pre)* A printing plate that has been exposed through positive film, as distinct from one exposed through negative film ('negative-working plate'). → *negative-working plate*

post binder *(fin)* A method of binding loose leaves (including covers) by individual posts punched through holes.

poster board *(pap)* Cardboard with a 24-point caliper thickness, in standard sheet sizes of 559 x 711mm (22 x 28in) and 711 x 1118mm (28 x 44in).

posterize/posterization *(pho)* To divide, by photographic or digital means, a continuous tone image into either a predefined or arbitrary number of flat tones. Also called 'tone separation'. → *solarize/solarization*

postlims *(gen)* → *end/back matter*

Post Office Protocol (POP) *(int)* An e-mail protocol for retrieval and storage – a 'POP account' is what you tell your e-mail software to use to send and retrieve your mail.

post-production *(gen)* In the film and photographic industries, all processes that take place after the camera work has been completed, such as editing, retouching, special effects, and so on.

This image has been run through a **posterize** filter

PostScript *(com)* Adobe Systems Inc's proprietary 'page description language' (PDL) for image output to laser printers and high-resolution imagesetters. ➔ *page description language*

PostScript font *(com)* ➔ *Type 1 font*

PostScript interpreter *(com)* The code used by printing devices to understand PostScript instructions. ➔ *interpreter*

PostScript printer *(com)* Any printing device that uses the Adobe-licensed PostScript page description language (PDL). ➔ *PostScript; page description language (PDL)*

PostScript Printer Description file (PPD) *(com)* A file that defines the characteristics of individual PostScript printers.

pothook *(typ)* The sharply curved terminal of a character, particularly noticeable in italic fonts.

POTS *(int)* Acronym for 'plain old telephone system'. A standard analog telephone system.

pouncing *(pap)* To improve a surface prior to writing or drawing. For example, parchment is rubbed with resin or chalk to make it smoother and whiter, whereas tracing paper is rubbed with pumice to remove grease from the surface.

powdered *(fin)* The effect of a decorative stippling technique used for traditional book covers.

powdering *(pri)* A printing fault in which the substrate and ink separate after printing. Also called 'dusting'.

powderless etching *(pri)* A method of etching metal plates, in which an agent in the acid protects the edges of the dots while etching the metal, resulting in a very clean etch. ➔ *etch*

PPC *(com) abb.:* program-to-program communication. ➔ *interapplication communication (IAC)*

PPD *(com) abb.:* PostScript Printer Description file. ➔ *PostScript Printer Description file (PPD)*

ppi *(com) abb.:* pixels per inch. ➔ *pixels per inch (ppi)*

PRAM *(com) abb.:* parameter RAM (random access memory). ➔ *parameter RAM*

PRAM chip *(com)* The hardware chip that stores parameter RAM. ➔ *parameter RAM; zapping the PRAM*

prebinding *(fin)* A heavy-duty binding used by libraries. It is characterized by extra sewing of the sections, reinforced endpapers and plastic lamination of the cover.

precoated plates *(pri)* Litho plates that have received a coating that will not become light-sensitive until they are washed with a sensitizing solution. ➔ *presensitized plates*

preface *(gen)* An introduction to a book, stating its scope and subject. ➔ *foreword*

*!?

P

preferences *(com)* A facility provided by most applications for modifying the default program settings (such as the unit of measurement). Modifications can often be applied to a single document or, sometimes, all documents.

preflighting *(com)* The process of checking and collating font, graphic, picture, and all other items associated with an electronic file that are required for output to imagesetter.

prefs file *(com)* An application file that records your preference settings so that when you reopen the application you don't need to reset the preferences. → *preferences*

pregather *(fin)* The binding of a single section prior to combining it with other sections.

prelims/preliminary pages *(gen)* The pages of a book before the main text starts, usually consisting of the half title, title, preface and contents pages. Also called 'front matter'. → *end/back matter*

premake ready *(pri)* The final checking of plates before they are made ready on press. → *make-ready*

premask *(pre)* A film positive that will be combined with negative to create a new mask.

prepress *(pre)* Any or all of the reproduction processes that may occur between design and printing, but often specifically used to describe colour separation and planning. Also called 'origination'.

prepress (colour) proofing *(pre)* → *off-press proof(ing)*

preprint *(pri)* An item printed in advance of a publication, later inserted loosely into bound copies. → *run of press(ing)*

preproofing (1) *(pre)* → *off-press proof(ing)*

preproofing (2) *(pre)* A proof made from a desktop printer (such as a laser printer), as distinct from one made by an imagesetter. → *off-press proof(ing)*

prescreen *(pre)* A halftone-screened positive print pasted down with line artwork to circumvent the need for film stripping.

prescreened film *(pre)* Film that has been pretreated so that it will generate a halftone image from a continuous tone original without the need for a halftone screen.

presensitized plates *(pri)* Ready-made litho plates that have received a light-sensitive coating and which are ready for exposure to a positive or negative. → *precoated plates*

presentation visual *(gen)* → *comprehensive*

presets *(com)* → *default*

press *(pri)* Any machine that transfers (prints) an impression, traditionally from a forme, block, plate or blanket onto paper or other material.

pressboards *(pap)* → *millboards*

press gain *(pri)* The mechanical enlargement of halftone dots while printing, as distinct from the 'dot gain' of the prepress photographic kind. → *dot gain*

pressing unit *(fin)* A unit of a binding line that presses freshly cased books with heated clamps, avoiding the need to leave them to stand for a time in a 'standing press'.

press mark *(pap)* → *impressed watermark*

press proof *(pri)* → *machine proof*

press revise *(pri)* A proof used as the final 'pass for press'. Also called a 'machine revise'. → *proof*

press run/run *(pri)* The total number of copies of a print job.

presswork *(pri)* All of the processes carried out on a printing press, from press make-ready through actual printing to finishing operations.

pretzel symbol *(com)* → *cloverleaf/pretzel/ propeller symbol*

preview *(com)* In some graphics applications, the facility to view an item by showing what it will eventually look like when printed, with any attributes, such as colours and fills, that may have been applied.

prima *(pri)* The first page of a set of printer's galley proofs.

primary binding *(fin)* The binding used for the first edition of a book.

primary colours *(gen)* Pure colours from which, theoretically (but not in practice), all other colours can be mixed. In printing, they are the 'subtractive' pigment primaries: cyan, magenta and yellow. The primary colours of light, or 'additive' primaries, are red, green and blue. → *additive colours; subtractive colour mixing*

primary letter *(typ)* Any lower-case character that does not have an ascender or descender – 'a', 'e', 'm', etc.

primes/prime marks *(typ)* → *ditto/prime marks*

primitive *(com)* The basic geometric element from which a complex object is built.

print (1) *(pho)* A photographic image, usually made from a negative.

print (2) *(pri)* The image etched, or otherwise generated, onto a printing plate.

print (3) *(pri)* The impression made from a plate, blanket, etc., onto paper or other material.

print buffer *(com)* A hardware device where items are stored ('queued') while waiting for a printer to become available, thus allowing you to continue working. As distinct from a print spooler. → *buffer; spool/spooler/ spooling*

print convertors *(fin)* The mechanized functions employed to complete a print job – for example, folding, cutting, collating, stitching, etc.

printed circuit board (PC board) *(com)* → *circuit board*

printed edges *(fin)* Printing on the cut edges of a book. → *sprinkled edges*

printer *(pre)* The single films of each of the four process colours – cyan, yellow, magenta and black ('cyan printer', 'yellow printer' and so on), which will produce an image when eventually printed on a four-colour press. → *colour separations*

printer description file *(com)* A file that defines the characteristics of individual printers. → *PostScript Printer Description file (PPD)*

printer driver *(com)* → *driver/device driver*

printer font *(com)* → *outline font*

printer port *(com)* The socket via which a computer is connected to a printer or, on Macintosh computers, a network or modem.

printer's flower *(typ)* → *flower*

printer's imprint *(gen)* → *imprint*

printer's mark *(gen)* → *device (2)*

printer's ornament *(typ)* → *ornament*

printer's reader *(pri)* → *reader*

printer's ream *(pap)* 516 sheets, or 16 more than the standard ream of 500 sheets. Also called a 'publisher's ream'. → *overs*

printing down *(pri)* The transfer of image from film to plate.

printing down frame *(pri)* → *vacuum frame*

printing-in *(pho)* A photographic printing technique by which the exposure is selectively increased over parts of the image.

printing plate *(pri)* → *plate (1)*

printing press *(pri)* → *press*

printing pressure *(pri)* The force required to transfer an impression between any of the image-bearing surfaces of a printing press, such as plate and paper, plate and blanket, blanket and impression cylinder, impression cylinder and paper.

printing processes *(pri)* There are four generic printing processes: 'intaglio' (e.g. gravure), 'planographic' (e.g. lithography), 'relief' (e.g. letterpress) and 'stencil' (e.g. screen printing). → *colour printing*

printing unit *(pri)* The unit that houses all the components required to print a single colour on a multicolour press (typically, the four-unit press that prints the process colours: cyan, magenta, yellow, and black).

printmaking *(pri)* The printing of fine art editions by a variety of processes.

PrintMonitor *(com)* Part of the Mac OS (prior to Mac OS X), a print spooling application that provides 'background' printing, allowing you to print while you carry on working. → *spool/spooler/spooling*

print origination *(pre)* → *prepress*

print-out *(com)* Digital data 'output' from a printer as a 'hard copy'. → *hard copy*

print run *(pri)* → *press run/run*

print spooler/spooling *(com)* → *spool/spooler/spooling*

print to paper *(pri)* An instruction to print as many sheets or copies as the paper supplied will permit, without specifying an exact quantity. Also called 'run of paper'.

prism *(pho)* A specially shaped transparent substance, usually glass, that refracts light in a controlled manner.

process block *(pri)* A plate made by 'photoengraving'. → *photoengraving*

process blue *(gen)* → *cyan (c)*

process camera *(pre)* A specially designed graphics art camera used in photomechanical reproduction. Also called a 'repro camera' or 'reproduction camera'. → *vertical camera*

process colour *(pri)* → *CMYK*

process colour printing *(pri)* → *four-colour process*

process colours *(pri)* The colours of the inks used in a particular printing process, usually assumed to be cyan, magenta, yellow and black unless otherwise specified. The process colours might be supplemented by spot colours that fall outside the gamut achievable using the primaries, such as very intense saturated colours and fluorescent or metallic colours.

process colour separation *(pre)* → *colour separation*

process engraving *(pri)* → *photoengraving*

process ink *(pri)* → *CMYK*

process ink gamut chart (PIG) *(pri)* A chart that compares the colours that can be obtained from a variety of ink and substrate combinations.

processor (chip) *(com)* A silicon 'chip' containing millions of micro 'switches' that respond to binary electrical pulses, which performs specific functions in a computer, such as the 'central processor' (CPU) and memory (RAM). Also known as a 'microprocessor' or 'microchip'. → *chip/microchip; coprocessor; CPU;*

processor direct slot (PDS) *(com)* An expansion slot that connects to the CPU directly rather than indirectly through a 'bus'. → *bus (1)*

process photography *(pre)* The photomechanical preparation of materials, such as colour separations, for print reproduction. → *separation*

process red *(gen)* → *magenta (m)*

process white *(gen)* Opaque, lead-free white paint used for masking and correction of camera-ready artwork.

process work *(pri)* The general preparation, usually by photomechanical means, of a surface for process printing. → *photoengraving*

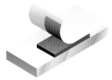

intaglio (gravure)

planographic (litho)

relief (letterpress)

stencil (screen)

The four **printing processes** are illustrated above, with black ink, silver printing surfaces and cream paper. In the stencil process the screen is below the (pink) stencil

process yellow *(gen)* → *yellow (y)*

production press *(pri)* The press used for printing a job, as opposed to the one used for proofing it; it is generally impractical to use the production press for proofing.

profile *(com)* The colorimetric description of the behaviour of an input or output device, which can be used by an ICC-aware application to ensure accurate transfer of colour data. There are usually some generic ICC profiles installed on your computer by ICC-compliant applications like Adobe Photoshop; you can also create your own or have them created for you by a colour consultant. A profile describing the colour space used during image creation or editing should ideally be embedded in the image, so that it can later be used as a reference by other users, other software applications or display and output devices.

Profile Connection Space (PCS) *(com)* → *PCS*

program *(com)* → *software*

program defaults *(com)* → *default*

programmer *(com)* An author of computer programs, as distinct from a user. → *software*

programming *(com)* Arranging coded instructions for the automatic execution of a particular task, such as those performed by a computer ('software program') or by a computer-controlled machine, such as a printing press.

programming language *(com)* The special languages devised for writing computer software. Programming languages are either 'high-level', which are based as closely as possible on English, or 'machine code', the lowest level, being the least like English but the easiest for a computer to understand. Typical languages are 'BASIC', 'C++', 'FORTRAN' and 'Pascal'. → *high-level language; machine code*

An example of **projection mapping**

progressive JPEG *(int)* A digital image format used for displaying JPEG images on webpages. The image is displayed in progressively increasing resolutions as the data is downloaded to the browser. Also called 'proJPEG'. → *interlacing/interlaced; interlaced GIF; JPEG*

progressive proofs/progs *(pre)* Proofs used in colour printing to show each colour printed separately, and progressively combined – in the order in which they will be printed – with the others.

projection mapping *(com)* Texture mapping onto a 3D object, where the texture appears to project through the image surface.

proJPEG *(int)* → *progressive JPEG*

PROM *(com)* abb.: programmable ROM (read-only memory). → *read-only memory (ROM)*

promotion *(gen)* The process of advocating a product or service in order to increase production or sales.

promotional books/edition *(gen)* An edition of a book created, printed and published specifically for the purpose of being 'marked down' (sold at a lower price) after having first been offered for sale at full price, albeit for a very short period. Also called 'bargain books', which are not to be confused with 'remainders', books that a publisher failed to sell at normal retail price, thus marked down to clear stocks.

promotion copies *(gen)* Copies of a newly published book presented to commercial buyers.

prompt *(com)* A symbol, i.e. '>', (or sometimes an audible alert), indicating that the computer is waiting for you to enter an instruction.

proof *(gen)* A prototype of a job, taken at various stages from laser printers, imagesetters, inked plates, stones, screens, block or type, in order to check the progress and accuracy of the work. Also called a 'pull'.

PROOF

proof correction marks *(gen)* A standard set of signs and symbols commonly understood by all those involved in preparing copy for publication. Text proof-correction marks vary from country to country, but colour correction signs are more or less internationally recognized.

proofing *(gen)* The production/correction of a prototype or simulation of a print job prior to its subsequent reproduction in quantity.

proofing chromo *(pap)* A superior coated paper used for proofing.

proof(ing) press *(pre)* A small press on which individual sheets are printed for proofing purposes. ➔ *proof*

proofreader *(gen)* Someone who reads proofs for errors and who marks corrections accordingly. ➔ *proofreader's marks*

proofreader's marks *(gen)* A collection of notations, symbols and marks used to identify errors on a proof and the necessary action needed to correct them. ➔ *proof correction marks; proofreader*

propellor symbol *(com)* ➔ *cloverleaf/pretzel/ propeller symbol*

property *(com)* The attributes of digital object, such as size, position, colour or orientation.

proportionality failure *(pri)* A problem that occurs in the value of an ink hue when the dot size of a halftone tint varies, changing the hue of the ink in relation to a solid ink colour.

proprietary *(gen)* A design, product or format developed, marketed and owned by a company or person, rather than one defined by a standards organization.

proprietary system *(gen)* ➔ *dedicated*

protocol *(com)* A set of mutual rules that hardware and software must observe in order to communicate with one another.

prove *(pre)* A seldom used alternative term for 'proof'.

provider *(int)* ➔ *Internet Service Provider (ISP)*

proximity effect *(aud)* Many condenser microphones emphasize the bass frequencies of a particular sound when it is close to the mike itself. This is known as the proximity effect, and it has influenced the singing style – or at least the recording style – of many vocalists since the 1930s, but it can also reduce intelligibility.

PSD *(com)* Photoshop Document. The native file format (with extension .psd) of Adobe Photoshop, containing the image and other relevant information, including layers, channels and preferences.

pseudepigraphia *(gen)* The collective term for those who are incorrectly identified as the author of a work.

pseudoclass *(int)* The differentiation between a piece of HTML code and the same one used as a selector.

pseudonymous *(gen)* A work published under an assumed name.

public domain (PD) *(gen)* A description of 'intellectual property' that is free of all copyrights, meaning that it can be used by anyone for any purpose, either because the copyright period has lapsed or because its author has declared it so. Not to be confused with 'shareware', for which a fee is usually required.

publicity face *(typ)* A traditional term for display sizes of typefaces, used for advertisements, catalogues, etc.

publisher *(gen)* The person or organization responsible for the creation (though not always), distribution and marketing of published works.

publisher's binding *(fin)* The standard binding used by a publisher selling to the book trade. Also called 'edition binding' or 'trade binding'.

publisher's cloth *(fin)* The traditional binding material for edition-bound books. ➔ *edition binding*

PROOF CORRECTION MARKS

publisher's imprint *(gen)* → *imprint*

publisher's ream *(pap)* → *printer's ream*

puck *(com)* The rather more complex 'mouse' used in CAD systems. → *CAD (1); digitizing tablet/pad; stylus*

puff *(gen)* A term, originating in the 17th century but still used today, describing the written hyperbole accompanying a new book. → *blurb*

pull *(pre)* → *proof*

pull-down menu *(com)* → *drop-down menu*

pulling *(pri)* → *picking*

pull out *(fin)* → *fold out*

pull-out section *(gen)* Pages of a publication that can be detached as one piece.

pull-processing *(pho)* Giving film a shorter development time than normal to compensate for overexposure or to reduce contrast. → *push-processing*

pull quote *(gen)* A sentence or phrase taken from the body of a text and set, within the text, in a larger size or in some other distinctive manner.

pull (sheet) *(pri)* Sheets removed from the press for examination during the print run. → *proof*

pull (technology) *(int)* → *Push (technology)*

pull test *(fin)* A method of testing the strength of a perfect-bound book by pulling it apart.

pulp *(pap)* The wet, raw material used in papermaking, usually prepared either 'mechanically' or 'chemically'. → *chemical pulp; mechanical (wood) pulp*

pulp board *(pap)* A board manufactured from pulp as a single homogenous sheet on a fourdrinier or cylinder machine.

pulpwood *(pap)* Wood, and its various forms of offcut, that has been ground or shredded prior to making pulp for papermaking. → *pulp*

A Mac OS X
push button

punch in/out *(aud)* Record function on most audio recorders (hardware and software), which enables you to drop in at any point of the recording with additional, or replacement recording, then drop out again, leaving the rest of the track intact.

punch register *(pre)* → *pin register*

punctuation mark *(typ)* A system of marks used to clarify text and separate sentences.

punctuation space *(typ)* A space the width of a period (full point) in a given font.

pure *(pap)* → *woodfree paper*

purity *(gen)* The degree of saturation of a colour.

push button *(com)* A button in a dialog box that, when clicked, invokes the command specified on the button.

pushout *(fin)* → *binder's creep*

push-processing *(pho)* Giving film a longer development time than normal to compensate for underexposure or to increase contrast. → *pull-processing*

Push (technology) *(int)* A Web-based technology by which information, distributed to designated groups of users via 'channels', can be updated immediately whenever changes are made. As distinct from the normal Web activity of browsing and requesting information at will ('pull'). → *channel (1)*

put down/up *(typ)* An instruction to the typesetter to change characters to lower case ('put down') or capitals ('put up'). As distinct from 'keep down' and 'keep up', which are instructions to set in lower case or caps in the first place. → *keep down/up*

put to bed *(pri)* → *bed (1)*

*!?

QA *(gen)* abb.: query author. A mark used by text editors.

qq.v. *(gen)* ➔ *q.v.*

quad (1) *(pap)* A traditional term used as a prefix to a sheet size. It denotes a current sheet that is four times the area of the original. For example, a demy sheet was 17½ x 22½ inches (393¾ square inches), while a quad demy was 35 x 45 inches (1575 square inches).

quad (2) *(typ)* A contraction of 'quadrat' (never used in full). In conventional typesetting, quads are inter-word spaces whose sizes are usually en, em, 2-em, 3-em or 4-em, thus 'to quad', or 'quadding', is to fill out a line with quad spaces. ➔ *em quad; en quad*

quad centre *(typ)* In traditional typesetting, a line that is centred. ➔ *quad (2)*

quad folder *(fin)* A machine that creases and folds single printed sheets of 64 pages into four 16-page signatures or two 32-page signatures.

quad left *(typ)* In traditional typesetting, a line that is ranged left. ➔ *quad (2)*

quad middle *(typ)* ➔ *quad centre*

quadracolour *(pre)* The ability of a scanner to output all four colours from/on one piece of film.

quadrata *(typ)* ➔ *square capitals*

quad right *(typ)* In traditional typesetting, a line that is ranged right. ➔ *quad (2)*

quadrophonic *(aud)* Obsolete standard that was meant to replace stereophonic sound in 1970s homes, but failed. However, surround sound is a similar concept.

quality control *(gen)* A procedure implemented to ensure that all stages of a production process are monitored and, if necessary, improved to ensure an end result that exactly matches the original specification.

quantize *(aud)* A standard function on all MIDI sequencers, which allows you to move note data onto the correct beats of the bar. For example, if you have played a synthesizer line manually that is meant to be in accurate sixteenths, or in accurate triplets, the Quantize function will shift all of the note information onto those beats if you request it. On strong settings, use with extreme care if you don't wish your work to sound 'mechanical'.

quarter-bound *(fin)* A case binding in which the back is covered in one material and the sides in another – for example, a leather back with cloth sides. ➔ *half-bound/ binding*

quarter bound/binding *(fin)* A hardback binding in which the back is covered in one material and the sides in another – for example, a leather back with cloth sides. ➔ *corners (2); full bound; half-bound/ binding; three-quarter bound*

quarternion *(gen)* The gathering of four sheets that are folded once, found in early printed books.

A **quarter-bound** book usually has a leather back and cloth sides

Photoshop's **Quick mask** button

A **QuickTime VR** movie of a computer

quartertone *(pre)* The area of a screened image where the dot is twenty-five per cent of solid.

quarto/4to *(pap)* A page size obtained by folding a sheet of paper in half twice, making quarters, or eight pages. The original size of the sheet is usually prefixed, as in 'Crown 4to', thus defining the final size. When a paper size is not stated, the final size can be assumed to be about 12 x 9½ in.

query *(gen)* An annotation by editor, author, proofreader or typesetter in the margin of a proof or galley, sometimes simply a '?', to draw attention to a potential mistake.

QuickDraw *(com)* The part of the Mac system that performs all display operations on your screen, and now incorporated into Mac OS X's 'Quartz' display technology. It is also responsible for outputting text and graphics to non-PostScript printers. → *PostScript*

Quick mask *(com)* Provides a quick method of creating a mask around a selection in applications like Photoshop. The mask can be drawn and precisely defined by using any of the painting tools or the eraser respectively.

quick printing *(pri)* → *jobbing*

quick-set inks *(pri)* A type of ink that usually contains mineral oil (that is rapidly absorbed into the paper and allows for quicker handling), with varnish and pigment (which are left on the surface). These set more slowly and so are particularly suited to multicolour printing.

QuickTime *(com)* Apple's software program and system extension, which enables computers running either Windows or the Mac OS to play film and sound files, particularly over the Internet and in multimedia applications. Provides cut, copy and paste features for moving images and automatic compression and decompression of image files. → *AVI; codec (1)*

QuickTime VR *(com)* Acronym for QuickTime 'virtual reality'. An Apple extension that provides features for the creation and playback of 3D objects and panoramic scenes. → *QuickTime*

quire (1) *(pap)* 25 sheets of paper (formerly 24 sheets plus one 'outside').

quire (2) *(fin)* A gathering of four sheets folded once to make eight leaves, or 16 pages. Synonymous with 'quaternion'.
→ *quaternion*

quires/quire stock *(fin)* Printed sheets that are folded but not yet bound. Also called 'sheet stock'.

quirewise *(fin)* A collection of unbound leaves, folded one within another. They are subsequently stitched.

quit *(com)* The command by which you 'shut down' an application, as distinct from closing a document within the application, in which case the document disappears but the application remains open.

quotations *(gen)* Passages in a published work that repeat verbatim the words spoken or text written by another, usually distinguished from the narrative by quotation marks.
→ *inverted commas; single quotes*

quotation/quote marks/quotes *(typ)* Inverted commas and apostrophes, either single (' ') or double (" "), used before and after a word or phrase to indicate that it is a quotation, title, jargon, or slang. → *smart quotes*

q.v. *(gen)* abb.: *quod vide*. A Latin term meaning 'which see', used to accompany an item that is cross-referenced to another. The plural form is 'qq.v.'.

qwerty *(com)* The standard typewriter-based keyboard layout used by most computer keyboards. The name comes from the first six characters of the top row of letter keys.

Rr

RA *(aud) abb.:* RealAudio → *RealAudio*

rack-jobbing distribution *(gen)* → *impulse outlet*

radial fill *(com)* A feature of some applications by which an item can be filled with a pattern of concentric circles of graduated tints.

radiation shield/screen *(com)* A wire mesh or glass filter that fits over a monitor to reduce the level of radiation being emitted. → *ELF*

rag content *(pap)* The amount of cotton or linen fibre to be found in a paper.

ragged left/right *(typ)* → *unjustified*

rag paper/pulp *(pap)* Paper manufactured from cotton or linen fibre, using either new or recycled rags, and commonly used for writing and ledger papers.

RAID *(com) abb.:* redundant array of independent disks. → *redundant array of independent disks (RAID)*

raised bands *(fin)* Ridges on the spine of a book that cover the cords securing the sections.

raised cap(ital) *(typ)* A capital letter that projects above the cap height of the first line of type, but remains on the same baseline. Also called a 'cock-up initial' or 'raised initial'. → *raised initial*

raised dot *(typ)* → *raised point*

raised initial *(typ)* A bold face capital that projects above the line of type. Also called a 'raised cap', 'stickup initial' or 'cock-up initial'. → *raised cap(ital)*

raised period *(typ)* → *raised point*

raised point *(typ)* A period (full point) placed at the mid-height of capitals rather than on the baseline.

RAM *(com) abb.:* random access memory. → *DRAM; random access memory (RAM)*

RAM cache *(com) pron.:* 'kash'. A piece of RAM that stores the most recent actions your software carried out so that they do not need to be retrieved from disk if you need them again. → *cache*

RAM chip *(com)* → *DIMM; SIMM*

RAM disk *(com)* A feature of some operating systems or utility software, by which a part of RAM can be temporarily put to use as a virtual disk drive. Since the process of retrieving data from RAM is so much faster than from disk, operations performed by the RAM 'disk' will speed up. This 'disk' is erased when you switch your computer off. → *RAM*

R&D *(gen) abb.:* research and development.

random access *(com)* Digital data that can be retrieved at random, such as from a disk or from memory, as distinct from data that can be retrieved only sequentially, such as from a tape.

A white-to-red
radial fill

RA

A SIMM **RAM chip**

random access memory (RAM) *(com)*
A type of computer memory that can be accessed randomly, which means that any byte of memory can be used by any program without having to access any of the preceding bytes. RAM modules are often used in various audio devices, such as MP3 players or DAWs. As opposed to ROM, RAM can be written to and read, while ROM can only be read. ➜ *read-only memory (ROM)*

random proof *(pre)* ➜ *scatter proof*

ranged left/right *(typ)* ➜ *unjustified*

ranged/ranging figures *(typ)* ➜ *lining figures/numerals*

RA paper sizes *(pap)* The designation of untrimmed paper sizes in the ISO series of paper sizes. ➜ *ISO A-series paper sizes*

raster *(com)* An image created by building up rows of pixels or dots. CRT TV and computer monitors show raster images.

raster image processor (RIP) *(pre)* A device that converts data generated by a page description language, such as PostScript, into a form that can be output by a high-resolution imagesetter for use in commercial printing.

raster(ization) *(com)* Deriving from the Latin word *rastrum*, meaning 'rake', and refers to the method of display (and of creating images) employed by video screens, and thus computer monitors. The screen image is made up of a pattern of several hundred parallel lines created by an electron beam 'raking' the screen from top to bottom at a speed of about one-sixtieth of a second. An image is created by the varying intensity of brightness of the beam at successive points along the raster. The speed at which a complete screen image, or frame, is created is called the 'frame' or 'refresh' rate. ➜ *raster image processor*

rasterize *(com)* The electronic conversion of a vector graphic into a bitmap image. The process may introduce aliasing problems, but is often necessary when preparing vector images, including text, for use on the Web.

rate determining factor (RDF) *(gen)* The rate at which progress is determined, defined as the slowest part of any procedure or process. For example, the rate at which you may be able to complete a design job will depend on how long it takes the slowest contributor to complete his or her task – in which case, that person is the rate determining factor. It could even be you.

raw *(com)* A digital file format that saves image data for transferring between applications and computer platforms.

raycasting *(com)* A no-bounce raytracing technique. ➜ *raytracing*

raytracing *(com)* Rendering algorithm that simulates the physical and optical properties of light rays as they reflect off a 3D model, producing realistic shadows and reflections. ➜ *VRML*

RDF *(gen) abb.:* rate determining factor. ➜ *rate determining factor (RDF)*

reader *(pre)* A person who compares a typeset text with the original and annotates it with corrections. Also called a 'printer's reader'.

reader's spread *(gen)* ➜ *breakacross*

reading gravity *(gen)* The propensity for most people, at least in the Western hemisphere, to begin reading from the upper left to the lower right of a page.

read only *(com)* Disks, memory and documents that can only be read from, and not written to.

read-only memory (ROM) *(com)* Memory that can be read from but not written to. As distinct from RAM, in which data can be written to memory but is lost when power to the computer is switched off. ➜ *random access memory (RAM)*

read/write head *(com)* The part of a disk drive that 'reads' data from, and 'writes' data to, a disk. One read/write head is positioned above each side of every disk platter in a drive, which may consist of several platters. These move, on rails, over the surface of the platter, which rotates at speed. ➔ *disk*

RealAudio *(int)* A proprietary helper application that enables audio playback in Web browsers. ➔ *helper application*

RealMedia *(int)* A Web technology for delivery and playback of multimedia across the Internet, supporting both live and on-demand video ('RealVideo'), and sound ('RealAudio').

real-time *(com)* The actual time in which things happen on your computer. For example, at its simplest, a character appearing on screen at the moment you type it is said to be real-time, as is a video sequence that plays back as it is being filmed. Also called 'interactive mode'. ➔ *interactive mode*

ream *(pap)* A standard quantity of paper, usually 500 sheets. In some circumstances, an extra number may be allowed for wastage, such as in a 'printer's ream', which is 516 sheets. ➔ *printer's ream*

reboot *(com)* To reload a computer's operating system (or an application) into memory. This can be achieved either by switching the power off ('shutting down') and switching it on again ('cold boot'), or by using the 'restart' command, if available ('warm boot'). Also referred to as 'restart'. ➔ *boot/boot up/booting up; startup*

rebuild desktop *(com)* On pre-OS X Macintosh computers, to flush out obsolete information from the invisible desktop file in order to speed up operations. The desktop file records not only new files, but deleted ones as well, so that the more files you add and delete, the more the desktop file keeps growing.

A **RealMedia** file needs RealOne Player

receptivity *(pri)* ➔ *ink receptivity*

recessed cords *(fin)* In traditional bookbinding, the use of flax or hemp cords that run along grooves sawn across the gathered sections of a book. This enables the spine to be flat. ➔ *sunken cords*

recess printing *(pri)* An intaglio printing process by which the ink is held in recesses in the plate or cylinder, such as photogravure. ➔ *intaglio; photogravure*

reciprocity failure *(pho)* An exception to mathematical law in photographic processing. A short exposure under a bright light does not produce the same result as a long exposure in a dim light, although mathematically it should. In other words, at very short and very long exposures, the reciprocity law ceases to hold true, and an extra exposure is needed. The effect produced varies with film types, but on colour film the three dye layers suffer differently and a colour caste may occur, so only the exposure range that the film was designed for should be used. ➔ *reciprocity law*

reciprocity law *(pho)* A law that states that photographic exposure is the result of both the intensity of light and the time taken to make the exposure. ➔ *reciprocity failure*

record *(com)* An individual entry on one subject – such as a person – in a database, comprising a set of related fields, such as that person's name, address and telephone number. ➔ *database; database manager*

recorder element *(com)* ➔ *machine dot*

recto *(gen)* The right-hand page of a book, or the front of a leaf.

recycled paper *(pap)* Paper made from existing printed paper that has been de-inked, or from unprinted waste and material left over from the papermaking process.

red *(gen)* One of the three additive primary colours of red, green and blue. ➔ *additive colours*

Red Book *(com)* The document that specifies all parameters for the original Compact Disc Digital Audio (CD-DA) technology developed by Sony and Philips. As well as defining the format in which an audio CD must be recorded so that it is playable in every CD player, it also specifies what the CD player must do to play CDs correctly. ➔ *CD-DA*

red lake C *(pri)* A pigment used in printing ink.

redraw rate *(com)* The speed at which an image is rendered on-screen after a change has been made. Sometimes confused (erroneously) with the 'refresh rate'. ➔ *refresh rate*

reduced instruction set computing (RISC) *(com)* A microprocessor that provides high-speed processing while requiring only a limited number of instructions. As distinct from 'complex instruction set computing' (CISK), which deals with more instructions and is thus (in theory) slower.

reducer (1) *(pri)* A softening agent in printing ink that also reduces its tack. ➔ *tack*

reducer (2) *(pho)* A chemical used to remove silver from a developed image, thus reducing its density. A useful technique for adjusting overexposed or underdeveloped negatives.

reduction glass/tool *(com)* ➔ *Magnify tool*

redundant array of independent disks (RAID) *(com)* A collection of hard disks that function as one system. They are often used for backing up data as well as processing vast amounts of data.

red under gilt edges *(fin)* Book edges that have been sprayed red and then gilded – used for Bibles, prayer books, etc. ➔ *edge gilding; gild*

reel gold *(fin)* A reel of imitation gold blocking foil, usually made from bronze.

reel-fed *(pri)* ➔ *web-fed*

reference colours *(gen)* Colours that are most familiar and thus easy to remember, such as sky blue, grass green, etc.

reference mark *(typ)* Typographic term describing symbols used in text to refer to footnotes – for example, an asterisk (*) or dagger (†).

references *(gen)* An indication of further reading matter that is in some way related to the current text – for example, in footnotes, bibliography or sources, often identified with Latin abbreviations such as *ibid., loc. cit.*, or *id.*

refining *(pap)* The preparation of fibres used in the papermaking process.

reflectance *(gen)* A value determined by the amount of light reflected from an area of tone compared with the amount of light reflected from a pure white area. ➔ *gloss (1)*

reflected light reading *(pho)* Measurement of the light that is reflected from a subject in order to determine the exposure of a photograph. ➔ *incident light reading*

reflection copy *(pre)* Any flat item that is to be reproduced photographically by light reflected from its surface. As distinct from a 'transparency', or 'slide', where the light is passed through it. ➔ *transparency (1)*

R

Reflection tool *(com)* In some applications, a tool for transforming an item into its mirror image, or for making a mirror-image copy of an item. ➔ *lateral reverse*

reflector *(gen)* An object or material used to bounce available light or studio lighting onto a subject, often softening and dispersing the light for a more attractive end result.

reflex copy *(pre)* A method of producing a contact copy by shining light through a sensitized material that is in contact with the original – the light bounces back onto the sensitized emulsion, creating an image.

reflow *(gen)* The automatic repositioning of continuous text as a result of editing.

refraction *(gen)* Light that is bent, typically when passing through one medium to another, such as air to water. ➔ *refractive index*

refractive index *(gen)* The measurement of the degree to which light is bent by passing through one medium to another, expressed as a ratio of the speed of light between the two. ➔ *refraction*

refresh rate *(com)* The frequency at which a screen image, or 'frame' (a single pass of an electron beam that 'rakes' the screen from top to bottom) is redrawn. Measured in hertz (Hz), a refresh rate of 72Hz means that the image is 'refreshed' 72 times every second. A screen with a slow refresh rate may produce undesirable flicker. The refresh rate is often confused (erroneously) with the 'redraw rate'. ➔ *redraw rate*

registered design *(gen)* A design officially registered with a patent office to protect it from copyright violations.

register marks/registration marks *(pre)* The marks used on artwork, film and printing plates that are superimposed during printing to make sure that the work is in register. Many graphics applications automatically generate register marks outside the page area. Also called 'crossmarks' or 'T-marks'. ➔ *corner marks; register/ registration*

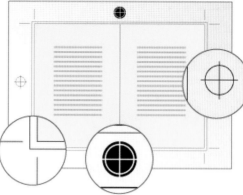

Registration marks ensure film separations align

register/registration *(pri)* The correct positioning of colour plates when printed one on top of another, or of the pages on one side of a sheet relative to the other (called 'backing up'). When a colour or page is incorrectly positioned, it is said to be 'out-of-register' or 'misregistered'. As distinct from 'fit', which applies to the correct positioning of individual items on a sheet. ➔ *back up/backing up (2); fit (2)*

register ribbon *(fin)* A ribbon fastened at the back of a book and used as a book marker.

register sheet *(pri)* A sheet used to obtain correct position and register when printing.

register table *(pre)* A large light table used to prepare and check paste-up, flats, etc., and to obtain correct position and register. It will generally be comprised of an illuminated surface grid with movable scales. Also known as 'lining up table', 'lineup table' or 'shining-up table'.

registration colour *(com)* In many graphics applications, a default colour that, when applied to items such as crop marks, will print on every separation plate.

reinforced binding *(fin)* A heavy-duty binding for public library use.

reinforced signatures *(fin)* Additional material used in the fold or around the outer signatures to strengthen them at the point that takes the most strain.

REFLECTION TOOL

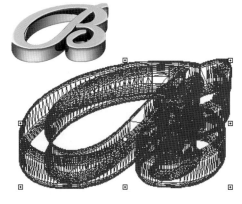

relational database *(com)* A database application in which the information that is contained in separate files or categories is interchangeable. This differs from a 'flat-file' database, in which each file is self-contained and is unable to exchange information with another file. → *database; database manager; flat-file database*

A 3D shape before and after **rendering** (left)

relative humidity (RH) *(gen)* A value determined by the percentage of water vapour in a given environment when compared with the amount that would be present if the atmosphere was fully saturated with water vapour at the same temperature. Relative humidity is an important factor when printing in countries with particularly humid climates, because it can have a dramatic effect on print quality in certain processes such as lithography (which uses water to repel ink) and also in paper storage, because humidity can affect dimensional stability along with other properties.

relative URL *(int)* A link that is connected to the current webpage's URL so that a browser looks for the link in the same location as the current page.

release version *(com)* A software program that is finally ready for general sale, following the alpha- and beta-tested versions. → *alpha version; beta version*

A **relief map** of France

relief block *(pri)* A letterpress line or halftone block.

relief map *(gen)* A cartographic map in which elevation is rendered to simulate three dimensions. → *DEM; mapping resource*

relief offset *(pri)* → *letterset*

relief plate *(pri)* A printing plate with a raised printing surface.

relief printing *(pri)* Printing from a raised surface – for example, letterpress printing. → *letterpress*

relief stamping *(fin)* → *die stamping*

remainders *(gen)* Unsold books returned to publisher. → *promotional books/edition*

remix *(aud)* A process in which the entire mixing phase of song production is redone. While the same sounds and tracks are generally reused in a remix, it usually involves a fairly drastic restructuring of a song to bring out certain interesting elements at the expense of others.

removable media *(com)* Hard disks or optical discs that can be ejected, thus making it easier to transport large amounts of data between computers that are not networked. Very useful when backing up data.

removes *(gen)* Text set at the foot of a page in a smaller type size, used typically for notes or references.

render(ing) *(com)* The process of creating a 2D image from 3D geometry to which lighting effects and surface textures have been applied.

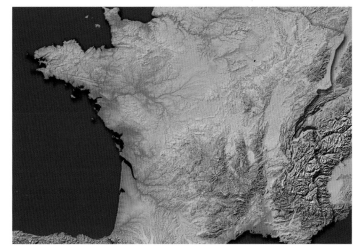

R

replenisher *(pho)* Chemical additions made to photographic solutions to prolong their active life.

reportage *(pho)* A type of photojournalism in which images that encapsulate a news story are recorded.

repped *(pap)* → *ribbed paper*

reprint *(gen)* A second or subsequent printing of a publication, with no changes other than minor corrections.

repro (1) *(pre) abb.:* reproduction. Literally describes the entire printing process from the completion of artwork to printing, although it is more frequently used to describe the processes that take place up to the printing stage. Also called 'origination' or 'prepress'. → *prepress*

repro (2) *(pre)* Any clean, sharp image of appropriate quality printed onto a suitable paper (such as bromide) for line or halftone reproduction. Also called a 'repro pull' or 'repro pull'.

repro(duction) camera *(pre)* → *process camera*

reproduction copy *(pre)* → *repro (2)*

reproduction percentage *(gen)*
→ *reproduction ratio*

reproduction ratio *(gen)* An instruction to reduce or enlarge an original when it is reproduced, expressed as a ratio (e.g. 2:1, which is half size), as an absolute size (e.g. 210mm) or as a percentage of the linear dimensions (e.g. 75%).

reproduction size *(gen)* → *reproduction ratio*

reprographic printing *(pre)* Individual or short-run or copying printing, typically using photocopiers or diazo processes rather than commercial printing presses. → *diazo(type)/ diazo process*

reprography *(gen)* Copying and duplicating printed matter. → *reprographic printing*

Original 300dpi

Sampled down to 150dpi   Sampled up to 600dpi

Resampled images showing quality change

repro proof/reproduction proof *(pre)*
→ *repro (2)*

repro pull/reproduction pull *(pre)*
→ *repro (2)*

request *(int)* The act of clicking on a button or link in a Web browser. You are, in fact, making a request to a remote server for some form of document.

resample *(com)* Altering an image by modifying pixels to either increase or decrease its resolution. Increasing the number of pixels is called 'resampling up', while reducing the number is called 'resampling down' or 'downsampling'. → *dithering (1); interpolate/interpolation; sampling rate*

resampling *(com)* Changing the resolution of an image, either by removing pixels (thus lowering the resolution) or adding them by interpolation (thus increasing the resolution).

rescale *(com)* Amending the size of an image by proportionally reducing its height and width. → *scale/scaling*

rescreened halftone *(pre)* A positive or negative halftone made from a previously screened image. A diffusion filter is often used to eliminate a potential moiré pattern, and this is known as 'descreening'.
→ *descreen(ing); halftone (1)*

ResEdit *(com)* An older Apple application for editing resources (icons, sounds, menus), used in modification of any Macintosh file or software program – system or otherwise.
→ *resource (3); resource fork*

resident font *(com)* A font stored in the printer ROM, as distinct from a 'permanent font' that exists in the printer memory only while the printer is switched on.
→ *permanent font*

resin *(pri)* An ingredient in ink that helps bind pigment to the substrate. It also adds gloss and hardness and can provide resistance to chemicals and heat. Can be used to add hardness to the surface of litho plates.

resin-coated paper *(pho)* A photographic paper with good dimensional stability, coated on one side with emulsion and on both sides with water-resistant resin or polyethylene.

resist *(pri)* The coating applied to a printing plate to protect the non-image areas from acid corrosion.

resolution (1) *(com)* The degree of quality, definition or clarity with which an image is reproduced or displayed, in a photograph or via a scanner, monitor screen, printer or other output device. The more pixels in an image, the sharper that image will be and the greater the detail. The likelihood of jaggies is also reduced the higher the image resolution. → *input resolution; machine dot; output resolution; pixels per inch (ppi); scan dot*

resolution (2)/monitor or screen resolution *(com)* The number of pixels across by pixels down. Common resolutions are 640 x 480, 800 x 600 and 1024 x 768. Most Web designers plan for 800 x 600.

resolving power *(pho)* The ability of a photographic emulsion or lens to record fineness of detail.

resource (1) *(com)* A system file that provides information to the central processing unit so that it can communicate with a peripheral device.

resource (2) *(com)* → *image resource*

resource (3) *(com)* An integral part of the Mac OS, which makes provision for user-definable elements such as dialog boxes, windows, fonts, icons, sounds and so on. It can be unique to any file or application, including the operating system itself.
→ *data fork; resource fork*

resource fork *(com)* On computers running the Mac OS, the part of a file that contains resources such as icons and sounds (on Macintosh computers, there are two 'forks' to every file unless the file contains only data). As distinct from the 'data fork', which contains user-created data such as text or graphics. Resources contained in the resource fork of a file can be modified with resource editors such as 'ResEdit'. Resource forks are becoming less common in the more recent versions of Mac OS.
→ *data fork; ResEdit; resource (3)*

response *(com)* On a network, the server's reply to a request for information from a user. → *request*

restart *(com)* → *reboot*

rest in pro(portion) *(gen)* An instruction to enlarge or reduce other dimensions of an image or artwork in proportion to the one given.

restore (1) *(com)* To copy backed-up files to disk from an archive if the originals are damaged or have been deleted.

restore (2) *(com)* To restore something to its original state or, in the case of a document, to its last 'saved' version. Also called 'revert'.

result code *(com)* → *error code*

reticulation *(pho)* A variously desirable or undesirable aberration in photographic processing, in which the film emulsion adopts a disrupted, 'crazed' pattern as a result of temperature changes in processing.

retina *(gen)* The sensory membrane lining the back of the eye, consisting of several layers, including one containing the rods and cones. The retina responds to light coming through the eye's lens and passes it to the optic nerve for transformation into an image by the brain.

retouching *(gen)* Altering an image, artwork or film to make modifications or remove imperfections. Scanned images are usually retouched electronically using appropriate software. ➔ *spotting*

retransfer *(pri)* The process of duplicating the image on one lithographic plate so that it can be transferred to another.

retree *(pap)* Damaged sheets in several reams of paper, usually marked 'XXX' or 'XX' to indicate the degree of damage.

retree copy *(pri)* A limited-edition book made from 'retree' or spare sheets. It is sold 'out of series' – the books are unnumbered and bound as 'overs'.

retroussage *(pri)* A technique used to soften the image and improve the dark tones when printing from an intaglio plate. A fine muslin rag is passed or flicked over the surface, drawing ink from the recesses and onto the surrounding areas.

retting *(pap)* The soaking of paper fibres in water to partially disintegrate them.

Return key *(com)* The key on a computer keyboard that performs operations similar to a typewriter 'carriage return' key, in that it moves the text insertion point to the beginning of the next line. In many applications and dialog boxes, it also duplicates the actions of the Enter key – for example, confirming a command. ➔ *Enter key*

returns *(gen)* Publications that are returned to the publisher by the retailer if they remain unsold. Such publications will have been supplied to the retailer on a 'sale or return' basis.

reversal developing/processing *(pho)* A method of making a positive copy from a positive image (or a negative from a negative).

reversal film *(pho)* Film emulsion that produces a positive image, as in colour transparencies ('slides').

reverse b to w *(typ)* abb.: reverse black to white. An instruction to reverse out an image or type. ➔ *reverse out*

reversed calf *(fin)* ➔ *rough calf*

reversed type *(typ)* ➔ *reverse out/ reverse type*

A photo affected by **reticulation**

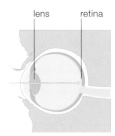

lens   retina

In the eye, light passes through the lens to the **retina**

reverse image *(gen)* An image that has been reversed, either horizontally or vertically. What was on the left of the image is now on the right, or what was at the top is now at the bottom, as in a mirror-image.
→ *flip/flop*

reverse indent *(typ)* → *hanging indent*

reverse l to r *(gen) abb.:* reverse left to right.
→ *lateral reverse*

reverse out/reverse type *(gen)* To reverse the tones of an image or type so that it appears white (or another colour) in a black or coloured background. Also called 'dropout', 'save out' or 'knockout'.
→ *dropped-out type*

reverse P *(typ)* → *blind P*

reverse printing *(pri)* → *back printing*

reverse reading *(pre)* → *wrong reading*

reversing *(pri)* A term used in photoengraving to describe a change from black to white or from left to right.

revise *(pre)* A proof on which the revisions marked on an earlier proof have been implemented.

revised edition *(gen)* The reprinting of a book that is essentially the same as the original except that the content has been amended or updated. Also known as an 'enlarged edition' or 'new edition'.

ReWire *(aud)* Mac/PC system common to most MIDI and audio software suites. It allows you to transfer MIDI and audio data seamlessly between ReWire-compatible products. For example, you could import a Reason track into Cubase to add vocals and external audio.

REX *(aud)* Loop format developed by Propellerhead for its Reason virtual studio and ReCycle loop editor.

RGB *(gen) abb.:* red, green, blue. The 'additive' colour model used by TV and computer screens, where all colours are formed from combinations of red, green and blue light.
→ *additive colours*

RH *(gen) abb.:* relative humidity. → *relative humidity (RH)*

rhodamine *(pri)* A component of magenta process ink with a blueish pigment.

ribbed paper *(pap)* An unusual type of woven paper with a ribbed effect produced by pressing before the web is dry. Also known as 'repped' paper.

rich black *(pri)* A percentage of another colour – usually 20–40 per cent black or magenta – which is printed under solid black in colour printing to produce a more dense black.

rich text format (RTF) *(com)* A Microsoft file format for transferring formatted text documents. It is an intermediate format between plain ASCII text and sophisticated word-processing formats.

rider roller *(pri)* A printing press cylinder that has no motive power of its own but rotates only when in contact with another cylinder.

RIFF (1) *(com) abb.:* raster image file format. A seldom-used proprietary file format (devised by Letraset) for storing images.

RIFF (2) *(aud)* Resource Interchange File Format, an owner-definable mix of MIDI, WAV, AIF and other files in a portable format.

rifle stock *(pho)* A camera support that helps to hold steady a camera with a long lens (like a rifle).

right-aligned/justified *(typ)* → *unjustified*

right-angle fold *(fin)* The standard method of folding a printed sheet. It is folded in half and then again at right angles to the first fold. Also known as a 'chopper fold'.

right indent *(typ)* The distance between the right edge of a text column and the right edge of a line of text. → *indent(ed)*

right reading *(pre)* The way of viewing negative or positive film so that any text can be read as normal – i.e. from left to right, top to bottom – and used to specify the side of the film on which the emulsion is required for

R

film duplication or platemaking. For example, if the request is for film that is 'right reading, emulsion down' ('RRED'), the emulsion is on the underside, whereas 'right reading emulsion up' ('RREU') means that it is on the top surface.

right side *(pap)* ➔ *felt side*

rim lighting *(pho)* A variation on backlighting where a strong light source is placed behind (and completely concealed by) the subject. In portraits, this light is diffused through the hair to create a rim of bright light. Careful metering is often called for to balance the rim light with that directed at the subject from the front.

ringflash *(pho)* An electronic flash, in the shape of a ring, surrounding the camera lens. This produces virtually shadowless lighting.

RIP (1) *(pre)* abb.: raster image processor. ➔ *raster(ization); raster image processor (RIP)*

RIP (2) *(gen)* abb.: rest in proportion. ➔ *rest in pro(portion)*

Ripple Distort filter *(com)* Simulates random pond-like ripples. The wave filter provides similar results but provides more control.

RISC *(com)* abb.: reduced instruction set computing. ➔ *microprocessor*

river *(typ)* An aberration in typeset text in which a series of word spaces form a continuous stream of white space down a page. Sometimes caused by badly justified type.

RM/RAM *(aud)* abb.: RealMedia ➔ *RealMedia*

roan *(fin)* A cover material made from dyed sheepskin, which is sometimes used in bookbinding instead of morocco.

robot *(int)* Referred to colloquially as a 'bot', a robot is a program that roams the World Wide Web, gathering and cataloguing information, usually for use by various Web search engines such as Yahoo and Google. The word 'robots', of course, also refers to mechanical devices, which no longer live only in the realms of science fiction. ➔ *information agent; search engine; spider*

rod *(gen)* The most common form of photoreceptor found on the retina. Rods are more sensitive to intensity than cones, but are not sensitive to colour. There are eighteen times more rods than cones in the human eye.

roll (1) *(gen)* An ancient manuscript usually made from parchment or vellum and kept rolled rather than folded.

roll (2) *(com)* In a 3D environment, the rotation of an object or camera around the z-axis. ➔ *camera moves*

roll (3) *(fin)* A tool comprising a brass wheel, sometimes decorated with a repeating pattern, that is used in traditional bookbinding to impress a continuous line on a cover.

roll (4) *(aud)* A common form of moving title, most often seen in end-credits, where text scrolls upwards from the bottom of the screen.

roller *(pri)* A cylinder that is used to apply ink to a plate or forme. Also used on small presses to roll out the ink to the correct consistency.

roller stripping *(pri)* The failure of ink to adhere to the inking roller.

The Photoshop Ocean
Ripple Distort filter

roller train *(pri)* A series of inking rollers through which stiff ink travels until it reaches the correct consistency.

roll-fed *(pri)* → *web-fed*

roll film *(pho)* Film rolled onto a spool with a paper backing. The most common roll film format is 120.

rollover *(int)* The rapid substitution of one or more images when the mouse pointer is rolled over the original image. Used extensively for navigation buttons on webpages and multimedia presentations. → *navigation button*

roll set curl *(pap)* The paper curl that occurs when a web has been stored in roll form for too long. Also known as 'wrap curl'.

roll stand *(pap)* A device used to support a roll of paper as it is fed into a press.

roll-to-roll printing *(pri)* Rewinding a continuous printed web onto another roll.

roll-to-sheet *(pri)* A system that cuts sheets from a roll and delivers them into a sheet-fed press. → *sheeter*

roll-up *(pri)* A check of the first printed sheets to emerge from a press while the plate is still being inked.

ROM *(com) abb.:* read-only memory. → *random access memory (RAM); read–only memory (ROM)*

Roman notation *(gen)* Using Roman numerals to record dates, still common practice today. → *Roman numerals*

Roman numerals *(gen)* A system of numerical notation, which uses letters rather than numbers: I (one), V (five), X (10), L (50), C (100), D (500) and M (1,000). The letters are used in combinations to represent any number. → *Roman notation*

roman (type) *(typ)* A font design in which the characters are upright, as distinct from italic.

The Adobe Illustrator
Rotation tool

root directory/level *(com)* The first level at which files and folders are placed, represented by the window that appears when you double-click on (in order to open) a disk icon.

ROP (1) *(pri) abb.:* run of paper. → *print to paper*

ROP (2) *(pri) abb.:* run of press. → *run of press*

rosette(s) *(pri)* → *dot pattern*

rosin *(pap)* A natural by-product left after turpentine has been tapped from pine trees. It is used in the manufacture of engine-sized paper, making it more impervious to ink and moisture. → *engine-sized*

rotary press *(pri)* Any printing press in which the printing surface is on a rotating cylinder. Paper can be delivered to rotary presses in either sheet or web form.

Rotation tool *(com)* In some graphics applications, a tool that enables you to rotate an item around a fixed point.

rotogravure *(pri)* A rotary press that uses intaglio gravure cylinders to produce an impression rather than litho plates or cast letterpress stereos. → *gravure; intaglio; lithography; rotary press*

rough *(gen)* A preliminary drawing showing a proposed design. Also called a 'scamp', or 'visual'. → *layout; tissue*

rough calf *(fin)* A traditional calfskin binding with the flesh side outermost. Also known as 'reversed calf'.

rough draft/draught *(gen)* → *draft/draught*

rough etch *(pri)* The initial etching of a descummed copper or zinc plate in order to reduce the dot size, ultimately giving contrast and depth to the printed image. Also known as 'flat etch', although this term also applies to reducing the size of halftone dots on film. Rough etching is followed by 'fine etching'. → *fine etch; flat etch*

rough gilt *(fin)* Uncut edges that are gilded before they are sewn. ➔ *edge gilding; gild*

roughness map *(com)* In some 3D applications, the use of a texture map to control surface roughness. ➔ *texture map(ping)/surface mapping*

rough proof/pull *(pre)* A proof that does not necessarily show copy in its correct position or on the correct paper. Also called a 'flat pull'.

round dot *(pre)* The shape of each dot in a halftone screen, although – in the midtones – dots take on a square shape. ➔ *dot shape*

rounded and backed *(fin)* ➔ *rounding and backing/rounded and backed*

rounding and backing/rounded and backed *(fin)* The style of binding in which a cased book has a convex back, thus making the fore-edge concave. Backing provides the 'joints' (the point at which the spine and the boards of a casebound book are hinged). ➔ *flat back(ed) (book)*

router *(int)* ➔ *gateway*

routine *(com)* A piece of programming code designed to perform a specific task.

royalty-free *(gen)* A term, usually applied to images (either photographs or illustrations), that states that once a flat fee has been paid, the image can be used by the purchaser wherever and how often desired (unless otherwise stipulated), and that no additional fee need be paid to the copyright holder. ➔ *clip art/clip media*

RTF *(com)* abb.: rich text format. ➔ *rich text format (RTF)*

rubber sheeting *(com)* ➔ *mesh warp*

Rubber Stamp tool *(com)* Sometimes called the *Cloning tool* (on account of its action), the *Rubber Stamp* tool is often used for removing unwanted image elements. Later Photoshop versions (and some other editors) feature two *Rubber Stamp* tools, the

basic tool and the *Pattern Stamp*. The basic tool is normally used as a brush (and shares the common *Brushes* palette for brush type selection) but 'paints' with image elements drawn from another part of the image, or a separate image.

Using Adobe Photoshop's **Rubber Stamp** (cloning) tool to copy from the crosshairs (right) to the left.

rubber stereo *(pri)* A stereo made in a moulding press by pressing a rubber plate against a heated matrix. The rubber is vulcanized by the heat, creating a permanent impression. ➔ *matrix; stereo*

rub-down lettering/type *(typ)* ➔ *dry transfer lettering*

rub-off *(pri)* The occurrence of dry, printed ink transferring from one printed surface to another.

rub-off lettering/type *(typ)* ➔ *dry transfer lettering*

rub-ons *(gen)* ➔ *dry transfer lettering*

rubric *(gen)* In a book printed predominantly in black ink, text printed in red, usually chapter headings or other divisional headings.

ruby *(typ)* A traditional name for a size of type, approximately 5½ point.

A **rounding and backing** book binding

ROUGH GILT

Rubylith *(pre)* The brand name for a widely used type of peelable masking film used for film make-up.

rule *(gen)* A printed line. The term derives from the Latin *regula* (meaning 'straight stick') and was used to describe the metal strips of type height, in various widths, lengths and styles, which were used by traditional typesetters for printing lines.

ruler *(com)* In some publications, this refers to the calibrated ruler at the edges of a document window, in a preferred unit of measure. ➔ *ruler guide*

ruler guide *(com)* In some applications, a non-printing guide that you position by clicking on the ruler and dragging it to the desired location. ➔ *ruler*

ruler origin *(com)* ➔ *origin*

il utem nim dionums t praesed dolore aciniam, conse- ea am alit alit el endre exeros llaortis alismod n endrem zzrilis lestrud quipisc vel de- utat ver ectet utem dio gnim vulla con e corem niam- rud diat aut au- gue dolor sum Visl utat landit, ptat inisisit ute cilit, quamcom s nostio conul- am,Im zzrit prat. digna adipis aut tat, con ulputpat met, sis am estrud Cum dolesto od tin vel ing et at r augue facilit faccum veriusc s dit praestrud tatinci i faciliquat. Lore del augait nim venim dit m niamcon sequam

In hent nostrud et venit zzriure dui bla facilis estrud magnis nos ex con hent irilit prat a erosto dolor incidu etuerat, quam dit wis nim e aut aut ni wisim iri autpatie Tet ilisit dolorero od am, conulput eugait del ex el ilit atuerit del ipsusci am etum inim dol cum irit ulla feuis commolore dolup secte tat, commy num dipsustis ad vercil in vendio diat. Igniamet lore commod e eros dolore dol eugue mincing ulputat. Erate f nonsed magna enim dunt ad vel doloborerit a luptat, corpera estrud deler eu feum ero corer se et, co acip er susci enis nullum at

Here the text is following a clipping path to **runaround** the woman

ruling machine *(pri)* A machine designed specifically for drawing the lines on music and ledger paper.

run *(pri)* ➔ *press run/run*

runaround/run round *(typ)* Text that flows around a shape, such as an illustration. Also called 'text wrap'.

run back *(typ)* Words that move back from a line to the previous line as a consequence of a text deletion or correction. The opposite of 'overrun'. ➔ *overrun*

run chart *(gen)* ➔ *trend chart*

run down *(typ)* A proofreading instruction to break a line at a specific place, forcing the remaining text to the next line. ➔ *take down*

run-in *(typ)* ➔ *run on (2)*

run-in head/heading *(gen)* A heading starting on the same line as the text, as distinct from a heading placed above the text.

run-in sheets *(pri)* The printed (spoil) sheets produced between the start of a print run and the point at which a printed sheet of acceptable quality is produced. ➔ *run up; spoils*

runners *(typ)* The numbers placed in the margin of a text to form references for identifying particular lines of that text.

running feet *(gen)* ➔ *headline (1)*

running foot *(gen)* ➔ *footer (2)*

running head(ing)/headline *(gen)* ➔ *headline (1)*

running text *(typ)* The main text that runs from page to page, even though it may be broken up by illustrations.

running title *(gen)* ➔ *headline (1)*

run-of-paper *(gen)* Those advertisement positions that are sold in a publication without the client specifying a particular location – such as the inside front cover – and which may thus appear anywhere in the publication.

*!?

R

run of press *(pri)* Printing work carried out at the same time as the main run, rather than supplied to the printer as a preprinted item for later insertion. ➔ *preprint*

run on (1) *(pri)* A specified number of sheets printed in addition to the originally specified quantity. ➔ *overs*

run on (2) *(typ)* An instruction that two paragraphs are to be set as one. Also referred to as 'follow on'.

run on chapters *(typ)* Chapters that do not start on a new page but immediately follow the preceding chapter.

run out and indented *(typ)* A paragraph in which the first line is full out with the remainder being indented. More commonly referred to as a 'hanging indent'.
➔ *full out; hanging indent*

run ragged *(typ)* Ragged right. ➔ *unjustified*

run through work *(pri)* The printing of even parallel lines across a sheet using a specialized press. ➔ *feint ruling; ruling machine*

run up *(pri)* The period between the start of a print run (i.e. switching the press on) and the point at which a printed sheet of acceptable quality is produced. This period normally generates a certain amount of spoiled sheets. ➔ *run-in sheets*

run-up spine *(fin)* A standard decoration on the tooled spine of a book, consisting of twin lines running up the spine edges and across the width to form panels.

rush changes *(gen)* A questionable practice in which additional fees are paid to a supplier for completing a job in less time than would normally be taken. Also referred to as 'expediting changes'.

Russia cowhide *(fin)* A traditional, lesser-quality binding material made from cowhide, often impregnated with Russian oil in order to resemble genuine Russia leather. Also called 'American Russia'. ➔ *American russia; Russia leather*

Russia leather *(fin)* A traditional, high-quality cover material made from calfskin impregnated with aromatic birch tar oil.
➔ *Russia cowhide*

R

Ss

sabattier effect *(pho)* The partial reversal of tone or colour in a photographic emulsion due to brief exposure to light during development.

SACD (super audio CD) *(aud)* Offers a staggering frequency range above and below the normal range of human hearing, and ultra-high ('1-bit' direct stream) sampling. Special players are needed, and digital amplification is essential for the best results. Sampling rate: 2.8 MHz (2.8 million samples a second); Frequency range: 2 Hz–100 kHz; Dynamic range: 105 dB; Capacity: 4.2 GB.

saddleback book *(fin)* A book with inset pages secured by stitching with thread through the fold line. ➔ *insert (1)*

saddle-sewn *(fin)* A method of securing multiple pages by stitching them with thread through the fold line while the pages are supported on a saddle-shaped mount.

saddle-stitched *(fin)* A method of securing pages in pamphlets or brochures by stitching them through the fold line with wire staples while the sheets rest on a saddle-shaped mount. ➔ *saddle-sewn; saddleback book*

sad Mac icon *(com)* A picture of an unhappy face that can appear at the beginning of startup on Macintosh computers, indicating that a fault has been diagnosed during the startup tests performed by the computer. Often accompanied by a sound that differs from the usual harmonious startup chord. ➔ *icon*

safelight *(pho)* ➔ *non-actinic (light)*

safety paper *(pap)* Chemically treated paper with special properties that make it easier to distinguish it from forgeries, used especially for cheques and legal documents.

sale or return *(gen)* ➔ *returns*

same size (S/S) *(gen)* An instruction that original artwork/illustrations should be reproduced without enlargement or reduction.

sample *(com)* Usually used to describe a piece of audio, but can also refer to a unit of anything – pixels, for example. ➔ *sampling rate*

The White House with the **sabattier effect** simulated using Photoshop's *Curves* tool

sample point *(gen)* The point or area sampled using an Eyedropper tool. → *Eyedropper tool*

sampler (1) *(com)* A device used to digitize sound so that it can be manipulated by a computer. → *digitize*

sampler (2) *(gen)* A demonstration of a product, such as software distributed on disks.

sample size *(com)* The number of pixels, or the amount of data, used as a sample to assess information about an image or about other digital files such as sounds. → *pixel*

sampling rate *(aud)* This refers to the number of samples taken of a piece of audio in one second during a digital recording. For example, the standard for CD audio is 44,100 samples per second, or 44.1 kHz. According to the Nyquist Theorem, the sampling rate must be twice the amount of the highest frequency to be reproduced.

sans serif *(typ)* Generic description of type designs that lack the small extensions ('serifs') at the ends of the main strokes of the letters, and which are usually without stroke contrast. Also called 'lineal type'. → *serif*

sarsanet *(fin)* A type of lining material of stiffened silk.

satin finish *(pap)* Paper with a smooth finish and a satin sheen.

satin white *(pap)* White paper with a smooth finish and slight sheen. → *china clay; satin finish*

saturation *(gen)* The variation in colour of the same tonal brightness from none (grey) through pastel shades (low saturation) to pure colour with no grey (high saturation, or 'fully saturated'). Also called 'purity' or 'chroma'. → *HSB*

save *(com)* The computer command that transfers data from memory to disk, ensuring that work is preserved. → *memory; save as*

save as *(com)* The computer command that allows documents to be saved in another location or in another format. → *file format; save*

Save dialog box *(com)* A box that appears on-screen the first time a document is saved, requiring the user to supply its title and location. → *dialog/dialog box; save*

save out *(gen)* → *reverse out/reverse type*

sawtooth *(pri)* An aberration in screen printing, in which lines of a design cross the fabric mesh diagonally, giving them a jagged look. → *screen printing*

SC *(typ) abb.:* small capitals. → *small capitals/ caps*

sc. *(gen) abb.: scilicet.* The Latin term for 'namely'.

scalable font *(com)* → *outline font*

scalar processor architecture (SPARC) *(com)* A powerful microprocessor developed by Sun Microsystems. Forms the basis of the UNIX Operating System.

scale drawing *(gen)* A drawing such as a map or plan, which represents the subject matter in proportion to its actual size and to a specified scale. For example, an object drawn to a scale of 1:10 means that one unit of measurement on the drawing is equivalent to 10 of the same units on the object at full size – so 1 inch on the drawing equals 10 inches at full size.

scale/scaling *(gen)* The process of working out the the degree of enlargement or reduction required to bring an image to its correct reproduction size. → *sizing (2)*

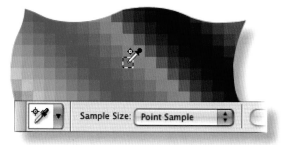

Saturation, from 100% (left) to 0% (right)

A **sample point** being selected by the *Eyedropper* tool

scaling text *(typ)* → *horizontal scaling*

scamp *(gen)* → *rough*

scan dot *(com)* The resolution of a scanning device, measured – like machine dots – in dots per inch (strictly speaking, this is actually pixels per inch, or ppi). However, the formula for calculating scan dot resolution does not relate to that of calculating machine dot resolution. A rough rule of thumb is that for images that will eventually be printed with a halftone screen ruling greater than 133lpi, the scan resolution should be 1.5 times the lpi screen ruling, and for screens equal to, or less than, 133lpi, the scan resolution should be 2.0 times the lpi ruling. Scanning at higher resolutions will not make any difference because the halftone dots will not be small enough to reproduce the extra detail. → *halftone dot; machine dot; pixels per inch (ppi)*

scanned image *(pre)* An image that has been recorded by a scanner and converted to a suitable form for reproduction, such as film or a digital file. → *scan(ning); scan dot*

scanner *(com)* An electronic device that uses a sequentially moving light beam to convert artwork or photographs into digital form so that they can be manipulated by a computer or output to separated film. A scanner can be a simple flatbed type, used on the desktop for positioning pictures only, or a sophisticated reprographic device ('drum scanner') used for high-quality colour separation. → *commercial colour; desktop scanner; drum scanner*

scan(ning) *(pre)* An electronic process that converts an image into digital form by sequential exposure to a moving light beam such as a laser. The scanned image can then be manipulated by a computer or output to separated film. → *desktop scanner; drum scanner; laser*

scan plates *(pri)* Plates made on an electronic engraving machine. → *engraving (2)*

s caps *(typ)* abb.: small capitals. → *small capitals/caps*

scatter diagram *(gen)* A graph used to analyze the cause and effect relationship between two variables where two sets of data are plotted on x and y axes, the result being a scattering of unconnected dots.

scatter proof *(pre)* A single colour proof containing unrelated images placed randomly and without reference to their final position. The process is used to cut costs when large numbers of pictures are needed – for example, in a magazine or illustrated book. Also called a 'random proof'.

school edition *(gen)* An edition of a book, printed from the original plates but generally in a different format and with different binding, and sometimes annotated.

scoop *(pho)* Smoothly curving background in a photography studio, used principally to eliminate the horizon line. Also called a 'cove'.

scorcher *(pri)* A machine used to heat and curve stereo matrices for use on a rotary press.

score (1) *(fin)* Marking the line of a crease in paper or card so that it can be folded cleanly. Also called 'creasing'.

score (2) *(com)* The term describing time information about each object and property in a scene in some 3D applications. Based on the idea of a musical score.

scraperboard *(gen)* A board coated with ink (white on black or black on white), at one time used widely in commercial work by artists preparing illustrations for line reproduction, mostly as press advertisements.

scratch comma *(typ)* A comma rendered as a short, straight oblique line.

scratch pad *(gen)* Any space set aside for experimenting with ideas, techniques, and so on.

scratch (space/disk) *(com)* Disk space that is not needed for normal data storage and which has been set aside as 'virtual memory' for temporary storage, typically by image-editing applications. → *virtual memory*

screamer *(gen)* A slang term for exclamation mark used by printers and journalists.

screen (1) *(com)* → *monitor*

screen (2) *(pre)* → *halftone screen*

screen (3) *(pri)* The porous silk or synthetic mesh used as an image carrier in the screen printing process. → *screen printing; silkscreen printing*

screen angle *(pre)* The angle at which halftone screens of images printing in two or more colours are positioned to minimize undesirable dot patterns (moiré) when printed. The angle at which screens should be positioned depends upon the number of colours being printed, but the normal angles for four-colour process printing are: cyan 105; magenta 75; yellow 90; black 45. → *dot pattern; moiré*

screen capture *(com)* → *screen grab*

screen clash *(pre)* → *moiré*

screen distance *(pre)* The space between the surface of a halftone screen and the plate or film during halftone photography. The distance depends on the screen ruling. → *halftone screen*

screen dump *(com)* → *screen capture*

screened print *(pre)* A image reproduced through a halftone screen and printed as a one-off print, usually on photographic bromide paper, so that it can be photographed as a line original as part of camera-ready art. → *dot-for-dot (2)*

screen filter *(com)* → *radiation shield/screen*

screen font *(com)* → *bitmapped font*

screen frequency *(pre)* The number of line rulings per inch (lpi) on a halftone screen. → *halftone screen; screen ruling*

screen grab *(com)* A 'snapshot' of part or all of a monitor display. Also called a 'screen shot', 'screen capture' or 'screen dump'.

screening *(pre)* Turning a continuous-tone image into a pattern of dots of various size by photographing it through a halftone screen placed in front of the photographic emulsion. → *halftone screen*

screenless printing *(pre)* → *stochastic screening*

screen marks *(pri)* → *mesh marks*

screen negative *(pre)* A photographic reproduction of an image made through a halftone screen onto negative film. → *halftone screen; screen positive*

screen positive *(pre)* A photographic reproduction of an image made either through a halftone screen onto positive film, or by 'contact' duplicating a screen negative. → *screen negative; halftone screen*

screen printing *(pri)* A printing process in which ink is forced through a porous mesh screen stretched across a frame. The image is formed by means of a hand-cut or

This image, like many in this book, is a **screen grab**. Additionally, an area of this screen is being selected and grabbed using the Mac OS X command Shift+Apple+4

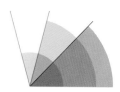

The relative halftone **screen angles**

Script typefaces resemble handwriting

photomechanically generated stencil, which is bonded to the screen, blocking the non-image areas. → *curved screen*

screen process work *(pre)* The basis of the halftone process in printing where continuous tone images are reproduced by means of exposure through a screen. → *halftone screen*

screen resolution *(pre)* → *screen ruling*

screen ruling *(pre)* In halftone screens, the number of ruled lines per inch or centimetre. The greater the number, the finer the resolution. The range in common use varies between around 85lpi for halftones printed on newsprint, to 150lpi or more for those printed on art papers. The default setting on laser printers is usually around 80lpi. Although the abbreviated form, lpi, is sometimes used, it is more usual to express, say, a '150 lpi' screen as a '150-line' screen. → *halftone screen*

screen-safe *(aud)* Most conventional TV screens will cut off a certain area around the border of the video image during playback.

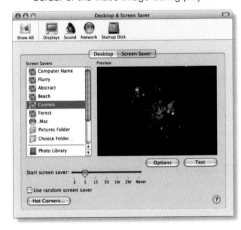

Most operating systems have an option to select a **screen saver** from their display options

The screen safe (or title-safe) area is the central region of the video frame that will be safe from this involuntary exclusion.

screen saver/blanker *(com)* A means of dimming the screen image or replacing it with a pattern after a preset time of inactivity in order to preserve the phosphor coating on the monitor.

screen shot *(com)* → *screen capture*

screen size *(com)* → *monitor*

screen tester *(pre)* A piece of equipment used to identify the screen resolution, or number of lines per inch, of a printed halftone image. → *halftone screen*

screen tint/tone *(pre)* → *halftone tint*

screen type *(pre)* → *dot shape*

scribing *(pri)* Making corrections to an image on film or plate by scratching the surface.

scrim (1) *(fin)* → *mull*

scrim (2) *(pho)* Mesh fabric placed in front of a photography lamp in order to diffuse the light.

script (1)/scripting language *(com)* Simplified programming languages that certain 'authoring' applications allow you to write to create your own programs. Scripting is used extensively in multimedia applications, such as Macromedia Director's 'Lingo', and in software creation tools such as SuperCard and Revolution. → *programming language*

script (2) *(typ)* A typeface designed to resemble handwriting.

scroll (1) *(gen)* A document presented as a roll of parchment or paper, usually handwritten.

scroll (2) *(com)* To move the contents of a window or directory listing up or down (or, sometimes, sideways), in order to view a part of a document that was hidden beyond the edges of the window. Scrolling is done by means of 'scroll bars', 'scroll boxes' and 'scroll arrows'.

scroll arrow *(com)* An arrow that, when clicked on, moves the contents of a window up, down or sideways. → *scroll (2)*

scroll bar *(com)* The bar at the side and, usually, the bottom of a window, within which the scroll box operates and which indicates if there are parts of the document hidden from view. → *scroll (2)*

scroll box *(com)* A box sitting within the scroll bar of a window, which can be moved up and down to access different parts of the open document. The position of the scroll box in the bar indicates position in relation to the size of the entire document.
→ *scroll (2)*

scrubbing *(aud)* The action of moving through a video, frame by frame.

SCSI *(com) abb.:* small computer system interface. → *small computer system interface (SCSI)*

SCSI bus *(com)* The data path that links SCSI devices to a computer. → *small computer system interface (SCSI)*

SCSI chain *(com)* Sequential linking of a number of SCSI devices to a computer. Also called a 'daisy-chain'. → *daisy-chain; small computer system interface (SCSI)*

SCSI device *(com)* A device, such as a disk drive or scanner, that can be attached to a computer by means of a SCSI connection. SCSI devices may be inside the computer ('internal device') or outside ('external device'). → *device (1); small computer system interface (SCSI)*

SCSI ID (number) *(com)* The identifying number or 'address' assigned to each SCSI device attached to a computer. Each number must be unique. → *DIP switch; SCSI chain; SCSI device*

SCSI partition *(com)* → *partition(ing)*

SCSI port *(com)* The point at which the SCSI chain connects to the computer by means of a connecting plug. SCSI ports can be of the 25-pin or 50-pin variety. The devices themselves almost always have 50-pin ports, whilst some computers (Macintosh, for example) have 25-pin ports. → *small computer system interface (SCSI)*

SCSI terminator *(com)* A device for protecting the SCSI bus from 'signal echo', which can corrupt data transfer. → *small computer system interface (SCSI)*

scuffing *(pap)* Degradation of the surface of paper caused by prolonged contact with another surface. Also called 'abrasion'.

scum/scumming *(pri)* A fault occurring in lithographic printing when the ink adheres to the non-image areas of the plate.
→ *catch-up*

SDK *(com) abb.:* software developer's kit.
→ *software developer's kit (SDK)*

SEA *(com) abb.:* self–extracting archive. → *self-extracting archive (SEA)*

seal *(fin)* The skin of the Newfoundland seal, used in bookbinding for limp covers.

search and replace *(com)* The automated process of finding specified data, such as text or images, within a document and substituting it with replacement data.
→ *batch mode/processing*

search engine *(com)* The part of a program, such as a database, that seeks out information in response to requests made by the user. On the Web, search engines such as Yahoo, HotBot and Alta Vista provide sophisticated criteria for searching, and provide summaries of each result as well as the website addresses for retrieving more information. → *robot; search tool*

search path *(com)* The route taken by software when it looks for a file. → *search engine*

Search tool *(int)* A program that enables specific webpages to be searchable.
→ *search engine*

SECAM *(com) abb.:* Système Electronique pour Couleur avec Mémoire. A colour television standard used in France, eastern Europe, Russia and the Middle East (where it is called 'MESECAM'). It uses 625 lines and displays images at 25 frames per second.
→ *NTSC; PAL*

secondary binding *(fin)* A variant of binding materials, which may occur when a single printing of a book is bound in batches over a period of time.

Mac OS's Sherlock
is a Web **Search tool**

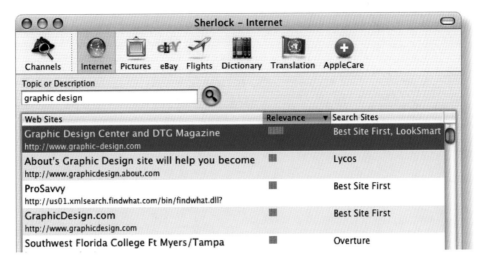

secondary colour *(pri)* Colour produced by overprinting two primary colours. Also called 'overprint colour'.

second cover *(pri)* An alternative term for the inside front cover of a publication.

section (1) *(com)* In some page-layout applications, any group of sequentially numbered pages.

section (2) *(fin)* A printed sheet folded to form four or more pages of a book, ready for gathering and sewing. The term is now used synonymously with 'signature'. ➔ *signature (1)*

section (3) *(typ)* A symbol ('§') used as a reference mark in text to draw the reader's attention to a footnote.

section-sewn book *(fin)* A book in which the gathered sections are sewn together with thread.

sector *(com)* A segment of a track on a disk and the smallest contiguous space in which data can be stored, usually allowing space for 512 consecutive bytes. ➔ *block (3)*

sector interleave factor *(com)* ➔ *interleave ratio*

secure area *(int)* The area of a website in which personal or sensitive information can be entered by users. Secure areas are usually identified by the prefix 'https' in the URL and are particularly important for commercial transactions made via the Web. ➔ *https*

see copy *(gen)* A proof mark signalling an omission that is too large to be inserted on the proof. The omission is indicated on the attached copy for the guidance of the compositor. Also used to indicate to the author that the reader is uncertain about a part of the copy.

seek time *(com)* The time it takes for a disk head to move from whatever track it is on to whatever track you tell it to read next. ➔ *access time*

see-through *(pri)* ➔ *look-through*

segment *(com)* A part of an application. Several segments may make up an application; not all of these segments need to be in RAM at the same time. ➔ *application*

selectasine *(pri)* A colour printing process that employs a single silk screen for all colours used.

select(ing) *(com)* The choosing of an item, such as a piece of text, graphic symbol or icon, in order for it to be altered, moved or manipulated. Any item must be selected, or made active, before its state can be altered in

any way. If no part of a document has been selected, but a function such as a spelling check is requested, some applications will continue on the basis that the entire document is selected, therefore the entire document will be checked for spelling.

selection *(com)* In image-editing, a part of an on-screen image that is chosen and defined by a border in preparation for manipulation or movement.

selection marquee/rectangle/box *(com)* A dotted line that forms a rectangle or box. The line is drawn by means of the pointer or a selection tool, and vanishes immediately the selection is made, or becomes a marquee. ➔ *marquee*

selector *(com)* The rules applied to a set of properties and values by which you make a selection.

self ends *(fin)* When the same paper stock that is used for the text and part of the first and last sections is also used to form the endpapers of a book, these are known as 'self ends' or 'own ends'. ➔ *endpapers*

self-extracting archive (SEA) *(com)* One or more files stored in a compressed format along with the extra programming code needed to expand the items to their original state without using any external software. This is usually achieved by double-clicking. Such files are usually suffixed with '.SEA'. ➔ *compression (1)*

self wrapper/cover *(fin)* A cover or wrapper formed of the same paper stock as the text. It is usually printed, as in a pamphlet, for example.

semi-concealed cover *(fin)* A piece of material that is slotted, or punched and scored, and used in combination with the actual binding device to form the closed backbone of a book or booklet in the mechanical binding process.

semi-uncial *(typ)* ➔ *half-uncial*

semi-Yapp *(fin)* A style of binding midway between limp and Yapp bindings. The protective cover turns over just beyond the book's edges. ➔ *Yapp binding*

sensitize *(gen)* To make something, such as a piece of paper, sensitive to something else, such as light. In printing, this includes making the image areas of a printing plate ink-receptive by applying a special coating to an aluminium printing plate.

separate *(gen)* An article from or a part of a periodical reprinted and issued separately. Sometimes called an 'off-print'. ➔ *off-print*

separation *(pre)* ➔ *colour separation*

separation artwork *(pre)* Artwork that consists of separate layers for each of the colours used. ➔ *colour separation*

separation filters *(pre)* The filters used to separate colours so that they can be printed individually. They each transmit about one-third of the spectrum. ➔ *colour separation*

separation guide *(pho)* A printed guide containing a set of standard colours. When photographed alongside a colour-critical subject (like a painting), this allows the separation to be matched against the colour control bar printed alongside the image.

A **selection marquee** is used when selecting files in Mac OS

The Mac OS icon for a **self-extracting archive**

A photograph in classic **sepia** tones

SELECTION

separations *(pri)* The 'split' versions of a page or image that has been prepared for process printing. Each separation is used to print a single process colour or spot colour.

separator *(typ)* The line separating the 'denominator' from the 'separator' in a fraction. → *denominator; fraction*

sepia *(gen)* A brown colour and also a monochrome print in which the normal shades of grey appear as shades of brown. → *sepia toning*

sepia toning *(pho)* A process of making sepia prints from standard black-and-white prints. Various bleaches and dyes are employed in the process. → *sepia*

sequencing *(aud)* A process first developed with analog synthesizers whereby timed electronic pulses were used to trigger sounds in a rhythmic fashion. Sequencing now covers a range of digital audio functions, and is used to trigger MIDI, percussive elements, prerecorded audio clips and effects.

serial (1) *(com)* The process of transmitting data sequentially, or consecutively in a sequence, as opposed to simultaneously.

serial (2) *(gen)* The publication of a book in serial form, i.e. in parts that appear at regular intervals.

serial flash *(pho)* → *multiple flash*

serial interface *(com)* The connection between computer hardware devices in which data is transmitted sequentially, one at a time. As distinct from parallel interface. → *parallel interface*

serial line Internet protocol (SLIP) *(int)* A communications protocol that supports an Internet connection over a dial-up line. Now superseded by PPP.

serial port *(com)* The socket or port on a computer used for the connection of devices that use a serial interface – modems or printers, for example. → *serial interface*

serif *(typ)* The short counterstroke or finishing stroke at the end of the main stroke of a type character. Serifs on older 'classic' typefaces tend to be bracketed and curve out from the main stroke to a point. Modern serifs are flat hair-lines at the end of the main stroke. → *bracketed type; sans serif*

serigraphy *(pri)* The silkscreen printing process. → *silkscreen printing*

server *(com)* A networked computer that serves client computers, providing a central location for files and services, and typically handling such things as e-mail and Web access. → *client*

server-side *(com)* Processing done by a network server rather than by your own computer ('client-side'). → *client-side*

server-side image map *(int)* A means of navigating a webpage via an image map. It sends the coordinates of your mouse pointer (in relation to the page) back to the server where the page came from, so that it can determine where to direct you next. → *client-side image map*

service bureau *(pre)* A company that provides digital image services such as colour scanning and high-resolution imagesetting.

service provider *(int)* A commercial organization specializing in providing connections to the Internet. → *BBS; ISP*

set (1) *(typ)* The width of an individual type character.

set (2) *(typ)* A contraction of 'typesetting', meaning to set type.

set and hold *(pri)* An instruction to the printer to prepare matter in readiness for printing, but not to print.

N

An example of a
serif typeface

setback *(pri)* The distance between the front edge of a printing plate and the start of the image area. Allows for the gripper margin. ➔ *gripper margin*

set close *(typ)* Type that is set with the minimum of space between words and sentences.

set flush *(typ)* Text set without any indented lines. ➔ *flush paragraphs*

set-off *(pri)* The accidental transfer of wet ink on a freshly printed sheet to the back of the next on the delivery pile. ➔ *cure*

set-off reel *(pri)* In reel-fed ('web') printing machines, an extra reel that prevents ink from the printed reel setting off on the packing of the impression cylinder. ➔ *set-off*

set solid *(typ)* Text set with no extra space ('leading') between the lines. Also called 'solid matter'. ➔ *leading*

set-top *(int)* A network computer designed to use a domestic television for display rather than a computer monitor. ➔ *netTV*

set width/size *(typ)* The space allowed across the body of each character in a line of text. ➔ *set (1)*

sewing *(fin)* The fastening together of sections of a book by means of thread. Can be performed manually or mechanically. ➔ *stitching (1)*

sewn book *(fin)* A book fastened together by the sewing process. ➔ *sewing*

sexto-decimo *(gen)* ➔ *sixteenmo/16mo*

sexto/6to *(pap)* A sheet either cut or folded to one sixth its original size.

SGML *(int) abb.:* Standard Generalized Markup Language. ➔ *ISO (1); Standard Generalized Markup Language (SGML)*

sgraffito *(pri)* A woodcut printing technique that produces a design in white on a black or red ground.

shade *(pri)* Equivalent to hue in the description and manufacture of printing inks.

shaded letter (1) *(typ)* ➔ *shadow font*

shaded letter (2) *(typ)* A type character filled with cross-hatched lines rather than with a solid tone.

shading *(com)* In 3D applications, the resulting colour of a surface due to light striking it at an angle.

shadow (area) *(gen)* The areas of an image that are darkest or densest. ➔ *density (3)*

shadow font *(typ)* Characters given a 3D appearance by heavily shaded areas beside the main strokes.

shared disk *(com)* Any hard disk attached to a networked computer, which other computers on the network can access. ➔ *network*

shareware *(com)* Software that is available through user groups (like magazine cover disks) and which is usually paid for only by those who decide to continue using it. Although shareware is not 'copy protected', it is nonetheless protected by copyright and a fee is normally payable for using it, unlike 'freeware'. ➔ *freeware*

sharpen edges *(com)* ➔ *peaking*

sharpen(ing) *(com)* Enhancing the apparent sharpness of an image by increasing the contrast between adjacent pixels. ➔ *interpolate/interpolation; sharpness*

sharpness *(pho)* A measure of the clarity of focus present in a photographic image. ➔ *definition*

sheet *(pap)* A single piece of paper, plain or printed.

sheeter *(pap)* A machine that cuts paper from a roll into sheets.

sheet-fed (press) *(pri)* A printing press into which single sheets are fed. ➔ *continuous feeder*

sheet proof *(pri)* ➔ *imposed proof*

sheet stock *(fin)* ➔ *quires/quire stock*

sheetwise (imposition) *(pri)* The technique whereby separate plates are used to print either side of a sheet. ➔ *imposition/impose*

The cross-hatching of **shaded letters**

Shadow fonts have a 3D appearance

Before (top) and after (below) applying **sharpen**

Creating a **Shockwave**
file using Director

sheet work *(pri)* A particular printing technique that involves printing on both sides of a sheet.

shelf back *(fin)* The spine of a book.

shift-click(ing) *(com)* The process of holding down the shift key whilst clicking on several items or passages of text on the screen, thus making multiple selections.

shift key *(com)* The modifier key used to generate upper case, and other characters, on a keyboard.

shift lens *(pho)* → *perspective correction (PC) lens*

shiners *(pap)* Impurities or tiny flaws in a sheet of paper, which show on the surface as shining specks.

shingle/shingling *(fin)* → *binder's creep*

shining *(fin)* The technique of holding printed sheets up to a light source to ensure that they are in register prior to folding.

shining-up table *(pre)* → *register table*

shocked *(int)* The term applied to webpages that contain material prepared with Macromedia's Shockwave technology, and which therefore require the Shockwave plug-in in order to be viewed. → *Shockwave*

Shockwave *(int)* A technology developed by Macromedia for creating Director presentations that can be delivered across the Internet and viewed with a Web browser. → *shocked; Flash (1)*

shoes *(fin)* Small, protective corners made of brass or silver, fitted to cover the corners of large handbound books.

shopping cart *(int)* → *virtual shopping cart*

short and *(typ)* → *ampersand*

short-focus lens *(pho)* A camera lens with a focal length shorter than the diagonal measurement of the film format. Thus, for 35mm film, a lens shorter than 35mm is short-focus. → *long-focus lens*

short grain *(pap)* → *machine direction*

short ink *(pri)* Printing ink that is heavily viscous and does not flow easily. The opposite of 'long ink'. → *long ink*

short page *(gen)* A page with less text printed on it than the standard length on other pages. Often employed at the beginning and end of chapters in a book.

short ream *(pap)* 480 sheets of paper.

shoulder (1) *(typ)* The non-printing area surrounding a face of type.

shoulder (2) *(fin)* The edges of the backbone of a book that project slightly from the cover faces.

shoulder-heads *(gen)* Headings that mark the second division of text within a chapter.

shoulder-notes *(gen)* Marginal notes situated at the top outer corners of a page.

show side *(fin)* The best, or face, side of any material that will ultimately be visible in the finished article. Often used to describe book cloths.

show-through *(pap)* → *look-through*

S

shrink wrap(ping) *(gen)* A packing technique involving the wrapping of products such as books or pamphlets in a plastic film, followed by an application of heat, causing the film to shrink to form a tight and neat package.

shuffling *(com)* In some page make-up applications, the re-ordering of document pages whilst retaining a logical sequence of numbering.

shut down *(com)* To switch off your computer in a safe manner – i.e. having first saved and closed any open files and ejected any removable disks.

shutter *(pho)* The device inside a conventional camera to control the length of time during which the film is exposed to light. Many digital cameras don't have a shutter, but the term is still used as shorthand to describe the electronic mechanism that controls the length of exposure for the CCD.

shutter priority *(pho)* A mode in automatic cameras in which you select the shutter speed manually, the aperture then being set automatically according to the camera's metering system. The opposite of aperture priority. → *aperture priority; shutter speed*

shutter speed *(pho)* The speed at which a camera shutter opens and closes, which, in turn, governs the exposure of the film. → *shutter priority*

sic *(gen)* A Latin word meaning 'thus'. Used in brackets immediately after a quoted passage that was misused or contained an error of spelling or grammar, to indicate the existence of this error in the original.

sidebar *(gen)* → *box feature/story*

sidebearing *(typ)* A space assigned to each side of a font character, adjustable if the application permits.

side gluing *(fin)* The securing of the cover on a perfect-bound book by means of adhesive on the outside of the outermost signature. → *perfect binding*

side-heads *(gen)* The headings that mark the third division of text within a chapter, subsidiary to shoulder-heads. → *shoulder-heads*

sidelighting *(pho)* Lighting that hits the subject from the side, causing sharp and often very profound shadows.

side notes *(gen)* Notes placed outside the normal type area of a page, usually in the fore-edge margin or occasionally in the gutter.

sides *(fin)* The front and rear boards of a book.

side-sewing *(fin)* A form of bookbinding in which the whole book is sewn in one single section, instead of in individual sections. Books made in this way tend not to lie flat when open.

side sorts *(typ)* In traditional metal typesetting, those characters in a font of type that are less frequently needed and are therefore kept in small boxes at the side of the drawer or case.

side-stitch/stab *(fin)* The process of binding a booklet or pamphlet by stitching the sheets together along the side close to the gutter. If wire is used, this is known as 'sidewiring'.

sidewire/sidewiring *(fin)* → *side-stitch/stab*

siding *(fin)* The process of fitting and/or gluing the cloth or paper sides of a quarter- or half-bound book to the boards.

signal processor *(com)* An electronic effects component or a virtual effects plug-in.

signal-to-noise (ratio)/SN *(aud)* The gap between the strength of the signal and the noise floor. A higher signal-to-noise ratio is best, since noise is less noticeable. SN is measured in decibels.

signature (1) *(pri)* A mark, usually a small capital or a numeral, normally placed in the tail margin at the beginning of each section of a book, which serves as a guide for

Thanks to the optical effect of **simultaneous contrast**, these squares may appear different

This is a view using **simplified geometry**, in this case polygons with no shading

finishing and binding. The term also describes the folded sheet itself.
→ *conjugate leaves; designation marks; section (2)*

signature (2) *(int)* A user-defined 'footer' automatically attached to an e-mail message, identifying its sender.

signature rotary *(pri)* A web-fed rotary letterpress incorporating rubber or plastic plates, used for long print runs.

signature title *(gen)* An abbreviated indication of the author's name and title, printed in the signature line on the first page of each section of a book. Also called a 'catch title'.

signet *(fin)* A ribbon bookmark that is stitched into the binding of a book.

silhouette (halftone) *(gen)* → *cutout (1)*

silkscreen printing *(pri)* A traditional method of 'serigraphic' printing in which ink is forced through a stencil fixed to a screen made of silk. Nowadays the screen is made of synthetic material and the process is generally called 'screen printing'. → *screen printing*

silurian *(pap)* A paper into which small amounts of coloured fibres have been incorporated, giving a flecked effect.

silver nitrate *(pho)* A light-sensitive compound that is a fundamental base of many photographic chemicals.

silverprint *(pho)* A brown-hued photographic print made using silver chloride. → *Vandyke print*

SIMM *(com) abb.*: single in-line memory module. A computer chip that provides RAM.
→ *DIP SIMM; dual-inline memory module (DIMM); random access memory (RAM)*

Simple Mail Transfer Protocol (SMTP) *(int)* A text-based TCP/IP protocol used to transfer mail messages over the Internet.

simplex *(pri)* Printing, photocopying or duplicating on one side of a sheet of paper only. → *duplex*

simplex decal *(pri)* → *decal*

simplified geometry *(com)* The successive simplification of the construction of a 3D object, from a rendered view (most complex) through to the geometry as represented by a set of polygons (most basic).

simultaneous contrast *(gen)* A human perceptual anomaly whereby colours or shapes are affected by surrounding colours or shapes. For example, a red square surrounded by a thick black border will seem brighter than the same red square surrounded by a white border.

sine wave *(aud)* A perfect sound wave in which the positive and negative peaks are equal. Test tone generators can produce these pure waveforms and they are often used for testing purposes.

single-colour press *(pri)* A printing press capable of handling only one colour at a time.

single lens reflex camera *(pho)* → *SLR camera*

single-line halftone *(pre)* A half tone image created with a screen that has uniform parallel lines, as opposed to one with lines crossing at right angles. → *dot shape; halftone screen*

single printing *(pri)* The process of printing a sheet of paper first on one side and then the other. Also called 'work and turn'.
→ *work and turn*

single quotes *(gen)* Single, as opposed to double, inverted commas used in marking quotations in a body of text.

singleton *(int)* An HTML tag without a corresponding closing tag. In modern HTML, virtually all instructions must have opening and closing tags if they are to work properly. For example, a lone <p> is incorrect, while a <p> paired with a closing </p> is correct.

sinkage *(gen)* The amount of space between the top of the page text column and the first line of text in a new chapter.

sit *(com)* The suffix of files that have been compressed using Stuffit, a file compression utility. → *compression (1)*

sitemap *(int)* An outline view of all the pages on a particular website. → *World Wide Web (WWW)*

sixteenmo/16mo *(gen)* A book size generated by folding a sheet with four right-angle folds, forming a page size one sixteenth of the original sheet, with a thirty-two page section. Also known as 'sexto-decimo'.

sixteen sheet *(gen)* A standard poster sheet size of 3050 x 2030mm.

sixty-fourmo/64mo *(gen)* A book size generated (theoretically) by folding a sheet with six right-angle folds, forming a page size one sixty-fourth of the original sheet. Since this is not practically possible, a quarter sheet would be folded four times to arrive at this size.

size *(pap)* A glue-like substance that is applied to paper or used in its manufacture to alter qualities such as absorbency.

sizing (1) *(pap)* Treating paper with size. → *size*

sizing (2) *(gen)* The process of defining the dimensions of enlargement or reduction of a photographic image for reproduction.
→ *scale/scaling*

SKD *(aud) abb.:* Sseyo Koan Design. Native instruction set format of Sseyo's generative music composition program, Koan (now owned by Tao Group). It tells your soundcard what to play, and also builds the 'instrument' to play it.

skeleton black *(pri)* A technique involving the use of black to sharpen contrast and enhance detail in four-colour reproduction. Also called 'halfscale black'. → *full-scale black*

skew(ing) *(com)* A feature built into some graphics applications, allowing type characters or images to be slanted.

skewings *(fin)* Scraps of waste gold leaf left over from the gold blocking process.

skin *(com)* In 3D applications, a surface stretched over a series of 'ribs', such as an aircraft wing.

skinny *(pre)* → *choke*

skylight *(pho)* In a photography setup, light provided by a blue sky as opposed to direct sunlight.

slab/square serif *(typ)* In certain type designs, notably Egyptian, serifs that are of almost the same thickness as the uprights.
→ *Egyptian*

Most image-editing applications can **skew** images

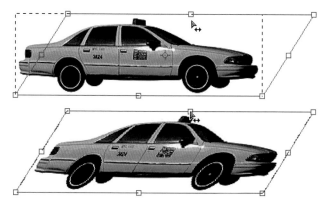

slash *(typ)* An obliquely sloping line, or 'forward slash' (/). Reversal forms a 'backslash' (\). Also called a 'solidus'.

slave unit *(pho)* In a photographic setup, a remote device that responds to the light emitted from a single flash unit, activating additional remote flash units simultaneously.

slice *(pap)* A long, flat, vertical plate, over which pulp is passed during the paper manufacturing process.

slide *(pho)* → *colour transparency (film)*

SLIP *(int)* abb.: serial line Internet Protocol.
→ *serial line Internet Protocol (SLIP)*

slipcase *(gen)* An open-ended box that holds a book or a set of books, their spines remaining visible.

slip page/proof *(gen)* → *galley proof*

slips *(fin)* In the binding of a sewn book, the loose ends of the cords that protrude after sewing. The slips are frayed and then attached to the boards.

slip-sheeting *(pri)* → *interleaved*

slipsheeting *(pri)* Sheets of paper placed between freshly printed pages to prevent set-off. → *set-off*

slit *(pri)* A cut made by a sharp rotary knife on a press, between the impression cylinder and delivery.

slitter *(fin)* A sharp rotary blade, which cuts a moving sheet into strips. → *slit*

sloped roman/type *(typ)* A sloped version of a font or typeface that is based on the roman letterform, as opposed to a specifically designed italic type. → *italic*

slot *(com)* → *expansion slot*

SLR camera *(pho)* A camera that transmits the same image via a mirror to the film and viewfinder, ensuring that you get exactly what you see in terms of focus and composition.

slug (1) *(typ)* In hot metal typesetting, the name for a line of type set as a single piece of metal. → *hot metal (type); Linotype*

slug (2) *(gen)* In newspapers, a single line that indicates that the story is continued on another page, similar to a 'jump line'.
→ *jump line*

slur *(pri)* In printing, the 'skidding', or smudged, appearance of an image, with blurred or doubled halftone dots or characters, a fault that is caused by excessive movement between plate and paper during impression.

slurry *(pap)* → *stuff*

slushing *(pap)* The action of liquidizing or pulping the ingredients in the paper manufacturing process.

small ad *(gen)* → *classified ad(vertisement)*

small capitals/caps *(typ)* Capital letters that are designed to a smaller size than the capitals of the font to which they belong. Many computer applications make provision for small caps, but these are invariably mere reductions in size of the regular capitals, resulting in weight or 'colour' that is too light. Special fonts, called 'expert sets', are available, which have specially designed small caps. → *capital; caps and smalls; even s. caps/even smalls; expert set*

small computer system interface (SCSI) *(com)* pron.: *'skuzzy'*. A computer industry standard for interconnecting peripheral devices such as hard disk drives and scanners.

small pica *(typ)* An old name for a size of type, now standardized as 11 point. → *pica*

smart quotes *(typ)* A feature in many applications that automatically converts inverted commas ('prime' marks) to correct quotation marks by gauging their positions in the text. Also referred to colloquially as 'curly' quotes. → *dumb quotes; primes/ prime marks; quotation/quote marks/ quotes*

smash(ing) *(fin)* The compression of the pages of a finished book, using heavy pressure to expel all air and fully flatten pages and boards. Sometimes called 'nipping', although this term is more correctly applied to books printed on hard paper. → *nipping*

SMF *(aud)* Standard MIDI File. There are three types of this audio file format. Type 0 contains one track of information in one song, Type 1 contains all the original track structure of one song (one track per channel) and Type 2 contains all the original track information for an unlimited number of songs.

smoothing *(com)* The refinement of bitmapped images and text by a technique called 'anti-aliasing' (adding pixels of an 'in-between' tone). Smoothing is also used in some drawing and 3D applications, where it is applied to a path to smooth a line, or to 'polygons' to tweak resolution in the final render. → *antialiasing; polygon*

smoothness *(pap)* The measure of quality of the surface of blemish-free finished paper.

smooth point *(com)* A Bézier control point that connects two curved lines, forming a continuous curve. → *Bézier curve*

smooth washed *(fin)* Ungrained bookcloth, i.e. cloth that is not mechanically grained.

SMPTE (timecode) *(aud)* pron.: 'sum-tee'. This stands for the Society of Motion Picture and Television Engineers. The SMPTE timecode is a standard method of synchronizing both audio and video devices. In a digital process, the software generates the code; in an analog process, the code is 'striped' onto one track of tape. The EBU (European Broadcasting Union) also promotes its own synchronization standards.

SMTP *(int)* abb.: Simple Mail Transfer Protocol. → *POP (2); Simple Mail Transfer Protocol (SMTP); TCP (TCP/IP)*

Smyth sewn/sewing *(fin)* A sewn binding method in which sections of a book are sewn together to give flexibility; the finished book should lie flat when opened at any given page.

snail mail *(gen)* The standard postal system.

snap to *(com)* In many applications, a facility that automatically guides the positioning of items along invisible grid lines, which act like magnets, aiding design and layout.

SND *(aud)* A sound file format found on the Mac.

snoot *(pho)* A cylinder fitted to a photographic light source, throwing a circle of light.

snowflaking *(pri)* Minute white specks in type and solid ink areas in offset printing.

socialware *(com)* Software designed to help users engage in social activities.

socket *(int)* A type of Internet address, which is a combination of an Internet protocol address and a port number, the latter providing the identity of applications such as WWW and FTP. → *FTP; World Wide Web (WWW)*

A studio light with a **snoot** fitted

soft *(pho)* A photographic image with low tonal contrast or a photographic paper specifically designed to produce such images.

softback edition *(gen)* A paperback edition, a cheaper alternative to a hardback edition.

softback/soft cover *(fin)* → *paperback*

soft-box *(pho)* A studio lighting accessory, consisting of a flexible box that attaches to a light source at one end and has a diffusion screen at the other, softening the light and any shadows cast by the subject.

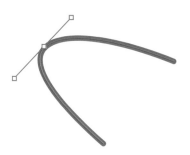

Smooth points act as control points on a Bézier curve

A plain (top) and a **soft focus** (below) image

soft copy (1) *(com)* A copy of a document made as data on a computer disk and viewed on screen, as opposed to a 'hard copy' printout on paper. → *hard copy*

soft copy (2) *(typ)* In traditional typesetting, the term given to copy that is used for checking text prior to final layout. Curiously, the same thing produced nowadays by a computer is referred to as the opposite, i.e. a 'hard copy'.

soft dot *(pre)* A halftone dot on film that is less dense at the edge than at the centre and is thus easier to etch for correction purposes. As distinct from a 'hard dot', which has less tolerance for alteration and is thus used as final film for platemaking. → *final film; halftone (1); hard dot*

soft focus *(pho)* An effect that 'softens' or slightly diffuses the lines and edges of an image without altering the actual focus. Slightly opaque filters are employed. → *diffuse*

soft proof *(com)* A feature in professional publishing and graphics applications whereby the effects of a CMYK or RGB conversion on final output are simulated onscreen as accurately as possible within the gamut limitations of the screen used.

soft-sized *(pap)* Low-grade paper, of the type used for newsprint. Minimal amounts of size and other materials are used in its manufacture.

software *(com)* Specially written 'pieces' of data, called programs, which make it possible for a computer or any other item of computer-related hardware to perform its tasks. Software comes in the form of the 'operating system' and related files ('extensions') that make your computer work, 'utilities' for performing specific day-to-day tasks such as virus-checking and backups, and 'applications' that are used to produce work, whether it be page-layout (Adobe InDesign or QuarkXPress), image

The effect of a **solarize** filter

manipulation (Adobe Photoshop), drawing (Adobe Illustrator or Macromedia FreeHand) or word processing (Microsoft Word). → *hardware*

software developer's kit (SDK) *(com)* A kit containing information and special software to help programmers write programs for a particular software product.

solarize/solarization *(gen)* An effect involving the 'simplification' of colour differences. Subtle changes in colour become flat tones, or are replaced by different colours. Solarization can be achieved digitally or by photographic processing. → *posterize/ posterization*

solid *(pri)* An area printed with 100 per cent of a colour.

solid matter *(typ)* → *set solid*

solidus *(typ)* → *slash*

solus position *(gen)* An advertisement placed on a page on which no others are present.

SONET *(com)* Acronym for synchronous optical network. → *synchronous optical network (SONET)*

sophisticated *(fin)* A book in which a page or pages were found to be missing and have been replaced with those from an identical copy, which can include high-quality photocopied pages.

S

sort (1) *(com)* In certain applications, particularly spreadsheet and database applications, a facility for arranging data into a sequence (e.g. alphabetical or numerical).

sort (2) *(typ)* A character used in text, which is not part of the main font used, such as a 'dingbat' or 'pi' character. ➔ *dingbat; pi character*

sorts *(typ)* ➔ *character (1)*

soundcard *(aud)* A component that adds higher audio functions to a computer system. High-end audio work usually requires an external soundcard that sits outside of the desktop tower or notebook case, so as to minimize the noise inherent in any computer system.

Soundmanager *(aud)* The standard audio driver on all Macs – the Apple counterpart to MME and DirectSound. A solid, swift and reliable system that, in the most recent versions of Mac OS, handles ultra-low latency times with ease.

sound wave *(aud)* A sound or a graphical representation of a sound. ➔ *sine wave*

source (1) *(com)* Any document, file or disk that is original, as opposed to a copy.

source (2) *(com)* Documents, files or disks from which copied, transmitted or linked data originates. As distinct from the 'target', or destination, of such data. ➔ *target*

source code *(int)* The original or base code for a software program or for a web page. ➔ *HTML*

source document *(pre)* Any original used as a master for reproduction.

source volume *(com)* ➔ *source (2)*

space *(typ)* A 'blank' (non-printing) spacer piece, used singly or in multiples, to create the spaces in text. Deriving from metal typesetting, which used graded units of size; a standard word space (called a 'mid' space) measures one quarter of an em, although in computer applications it is sometimes possible to define this to your own preference. ➔ *mid(dle) space; thick space; thin space*

spacer *(int)* A blank, transparent GIF, one pixel wide, used to space elements on a webpage.

spam/spamming *(int)* A colloquial term for an unsolicited e-mail or newsgroup posting, usually advertising material. The term derives from the television comedy show 'Monty Python's Flying Circus' where, in one sketch, a restaurant menu lists food items that can be ordered only if accompanied by 'spam'. ➔ *e-mail; newsgroup; troll/trolling*

SPARC *(com)* Acronym for scalar processor architecture. ➔ *scalar processor architecture (SPARC); UNIX*

S/PDIF (Sony/Phillips Digital InterFace) *(aud)* A high-quality, audio-specific file transfer format that can be used with a variety of digital audio equipment, through an RCA-style connection or an optical cable. It can also be used with specialized speakers.

special character *(typ)* A character obtained by pressing modifier, or combinations of, keyboard keys.

special sorts *(typ)* Characters not usually included in a font of type, such as fractions or ornaments. Also called 'peculiars' or 'pi characters'. Not to be confused with 'pie' type (accidentally mixed type). ➔ *pi font; sort (2)*

spec(ification) *(gen)* A detailed description of the components of a job, product or activity, detailing final requirements, preferred methods by which these are achieved, and so on.

Specifications for Web Offset Publications (SWOP) *(pre)* A system of standards developed for the printing industry to aid consistency in the use of colour separation films and colour proofing.

specimen book *(gen)* A catalogue of a manufacturer's products with actual samples, such as an ink manufacturer's catalogue of colours, normally showing basic colours and often including halftones or a catalogue of typefaces, showing fonts, sizes, etc. → *specimen page/sheet*

specimen page/sheet *(gen)* A page or group of pages printed as a sample to show the design, style of setting, fonts, paper quality and so on.

spectral response/sensitivity *(pho)* The manner or rate in which a light-sensitive component, such as film emulsion, responds to different wavelengths of light, both visible and non-visible.

spectrophotometer *(gen)* Device for measuring emitted or reflected luminous energy at various frequencies throughout the spectrum. Spectral data can be displayed as CMY, density, LAB or XYZ values.

spectrum *(gen)* The series of colours that results when normal white light is dispersed into its component parts by refraction through a prism.

specular highlight *(pre)* The lightest highlighted area in a reproduced photograph, usually reproduced as unprinted white paper.

specular map *(com)* In 3D applications, a texture map – such as those created by noise filters – which is used instead of specular colour to control highlights.

specular reflectance *(gen)* The reflection (as by a mirror) of light rays at an angle equal to the angle at which it strikes a surface (angle of incidence).

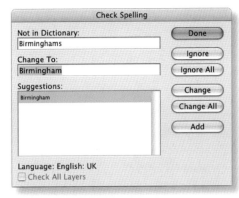

A typical
spell checker

The full **spectrum** of white light

spell(ing) checker *(com)* A facility built into most word processing applications, which uses a built–in dictionary to check for and correct spelling errors.

SPH *(pri) abb.:* sheets per hour. The speed of a printing press.

spherical aberration *(pho)* The failure of a lens to focus light rays exactly at its centre and at its edges.

spherical map(ping) *(com)* A 3D technique of mapping a rectangular image to a sphere. The rectangle first becomes a cylinder, which is then wrapped around a sphere by pinching the top and bottom of the cylinder into single points, or 'poles'.

spider *(int)* A program that tirelessly roams the World Wide Web, gathering and cataloguing information, typically for use by Web search engines. → *information agent; robot; search engine*

spike suppressor *(com)* A device installed in the in-line power supply of computing equipment. Its function is to eliminate power surges and voltage fluctuations. Also called a 'surge suppressor' or 'power filter'.

spine *(fin)* The part of the outer cover of a book that encloses the back, and usually carries the title, author's name, etc. → *binding*

spinner *(gen)* A revolving display stand in a retail outlet.

spiral binding *(fin)* A binding method in which the sections of a book are hole-punched and then held together by a spiral wire coil. Also called 'spirex binding'. → *plastic comb/coil binding; twin-wire binder*

SPL (sound pressure level) *(aud)* Put simply, this is the volume of a sound measured in decibels.

splayed M *(typ)* A character 'M' with outwardly sloping or splayed sides.

spline *(com)* The digital representation of a curved line that is defined by three or more control points, common in 3D applications. → *vector*

split boards *(fin)* Outer cover boards for books, consisting of a thick and a thin board glued together, leaving a split into which endpapers and tapes are inserted. Used for library binding.

split dash/rule *(gen)* A decorative rule, split at its centre with a star or similar ornament, and tapering off at the ends.

split-duct printing/working, split fountain *(pri)* A printing technique involving the use of two or more colours on a normal single-colour press, achieved by dividing the ink duct into sections for the different inks, and preventing mixing on the forme. Also called 'split fountain'.

split fountain *(pri)* → *split-duct printing/ working, split fountain*

split fraction *(typ)* Type for fractions. This comes in two parts, the upper bearing a numeral only, and the lower a numeral and a dividing line above it. → *built fraction*

spoils *(pap)* Sheets of paper with flaws or imperfections. The term spoils is used to describe both printed and unprinted sheets. → *run-in sheets*

spool/spooler/spooling *(com)* Software that intercepts data on its way to another computer or device and temporarily stores it on disk until the target device, such as a printer, is available, thus allowing you to carry on working. As distinct from a 'buffer', which is temporary storage in memory. → *buffer*

spot colour *(pri)* Any colour used for printing, which has been 'custom mixed' for the job, as opposed to one of the four standard process colours.

spot glue *(fin)* Spots of glue used as a temporary fastening to hold gatefolds closed during the binding process, later trimmed off so that the gatefold opens when read.

spotlight (1) *(com)* In 3D applications, a beam of light whose beam is shone as a cone. → *spotlight (2)*

spotlight (2) *(pho)* A photographic lamp that concentrates a controllable narrow beam of light. → *spotlight (1)*

spot meter *(pho)* A specialized light meter, or function of the camera light meter, that takes an exposure reading for a precise area of a scene.

spotting *(pho)* The retouching of photographic film or prints in order to remove tiny blemishes or imperfections. → *retouching*

spot varnishing *(pri)* Selective application of varnish to a sheet after printing, usually for graphic effect. → *varnish*

spray powder *(pri)* A powder-like substance that can be applied to freshly printed work to prevent ink set-off. Also called 'anti-set-off' spray. → *set-off*

spread (1) *(gen)* → *double-(page) spread*

spread (2) *(pre)* One of the 'trapping' techniques (along with 'choke') used in print preparation to ensure that two abutting areas of ink print without gaps. A spread traps a light foreground object to a surrounding dark background by expanding

An example of **spiral binding**

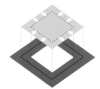

A **split dash** is used for decoration

Here the blue ink has been **spread** over the lighter yellow as part of the trapping process

the edge of the inner object so that the two colours overlap. Because the darker of the two adjacent colours defines the visible edge of the object, it is always preferable to extend the lighter colour into the darker. → *choke; trapping*

spreadsheet *(com)* An application that enables you to make complex calculations to almost any user-defined criteria. A spreadsheet employs a table of rows and columns, and the spaces in the grid, known as 'cells', can be moved and mathematically manipulated. Some spreadsheet applications will also generate graphics (3D in some cases) from the data entered into cells. → *DIF*

sprinkled calf *(fin)* Fine calfskin leather used for book covering in approximately the 17th century. A speckled finish was achieved by sprinkling acid on to the leather.

sprinkled edges *(fin)* A decoration on the cut edges of a book that gives a sprinkled ink effect. Helps to disguise soiling caused by excessive handling, etc.

square back (book) *(fin)* → *flat back(ed) (book)*

square capitals *(typ)* Capital letters adapted from Roman lapidary capitals. They are thick, and finished with wide, square serifs. Also known as 'quadrata'.

Microsoft Excel is a popular **spreadsheet**

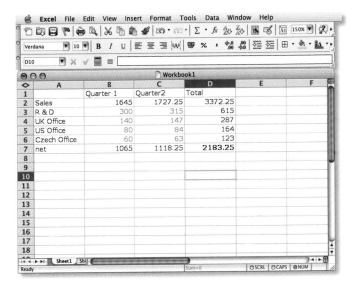

Square corner tool *(com)* A feature of most graphics applications, this is a tool used for drawing squares and rectangles. Also called a 'Rectangle tool'.

square dot *(pre)* A halftone screen in which the dots are square in shape. → *dot shape*

squared(-up) halftone *(pre)* Trimming ('cropping') or resizing a halftone image to a square or rectangular shape, as opposed to a cutout halftone. → *cutout (1)*

square folding *(fin)* A folding technique in which printed sheets are folded with the second fold at right angles to the first, the third to the second, and so on.

squares *(fin)* The portion of the case covers of a book that protrude beyond the edge of the pages when the book is closed, thus protecting the pages themselves.

square serif *(typ)* → *slab/square serif*

squash *(pri)* → *ink squash*

squeegee *(pri)* A blade or paddle device, usually made of rubber or plastic. It forces ink through the open areas of the mesh and stencil in the screen printing process.

SRA paper sizes *(pap)* The designation of untrimmed paper sizes for bleed printing work in the ISO series of paper sizes. → *ISO A-series paper sizes*

sRGB *(gen)* A common RGB colour space with a relatively small gamut, originally designed to characterize a 'typical' PC monitor, but also frequently used as a colour profile for consumer-level digital cameras. sRGB is gaining in popularity, and is not as bad a working space as its limited gamut makes it appear.

S/S *(gen)* abb.: same size. → *same size*

SSL *(int)* abb.: Secure Sockets Library. A programming 'library' devised by Netscape for helping programmers add secure areas to websites. → *https; secure area*

S

stabbing (1) *(fin)* Stapling together a pamphlet or closed section near the back edge.

stabbing (2) *(fin)* Using a sharp tool such as an awl to pierce holes in the side of a section prior to stitching.

stabilization paper *(pho)* Photographic paper used in 'rapid-access' processing (fast processing), the emulsion of which incorporates a developing agent.

stacking order *(com)* The position of items relative to others in front of or behind in graphics applications.

staging out *(pri)* → *stopping out/stop out*

stained edges *(fin)* → *coloured edges/tops*

staircasing/stairstepping *(com)* → *aliasing*

stamp (1) *(typ)* In conventional metal typesetting, the compositor's term for a single piece of type.

stamp (2)/stamping *(fin)* The process of impressing a design into a page or cover, etc. by means of a die pressed with considerable force. Various coloured foils or gold leaf can be used, or the die may be used without colour ('blind', or 'blank' stamping). → *emboss(ing)*

stamping die *(fin)* → *block (2)*

standalone (system) *(com)* The ability of a computer or system to operate independently of others, usually referring to one that is not networked or dependent on other devices.

standard character set *(com)* → *character set*

Standard Generalized Markup Language (SGML) *(int)* An ISO markup standard for defining documents that can be used by any computer, regardless of platform.

standard MIDI file (SMF) *(aud)* → *SMF*

standing time *(gen)* → *open/standing time*

standing type/matter *(pre)* Any material – typeset, film or stored data – that is held over for revision or reprinting.

stapling *(fin)* A binding method that uses one or more pressed wire staples to secure pages.

star *(typ)* A typographical ornament or device. → *dingbat*

starburst *(com)* In some applications, the shape that the pointer assumes when certain transformation tools are selected.

starburst (filter) *(pho)* The photographic effect of light rays radiating from a highlight in lines, achieved by the use of a filter that diffuses light from a strong concentrated source.

star network *(com)* A common network configuration in which every device ('node') is wired directly to a central hub, radiating from it in a star shape. → *network*

star signature *(fin)* The inner 16 pages of a 32-page section, identified by the signature letter followed by a star (e.g. 'A*'). The outer 16 pages are identified by the signature letter alone (e.g. 'A'). → *insert (1)*

start *(fin)* A binding fault that occurs – particularly in books with many sections – when one section or signature is thrown forward of the others, making it difficult to achieve a strong binding.

start bit *(com)* A single bit used in data communication to indicate the beginning of transmission. → *bit; stop bit*

start-of-print line *(pri)* The trim line delineated by the trim marks closest to the gripper edge of the printing plate. → *trim marks*

start time *(com)* In 3D and multimedia applications, the beginning of an animation.

startup *(com)* The process of turning on the power to a computer and the startup procedure it goes through in which certain checks are made. These include checking the RAM and loading the operating system into memory. If there is a fault, it will be reported accordingly, or the computer may fail to start altogether. Also called 'booting up'. → *boot/boot up/booting up; reboot*

STABBING

startup disk *(com)* Any hard drive, floppy disk, zip disk or CD disk containing an operating system and used to start up a computer. Also called a 'boot disk'. → *startup*

startup document *(com)* → *init*

static RAM *(com)* → *DRAM*

stationery *(com)* Any document used as a template, i.e. one that is automatically duplicated on opening, leaving the original intact. → *template (2)*

stationery binding *(fin)* → *letterpress binding*

A browser **status bar** showing progress

status bar *(com)* In most applications, a bar in a dialog box that tells you what is happening – for example, the progress being made during the rendering of an image or the copying of a file.

steel engraving *(pri)* A print made from an engraved steel plate. The process was invented in the early 19th century and used initially for making forgery-proof banknotes. Books illustrated with steel engravings were produced until the 1880s. → *engraving (1)*

stem *(typ)* The main vertical stroke in a text character, such as in a t, p or f.

stencil *(pri)* In screen printing, the material used to prevent ink transferring through the screen to the non-image areas of the paper.

step and repeat *(com)* A method of producing multiple copies of an image at different sizes in defined incremental stages.

step index *(fin)* → *thumb index*

step tablet *(pho)* → *greyscale (1)*

step wedge *(pre)* → *greyscale (1)*

stereography *(pho)* A type of photograph in which two simultaneous exposures are made in such a way as to give the impression of 3D depth.

stereophonic (stereo) *(aud)* Describing sound that is stored and played back using two channels, a left and a right, to resemble sound more closely as we hear it in nature. Surround sound takes this a step further by incorporating more than two speakers to add artificial depth.

stereo(type) *(pri)* A duplicate printing plate made by taking an impression of the original in a mould of plaster of Paris or papier mâché and casting another in lead alloy. → *cliché; electro(type); flong*

stet *(gen)* Derived from the Latin term meaning 'let it stand'. Used by proofreaders when marking up copy to cancel a previous correction.

sticking *(pri)* Sheets of printing paper can stick together if they have been guillotined with a blunt knife or stored incorrectly. Sticking after printing is caused by ink remaining wet on the paper, especially hard surface paper, or sometimes by static electricity.

stickup initial *(typ)* → *raised initial*

stiffened and cut flush *(fin)* → *cut flush*

stiff leaves *(fin)* Endpapers that are glued across the full width of the first and last leaves of a book. → *endpapers*

stigmatypy *(typ)* The technique of making a design or portrait out of small type characters.

stilted covers *(fin)* A description of a book that has been bound in larger covers than necessary in order to make it uniform with the shelf with larger books.

stipple engraving *(pri)* A technique that combines etching and engraving.

S

stitching (1) *(fin)* A binding technique in which all sections of a book are pierced and secured with wire or thread. → *sewing*

stitching (2) *(gen)* In image editing, the process of merging a number of frames to form a larger, usually panoramic, image.

stochastic screening *(pre)* A method of reproducing an image by applying a 'screen' of scattered microdots, each one no larger than a machine dot, and by which 256 greys (or more) can be rendered without varying the dot size. It differs from conventional halftoning in that the dots are not distributed in a grid pattern but placed in accordance with an algorithm that statistically evaluates their distribution within a fixed set of parameters. Stochastic screening offers many advantages over conventional halftone screening, since it eliminates 'moiré' patterns, allows a wider range of colours and does not cause a shift in colours if there is misregister during printing. Also called 'FM (frequency modulated) screening'. → *FM screening; machine dot*

stock (1) *(pap)* The printer's term for the paper to be used in printing.

stock (2) *(pap)* → *stuff*

stock sizes *(pap)* Readily available sizes of printing paper.

stop *(pho)* The aperture size of a camera lens. → *f-number/f-stop*

stop bath *(pho)* An acid solution used to stop the developing process of a photographic negative or print.

stop bit *(com)* In data communication, the bit that indicates the end of one byte. → *asynchronous; start bit*

stopping out/stop out *(pri)* The process of covering with varnish those parts of the etching plate that do not require further etching by acid. Also called 'staging out'.

storage *(com)* The preservation of data (on disk, tape, etc.) so that it can be accessed at a future date, as distinct from 'memory' where data is in transit.

storage media *(com)* → *media (2)*

storage set *(com)* → *backup set*

straight matter *(typ)* A body of continuous running text with no breaks for sub-headings, illustrations, tabulated material, and so on.

strap *(gen)* A sub-heading that appears above the headline in a magazine or newspaper article to identify the subject matter, page or section.

Stitching augments a book's longevity

strawboards *(pap)* Boards traditionally made from straw (now more commonly from pulped waste paper), that are used to make covers of cased books. Strawboards are cheaper than millboard, which is the preferred choice of handbinders. → *millboards*

streak photography *(pho)* A type of photography in which the camera or subject is moved during a long exposure, the resulting image showing a trace of the movement.

A classic example of **streak photography**

streamer *(gen)* A publicity poster (usually a strip of paper) supplied by publishers to booksellers for displaying with copies of a new book. → *crowner*

streaming *(aud)* Term used to describe audio or video that can be listened to (or viewed) at the same time as it is downloaded over the Internet. Due to the limitations of bandwidth, it is usually compressed to a

STITCHING

The pink line represents a calligraphic **stroke**

A painted stroke on a **stroke path**

very low quality so that there is less data to download (or 'buffer') and fewer interruptions required in the broadcast to catch up with the download.

stress *(typ)* The emphasis of a letterform, as perceived in the heaviest part of a curved stroke.

strike on *(typ)* → *cold composition*

strike-on composition *(typ)* → *cold composition*

strike through (1) *(pri)* A fault caused by the oily medium in printing ink soaking through the paper and causing it to become transparent.

strike through (2)/strike thru *(typ)* Type characters with a horizontal rule passing through the centre. Also called 'lined characters' or 'erased characters'.

striking *(typ)* The method used by calligraphers to achieve an elaborate freehand embellishment without the use of underlying guidelines. Perfected in 1605 by Jan van den Velde. Also referred to as 'by command of hand'.

string *(com)* All characters within a given sequence, including spaces and special characters. → *text string*

stripe pitch *(com)* → *dot/stripe pitch*

stripping (1) *(pre)* → *assembly*

stripping (2) *(pre)* Inserting a typeset correction into film or camera-ready art.

stripping up as one *(pre)* In photomechanical reproduction, the process of putting together two or more images in order to combine them as a single piece of film. → *assembly*

strobe *(pho)* abb.: 'stroboscopic' (light). A rapidly repeating flash unit, used for multiple-exposure photographs of moving subjects.

strobe effect *(com)* → *flicker*

stroke (1) *(gen)* A line drawn around or inside a screen object, such as a letter or shape. Strokes may have different widths, colours, styles and/or textures. The opposite of 'fill'.

stroke (2) *(typ)* In calligraphy, the part of a character that can be drawn in a single movement.

stroke path *(com)* The *Stroke Path* command in Photoshop enables a previously constructed path to be painted using one of the painting tools.

strongfold paper *(pap)* Strong paper coated with a surface that will not crack when folded.

stub (1) *(typ)* The first column of text set in a tabular form.

stub (2) *(fin)* The narrow margin of a leaf, which remains when a cancelled page is removed and onto which the correct page is fixed.

stuff *(pap)* The pulp that is poured onto the wire of a fourdrinier machine. Also called 'slurry' or 'stock'. → *fourdrinier; half-stuff*

stuffer *(gen)* A publisher's advertising leaflet, which is 'stuffed' into envelopes when sending other material through the post, or inserted into books sold over the counter.

style (1) *(com)* → *type style*

style (2) *(int)* The rules that control all attributes of a webpage, such as font, alignment or background colour. → *cascading style sheet (CSS); embedded style sheet; style sheet*

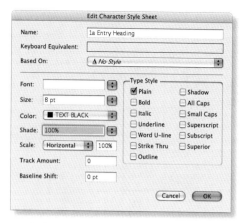

Edit Character Style Sheet

Name: 1a Entry Heading
Keyboard Equivalent:
Based On: △ No Style

Font:
Size: 8 pt
Color: ■ TEXT BLACK
Shade: 100%
Scale: Horizontal 100%
Track Amount: 0
Baseline Shift: 0 pt

Type Style
☑ Plain   ☐ Shadow
☐ Bold   ☐ All Caps
☐ Italic   ☐ Small Caps
☐ Underline   ☐ Superscript
☐ Word U-line   ☐ Subscript
☐ Strike Thru   ☐ Superior
☐ Outline

Cancel   OK

style library *(gen)* A collection of preset styles or templates, which may contain fonts, colours, layouts, animations and effects.

style sheet *(com)* In applications such as those used for page-layout and graphics and the construction of HTML pages, the facility to apply a range of specific, frequently used attributes such as typographic or graphic formats to text and graphic elements in a document. → *format (2)*

stylus *(com)* The pen-like pointing device used with digitizing tablets, replacing the mouse. → *digitizing tablet/pad*

subdirectory *(com)* Any directory that is secondary to the principal, or 'root', directory. → *root directory/level*

subdomain *(int)* → *Domain Name Service (DNS)*

sub-head/sub-heading *(gen)* A secondary heading after a headline or chapter heading, usually rendered in less prominent type. → *cross-head*

subject *(gen)* The general term used to denote any single image that is originated or reproduced.

submenu *(com)* → *hierarchical menu*

subscript *(com)* → *inferior character*

subsidiaries *(gen)* Those sections found at the end of a book, including the appendix, glossary, bibliography and index.

subsidy publishing *(gen)* → *vanity publishing*

substance *(pap)* → *paper substance*

substrate *(pap)* A general term for the material (paper, card, cloth, etc.) that receives a printed image by means of inked type or an inked plate.

subtitle *(gen)* A phrase that follows the title, offering a brief explanation of the subject matter.

subtractive *(pri)* The colour model describing the primary colours of reflected light: cyan, magenta and yellow (CMY). Subtractive colours form the basis for printed process colours. → *CMY*

subtractive colour mixing *(pri)* The colour model describing the primary colours of reflected light: cyan, magenta and yellow (CMY). Subtractive colour mixing is the basis of printed colour.

suction feed *(pri)* A device on a printing press that uses air suction to deliver sheets to the press.

suitcase file *(com)* A font file (TrueType) on computers running Mac OS, screen font file (PostScript 'Type 1'), or collection of sound files, represented by an icon of a suitcase. → *TrueType; Type 1 font*

sunken cords *(fin)* A binding process invented in the 16th century and still used in a modified form for handbound books. Cords or leather thongs are laid in grooves made across the assembled sections of the book. After sewing and lacing to the boards, the spine of the book is flat. → *recessed cords*

sunken flexible *(fin)* A method of sewing the sections of a book, in which grooves are made and thin cords inserted, which are then completely encircled with the sewing thread.

Editing the **style library** in Adobe InDesign

System

Helvetica

Mac OS (Classic) **suitcase** icons

STYLE LIBRARY

The effect of a **surface geometry** render

An ornamental **swelled dash**

sunk joints *(fin)* → *French joints*

super *(fin)* The US term for 'mull'. → *mull*

super-calender *(pap)* A machine that consists of a series of heated metal rollers through which paper is passed to give it a high gloss finish. → *calender*

super-calendered paper *(pap)* Paper that has been through a series of heated metal rollers called a super-calender to give it an extra smooth finish. → *super-calender*

superior character *(typ)* A figure or letter that is smaller than the text size and aligned with the height of the capitals. Superior characters are distinct from superscript, which appears above capital height. Also called 'cock-up figures', 'cock-up letters', 'superior figures' or 'superior letters'. → *inferior character; superscript*

superior figure *(typ)* → *superior character*

superior letter *(typ)* → *superior character*

superscript *(typ)* Figures or letters that are smaller than the text size and raised above the height of capital letters. As distinct from 'superior characters', which are aligned at capital letter height. → *subscript; superior character*

SuperVGA (SVGA) *(com)* A video display standard that supports 256 colours or more in a variety of resolutions. → *monitor*

supplement *(gen)* Additional printed material forming part of a related work and issued at the same time, usually with its own title page and cover.

support *(gen)* After-sales assistance from a product supplier.

supra *(gen)* → *vide*

surface *(com)* In 3D applications, the matrix of control points and line end points underlying a mapped texture or colour.

surface geometry *(com)* In 3D applications, the geometry that underlies a surface, becoming visible when a surface is simplified.

surface mapping *(com)* → *texture mapping/ surface mapping*

surface paper *(pap)* → *coated paper*

surface sizing *(pap)* The application of size to paper during the manufacturing process. Both sides of the paper are treated at the 'waterleaf' stage when the sheet or web has been formed. The size is applied to the paper in a size press. → *waterleaf*

surge suppressor *(com)* → *spike suppressor*

surprinting *(pri)* → *overprint (1)*

surround sound *(aud)* Six or more-channel sound: left, centre, right, left surround, right surround, plus a low-frequency effects channel. It is essentially quadrophonic, plus the centre and low-frequency (bass boost, subwoofer) channels.

SVGA *(com) abb.:* SuperVGA. → *SuperVGA (SVGA)*

S-VHS (Super VHS) *(aud)* While VHS is an acronym for Video Home System, Super VHS offers 20-bit audio and can also be used in ADAT machines.

swash characters *(typ)* Ornamental italic characters with decorative tails and embellishments. For example, certain Caslon Old Face italic characters.

swatch *(gen)* A colour sample.

sweep *(com)* The process of creating a 3D object by moving a profile along a path.

swelled dash/rule *(gen)* Ornamental rules for dividing up text, particularly on a title page. Originating in 18th century typography, the swelled rule is characterized by a thickening in the centre of the rule. Also called a 'French dash'.

SWF *(int) abb.:* Shockwave Flash. Macromedia's proprietary file format for animations created in Flash. → *Flash*

SWOP *(pre)* Acronym for Specifications for Web Offset Publications. → *Specifications for Web Offset Publications (SWOP)*

SYLK *(com) abb.:* symbolic link. A file format for transferring spreadsheet data between applications.

symbol *(gen)* A figure, sign or letter that represents an object, process or activity. A computer icon, for example, is a pictorial symbol. ➔ *pictogram/pictograph; icon*

symmetrical point *(com)* A Bézier control point that connects two curved lines, forming a continuous curve. Also called a 'curve point'. ➔ *Bézier curve*

synchronous communication/ transmission *(com)* High-speed data transmission where data is sent in chunks between rigid electronic timing signals.

synchronous optical network (SONET) *(int)* A high-speed digital transmission system, capable of transmitting large amounts of data at high speed.

synopsis *(gen)* A concise version of a longer work, which conveys only the essential information.

syntax *(com)* The arrangement of words, showing their grammatical relationship. In programming languages, such as those used for creating multimedia presentations and HTML documents for the Web, syntax describes the correct use of the language according to a given set of rules. ➔ *HTML; syntax checker*

syntax checker *(com)* A program that checks a programmer's use of a particular programming language against the rules set for that language. ➔ *syntax*

synthesis *(aud)* This refers to the process of creating or developing sounds. There are many types of synthesis, including additive (constructs sounds by combining various simple waves), subtractive (filters a complex waveform to achieve a desired result), granular (putting a variety of short sound samples together to form a longer, more complex sound), amplitude modulation

(source signal multiplied by a simple positive signal), ring modulation (like AM but multiplied with a more complex bipolar modulation signal), frequency modulation (oscillating the frequency of the source signal), wavetable (similar to sampling, but in this case a sustainable portion of the sound that can be held) and physical modelling (very complex but closer to the actual creation of the sound that is being synthesized).

A group of **symbols**

synthesizer *(aud)* Synthesizers began as analog instruments that used oscillators to generate tones and a variety of other components to modify those tones, but most of these sounds can now be reproduced fairly accurately using digital emulators. Most virtual synthesizers or even the stand-alone electronic synths use the same analog-style parameters to create and modify sounds.

sysop *(int)* Acronym for 'system operator'. The operator of a bulletin board service. ➔ *bulletin board service (BBS)*

system *(com)* The complete configuration of software and hardware components necessary to perform electronic processing operations.

system disk *(com)* A disk containing all the files of an operating system necessary to start up the computer and carry out processing operations.

system error *(com)* ➔ *crash (1)*

system extension *(com)* ➔ *extension (1)*

System Folder *(com)* On computers running the Mac OS, specifically versions prior to Mac OS X, a folder that contains all the files, including System and Finder files, necessary for running the operating system. Also called the 'blessed folder'. ➔ *operating system*

system heap *(com)* ➔ *heap*

system operator *(int)* ➔ *sysop*

system software *(com)* ➔ *operating system*

Tt

T1 *(int)* A high-speed digital communications link that runs at 1.544Mbps. → *megabit (Mb/Mbit)*

tab-delimit *(com)* To separate elements of data, such as records or fields in a database, using the 'tab' key. → *comma-delimit*

tab index *(gen)* An index guide similar to a 'thumb index' except that the reference guides, or tabs, project from the pages of the book instead of being cut into them. → *thumb index*

table (1) *(fin)* → *bed (2)*

table (2) *(int)* The arrangement of information in 'cells' on a webpage, which are organized in rows and columns, similar to a spreadsheet. → *spreadsheet*

tablet *(com)* → *digitizing tablet/pad*

tabloid *(gen)* A page that is half the size of a 'broadsheet' or 'broadside'. → *broadside/broadsheet*

tab stop *(com)* The place at which the text insertion point stops when the 'Tab key' is pressed.

tabular work *(typ)* Type matter set in columns.

tabulate *(typ)* To arrange text or figures in the form of rows and columns, according to fixed measures.

tack *(pri)* The degree of 'stickiness' of printing ink, i.e. the degree to which it will divide ('split') between two surfaces so that some prints on the substrate (without damaging it) while some remains on the printing surface. → *delamination; viscosity*

An example of a
tab index

tag (1) *(com)* The formal name for a formatting command in a markup language such as HTML or XML. A tag is switched on by placing a command inside angle brackets '< >' and switched off again by repeating the same command but inserting a forward slash before the command. For example, <bold> makes text that follows appear in bold and </bold> switches the bold style off. → *markup (2); metacharacter; singleton*

tag (2) *(gen)* A colour profile embedded in a digital image for colour management purposes. A 'tagged' image is one that contains a profile.

tagged image file format (TIFF/TIF) *(com)* → *TIFF/TIF*

tail *(gen)* The bottom edge of a book, or the margin at the foot of a page.

tail band *(fin)* → *head/tail band*

tail-end hook *(pri)* → *back edge curl/tail-end hook*

tail margin *(gen)* → *feet/margin*

tail-piece *(gen)* A design, or graphic, at the end of a section, chapter or book.

take *(typ)* The portion of a manuscript that a compositor sets at one time.

take back *(typ)* An instruction to take back characters, words or lines to the preceding line, column or page. → *take over/take forward*

take down *(fin)* The process of disassembling a book into its original component parts prior to rebinding it.

take in *(gen)* An instruction to include additional copy supplied.

take over/take forward *(gen)* An instruction to take over characters, words or lines to the following line, column or page. Also referred to as 'carrying over'.

tall copy *(pri)* A book that has been printed with larger head and foot margins than others in the same print run. → *narrow copy*

tangent line *(com)* In a 3D environment, a line passing through a control point of a spline at a tangent to the curve. The tangent line is used to adjust the curve. → *spline*

tanned leather *(fin)* The traditional process of converting an animal skin into leather by soaking it in an infusion of the bark of an oak tree, staining it a dark brown.

tape drive *(com)* A device used for copying data from a primary storage device, such as a hard disk, for backup archiving purposes. A tape drive uses magnetic tape housed in removable cartridges. Tape drives are not used for primary storage because the data is stored on them 'sequentially' (in a linear form, from end to end), and cannot be accessed at random, as it can on disks.

taper *(com)* Referring to graduated tones and colours, the progression of one tone or colour to the next.

taper angle *(com)* The direction in which graduated tones or colours merge into one another.

Targa *(com)* A digital image format for 24-bit image files, commonly used by computer systems in the MS-DOS environment that contain the 'Truevision' video board.

target *(com)* A description of where documents, files or disks are being copied, transmitted, or linked to, as distinct from the source, from whence they originated. Also known as the 'destination'.
→ *source (2)*

target document *(com)* → *target*

target printer *(com)* The device that a document is sent to for printing. → *target*

TCP (TCP/IP) *(int) abb.:* Transmission Control Protocol/Interface Program (or Internet protocol). → *Transmission Control Protocol (TCP)*

TDMA *(com) abb.:* time division multiple access. → *time division multiple access (TDMA)*

TDM/HTDM *(aud) abb.:* (Host) Time Division Multiplexing. Describes the Digidesign architecture beneath its Pro Tools software and hardware environment (available for both Mac/PC). The HTDM evolution allows compatible virtual instruments and plug-ins to be bolted onto the Pro Tools family. In the Mac OS X environment, non-TDM-compatible instruments may work with the use of the authorizing system iLok.

A typical external **tape drive** for backups

tear-off menu *(com)* In some applications, a menu that can be 'torn' away from the menu bar by dragging it onto the desktop, where it can be moved around as you need it. → *floating palette*

tear sheet *(gen)* A page removed from a publication and used or filed for future reference.

technical camera *(pho)* A view camera that is similar in basic construction to a field camera, but of metal and made with greater precision. → *field camera; view camera*

t.e.g. *(fin) abb.:* top edge gilt. → *top edge gilt*

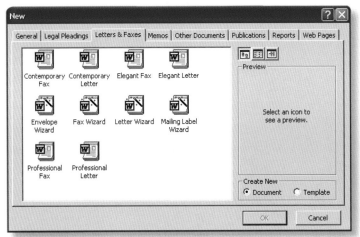

Microsoft Word includes a number of standard document **templates**

Telecine *(aud)* The conversion of film to a TV or video format.

telecommunications *(com)* The transmission of data by any means, but primarily via telephone lines.

telephoto lens *(pho)* A photographic lens with a long focal length, enabling distant objects to be enlarged but with a limited depth of field. → *long-focus lens; mirror lens; zoom lens*

television service provider (TVSP) *(int)* A company that connects the subscriber to the Internet via a TV and set top box. → *netTV*

Telnet *(int)* The Internet standard protocol that enables you to connect to a remote computer and control it as if you were there, even if you are thousands of miles away from it. → *dumb terminal*

tempera *(gen)* A type of paint in which the pigment is bound by egg yolk rather than by gum or oil.

temp file *(com)* A temporary file, used by the application that created it.

template (1) *(gen)* A shape used as a drawing aid.

template (2) *(com)* A document that has been created with prepositioned text and images, used as a basis for repeatedly creating other similar documents. → *master page; stationery*

tempo *(aud)* The rate or pace of a piece of music. In digital audio, this is usually measured in BPM (beats per minute).

tenant *(int)* People who administer a website that is located on another person's server, typically one belonging to an Internet Service Provider (ISP). → *Internet Service Provider (ISP)*

tensile strength *(pap)* The ability of paper to withstand breaking. → *mullen tester*

terabyte *(com)* 1024 gigabytes or 1,048,576 megabytes of data. → *gigabyte (GB/G/gig); kilobyte (KB/Kbyte); megabyte*

terminal *(com)* Any device used to communicate with another computer via a network. → *network*

terminal emulation *(int)* Software that allows your computer to mimic another (remote) computer by acting as a terminal for the other machine – in other words, it is as though you are actually working on that remote computer. → *terminal*

terminator/terminating resistor *(com)* → *SCSI terminator*

tertiary *(gen)* The resulting colour when two secondary colours are mixed.

text (1) *(typ)* Information rendered as readable characters.

text (2) *(gen)* Typeset matter forming the main body of a publication.

textbook *(gen)* A book about a particular subject, designed for study.

text box *(com)* In frame-based applications, a container in which text can be entered and edited.

text chain *(com)* A set of linked text boxes, with text flowing from one to another. → *text box*

4 | 5 | 6 | 7 | 8 | 9

The do-it-yourself displacement map operates on the same basis as the built-in version. Here the intention was to make one large 'lens', rather than tiling the same effect overall. In this sequence, one letter

only is used to demonstrate the technique. Imported type *(4)* was placed in a channel, resized and moved to fit the background image. Additionally, the word was split to allow for the loss of image in

the gutter of the book *(below left)* – not a problem with a web page. A duplicate of the type channel was created, and the image blurred *(5)* with Gaussian blur, set at 15 pixels in this case. A selection was then

made of the hard-edged t inverted to se type backgrou and used to sh the edge of th blurred versi filling the se with black (channel was

Arrows indicating the links in a **text chain**

text editor *(com)* Any application, such as a word processing application, used to enter and edit text.

text field *(com)* Any 'field', such as in a dialog box or database record, into which you enter text. → *field; lookup field*

text file *(com)* A file containing only ASCII text data, with no formatting, which can be 'read' on any operating system.

textile bindings *(fin)* Traditional bookbindings made from fabrics such as silk brocade and velvet, which are sometimes embroidered.

text insertion bar *(com)* → *insertion point*

text inset *(com)* A user-specified measurement that defines the space between the text box or column and the text frame or box.

text letter *(typ)* Traditional black or gothic letterforms. → *black letter*

text marker *(typ)* In word processing applications, a symbol or string of characters positioned in the text to provide a reference marker so that you can return there instantly (by using the 'Find' command). 'XXX' is common since no words contain three 'Xs' – unless you design for the brewing industry. Also called a 'wildcard'.

text mode *(int)* → *character/text mode*

text path *(com)* An invisible line, either straight, curved or irregular, along which text can be forced to flow.

text reflow *(typ)* → *reflow*

text retrieval terminal *(typ)* In typesetter's parlance, a device, such as a disk or tape, used to transfer data from one computer to another. Referred to colloquially as a 'milking machine' or 'fart box'.

text string *(com)* Strictly speaking, any sequence of type characters, but often used to distinguish actual text from that which contains formatting instructions. → *string*

text tool *(com)* → *I-beam pointer*

text type/matter *(typ)* Any typeface of a suitable size for printing a body of text, usually in a range of 8pt to 14pt. Also called 'composition sizes'. → *composition size(s)*

texture filtering *(com)* A method for improving (or reducing) the quality of textures for use in 3D programs.

texture mapping/surface mapping *(com)* In 3D environments, the technique of wrapping a 2D image around a 3D object. → *cubic mapping*

Text following a **text path**

text wrap *(typ)* → *runaround/run round*

thermal ink jet *(com)* → *bubblejet printer*

thermal printer *(com)* A device that uses a heat-sensitive paper to produce an image, sometimes found in older fax machines.

thermal transfer *(com)* A method of transferring an image by melting wax-based ink on a ribbon.

thermography *(pri)* A printing process that emulates die stamping (but without embossing), in which sheets are printed with a sticky ink or varnish and then dusted with a fine, pigmented powder that forms a raised surface when fused to the paper by heat. → *die stamping*

thermoplastic binder *(fin)* A device used for adhesive binding.

thesaurus *(gen)* From the Greek *thesauros* meaning 'treasure', a reference book first published in 1852, which lists words in related groups. It has long been associated with, and devised by, Peter Mark Roget. In the recent past, a thesaurus has been included in many word-processing applications and typically contains synonyms and antonyms as well as definitions.

thickening *(pri)* The spreading of ink on a litho plate beyond the image areas. → *ink spread; spread (2)*

thickness copy *(gen)* → *bulking dummy*

thick space *(typ)* In traditional metal typesetting, a word space measuring one-third of an em. → *thin space*

thin *(pho)* → *underexpose/underexposure*

thin space *(typ)* In traditional metal typesetting, a word space measuring one-fifth of an em. → *thick space*

third-party *(gen)* → *OEM*

thirty-twomo/32mo *(pap)* A sheet cut or folded to one thirty-secondth of its basic size.

thirty-two sheet *(gen)* A standard poster size, measuring 3040 x 4060mm (120 x 160in).

thread (1) *(int)* Postings to an online newsgroup or e-mail distributions on a theme or subject in which a group of subscribers have a particular interest. The messages are usually followed by any replies, and the replies to those replies.

thread (2) *(fin)* The material used to 'sew' books together.

threadless binding *(fin)* A binding method in which the leaves of a book are trimmed at the back and glued, but not sewn. Also called 'unsewn binding'. → *adhesive binding; perfect binding*

three-colour black *(pri)* The black that would theoretically result from overprinting solids of cyan, magenta and yellow. In practice, however, this process often produces a dark brown.

three-colour (process) reproduction *(pri)* The now defunct method of printing using the three process colours – cyan, magenta and yellow – but without black. The four-colour process, with black used to add density, is now the norm. → *four-colour process*

three-quarter bound *(fin)* A method of bookbinding in which cloth- or paper-covered sides are partially overlaid with another material, typically leather, covering the spine and a good part of the sides. → *corners (2); half-bound/binding; quarter-bound*

threshold *(gen)* A set level designed to limit the values or settings used in a project, or show up where the project goes beyond those limits. For example, a threshold might be used to show where chroma levels go beyond legal colour boundaries.

*!?

through-the-lens (TTL) meter *(pho)* An exposure meter built into a camera that calculates an exposure based on the amount of light passing through the camera lens.

throughput (1) *(com)* A unit of time measured as the period elapsing between the start and finish of a particular activity. For example, the amount of data that is passed along a communications line in a given period of time.

throughput (2) *(pri)* A unit of time measured as the period elapsing between the start and finish of a particular job, expressed in units per hour or per minute, such as impressions or pages.

throw in *(fin)* ➔ *insert (2)*

thrown clear *(fin)* A method of adding folded illustrations to a book, usually maps, plans or equipment diagrams, which are printed alongside a blank page (called a 'guard') and which open out entirely beyond the page area for ease of reference. ➔ *fold out*

thrown out *(fin)* ➔ *fold out*

thrust *(fin)* ➔ *binder's creep*

thumb edge *(gen)* The outside edge of a book, opposite the spine.

thumb index *(fin)* An index guide in a book, in which steps are cut down the fore-edges of the page to provide a reference guide to the contents. Also called a 'step index'.
➔ *tab index*

thumbnail (1) *(gen)* A miniature rough layout of a design or publication, showing a possible treatment or the order of chapters, etc.

thumbnail (2) *(com)* A small representation of an image used mainly for identification purposes in a file browser or, within Photoshop, to illustrate the current status of layers and channels.

tied letters *(typ)* ➔ *ligature*

ties *(fin)* Tapes or ribbons fixed to the covers of a book, which, when tied, stop it from opening.

TIFF/TIF *(com)* Acronym for Tagged Image File Format. A standard and popular graphics file format originally developed by Aldus (now merged with Adobe) and Microsoft, used for scanned, high-resolution, bitmapped images and colour separations. The TIFF format can be used for black-and-white, greyscale and colour images that have been generated on different computer platforms.

tight *(gen)* A general design term describing a design, or text, that is very closely-packed and with little blank space.

tight back *(fin)* A rarely used method of bookbinding, in which the body of the book (book block) is glued directly to the spine, so no hollow is formed.

tile/tiling (1) *(com)* The repetition of a graphic item, with the repetitions placed side-by-side in all directions so that they form a pattern just like tiles.

tile/tiling (2) *(pri)* The printing of a document that is larger than the maximum size paper the printer can accommodate. The document is printed on several pieces of paper, to be assembled by hand to form a whole image.

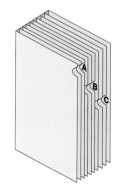

A **thumb index** is sometimes used in reference books

In this print dialog box, **tiling** is indicated by the lines in the preview

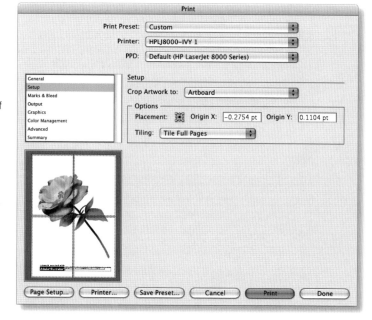

tilt *(com)* In a 3D environment, a camera that performs vertical pans (up and down) about its horizontal axis. ➔ *camera moves*

time division multiple access (TDMA) *(com)* A communications protocol for sending multiple signals along a single line.

time exposure *(pho)* A photographic exposure of several seconds or more.

timeline *(com)* In 3D animation applications, this refers to the display of the duration of a sequence in frames per second. Also refers to the time reference meter along which audio elements are arranged in most music software. In video editing, it represents the workspace in which audio and video clips can be placed or layered on top of each other in order to assemble a project.

time scale *(com)* In a 3D animation, a method of displaying key frames within a score.

time-slicing *(com)* Dividing time into small chunks in order to get several things done at once (actually a delusion, since the aggregate time is the same). On a computer, however, time-slicing works more efficiently if the central processing unit is involved rather than yourself. A computer can usually run two or more applications at the same time, appearing to work on them simultaneously by switching processing time very rapidly from one to the other. ➔ *multitasking*

time-stretching *(aud)* The analogous process to beat matching/mapping. ➔ *Beat matching/mapping*

time value *(com)* In a 3D animation, a value given to a key frame, comprising the animation value and the motion style.

time zero *(com)* The start point for a 3D animation sequence.

tint (1) *(gen)* The resulting shade after white is added to a solid colour.

tint (2) *(pre)* ➔ *halftone tint*

tinting *(pri)* The effect of ink bleeding into the dampening solution on a litho press, causing unwanted artefacts to appear on the non-image areas.

tint sheet *(gen)* A preprinted sheet of halftone tints, patterns and other designs that are cut and pasted onto camera-ready artwork. ➔ *mechanical tint; Zip-a-tone/Zipatone*

tip in/on, tipped in/on *(pri)* A page or image inserted separately into a book and secured by pasting one edge.

tissue *(gen)* Transparent paper that overlays a design, with instructions for reproduction. Also called an 'overlay'. ➔ *layout*

title *(int)* Text that appears in the titlebar of a webpage.

title bar *(com)* The bar at the top of an open window, which contains its name. The window can be moved around the desktop by dragging its title bar. ➔ *menu bar*

title page *(gen)* The page, normally a right-hand page, at the front of a book, which gives its title, the name of the author, the publisher and any other relevant information.

title signature *(pri)* An identification, marked with a 'B' or '2', on the second sheet of a book, indicating that there is a preceding sheet (the 'title sheet'), which may be unmarked.

title verso (t/v) *(gen)* The verso (back) of the title page of a book, usually containing copyright information. ➔ *title page; verso*

titling (alphabet) *(typ)* ➔ *full face*

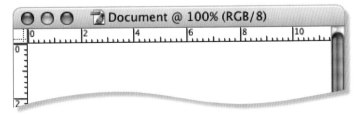

The **title bar** is at the top of the window

TITLING (ALPHABET)

TM *(gen) abb.:* trademark. → *trademark (TM)*

T-marks *(pre)* → *register marks/ registration marks*

toggle *(com)* Those buttons, menus and checkboxes that switch between off and on each time you select or click on them.

token ring *(com)* A method of linking computers in a ring network, now rarely used. Data can be sent from one to another only after a digital code or token is transmitted from one computer to the next. → *LAN; WAN*

tonal colour *(typ)* The general effect of darkness or lightness on a page of printed text, affected by the choice of typeface, leading, margins, etc.

tonal value/tone value *(gen)* The relative densities of tones in an image.

tone compression *(pri)* The inevitable consequence of printing an image, resulting in a reduction of the range of tones from light to dark.

tone correction *(com)* → *gamma correction*

toned paper *(pap)* Paper with a slight colour cast.

tone-line process *(pre)* A conventional technique of producing a line image from a continuous tone original by combining negative and positive film. Now done with software. Not to be confused with combination line and halftone.
→ *combination line and halftone*

toner *(com)* The plastic powder used in laser printers and photocopiers to produce an image.

tone separation *(gen)* → *posterize/ posterization*

toning *(pho)* Adding a brown or blue (usually) tone to a photographic print.

tool *(com)* A feature of most graphics applications, with which you perform specific tasks. A tool is a function represented by an icon that, when selected, is then used to perform the designated task.

toolbar *(com)* Some image-editing applications, such as Photoshop, in addition to the toolbox, feature a toolbar. This permits additional settings to be made to certain tools. → *toolbox*

toolbox *(gen)* The name given to the main tool window in many applications.

Toolbox *(com)* The part of the Mac OS written into the ROM chip that handles such things as dialog boxes, windows, fonts, mouse, keyboard and so on.

tooling *(fin)* Impressing or laying decorations and lettering onto book covers. → *deep gold*

tool palette *(com)* → *tool; toolbox*

tooth *(pap)* The ability of the surface of a paper to hold a painting, drawing or printing medium.

top and tails *(pri)* A traditional printer's description of preliminary and subsidiary matter.

top edge gilt *(fin)* The application of gilding to only the top edge of a book. → *gild*

topical head *(gen)* → *headline (1)*

top side *(pap)* → *felt side*

total harmonic distortion (THD) *(aud)* Absolute tape saturation or circuit overload. Three per cent THD is the point at which tape saturation or circuit overload introduces audible distortion. Three per cent THD is measured in the number of decibels above 0 dB at which this distortion occurs, normally using a 1-kHz (mid-range) reference signal. The gap between 0 dB and 3 per cent THD is called 'headroom', while the gap between the noise floor and 3 per cent THD is its overall dynamic range.

TOYO Colors *(pri)* A system of specifying spot colours, mainly used in Japan.

TPD *(com) abb.:* two-page display. → *two-page display (TPD)*

tps *(fin) abb.:* trimmed page size. → *finished page area; trimmed page size (tps)/ trimmed size*

The Adobe Photoshop **Toolbox**

TM

track (1) *(com)* The concentric 'rings' circumscribing a 'platter' in a hard disk drive, on which data is stored. Each track is divided into 'sectors'. → *platter; sector*

track (2) *(com)* In a film or animation sequence, a method of storing information relevant to a particular property, such as sounds. ('soundtrack').

track (3) *(pri)* The printing line from the front edge of a plate to the back. Items imposed in track will all be subject to the same inking adjustments on press.

trackball *(com)* A device that replaces the mouse, actually resembling an upturned mouse. You move the pointer by manipulating the ball. The device remains stationary, thus occupying less desk space than the conventional mouse.

tracking (1) *(com)* The adjustment of space between characters in a selected piece of text. As distinct from 'kerning', which involves only pairs of characters.

tracking (2)/tracking shot *(com)* In video and 3D animation, the smooth movement of a camera past its subject whilst remaining parallel to it. Also called a 'trucking shot'. → *camera moves*

trackpad *(com)* A device found on portable computers that replaces a mouse. The pad is sensitive to finger movements, which control the position of the cursor on screen.

trade binding *(fin)* → *publisher's binding*

trade books *(gen)* A general term describing adult fiction and non-fiction, paperbacks and children's books, as distinct from educational textbooks, scientific and technical manuals. → *trade edition*

trade edition *(gen)* An edition of a book – generally a trade book – sold to the book trade at the wholesale price. → *trade books*

trademark (™) *(gen)* A name or logo identifying a product or service and linking it to its maker or supplier. Trademarks are usually identified by an adjacent '™' or '®', meaning that the mark is registered.

tranny/trannies *(pho)* → *colour transparency (film)*

transduction *(aud)* The process by which electronic signals are converted to acoustic signals, as with a loudspeaker; it also applies to when the process is reversed, as with a microphone.

transfer *(pri)* → *decal*

transfer lettering *(gen)* → *dry transfer lettering*

transfer paper *(pri)* The substrate that contains an inked impression that will become the printing form for litho printing. → *form (2)/forme*

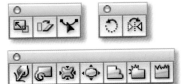

Transformation tool *(com)* In some applications, the name given to tools that change the location or appearance of an item, such as 'scale' or 'reflection'.

transient font *(typ)* An automatically downloaded font that lasts in a laser printer's memory only until the document currently being printed has finished. As distinct from a so-called 'permanent' font, which is permanent only for as long as the printer is switched on.

transition *(com)* A visual effect that blends two or more frames of an animation, video or sound. The most common transition is a dissolve (also known as a mix or crossfade). Other transitions include wipes (linear, rectangular and circular) and DVEs.

transitional *(typ)* A classification of typefaces that are neither old face nor modern, such as Baskerville and Fournier. → *Vox classification*

An assortment of
Transformation tools

*!?

T

TRANSITIONAL

translator *(com)* An application or operating system extension, which translates a document created by one application or operating system into a document that can be used by another.

translucent *(gen)* A material, with a property anywhere between transparent and opaque, that partially obscures the image beyond – frosted glass, for example.

Transmission Control Protocol (TCP) *(int)* The industry standard developed by the US Department of Defense for providing data communication between computers, such as across the Internet. It ensures reliability by retransmitting lost and corrupted data packets, and ensures that an application on the receiving end of a TCP connection will receive bits and bytes in the same order in which they were sent.

transmission copy *(pre)* An original such as a transparency, reproduced by means of transmitted light.

transparency (1) *(pho)* → *colour transparency (film)*

transparency (2) *(gen)* A degree of transparency applied to a pixel so that, when the image is used in conjunction with others, it can be seen through. Only some file formats allow for transparency, including TIFFs (which define transparency as an alpha channel), or GIFs, which allow only absolute transparency.

transparent *(com)* Any software or hardware item that operates without interaction on your part – apart from installing it in the first place.

transparent background *(int)* → *transparent GIF*

transparent GIF *(int)* A feature of the 'GIF89a' file format, which lets you place a non-rectangular image on the background colour of a webpage. → *GIF; interlaced GIF*

transpose/transposition *(gen)* To exchange the position of any two items of text, or two images, either by design or because they are in the wrong order.

trapping *(pre)* The slight overlap of two colours to eliminate gaps that may occur between them due to the normal fluctuations of registration during printing. Also refers to printing an ink colour before the previous one has dried – also called 'wet trapping'. → *choke; dry trapping; spread (2)*

trend chart *(gen)* A method of recording and evaluating the performance of a process such as a press or printing plant. Also called a 'run chart'.

trichromatic *(gen)* Comprising three colours.

trim *(fin)* To cut printed sheets to the required size.

trim curve *(com)* In a 3D environment, a curve on the surface of one object where it is intersected by another, allowing you to trim away parts of the surface.

trim marks *(pre)* → *corner marks*

trimmed edges *(fin)* In traditional bookbinding, the cutting of the leaves at the top edge but cutting only the larger projecting leaves on the tail and fore-edges, thus giving a rough appearance.

trimmed flush *(fin)* → *cut flush*

trimmed page size (tps)/trimmed size *(fin)* The size of a printed and bound book, but referring to the page size rather than the size including the binding.

trimming *(fin)* The process of cutting the edges of the pages of a publication to remove the folds and produce a regular finish.

triple coated *(pap)* A superior-quality paper that has been coated three times to give a very fine finish.

tritone *(gen)* A halftone image that is printed using three colours. Typically, a black-and-white image is enhanced by the addition of two colours – for example, process yellow and magenta when added to black will produce a sepia-coloured image.

A **tritone** image creating a sepia tone

troll/trolling *(int)* A newsgroup posting designed to exasperate, annoy or enrage its readers, the purpose being to create as much argument as possible. An analogy might be 'pointing the gun but hoping someone else pulls the trigger'.
→ *newsgroup; spam/spamming*

trs *(gen) abb.:* transpose. → *transpose/transposition*

truck *(gen)* → *double-(page) spread*

trucking shot *(com)* → *tracking (2)/tracking shot*

TrueDoc *(com)* A font format devised by the Bitstream Corp, which is completely independent of platform, operating system, application, resolution and device. → *font embedding*

true negative *(com)* An unmodified negative image.

TrueType *(com)* Apple Computer's digital font technology developed as an alternative to PostScript and now used by both Apple and Microsoft for their respective operating systems. A single TrueType file is used both for printing and for screen rendering, unlike PostScript fonts, which require a screen font file as well as a printer font file.
→ *OpenType; Type 1 font*

A typical promotional **tummy band**

TRUMATCH colours *(gen)* A system of colour matching used for specifying process colours.

TTF *(com) abb.:* TrueType font. → *TrueType*

TTL *(pho) abb.:* through-the-lens → *through-the-lens (TTL) meter*

tub-sized *(pap)* A method of sizing handmade paper in a tub containing animal glue, gelatine or starch, and sometimes a combination of the three.

tummy band *(gen)* A strip of paper containing a sales message fixed around the middle of a publication. Also called a 'belly band'.

tungsten film *(pho)* A photographic film that is used where the scene is to be illuminated by tungsten lamps (normal, domestic lamps).

tungsten lighting *(pho)* Artificial lighting created by a heated filament of tungsten, as used in a domestic light bulb and some photographic lamps. → *photoflood; tungsten film*

turned commas *(typ)* Inverted commas.

turned-over cover *(fin)* A binding in which the material used on the case is turned in around the edges so that the edges of the boards are not left exposed as they would be if cut flush. Also called 'turned-in covers'.

turning-in corners *(fin)* A method of stretching the pasted cover material across the cover boards of a book to enable neatly mitred joints to be made.

t/v *(gen) abb.:* title verso. → *title verso (t/v)*

TVSP *(int) abb.:* television service provider.
→ *television service provider (TVSP)*

tween *(com)* A contraction of 'in–between'. An animator's term for the process of creating extra frames to fill in-between keyframes in a 2D animation.

twelvemo/12mo *(pap)* A sheet folded or cut to one twelfth its basic size.

twenty-four-bit/24-bit colour *(com)* The allocation of 24 bits of memory to each pixel, giving a possible screen display of 16.7 million colours (a row of 24 bits can be written in 16.7 million different combinations of 0s and 1s). Twenty-four bits are required for CMYK separations – eight bits for each. → *colour depth*

twenty-fourmo/24mo *(gen)* A book comprising 48 pages (24 leaves), made by folding a sheet at right angles to each previous fold.

twice up *(gen)* Artwork prepared at twice the size at which it will be reproduced. Artwork that is drawn twice up will need to be reduced by one half, to fifty per cent, to print at its intended size. → *half-up*

twin-wire binder *(fin)* A method of bookbinding, in which a comb of plastic-covered wire with twin wire loops is used to secure the covers and pages. → *spiral binding*

twin-wire paper *(pap)* A method of papermaking where the two ends of the web are brought together with the wire side innermost so that the paper formed has two top ('felt') sides. Also called 'duplex paper'.

twitter *(com)* A colloquial term for the visible vibrations on a video display caused by 1-pixel-high images.

two-fold *(gen)* A publication that is folded twice on the same axis to form six panels, three on each side.

two-line letters *(typ)* Enlarged capital letters that extend to the depth of two lines, used as initial caps for chapter openers, etc. Also called 'drop capitals'.

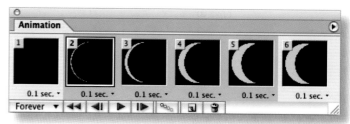

two on and two off *(fin)* → *one on and two off*

two-on binding *(fin)* A method of trimming two books, one on top of the other, at the same time. Also called 'two-up binding'.

two-page display (TPD) *(com)* Sometimes used to describe a 21in monitor.

two-revolution press *(pri)* A cylinder on a printing press, which rotates twice for each impression without reinking.

two-up *(pri)* A method of printing two copies of each page on a single sheet. They are eventually trimmed into separate entities after binding. → *four-up*

two-up binding *(fin)* → *two-on binding*

type (1) *(typ)* Originally, an individual text character cast in metal (called a 'stamp' by compositors), but latterly any letter, numeral or ornament drawn in a huge variety of designs (each one a 'typeface' belonging to a 'type family'), sizes and weights (each one a 'font'). → *font; font family; typeface*

type (2) *(com)* A four-character code used by the Mac OS to identify a document, such as 'TEXT' for a text document, 'XDOC' for a QuarkXPress document, 'AGD3' for a FreeHand document, and so on.

Type 1 font *(com)* The Adobe PostScript outline font technology containing 'hints' for improved rendering on-screen. Type 1 fonts come as two files: an outline printer file and a bitmapped screen file. → *hints/hinting; outline letter/outline font*

Type 3 font *(com)* A PostScript font format that does not contain hints and which is now virtually obsolete. → *Type 1 font*

Frames 2 to 5 of this sequence are **tweened**, in that they are created automatically to fill the gap between frames 1 and 6

type area *(gen)* The area of a page in which the main body of text falls, thus creating margins. Also called a 'type page'.

type effect *(com)* The digital modification of type characters to create a special effect, such as outline, zoom, etc.

typeface *(typ)* The term (based on 'face' – the printing surface of a metal type character) describes a type design of any size, including weight variations on that design such as light and bold, but excluding all other related designs such as italic and condensed. As distinct from a 'type family', which includes all related designs, and a 'font', which is one design of a single size, weight and style. Thus 'Baskerville' is a type family, whereas 'Baskerville Bold' is a typeface and '9pt Baskerville Bold Italic' is a font. ➔ *font; font family; type (1)*

type family *(typ)* ➔ *font family*

type high *(typ)* The depth of a piece of type or any other material, such as blocks, that are composed alongside it. In the US and UK this is 0.918 inches.

type markup *(typ)* To specify to a typesetter every single detail that is required to carry out a job satisfactorily, also the actual item produced to that effect. Also called a 'type spec' or 'type specification'. ➔ *markup (1)*

type page *(gen)* ➔ *type area*

type path *(gen)* A straight or curved line used to position a line of text across the screen. If you move the path, the text will shift to follow it.

type scale/gauge *(typ)* ➔ *line gauge*

typescript *(gen)* A typed manuscript.

typesetter *(typ)* ➔ *compositor*

typesetter's quotation marks *(typ)* The traditional 'curly' quotation marks and inverted commas used in typesetting, as opposed to straight 'dumb' quotes intended to be used as foot and inch marks but often used as quote marks by typewriters and computer software.

typesetting *(typ)* The process of converting a manuscript into text set in a specified font and producing it in a form suitable for printing. A person whose job it is to set type is known as a 'compositor', or 'comp'. ➔ *comp (2); composing room; compositor; filmsetting*

type size *(typ)* The measurement, usually in points, of the body of a particular size of type as it would be if cast in metal. ➔ *body size*

type specimen sheet *(typ)* ➔ *type synopsis/specimen sheet*

type spec/specification *(typ)* ➔ *type markup*

type style *(com)* A digital modification of a typeface, such as italic, shadow, outline, and so on, as distinct from the 'real' versions of those typefaces.

type synopsis/specimen sheet *(typ)* A printed sample of a font showing the full character set.

type to type *(fin)* ➔ *fold to print*

typo *(typ)* A contraction of 'typographic error', an error occurring during typesetting, such as the wrong font, as distinct from a 'literal', such as a spelling mistake. ➔ *literal*

typographer (1) *(typ)* A person whose art, craft or occupation is typography. ➔ *typography*

typographer (2) *(typ)* ➔ *compositor*

typography *(typ)* The art of type design and its arrangement on a page.

Uu

UC, u/c *(typ)* abb.: upper case. → *upper case*

UCA *(pri)* abb.: undercolour addition. A method of increasing the yellow, magenta and cyan dot percentages to increase saturation in black areas when 'grey component replacement' (GCR) – which does not produce good saturated black – is used. → *GCR; UCR*

UCC (1) *(gen)* abb.: Universal Copyright Convention. → *copyright*

UCC (2) *(gen)* abb.: Universal Code Council, Inc. → *Universal Product Code (UPC)*

UCR *(pre)* abb.: undercolour removal. A reproduction technique of removing colour from the shadow areas of scanned colour separations, either to reduce the amount of ink or because the colours cancel each other out. For example, if there is enough black and cyan to cover the page, the magenta and yellow dots are removed. UCR can also reduce trapping problems in printing. → *GCR; UCA; trapping*

u/lc *(typ)* abb.: upper and lower case. An instruction that the copy is to be typeset in both upper and lower case, as appropriate. → *lower case; upper case*

ultraviolet light (UV) *(gen)* Light waves beyond the visible violet part of the spectrum. Since they can be absorbed by certain photosensitive materials, they are used for platemaking, printing inks, etc.

umlaut *(typ)* A pair of dots placed over a vowel (ü) to indicate a vowel change in some languages, particularly German. → *diaeresis/dieresis*

unbleached *(pap)* A method of papermaking using unbleached pulp. The resultant paper is light brown in colour.

uncials *(typ)* A type design reflecting the rounded letterforms of the 'majuscule' (capital) script found in medieval manuscripts. → *capital; half-uncial*

uncoated *(pap)* A paper without a mineral surface coating but which is available in a variety of finishes from 'antique' (rough) to 'super-calendered' (smooth).

uncut *(fin)* A book with pages that have not been trimmed.

underbanding *(fin)* The use of false bands on a book cover.

undercolour addition (UCA) *(pri)* → *UCA*

undercolour removal (UCR) *(pre)* → *UCR*

underexpose/underexposure *(pho)* Insufficient light to effect the correct exposure of a photosensitive material. The result is a print or transparency that is too dark and a negative that is too 'thin' (resulting in a dark print).

underline, underscore *(typ)* A rule printed beneath a word or piece of text.

underset *(typ)* A line of type with excessive word spacing.

UCR takes ink away from areas where it is either not desired or not required

undo *(com)* A standard command found in most applications that allows you to reinstate the previous thing that you did. Some applications allow several levels of 'undo'.

ungrained plate *(pri)* A litho plate that is much smoother than normal. It is used to improve the merging of tones as well as to increase the range of darker tones. A normal litho plate uses the graining to hold water in the non-image areas, whereas an ungrained plate requires other methods.

ungroup *(com)* → group

Unicode *(com)* A character set system that makes provision for 65,000 characters, thus accommodating the languages of the world. → *character set*

Uniform Resource Identifier (URI) *(int)* → *URI*

Uniform Resource Locator (URL) *(int)* → *URL*

Uniform Resource Name *(int)* → *URN*

uniform smoothing *(com)* In some 3D applications, smoothing that converts the surface of a model into a grid of evenly spaced polygons.

union *(com)* In drawing applications, the combining of two or more shapes into one.

unit (1) *(gen)* An expression of measure without reference to any particular system such as inches.

unit (2) *(pri)* A single part of a multi-colour printing press, which may itself print more than one colour.

Joining two shapes in drawing software is known as **union**

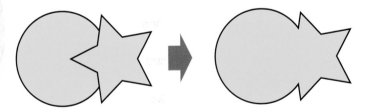

unit set (1) *(typ)* Type measured in unit dimensions rather than points.

unit set (2) *(pap)* A set of carbonless ('NCR') multi-part business forms. Older versions were interleaved with carbon tissue. → *NCR paper*

unit system *(typ)* Type design in which character widths conform to unit measurements associated with the 'set' (width) of the character. → *unit (1)*

Universal Copyright Convention (UCC) *(gen)* → *copyright*

universal film *(pri)* Colour separation film that produces the same results on both litho plates and gravure cylinders.

Universal Product Code (UPC) *(gen)* A product identification system for applying bar codes to products according to specifications provided by Uniform Code Council Inc. There are several specifications – for example, 'UPC-A' (or 'UPC 10') and 'UPC-E' (or 'UPC 6') are used mostly for retail items that will be scanned at point of sale, although variations of UPC-A are used in the publishing industry. 'UPC-Shipping' is used mostly on materials such as cardboard, where print quality is poor. → *bar code*

Universal Serial Bus *(com)* → *USB (Universal Serial Bus)*

UNIX *(com)* An operating system developed by AT&T, devised to be multitasking and portable from one machine to another. UNIX is used widely on Web servers, and is at the core of Mac OS X. → *A/UX; operating system*

unjustified *(typ)* Lines of type in which character or word spacing is consistent on every line, resulting in text lines of unequal length and leaving at least one side of the column of text uneven or 'ragged'. Distinct from 'justified' type, to which word and character spaces are added so that each line is of an equal length, uniformly aligning

*!?

with both left and right margins. Unjustified type may be ranged ('flush') left or right, or it may be centred with both sides ragged. The appearance of unjustified type is sometimes called 'free line fall'. Unjustified type is described in a wide variety of ways, with 'flush left' (or right) and 'ranged left/right' the most common, others being 'ragged left/right', 'left/right-aligned', 'left/right justified' and 'justified left/right'.
→ *justification*

unmount *(com)* To remove a volume (disk) from the desktop, either by disconnecting or ejecting it. → *disk*

unopened *(fin)* A term used to describe a bound book with untrimmed sections. Pages will need to be slit by hand with a paperknife. Also called 'untouched edges'.

unsewn binding *(fin)* → *threadless binding*

Unsharp Mask filter *(com)* One of the most potent Photoshop *Sharpen* filters, *Unsharp Mask* can sharpen edges whose definition has been softened by scanning, resampling or resizing. Differing adjacent pixels are identified and the contrast between them increased. The *Unsharp Mask* uses three control parameters: *Amount*, *Radius* and *Threshold*. *Amount* determines the amount of contrast added to boundary (edge) pixels. *Radius* describes the number of pixels adjacent to that boundary that are affected by the sharpening, and *Threshold* sets a minimum value for pixel contrast, below which the filter will have no effect. Once mastered, it is a powerful filter and can achieve more subtle, but more effective, results than any other sharpening filter.

unsharp masking (USM) *(pre)* A traditional film-compositing technique used for 'sharpening' an image. → *interpolate/ interpolation; sharpen(ing); sharpness*

untouched edges *(fin)* → *unopened*

unwanted colours *(pre)* Three colour patches on colour reproduction guides, which record the same as the white patch when separated. For example, the blue, cyan and magenta patches on a yellow separation record the same as the white patch.
→ *wanted colours*

UPC *(gen)* abb.: *Universal Product Code*
→ *Universal Product Code (UPC)*

upgrade *(com)* To modify or enhance the performance or capabilities of a computer, either by adding, for example, more memory or an accelerator card, or by installing a newer version of the operating system or application software.

upload *(com)* To send data from your computer to a distant computer such as a server. The opposite of download. → *download*

upper case *(typ)* The capital letters of a type font, the term deriving from the compositors 'case' – trays of type that were generally used in pairs, upper for capital letters and lower for small letters. → *capital; case (2); lower case*

upright (format) *(gen)* → *portrait, upright format*

upstroke *(typ)* The finer stroke in a type character derived from the downward stroke of a pen in calligraphic letterforms.

Before (top) and after (bottom) the **Unsharp Mask**

up vector *(com)* In a 3D environment, a line perpendicular to the viewpoint of the camera, which allows the camera object to be rolled around the viewpoint.

URI *(int) abb.:* Uniform Resource Identifier. Something that identifies resources available to the Web, such as a URL. ➔ *URL*

URL *(int) abb.:* Uniform Resource Locator. The unique address of a page on the Web. Each resource on the Internet has a unique URL, which begins with letters that identify the resource type (and thus the protocol to be used), such as 'http' or 'ftp', followed by a colon and two forward slashes, after which comes the 'domain name' ('host'). This can have several parts to it. After a forward slash comes the directory name, followed by pathnames to any particular file, e.g. 'http://www.digiwis.com/home.htm'. Usually if a file name is not stated, the server will normally supply the file named 'index.html' or 'index.htm', which is usually the home page. ➔ *absolute URL; DNS; http; relative URL*

URL-encoded text *(int)* A method of encoding text for passing requests from your Web browser to a server. ➔ *request; URL*

URN *(int) abb.:* Uniform Resource Name. A permanent name for a Web resource. ➔ *URL*

USB (Universal Serial Bus) *(com)* A digital data transfer technology for connecting peripheral devices to your computer. USB allows daisy-chaining (connecting one peripheral through another) and hot-swapping (plugging or unplugging without having to reboot). The standard was upgraded (to 'USB 2') in 2000 to increase speed. ➔ *daisy-chain; peripheral device; port*

UseNet *(int)* Acronym for user's network, in which a vast number of articles, categorized into newsgroups, are posted by individuals on every conceivable subject. These are hosted on servers throughout the world, in which you can post your own articles to people who subscribe to those newsgroups, using special 'newsreader' software. ➔ *forum; newsgroup*

user *(com)* A person who uses hardware and software, as distinct from someone who makes or creates it.

user group *(com)* A group of people who share their experiences, knowledge and problems, either generally or in relation to a specific software application or type of computer.

user interface *(com)* ➔ *interface*

user-specified defaults *(com)* Program defaults that have been specified or modified by its user, as distinct from 'factory' defaults, which are defined at the time of manufacture. ➔ *default*

USM *(pre) abb.:* unsharp masking. ➔ *unsharp masking (USM)*

utility (program) *(com)* A program that enhances or supports the way you use your computer generally, as distinct from those programs that enable you to do work specifically ('applications'). Typical utilities are programs for backup, font management, file-finding, disk management, file recovery, plug-ins, screen savers, and so on.

uudecode *(com)* Acronym for 'UNIX to UNIX decode'. A method of encoding and decoding binary data such as used by graphics files so that they may be transferred over the Internet in ASCII format, between computers running the UNIX operating system. ➔ *ASCII; UNIX*

UV coordinates *(com)* In a 3D environment, a system of rectangular 2D coordinates used to apply a texture map to a 3D surface.

UV light *(gen) abb.:* ultraviolet light. ➔ *ultraviolet light (UV)*

U

Vv

vacuum frame *(pre)* A device in which a film negative and a sensitized plate are held in tight contact by the creation of a vacuum between them. The plate is then exposed to the negative. Also called a 'printing down frame'.

value *(gen)* → *colour value*

Vandyke print *(pre)* A photocopy print, producing the image as a dark brown print, either negative or positive, and used as a final proof from flats before platemaking. Also called a 'brownline' or 'brownprint'. → *blueprint; Ozalid*

vanity publishing *(gen)* Book publishing enterprises based entirely on authors' willingness (vanity, in most cases) to underwrite all costs. Also called 'subsidy publishing'.

vantage *(pri)* The term describing a blank page on a printed sheet.

variable printing *(pri)* Printing in which variable data, such as names and addresses, is inserted during the print run.

varnish *(fin)* A liquid that dries with a hard surface and is generally insoluble in water. It is used in the manufacture of printing inks, in some drying agents and as a surface protector. → *spot varnishing*

varnishing *(fin)* The process of applying a protective covering to a book or periodical.

vat machine *(pap)* → *cylinder machine*

vat paper *(pap)* Hand-made paper.

VDT *(com)* abb.: video display terminal. → *monitor*

VDU *(com)* abb.: video display unit. → *monitor*

vector *(com)* A line defined by two or more control points; vectors are the building blocks of vector graphics. In vector graphics, shapes and objects are defined mathematically in terms of lines of various widths and colours, and fills of different colours and textures.

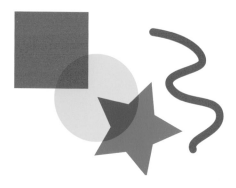
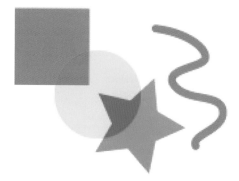

Vector graphics (left) can be magnified without loss of quality whereas jagged edges become apparent on bitmap images (right)

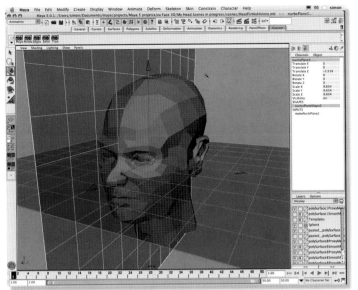

The X, Y and Z **vertices** for this 3D shape are indicated by the red, green and blue arrows

vector audio *(aud)* A concept developed by Koan and similar to that used with graphics and MIDI, vector audio uses the minimum possible information to describe musical parameters to a browser plug-in, thus generating music on the fly.

vector graphic *(gen)* Images made up of mathematically defined shapes, lines, curves and fills, which can be displayed at any size or resolution without loss of quality.

vegetable ink *(pri)* Ecologically sound printing inks made from vegetable oils.

vegetable parchment *(pap)* A type of greaseproof paper that, during manufacture, uses sulphuric acid to fuse the fibres together.

vehicle *(pri)* → *medium (1)*

vellum *(pap)* A fine-grained paper originally made from unsplit calfskin and used in bookbinding.

velocity *(com)* In 3D animation, the rate of change in an object's location relative to time. Also refers to the speed of sound (344 metres/1128 feet per second), or to the speed at which MIDI instructs a note to be played.

velox *(pre)* → *PMT (1)*

venetian types *(typ)* A style of typeface design that appeared in the 15th century, characterized by the wide set of the lower-case letters and bol serifs.

verbatim et literatim *(gen)* Latin phrase meaning 'word for word', describing a literal translation.

verification/verify *(com)* A term used to describe the process of testing the integrity of data or the data blocks on a disk drive by repeatedly writing and reading data to the disk. → *data*

verso *(gen)* From the Latin 'verso', meaning 'turned', this usually refers to the left-hand page of a book. More precisely, it describes the other side of a leaf from a 'recto' (right-hand page). → *recto*

vertex *(com)* In a 3D environment, the x, y and z locations at each corner of a polygon or control point.

vertex animation *(com)* In a 3D animation, the variation in the shape of an object by animating its surface control points.

vertex normals *(com)* → *normal(s)*

vertical alignment *(gen)* The placement of items such as images or lines of text in relation to the top and bottom of a page, column or box. → *alignment*

vertical bar pointer *(com)* → *I-beam pointer*

vertical blanking interval *(com)* → *blanking interval*

vertical camera *(pre)* A camera used for reproduction, typically with a fixed position camera and a horizontal copyboard that is moved up or down. → *process camera*

vertical centring *(gen)* The equidistant positioning of text ('vertical justification') or any other item from the top and bottom of a page, column or box. → *justification; vertical alignment*

vertical justification *(typ)* → *justification*

V

vertical page *(gen)* A page in which the copy is right-reading when the page is held in a vertical position. → *portrait, upright format*

very low frequency (VLF) *(com)* → *ELF*

VGA *(com) abb.:* video graphic array. Basic video display standard. → *monitor; SuperVGA (SVGA)*

vide *(gen)* A Latin term meaning 'see', used in a text as *vide infra* to indicate matter appearing subsequently, or as *vide supra* meaning 'see above'.

Video (1) *(com)* A QuickTime full motion video compression codec with fast compression but inferior quality and limited to 16-bit colour depth. Also called 'Apple Video'. → *codec (1); QuickTime*

video (2) *(gen)* A Latin term meaning 'I see', describing all television related products.

video card *(com)* A plug-in board that controls an external monitor.

video conferencing *(int)* The facility to conduct conferences over a computer network using sound and video pictures.

video digitizer *(com)* → *digitizer*

video display terminal (VDT) *(com)* → *monitor*

video display unit (VDU) *(com)* → *monitor*

video fades *(com)* The technique of starting and finishing a film sequence with a solid colour, such as black, blending it with the sequence at either end. Using this technique avoids an abrupt beginning or end.

Video Graphic Array (VGA) *(com)* → *VGA*

video RAM (VRAM) *(com)* → *VRAM*

view angle *(gen)* → *angle of view (1)*

view camera *(pho)* A large-format camera in which the image is projected onto a ground-glass viewing screen, behind the film plane at the back of the camera. After the scene is viewed, the film is placed in the same position as the viewing screen.

view distance *(com)* In a 3D environment, the distance between the eye point and view.

viewing conditions *(gen)* A standardized method (defined in the U.S. by ANSI) of maintaining consistent lighting conditions when viewing originals such as transparencies and flat copy, ensuring that a proof made from those originals can also be viewed in similar conditions, enabling a more accurate assessment of the quality of a proof.

ViewMovie *(int)* A Netscape plug-in for viewing animations. → *plug-in*

viewpoint *(gen)* The direction from which a subject is viewed to provide the best analytical or aesthetic study.

vigesimo-quarto *(pap)* → *twenty-fourmo/ 24mo*

vignette *(gen)* Strictly speaking, any image without a defined border, but also used to describe a halftone image in which the tones gradually fade out into the background. → *feather(ing)*

vignetted (halftone) dots *(pre)* Dots that reduce in intensity from their centres, fading to nothing at the edges. → *halftone dot*

vinyl *(aud)* Short for the analog vinyl record format, still the medium of choice for DJs.

virtual *(com)* Not physically existing, but made to appear as though it does. So 'virtual reality' is an imagined reality, indistinguishable from real life, provided that the means for experiencing it is enabled. Of course, in digital contexts, there's nothing imaginary about it at all since everything really does exist – if only as temporary data. → *virtual memory*

virtual machine *(int)* → *Java virtual machine*

virtual memory *(com)* A technique of making memory (RAM) seem larger than it really is by using other means of storing data elsewhere, such as on a hard disk. This means that you can work with as much memory as you have disk space, but the

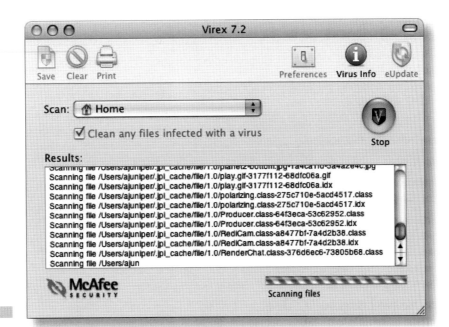

Virex is a **virus protection utility**

A digitally created **vignette** effect

trade-off for this luxury is speed – virtual memory is only as fast as the data transfer speed of the disk. Also called 'scratch space' in some applications. → *virtual*

virtual reality *(com)* → *virtual*

Virtual Reality Modeling Language (VRML) *(int)* → *VRML*

virtual server *(int)* A term used to describe a website that is hosted on a server run by an ISP (Internet Service Provider) rather than a server run by the creator of the site. This is convenient because a website server needs a permanent connection to the telephone network, and it is often more economic for an ISP to do this because a single server may host dozens of sites.
The Web address is unaffected by this arrangement – for example, the address, http://www.yourcompanyname.com can be hosted by any ISP. → *ISP*

virtual shopping cart *(int)* A method of providing Web shoppers with a means of selecting items for purchase as they browse a site, paying for them all at once when done – just as you would in any store.

virtual tracks *(com)* In both software and hardware multitrackers, virtual tracks allow you to store alternative takes of a performance, rather like the pasteboard on a word processor or image-editor.

virtual world *(com)* → *VRML*

virus *(com)* A computer program that is (illegally) written to alter or disrupt the normal operation of a computer. Viruses are spread from computer to computer across networks, via the Internet (increasingly) or simply via disks. A virus may infect some files, but not others (an application, perhaps, but not documents), and they manifest themselves in different ways, sometimes innocuously by simply beeping, displaying a message or causing strange behaviour, or sometimes cataclysmically by deleting files or even an entire hard disk. → *virus protection utility/ program*

virus protection utility/program *(com)* A utility program designed to, at the very least, alert you to the fact that a disk or file is infected and, at best, to eradicate the virus and prevent any other possible infections. There are many such utilities available, both commercial and shareware. → *virus*

viscosity *(pri)* The degree of resistance of a liquid to flow, expressed in 'poises', the unit of measurement used to describe viscosity. Printing inks used for high-speed rotary presses will have a viscosity in the range of 6–12 poises, whilst a hand letterpress machine might require 500 poises.

visible spectrum *(gen)* → *spectrum*

visual *(gen)* → *rough*

visual interface *(com)* → *graphical user interface (GUI)*

visualize/visualizer *(gen)* A term that describes a person (increasingly rare) who simulates the imagery used for advertisements or cover designs, typically using felt markers to render the image.

viz *(gen) abb.: videlicet*, Latin for 'namely', used when citing a reference in footnotes.

VLF *(com)* *abb.:* very low frequency. → *ELF*

volume (1) *(com)* A device or a partition where data is stored – in other words, a disk or tape or part of it.

volume (2) *(gen)* A term that describes a single book or even the parts of a book so long as each part is separated by its own title page.

volume bitmap *(com)* A record of the used blocks (represented by an 'on' bit) and unused blocks 'off' on a volume.

volume directory *(com)* → *directory (2)*

volume rights *(gen)* A term that describes the right of a publisher to publish a book in any volume form, most commonly paperback and hardback rights.

voucher copy *(gen)* A copy of a publication sent to a contributor, reference source or advertiser.

Vox classification *(typ)* Devised by Maximilien Vox in 1954, a method of classifying all typefaces according to their visual characteristics. There are ten: Humane, Garalde, Réale, Didone, Mécane, Linéale, Incise, Scripte, Manuaire and Fracture.

VRAM *(com) abb.:* video RAM (random access memory), special RAM reserved for monitor display. → *random access memory (RAM)*

VRML *(int) abb.:* Virtual Reality Modeling Language. An HTML-type programming language designed to create 3D scenes called 'virtual worlds'.

VST/VSTi *(aud)* (Mac/PC) Virtual Studio Technology (Instrument). Arguably the main plug-in standard for effects and virtual instruments, supported by Steinberg (Cubase SX), Emagic (Logic Audio) and others. VST, DirectX and HTDM have enabled audio production software to become fully integrated and expandable studio environments.

abc
abc
abc
abc
abc
abc
abc
abc
abc
𝔞𝔟𝔠

Styles representing the
Vox classifications

W3 *(int)* → *World Wide Web (WWW)*

W3C *(int)* → *World Wide Web Consortium*

waffling *(fin)* → *emboss(ing)*

WAIS *(int) abb.:* wide area Information Service. A system developed to access information in indexed databases across the Internet.
→ *gopher*

walk off *(pri)* Deterioration of the image on a printing plate during printing.

wall *(pri)* The divisions between cells on a gravure plate.

wallet edged *(fin)* A soft-covered book in which the back cover extends to enclose the fore-edge of the book block, fastening into a slot in the front cover.

wallet envelope *(pap)* An envelope with a rectangular flap along its long side.

wallet fold *(fin)* → *gatefold*

WAN *(com) abb.:* wide area network. A series of local area networks (LAN) connected together by terrestrial or satellite links.
→ *GAN; LAN; network*

wanderer *(int)* → *robot; spider*

wanted colours *(pre)* Three colour patches on colour reproduction guides, which record the same as the black patch when separated. For example, the yellow, red and green patches on a yellow separation record the same as the black patch. → *unwanted colours*

warehouse work *(pri)* All non-printing work carried out by a printer – for example, paper and ink handling, finishing and despatch.

warm boot *(com)* → *boot/boot up/booting up*

warm colours *(gen)* Any colour with a hue veering towards red or yellow, as distinct from cool colours, which veer towards blue or green. → *cool colours*

warping *(fin)* The distortion of hardback book covers due mainly to contraction or expansion of cloth, boards and end-papers, caused by a variety of reasons such as incorrect grain direction of the paper, changes in humidity during storage or shipping, and inadequate pressing during binding.

wash coating *(pap)* → *film coating*

wash drawing *(gen)* A brush-sketch using pale colour mixes.

washing up *(pri)* Cleaning ink from the printing plate or blanket.

wash marks *(pri)* Streaking on a printed image, caused by excessive water on the printing plate.

wash-out process *(pri)* Any printing process using photopolymer plates, in which the non-image areas of the plate are washed out after exposure, thus avoiding the need for routing.

watercolour printing *(pri)* Printing process using water soluble inks on porous paper, which results in the blending of overlapping layers of colour.

WATERCOLOUR PRINTING

water-colour/water-based inks *(pri)* Water-soluble-based, rather than oil-based inks, sometimes used for printing colours from a rubber surface.

watered silk *(fin)* Silk with a wavy pattern used sometimes for 'doublures' (decorative lining inside a handbound book).

water finish *(pap)* Dampened paper that is given a high finish by passing it through heated rollers. Used for making imitation art paper. → *art paper; imitation art (paper)*

waterleaf *(pap)* Semi-absorbent paper that requires sizing before use. → *surface sizing*

waterless lithography/printing *(pri)* A lithographic printing process that, rather than using water to repel ink on the non-image areas of the plate, uses instead a plate with an ink-repellent rubber layer. → *lithography*

water lines *(pap)* Alternative name for the lines in a laid paper. → *laid paper*

watermark (1) *(pap)* A mark or design impressed in paper during the manufacturing process, sometimes used to make forgery of a document more difficult, such as in banknote printing. → *counter-mark; cut ahead; imitation watermark; impressed watermark*

watermark (2) *(int)* The technique of applying a tiled graphic to the background of a webpage that remains fixed, no matter what foreground materials scroll across it.

watermark (3) *(com)* A technique of encoding a digital image with information such as copyright ownership, thus deterring unauthorized use.

water pan *(pri)* → *dampening fountain*

water streaks *(pri)* → *wash marks*

WAV *(aud)* Wave file format. The standard audio file format on Windows PCs.

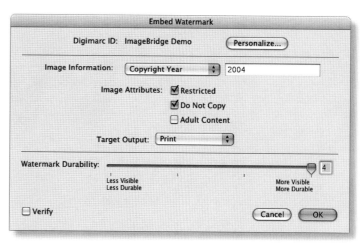

wave filter *(gen)* Version of the ripple distortion filter, which features customizable controls. Using 'wave generators', ripples are created. The number of wave generators can be specified, as can wavelength and wave height. Though waves are conventionally sinusoidal – i.e. following the shape of a sine curve – they can also be triangular or square.

WAVE PHF *(aud)* Acronym for 'Wavelength, Amplitude, Velocity, Envelope, Phasing, Harmonics and Frequency. The basic components of a waveform.

web (1) *(pap)* A continuous roll of substrate, particularly paper, that passes through a printing press or through converting or finishing equipment.

Web (2) *(int)* → *World Wide Web (WWW)*

Web authoring *(int)* The process of creating documents (usually in HTML or XML format) suitable for publishing on the World Wide Web. → *HTML; World Wide Web (WWW)*

web break *(pri)* The accidental breakage of a web of paper, while printing, on a high-speed web press. → *web (1)*

Web browser *(int)* → *browser (1)/Web browser*

Web crawler *(int)* → *spider*

Using technologies like Digimarc it's possible to add a **watermark** to protect the copyright of your image files

Web Embedding Font Tool (WEFT) *(int)*
→ *WEFT (2)*

web-fed *(pri)* Presses into which paper is fed continuously from a reel, as distinct from being fed individual sheets ('sheet-fed'). Also called 'reel-fed' or 'roll-fed'. → *web (1)*

Webmaster *(int)* The person responsible for managing a website.

web offset *(pri)* A rotary printing press using a continuous reel-fed paper 'web', where the impression (image) from the plate is offset onto a blanket (usually rubber) before being printed onto the paper. There are three main systems: 'blanket to blanket', in which two plates and two blanket cylinders on each unit print the web; three-cylinder systems, in which plate blanket and impression cylinders print one side of the paper only; and satellite or planetary systems, in which two, three or four plate and blanket cylinders are arranged around a common impression cylinder, printing one side of the web in as many colours as there are plate cylinders. → *web (1); web (printing) press*

webpage *(int)* An HTML document published on the World Wide Web. A group of such pages collectively forms a website.
→ *HTML; World Wide Web (WWW)*

web (printing) press *(pri)* A rotary printing press using continuous paper from a large roll that is fed through a series of rollers (cylinders) on which the plates are mounted. The impression from the plate is offset onto a blanket before being printed onto the paper. → *web (1); web offset*

Web server *(int)* A computer ('host') that is dedicated to providing Web services.

website *(int)* The address, location (on a server) and collection of documents and resources for any particular interlinked set of webpages.

Web spider *(int)* → *spider*

webTV *(com)* → *netTV*

wedding paper *(pap)* A low-glare paper with a very smooth surface.

weft (1) *(pri)* The weaker direction of a web offset blanket. → *blanket (1)*

WEFT (2) *(typ) abb.:* Web Embedding Font Tool. Microsoft's solution to the problem of downloading fonts without breach of copyright. WEFT does not require a plug-in.
→ *TrueDoc*

weight (1) *(typ)* The degree of boldness applied to a font, i.e. light, medium, bold, etc.

weight (2) *(pap)* → *paper weight*

well *(pri)* A single cell on a gravure printing plate.

wet-on-wet printing *(pri)* Printing subsequent colours on a multi-colour press while the previously printed colours are still wet.

wet pick *(pri)* The deterioration of the surface of coated paper, which can occur when it is re-run through an offset press.

wet plate *(pho)* A glass photographic plate that is exposed while the solution used to give it a photosensitive surface is still wet.

wet printing process inks *(pri)* Quick-drying inks used in multicolour printing; the last colour seals the surface.

wet rub *(pap)* The ability of a wet paper to resist scuffing. → *scuffing*

wet signal *(aud)* This refers to an audio signal with effects applied to it; the more effects that are applied, the 'wetter' it is.
→ *dry signal*

wet strength *(pap)* The bursting or tensile strength of paper after it has been saturated in water for a given time.

wet stripping *(pre)* The stripping away of the film base after the image has been processed but while the film is still wet.

wetting *(pri)* The process of adding varnish to ink pigments during manufacture, enabling them to be ground more easily, which, in turn, results in improved ink distribution.

wetting agent *(pho)* A soapy solution that weakens the surface tension of water, thus reducing the risk of drying marks on film.

wet trapping *(pri)* → *trapping*

w.f. *(typ)* abb.: wrong font. A proof correction mark used to indicate that type has been set in an incorrect font or is inconsistent with adjacent characters. → *font; proof correction marks*

what you see is what you get *(com)* → *WYSIWYG*

whipstitching *(fin)* A method of stitching books that are comprised of single sheets → *overcasting*

white balance *(pho)* A digital control used to balance exposure and colour settings for artificial lighting types. Can be applied to still images and video.

white letter *(typ)* An early description of roman type to distinguish it from a black or gothic letterform. → *black letter; gothic*

white light *(gen)* The colour of light that results from red, blue and green being combined in equal proportions. → *additive colours*

white line *(typ)* The space between two lines of type equivalent to the type size, including leading. → *leading*

white-lined black letter *(typ)* → *inline lettering*

white out (1) *(gen)* Typeset text that is reversed out of an image or background. → *reverse out/reverse type*

white out (2) *(typ)* To open out an area of type with spacing or leading either to improve its appearance or to fill a given area.

white point *(gen)* Point on a histogram denoting the position of those pixels that define white. Though nominally at the extreme end of the histogram, the white point should normally be moved to the position of the first white pixels in the histogram. In an RGB image, it corresponds to R, G and B values all at maximum, the brightest white that a monitor can show or scanner can read; in print or other CMYK hard-copy output, it usually means the paper or other substrate colour.

whiteprint *(pre)* → *diazo(type)/diazo process*

white space *(gen)* The term describing areas of white in a design or layout that contain no text or images, but which form an integral part of the design.

whole bound *(fin)* → *full bound*

wide-angle lens *(pho)* A photographic lens with wider field of view than a standard lens, so that more of the subject can be included – although the resulting image can be highly distorted. → *fish-eye lens; long-focus lens; short-focus lens*

wide area Information Service *(int)* → *WAIS*

wide area network *(com)* → *WAN*

wide gamut *(gen)* A large colour space (almost always RGB) or device (usually CMYK), which can represent or reproduce a larger range of colours than standard devices. Rarely used for commercial print, this is vital in high-quality photographic

Adjusting the **white point** in Photoshop

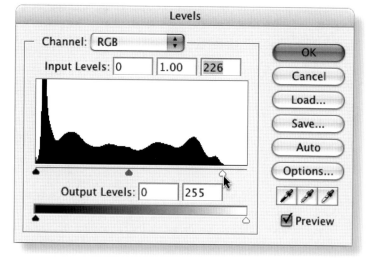

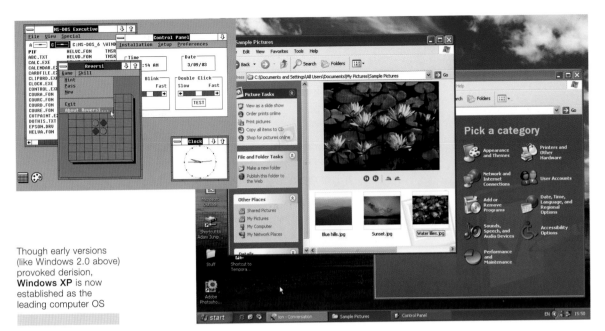

Though early versions (like Windows 2.0 above) provoked derision, **Windows XP** is now established as the leading computer OS

The **widow** is picked out in green (at the top)

work where final output is to transparency recorder, photographic printer or wide-gamut inkjet printer.

widget *(gen)* A colloquial term for any unspecified device.

widow (line) *(gen)* An unsightly short line or single word at the end of a paragraph, particularly objectionable at the top or bottom of a column of text. **→ orphan**

wildcard *(gen)* **→ text marker**

wild copy *(gen)* Typeset words that are separate from the main body of text, such as those used as annotation to an illustration or as part of a chart or diagram.

WIMPs *(com)* Acronym for windows, icon, mouse (or menu) and pointer. The constituent parts of a computer graphical user interface. **→ graphical user interface (GUI)**

window *(com)* Part of the graphical user interface (GUI) of a computer, a window is an area of a computer screen that displays the contents of disk, folder or document. A window can be resized and is scrollable if the contents are too large to fit within it. **→ graphical user interface (GUI)**

Windows *(com)* Operating system for PCs, developed by Microsoft, using a graphic interface that, like the Macintosh, took its inspiration from the pioneering work at Xerox Parc. Windows has become the most successful operating system available, installed on more than 90% of the world's personal computers. Despite that, some designers still regard it with suspicion because it was Apple computers that gained an early foothold in the design market.

WinSock *(int)* A software component of the Windows Operating System, used to connect PCs to the Internet. **→ Internet; Windows**

wipe *(pri)* A printing fault resulting in a blurred or double image.

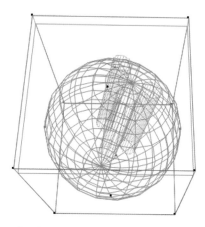

wire *(pap)* A wire (or Nylon) mesh typically 12–40 wires per cm, used as the moulding unit in a paper-making machine.

wireframe *(com)* The skeletal view of a computer-generated 3-D object before the surface rendering has been applied.

wire-mark *(pap)* The slight impression on the underside of paper left by the wire gauze during papermaking. → *wire side*

wire side *(pap)* The side of a sheet of paper that was in contact with the wire mesh during papermaking. → *felt side; wire-mark*

wire stabbing *(fin)* A rudimentary method of side-stitching a book using wire staples. Wire-stabbed books cannot be opened flat.

wire stitch(ing) *(fin)* A common method of saddle-stitching using wire, typically used for magazines and brochures. → *saddle-stitched*

witness *(fin)* The term describing a book that has had its fore-edge so slightly trimmed that some page edges are still rough.

WMV *(aud)* A Windows-specific video format.

woodcut *(pri)* A traditional method of printing using images and type that are carved – out of wood – in relief.

woodfree paper *(pap)* Paper made without mechanical wood pulp. Also called 'groundwood free' or 'pure'. → *chemical pulp; mechanical (wood) pulp*

wood letter/type *(typ)* Individual carved letterforms, a precursor of metal-based type.

wood pulp *(pap)* The raw material used in papermaking. Pulp is classified as being either mechanically or chemically produced.

word *(gen)* In digital terms, a word is a string of binary information. Word length refers to the amount of bits used to describe a digital sample. → *binary; bit-depth*

word break *(typ)* → *hyphenation (1)*

word processor *(com)* A software program used to create, store, retrieve and edit text, providing features for checking spelling, indexing, sorting, etc. A word processor also describes special computers dedicated to achieving the above.

word space *(typ)* The space between typeset words, based on the width of characters of the type size, and which is usually a constant if the text is unjustified but variable if it is justified. → *justification*

word underline *(typ)* → *underline/underscore*

word wrap *(com)* The automatic flow of text from one line to the next, not to be confused with 'text wrap', which is to run text around a shape. → *full word wrap; runaround/run round*

work and back *(pri)* → *sheet work*

work and tumble *(pri)* A printing technique where pages from both sides of the sheet are printed on one side using a single plate. After the first side is printed, the sheet is then turned, but this time with the back edge becoming the gripper edge (hence 'tumble'), and then passed through the press for a second time. The result is two copies of each page. → *work and turn; work and twist*

A **wireframe** of a 3D sphere shape

Wood lettering was the precursor to metal type

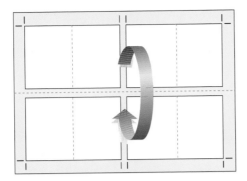

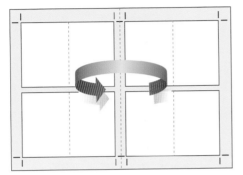

The illustrations (right) show the difference between **work and tumble** (top) and **work and turn** (below)

work and turn *(pri)* A printing technique where pages from both sides of the sheet are printed on one side using a single plate. After the first side is printed, the sheet is then turned over and, using the same gripper edge, passed through the press for a second time. The result is two copies of each page. Also called 'half sheet work'.
→ *work and tumble; work and twist*

work and twist *(pri)* An imposition (layout) technique for printing both sides of the sheet using a single plate. The printing film ('flat') is first exposed on one half of the plate and then rotated ('twisted') through 180° to expose the other half. When printed, this produces two copies of each page. → *work and tumble; work and turn*

working *(pri)* Any printing job in progress.

work off *(pri)* To print a job.

working space *(gen)* A device-independent colour space that, since it behaves more-or-less perceptually (changes to numerical values in any part of the colour space result in similar changes in the image) and is grey-balanced, can be used as a predictable and controllable working environment for image editing.

worksheet *(com)* A single page within a spreadsheet file. → *spreadsheet*

workstation (1) *(com)* Any single computer that may or may not be on a network but which is dedicated to one person's use.
→ *workstation (2)*

workstation (2) *(com)* A powerful computer – often UNIX-based – which is typically used for CAD/CAM and 3D applications.
→ *CAD/CAM*

world *(com)* In 3D applications, the term describing the simulated 'space' in which three-dimensional models and scenes are created.

World Wide Web Consortium *(int)* The organization responsible for maintaining and managing standards across the Web. Often abbreviated to the W3C.

World Wide Web (WWW) *(int)* The term used to describe the entire collection of web servers all over the world that are connected to the Internet. The term also describes the particular type of Internet access architecture, which uses a combination of HTML and various graphic formats, such as GIF and JPEG, to publish formatted text that can be read by web browsers. Colloquially called 'the Web'.

WORM *(com)* Acronym for write once read many. The term is used for storage media such as CD-recordable (CD-R) discs that can be written to only once and cannot be erased. → *CD-R/CD-RW; EO*

wove paper *(pap)* Paper with a smooth, fine 'woven' finish, as distinct from the lined pattern of 'laid' papers. → *laid paper*

wraparound (1) *(fin)* An insert placed around a signature before it is bound.

wraparound (2) *(fin)* A term describing the increased gutter width required for the outer pages of signatures to make allowances for 'creep'. ➔ *binder's creep; creep*

wraparound (3) *(typ)* ➔ *word wrap*

wraparound plates (1) *(fin)* Illustration plates printed separately from the text and bound on the outside of the text signature.
➔ *insert (1)*

wraparound plates (2) *(pri)* Flexible printing plates used on a 'wraparound' press (a sheet-fed rotary press).

wraparound press *(pri)* A high-speed, sheet-fed rotary press that uses relief plates.
➔ *wraparound plates (2)*

wrap curl *(pap)* ➔ *roll set curl*

wrapped round *(fin)* ➔ *insert (1); wraparound plates (1)*

wrapper *(fin)* A paper cover attached to a publication.

wrappered and overlapped *(fin)*
➔ *wrappering*

wrappering *(fin)* A strengthening process achieved by glueing unstiffened paper to the spine of a book. When large flaps are left at the fore-edge and then folded in, this is called 'wrappered and overlapped'.

wrapping *(typ)* The automatic flow of text from one line to the next. ➔ *word wrap*

wrinkle (1) *(pap)* A crease-like defect found in paper.

wrinkle (2) *(pri)* Marks occurring during the drying of the ink surface of a printed page, giving an uneven appearance.

wristwatch/hourglass pointer *(com)* The shape the pointer icon assumes to indicate that a process is underway but not yet complete. ➔ *pointer*

write-enable *(com)* To enable a computer drive or disk to receive data, the opposite of write-protect. ➔ *write-protect*

write-protect *(com)* To protect a computer disk from erasure or contamination by viruses, by preventing any data from being written to it or deleted from it – although the contents can still be read. Some removable media is equipped with a small tab that, when moved to reveal a hole, write-protects the disk. Sliding it back again to fill in the hole 'write-enables' the disk so that data can be added or deleted. ➔ *write-enable*

write/writing head *(com)* The part of a disk drive that retrieves (reads) data from, and deposits (writes) data to, a disk. One read/write head is positioned above each side of every disk platter (a hard drive may consist of several platters). These move, on rails, across the surface of the platter while the platter rotates at speed.

writings *(pap)* Smaller paper sizes used, suitably 'sized', for writing rather than printing upon.

wrong font/fount *(typ)* ➔ *w.f.*

wrong reading *(pre)* Negative or positive printing film on which the image reads backwards when viewed with the emulsion on the desired side. Also called 'reverse reading'. ➔ *right reading*

WYSIWYG *(com)* (pron. 'wizzywig') An acronym for 'what you see is what you get'. The display of a document on screen exactly as it appears when printed. All major computer operating systems now offer WYSIWYG displays.

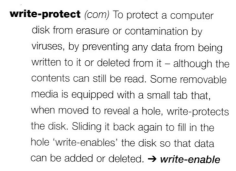

Some examples of the **wristwatch** or **hourglass** icon

x-axis *(gen)* → *x, y coordinates*

XCMD *(com) abb.:* external command.
→ *external command (XCMD)*

xerography *(gen)* A reproductive process where the surface of a drum is electrostatically charged so that it picks up particles of plastic toner (on the charged areas only) and transfers them to paper, to which they are fused by a heated roller. Xerography is the technology behind the photocopier and the laser printer and some 'digital' presses.

x-face *(int)* An encoded 48 x 48 bitmap image used by e-mail and news users to contain a picture of their face or company logo.

XFCN *(com) abb.:* external function. → *external function*

x-height *(typ)* The height of a lower case character without ascenders or descenders. The invisible line defined by x-height is called the 'x-line' or 'mean-line'.

The **x-height** of the letter 'X'

x-line *(typ)* → *x-height*

XMF *(aud) abb.:* Extensible Music Format.
→ *Extensible Music Format (XMF)*

XML *(int) abb.:* Extensible Markup Language.
→ *Extensible Markup Language (XML)*

XMODEM *(int)* A standard communications protocol that transfers data in blocks of 128K. → *YMODEM; ZMODEM*

Xobject *(com)* External objects, such as sounds and films, that are used in Macromedia Director presentations.

XON/XOFF *(com)* A 'handshaking' protocol used by computers when communicating via modems. → *handshake; protocol*

XSL *(int) abb.:* Extensible Style Language.
→ *Extensible Style Language (XSL)*

X Windows *(com)* A GUI used on UNIX computers, using an 'API' (application programming interface). → *application programming interface (API); GUI; UNIX*

x, y coordinates *(gen)* The point at which data is located on two-dimensional axes: horizontal (x) and vertical (y). Three-dimensional coordinates are known as 'x, y, z coordinates' (or axes).

xylograph *(pri)* A wood engraving.

Y *(gen) abb.:* process yellow. The special shade of yellow that is one of the four process colours used in four-colour printing.

Yapp binding *(fin)* A book-binding method in which a limp cover projects over the edges of the book's leaves. The term derives from the name of the London bookseller William Yapp who, in around 1860, designed the binding so that Bibles could be carried in the pocket. ➔ *circuit edges*

yaw *(com)* In a 3D environment, rotation around the y-axis. ➔ *x, y, coordinates*

y-axis *(gen)* ➔ *x, y coordinates*

y coordinates *(gen)* ➔ *x, y coordinates*

Yellow Book *(com)* The document that specifies all parameters for CD-ROM technology, guaranteeing that the discs can be read by all CD-ROM drives. ➔ *CD-ROM*

yellow printer *(pre)* In four-colour process printing, the plate or film used to print yellow ink.

yellow (y) *(gen)* With cyan and magenta, yellow is one of the three subtractive primaries, and one of the three process colours used in four-colour printing. Sometimes called 'process yellow'. ➔ *cyan (c); four-colour process; magenta (m)*

YMODEM *(int)* A standard communications protocol that provides error-checking whilst transferring data. ➔ *XMODEM; ZMODEM*

yon plane *(com)* ➔ *clipping plane*

In terms of the flight of an airliner, **yaw** is the side-to-side motion introduced by the rudder

Zz

zapping the PRAM *(com)* The term used to describe the re-setting of the parameter RAM (PRAM) on a Macintosh computer to its 'factory' settings. You do this by holding down the Option-Command-P-R keys while restarting your computer. Date and time settings, and of course your data itself, are not affected. ➔ *parameter RAM*

z-axis *(gen)* ➔ *x, y coordinates*

Z-buffer render *(com)* A 3D renderer that solves the problem of rendering two pixels in the same place (one in front of the other) by calculating and storing the distance of each pixel from the camera (the 'z-distance'), then rendering the nearest pixel last.

z-distance *(com)* ➔ *Z-buffer render*

zero point *(gen)* ➔ *origin*

z-fold *(fin)* ➔ *accordion fold*

z-height *(typ)* ➔ *x-height*

zigzag book *(fin)* A book made up of a continuous strip of paper folded in a concertina fold. If secured at the back, only one side of the sheet is printed. If it is printed on both sides, the book must be left unstitched. ➔ *accordion/ concertina fold*

zinco (1) *(fin)* A less durable but cheaper alternative to a 'binder's brass', but also producing less sharp results.

zinco (2)/zincograph *(pri)* An etching using a zinc plate. ➔ *etching*

zincography *(pri)* A former name for lithography, now obsolete. ➔ *lithography*

zinc plates *(pri)* Metal photoengraving plates used as an alternative to copper or magnesium alloy plates.

Zip-a-tone/Zipatone *(gen)* A patented collection of mechanical tint sheets, printed on cellophane.

ZMODEM *(int)* A standard communications protocol that can provide continuous data transfer despite interruptions or pauses. ➔ *XMODEM; YMODEM*

zone *(com)* One part of two or more connected networks. ➔ *network*

zoom (1) *(com)* A feature of some software applications that enables you to enlarge a portion of an image, making it easier to see and work with.

zoom (2) *(pho)* A camera lens with an adjustable focal length giving, in effect, a range of lenses in one. Drawbacks include a smaller maximum aperture and increased distortion over a prime lens (one with a fixed focal length).

zoom box *(com)* The box or button in some window title bars that, when clicked, expands or reduces the visible area of the window. ➔ *title bar*

zoom lens *(pho)* A camera lens with a continuously variable focal length, making it possible to determine the closeness of a subject to the camera without moving the camera. ➔ *telephoto lens*

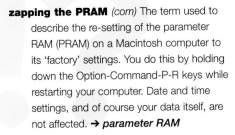

Selecting an object to **zoom**

Additional material

Apple Computer, Stuart Andrews, Tom Arah,
Neil Barstow, David Broad, Simon Danaher,
Graham Davis, Michael Freeman, Gianna
Galogavrou, Ed Gaskell, Barry Huggins, Adam
Juniper, Keith Martin, Chris Middleton, Simon
Phillips, Ben Renow-Clarke, Evelyn Shin,
Marilyn Tolhurst, Michael Walker.

ACKNOWLEDGEMENTS